The Arsonists' City

The
Arsonists'
City

Hala Alyan

Houghton Mifflin Harcourt
Boston   New York   2021

For information about permission to reproduce selections from
this book, write to trade.permissions@hmhco.com or to
Permissions, Houghton Mifflin Harcourt Publishing Company,
3 Park Avenue, 19th Floor, New York, New York 10016.

hmhbooks.com

Library of Congress Cataloging-in-Publication Data
Names: Alyan, Hala, 1986– author.
Title: The arsonists' city / Hala Alyan.
Description: Boston : Houghton Mifflin Harcourt, 2021.
Identifiers: LCCN 2020003643 (print) | LCCN 2020003644 (ebook) |
ISBN 9780358126553 (hardcover) | ISBN 9780358125099 (ebook)
Subjects: LCSH: Domestic fiction.
Classification: LCC PS3601.L92 A89 2021 (print) | LCC PS3601.L92 (ebook) |
DDC 813/.6 — dc23
LC record available at https://lccn.loc.gov/2020003643
LC ebook record available at https://lccn.loc.gov/2020003644

Book design by Greta D. Sibley

Printed in the United States of America
DOC 10 9 8 7 6 5 4 3 2 1

For Hanine and Nafez,

the suns of our solar system

The Wrong Ghosts

TONIGHT THE MAN will die. In some ways, the city already seems resigned to it, the Beirut dusk uncharacteristically flat, cloudy, a peculiar staleness rippling through the trees like wind. It's easy to costume the earth for grief, and tonight the birds perched upon the tangled electricity wires look like mourners in their black and white feathers, staring down at the concrete refugee camps without song.

There are orange trees in the courtyard, planted by the children the previous year; the NGO workers had wanted something bright and encouraged the youngest children to tie cheap ribbons to the branches, but they'd forgotten about the muddy season, and now the ribbons flap limply, streaked in dirt.

The man himself — Zakaria — knows it, or doesn't. He notices the queer feeling of the camps, the way his mother's makloubeh tastes perfectly fine but seems to be saltless, the meat stringier than usual. His sisters are gathered in the living room, cross-legged on the carpet, his mother's mother's carpet, the one that earned them a cuff on the ear back when they were children if they dropped crumbs or spilled Coke on it. *You think my mama, Allah rest her soul, Allah take her and Allah keep her, hauled this on her back, her* back, *all the way from Jerusalem to Ramallah to Amman to this godforsaken armpit of the world so that her heathen grandchildren could spill soda on it?* His mother hates the camps, hates Beirut, all of Lebanon, hates their neighbors, the aunties with their tattling and boring lives, always reminding her children, *We used to have gardens in Palestine, trees that belonged to us.*

His sisters are watching an Egyptian soap opera, one of their favorites, the one where the ingénue is kept from her love interest by his wicked mother. The screen is cracked from where one of his sisters — they always disagree about which one — threw a curling iron at it years ago, and it slices the starlet's torso in two as she cries on a park bench.

"What's wrong with you today?" Zakaria's mother asks him.

"Nothing," he lies. "I'm just not hungry." The truth is he's distracted. Something is nagging at him as it does when he forgets a song, the wispiest tune tugging at him. He thinks of the house across the city, the one where his mother has worked as a housekeeper for twenty years, the one he spent countless afternoons playing in as a boy with the son of the owner, the courtyard they'd transform into a battlefield, an ocean of sharks, lava. Idris was his first friend, his closest friend.

Whenever Zakaria thinks of the house, he sees it at dawn, the hour his mother would arrive for her daily duties after taking two buses from the south and walking from the final bus stop through the West Beirut streets, ignoring the vendors selling cigarettes and that sweet candy that made his teeth ache, to reach the gate, always latched, always easily unlocked.

He loved playing with Idris, of course, but he also loved those first couple of hours when the house was still quiet with the sleeping family, when his mother would fill buckets with warm soapy water to toss across the veranda, take down clothes she'd hung to dry in the garden the day before, whispering to him, "Silent as a mouse." When he was alone in the courtyard, it became his; he was the ruler of this inexplicable, beautiful place, a house with four bedrooms, bathtub faucets the shape of swans' necks.

Tonight he feels the house beckoning him with an invisible hand, feels greedy for those rooms, the silk-soft sheets that he'd slept in many times. But his best friend isn't speaking to him, their recent fight still raw as a burn, the insults they'd hurled at each other still echoing, each saying and not-saying the truth.

"You know what you did," Idris had finally said. "I trusted you. I've always trusted you."

Zakaria had fallen silent at that. He felt guilty and yet also unrepentant — how to apologize for the only truly good thing that'd ever happened to him? — which Idris had sniffed out like a dog. He'd called him a traitor.

"Not even a little plate?" his mother asks now, interrupting his thoughts.

"I'm just not hungry," Zakaria repeats. To stave off further questions, he tries to appear absorbed in the soap opera that his sisters, sprawled on the large sofa, are watching. The three girls are younger than him, all unmarried, with large noses and dark curly hair. They are branches of the same tree, rooted and yet always apart from him.

He must fall asleep at some point. One second, he is watching the woman on the television, and then he is with the woman, telling her he can't marry her, he's marrying Mazna. He'll never hear her response; he is shaken awake, and this is the last dream he will ever have. The television is off now and his sisters are huddled on the sofa, their faces alarmed and pale. His mother is leaning over him, blocking his view. He meets her eyes and sees panic.

"What have you done?" she murmurs.

He tries to sit up, but she keeps her palms on his shoulders. "What?" He shakes her off. "Mama, what —" She finally steps back, revealing what is behind her.

Zakaria understands. It's been three years, and yet everything falls into place in an instant — the night he and his friends manned the checkpoint in Beirut, the Maronites they stopped, the man who later died. He and Idris and the others, they'd hurt that young man for no reason other than that people were hurting people. The civil war had left the country riven — Shi'ite, Sunni, Maronite, Druze. Now they've found Zakaria. Not as an act of war, but one of love, of revenge. The tallest man is unfamiliar yet recognizable, the same comically thick eyebrows as his dead brother, his hair spiked with too much gel.

"Come, brother," the tallest one says, his voice almost languid.

"I told these men they have the wrong house. That you don't know them." The man holds up his hand, and his mother falls silent. These men aren't dressed like soldiers, but they are strangers and they are taking her son.

"Auntie, trust me, we've knocked on every door in this camp." His voice is surprisingly polite, earnest, and for some reason this strikes Zakaria with the first real needle of fear. The tall man fixes him with a steady gaze. "Brother, best for you to come now."

"Come? It's after ten. Come where? My son has work tomorrow. Zakaria, what are they saying?"

The man doesn't speak, simply holds out his hand as though helping a child who's fallen at the playground. Zakaria moves like a puppet, tipping forward until his fingers touch the other man's, letting himself be pulled up, gently, firmly, until they are standing a hairsbreadth away from each other, so close that, if this were a movie, and they were different men in a different city, they might have kissed. But instead, the tall man speaks in a low voice meant only for Zakaria.

"Say goodbye to your mother. Say goodbye to your sisters."

Zakaria waits for more fear, but there is a surprising absence. He understands. They will kill him in front of his mother, his sisters, or they will kill him away from them. This is the choice he has. It is the only choice he will ever have again.

It's not that Zakaria is particularly brave. But a few years ago, when those Phalangist men pointed their guns at the bus and killed thirty Palestinians and the country *fell into the hell it deserves,* as his mother says, he understood that his life had changed. The war made him understand his place in this country. He is a good man, or believes he is — most of the time. He has done only three terrible things in his life.

The first was the summer he'd spent stealing things from other inhabitants of the camps — a wristwatch and a pair of eyeglasses and other items that had no value and were thus priceless to their owners, things they'd clung to since arriving from Palestine. He was thirteen at the time, and angry; he had just read Marx and was certain that his people, the clear proletarians of the city, were chaining themselves to their possessions, that everything the world had robbed them of should be regarded with distaste, that they should not feel gratitude for what little they'd managed to keep. He'd kept his loot in a cookie tin under his bed. Then, toward the end of the summer, he took the box to the beach. One by one, he removed each item, gripped it in his fist, swam out into the cold and dirty water as far as his legs would allow, and let the object sink to its death. When the box was empty, he lay on the sand, panting, his muscles twitching with exhaustion.

The second terrible thing had happened this summer. This time he'd taken something — someone — from his best friend. A person he loved.

He's not all that familiar with love. If asked whether he loves his family, his three sisters and mother, he'd say yes. But there would be something rehearsed in that answer. He loves them because he ought to, and Zakaria is at heart an obedient man. (This is why he is following the men out of the house; this is why he walks deferentially to his death.) Love is what fills tables and waters gardens. It is Darwinian.

But this isn't how he loves Mazna. It isn't compliant; it's disruptive as a shark. He loves her hair. Her lips. He loves the way she says the word for to-mato, *bindura* — "ba-na-*du*-ra" — and the way she is tired of Damascus. He loves the one time he made her cry, one hand clenched in the other as her eyes filled. He loves the way she sulked the day she forgot her sunglasses. He loves that she wants to be an actress, to fill screens with her pretty, heart-shaped face. He'd spent twenty-five years in the camps, where the most ambitious people you came across were the likes of Abu Zaref, who wanted to open his own bar-bershop near the American University, so meeting someone so resolute and unembarrassed by her hunger — *Did you know Vivien Leigh started off as an extra?* she'd asked him the second night they met — was narcotic. He wants to write scripts for her. He wants to learn how to use movie cameras.

His mother is still prattling on about the time, her voice steady enough but her fingers, curled into fists, trembling, a tell (some primordial part of her brain must have been expecting her son to be taken). "Come *where?*"

"Mama." Zakaria's voice is convincing to his own ears. "These men are cus-tomers from the bakery. I promised our friend here that I'd help him with something." He turns to the tall man. "Ready?"

"When you are, brother."

"No," his mother whispers. Then, louder, "No! It is nearly eleven. You're not going anywhere with these men."

"Mama," he rasps. His throat is dry. His mind spins. "I'll be back soon. Yes?" He turns to the tall man, silently pleading. "Twenty, thirty minutes."

He nods. "An hour, tops." He gestures toward the door. Zakaria passes his mother, smells her familiar odor of fried onions and baby powder. He wants to kiss her temple, wants to tell his sisters to send a letter to Damascus. He passes his father's large framed photograph, the older man's eyes — frozen, forever, at forty-three — dark and wry as he watches his son walk out of the room.

The third terrible thing Zakaria had done happened soon after the war began in Lebanon. Idris had two close friends at his private school, Majed and Tarek, and the four boys had grown up together. Tarek's older brother Ali was a sergeant in the army, and even before the war, he'd known how to hold a rifle. Now, all over the country, men were getting involved. There was no longer one army; there were several, depending on which God you worshipped.

There was a checkpoint near the Green Line — the line that split the city into two, east and west, Christian and Muslim — and one night Ali told them they could join him. They were excited, pretending to be real officers. A car of university students — a young man and two women — pulled up.

Zakaria hates the memory of it. He can't explain how it happened, only that it felt like a game, the men egging one another on, forcing the man out of the car.

"I could make this Maronite trash do ballet for me if I wanted," Zakaria remembers Ali saying. The women had started to cry at some point; he'd felt nauseated. He knew they'd made a mistake.

It all happened quickly after that. The young man spat at them, shouted to be let go, and Ali rammed the butt of his rifle against his face. He did it over and over, the women screaming for him to stop. The boy staggered into the back of the car afterward; one of the women got behind the wheel and sobbed as she drove them off. He'd ended up dying from a brain injury. His family had money, and money bought information; it made finding the men at the checkpoint a matter of asking the right questions. They'd come for Ali a month later.

❈

They walk Zakaria to the edge of the camp, near the plot of meadow flowers the NGO workers had planted last year. They're all dead now, the stems brown and chalky. Zakaria thought the men would turn at the white gate, walk him to the city outside the camps. But no, they stop at the flowers, everyone looking to the taller man, waiting for him to speak. The man says nothing, simply pulls a knife from his pocket and looks at it closely.

"This was my brother's." His voice breaks.

Zakaria feels his knees buckle. The fear that surges in him is so full, so lushly animate, it's almost sensual, nudging up the hair on his arms. "This is slaughter," he croaks. "What you're doing. It's slaughter."

The man nods, almost kindly. "Yes, brother. Slaughter. Your men did it to mine. My men did it to others."

"I don't know your brother," Zakaria whispers. He remembers how the boy had cupped his broken nose, whimpering.

"This knife," the man continues, "it was on him when he died. But he never pulled it out. You bastards never gave him a chance. His face was mangled. Even my mother couldn't recognize him in the hospital." He began to move toward Zakaria. "But I have my God. I will leave your face alone."

"Please." Zakaria feels lightheaded. He remembers blood everywhere, Ali yelling at the women. "I had nothing to do with that, I swear."

"We'll find the other men as well," the man says caressingly, almost to himself. He looks around the camp as though one of them might appear. "After."

The men circle Zakaria, and he understands that they are blocking him from the view of any neighbors who might walk by. They are allowing him to die near his home; they won't make his mother search the hospitals for him. He is grateful; his mind is still understanding that gratitude when the tall man rushes toward him, and Zakaria feels something cold and gasping in his stomach. He registers moisture before pain. A week ago, he was drinking tea with Mazna and Idris in the garden; she'd gone off sugar and they were teasing her.

He looks down and sees the blood as the knife is pulled out, then plunged in, then pulled out, then plunged in for a third and final time. He sinks to the earth.

Minutes go by. The men leave; he can hear their footsteps. Someone cries out a name. His name. It slices the night, his mother's voice, the air suddenly alive with bird wings and footfalls, his name, his name, it is the last thing he knows of the world.

The main feature of exile is a double conscience, a double exposure of different times and spaces, a constant bifurcation.

— *Svetlana Boym,* The Future of Nostalgia

How alive the city is, how alive, how alive, how alive.

— *Alfred Kazin,* Journals

Part

I

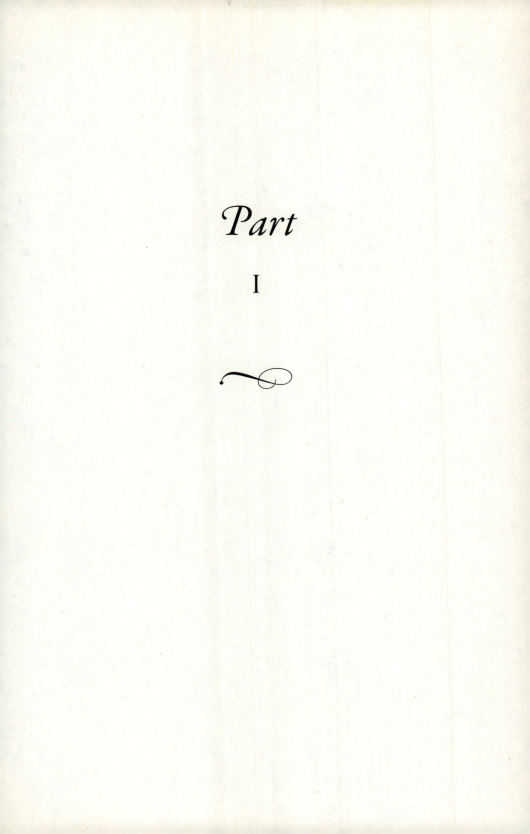

Park Slope Wives

THE PHONE RINGS as Ava and Nate are just finishing having sex. The frequency has been whittled down to two, three times a month since Zina's birth. Ava has come first, as is their tradition, on her belly, the vibrator between her legs, her mind furiously churning out fantasies — the Nigerian instructor at spin class, their boyish mailman — as Nate pets her and makes encouraging sounds. *Get it. That's it, baby.* Then there's the customary flipping over, Nate's face buried in Ava's neck as he shudders and groans. Then silence for six, seven seconds, during which they think of different things, before Nate pulls out slowly and takes off the condom, which looks like a collapsed jellyfish, and Ava gets up to pee. Which is when her cell begins to ring.

"'Mama,'" Nate announces, reading the screen. His limbs are long, but recently he's started carrying a slight gut. Nate holds the phone out questioningly. "She's trying to FaceTime."

Ava has a three-second internal debate — if she picks Mazna, she risks getting a urinary tract infection; if she picks the bathroom, she risks upsetting Mazna. She picks her mother.

"Toss it," Ava says. She catches the phone neatly. A photograph of her mother grins at her. Ava slips on her nightgown and clears her throat. She pats her bangs down. Holding the phone out in front of her, she presses the green button. "Mama?"

The video quality is sharp. Her mother is sitting in their kitchen in California. She's wearing her silky dressing robe and there's a bowl of tangerines in front of her. The phone is far enough away — tired of close-ups of their parents' noses and chins during FaceTime calls, her brother, Mimi, had ordered them a cell stand — that Ava can make out her father rustling around in the refrigerator. He's seemed a little quieter lately. He went to Beirut a couple of months ago, after her grandfather had died. It was a sore subject in the family; nobody else had been able to go to the funeral except Naj, though Ava privately thought her little sister's presence shouldn't count — she already lived there.

"Ava, we have news."

Ava sighs. Her mother was a thespian in her youth and her voice still commands. Speaking in English, Mazna dwindles a little, her musical accent whispery over the years. But speaking in Arabic, Mazna is a woman accustomed to being listened to.

"What is it?"

"Hi, Avey." Her father's head briefly emerges above the fridge door.

"Some *big* news," her mother clarifies. "Another one of your father's reckless, impulsive plans. I wish you children didn't have to be involved."

"Of course you'd say that, Mazna. If I said the sky was blue, you'd disagree."

"Idris, this isn't a sky-is-blue matter and you know it."

"*Mama.* Can someone explain what's going on?"

"I'm getting to it," Mazna says, wounded. "You children are all so impatient. Last week, I called Mimi, and, I swear to God, I barely got to hello before he rushed in with excuses to go, telling me that studio time was expensive."

Ava exhales. There is only one way through and it involves walking directly into the whirlwind that is her mother's way of talking. *Zwarib,* the Arabic word for it — alleyways and dead ends in speech, syntactical circles before getting to the point. Linguistic terrorism, Naj says.

"So he's going ahead with recording? Mimi?"

"Yes, yes, he said it's worth trying to have a new album on hand for some festival in the fall."

"Huh." A realization dawns on Ava; her body starts to bristle. "I know that's really costly. He'd told me he couldn't afford it."

"I don't understand why he's still recording," her father chimes in, his voice muffled. "He should focus on the restaurant."

"How many times have I told you not to say that in front of him? It'll *wreck* his confidence!" Mazna smacks the counter.

"Is Mimi here now? Is Ava hiding him in her cupboard?"

Ava says, ignoring them, "Yup, there's no way he could afford the studio time unless someone's helping him.

"How would I know about recording-studio costs?" her mother says, alert now. She switches to English, a strategy long recognized by her children as calculating. "What am I, a banker?"

"Like, really costly," Ava continues. "I'm pretty sure his salary from Olive wouldn't even begin to cover it."

"Mazna, what have you done," her father says. "The boy needs to stand on his own two feet. He's thirty-five!"

Her mother glares at Ava. "What am I, an accountant?"

"Unless Harper chips in," Ava says, almost enjoying herself now. "But we both know how much Mimi hates asking her for money. That poor girl is still living in that bungalow because Mimi can't afford a higher mortgage."

"Poor girl? What poor girl? Poor Mimi. She is a *millionaire*. She's making your brother live like that, and in sin. Just marry, I told her last time." Here they both pause, remembering different versions of a family friend's wedding in California two years ago, an altercation between Mazna and a slightly buzzed Harper. *You're almost thirty-five,* Mazna said as Ava had watched in horror. *Your body has two, maybe three eggs left.* Harper, Texas-bred, polite, smiled, shrugged, and said in her aw-shucks sort of way, *Well, Mrs. Nasr, I guess I'm gonna have to let them scramble, then,* leading the table in laughter, but Ava recognized Harper's defeat in saying the one thing that would deflate Mazna like a balloon.

"Mama, if Mimi wanted it, he could *own* the damn restaurant by now," Ava says.

"That's what I keep telling him," Idris says.

"You leave your brother alone, Ava." Mazna's voice sharpens. "It's not easy being an artist. He's doing the best he can."

"I buy all his music," she says defensively, stung.

"Well, you don't know what it's like, do you? To do gig after gig? You have to face failure every single day. It's like going to war."

Hyperbolic, but Ava knows she has hit a nerve; her mother mentions her failed acting career rarely and only when she's commenting on her children's lives. "Fine, Mama! But if it's not Harper paying for the studio and it's not the salary from Olive, that really leaves only one option."

"Ava, we called to tell you important news, not gossip-gossip."

In the background, her father is shaking his head, but he doesn't say anything. He's nervous, she realizes. This plan of his must be big.

"Okay, Mama, okay. What's the news?"

"Well . . ." Mazna says primly, then glances back toward Idris. "Why don't *you* share?" Her father says something low that Ava can't make out. "Of course you don't want to," Mazna snaps. "You know it's a terrible idea."

Idris, holding a plate with a pickle and a sandwich, joins Mazna at the counter. She turns her attention back to Ava. "You know the house in Beirut?" she asks.

"Yeah?"

"We're selling it," Mazna says flatly.

"Wait . . . what?" Ava's head swims. This happens so often in conversations with her mother. She is still absorbing the earlier point — her mother had given Mimi money! Again! Ava hadn't even gotten an allowance when she was a kid! — so her brain lags like a record skipping. The image of the Beirut house — large, given to swampy heat in the summers, mosaic tiles in the garden, the walls of the bedroom she shared with Naj speckled with black mosquito blood — rises in her mind. There had been a period of her life, after the civil war ended and before she moved east for college, when they went to the house almost every summer, spending June to August in Beirut, driving into Damascus to see her mother's family for a week. She is relieved by the interruption of her father's voice.

"Well, when you say it like that! Where's the context?"

"What context? That's the news."

"I don't understand. What do you mean, selling the house?" There is a pause. Her father eats a pickle. "Baba?"

Her father finally looks up. "Baba, the house is sitting empty."

"Naj lives in Beirut," Ava says nonsensically. "And Aunt Sara! Does she know about this?"

"Well." Idris shifts in his chair. "Legally, the deed goes to the son's family."

Ava and her mother groan. "Oh-ho, your father," Mazna says, kissing her teeth. "The modern feminist."

"I didn't write the law," he counters.

"Sara's going to kill you," Ava warns him.

"Forget Sara," Mazna says. "I told your father — this isn't just your house, Idris! It's Ava's and Mimi's and Naj's. I mean, Naj has made Beirut her home. Where do you expect her to live once she's done gallivanting around like a bachelor? It's not proper —"

"Wait a second," Ava interrupts, sensing a *zwarib* about her sister's feckless lifestyle. Her head is spinning. "Don't *you* hate Beirut? You're the one that's always saying there's no need to visit." Her mother's reluctance to sell is confusing; for years one of her favorite lines has been *That country can go underwater for all I care.* It wasn't just an expression; she meant literally underwater.

"It *is* needless," her mother says defensively. "But that doesn't mean we should sell the last family house that belongs to us. I don't make huge decisions on my own. I don't just clap my hands, click my heels, house is gone!"

Because it's not your house, Ava retorts silently. Of course her mother would want to do something for years and back off as soon as Idris wanted to do it as well. Maybe her father was right.

"That house has become a mausoleum," Idris says, pronouncing the word "moo-za-leem." "Just poor Merry cleaning those rooms over and over again. You didn't see it the way I did this last trip. Neither of you." There's indictment in his tone. "The life has been taken out of it."

"Baba," Ava says, trying to gentle her voice. Idris is impulsive and sentimental by turns, a dangerous combination. "Maybe you just need to take some time. After Jiddo —"

"God rest his soul," Mazna says with rare solemnity. The other two repeat the words.

"Yes, rest his soul. After Jiddo, you must be shaken up. But there's no rush. I'm sure Naj could even find tenants for it."

"This is why I said to call Ava." Mazna beams at her. Despite herself, Ava straightens. "She's logical. She knows how to think."

"I think," Idris says thoughtfully, like he's picking a letter on a game show, "I'm still going to sell the house."

"God grant me fortitude," her mother mutters. Idris takes a bite of his sandwich, and they all fall into silence. "This is a terrible idea," she announces to nobody in particular.

"Do you want some?" Idris holds the sandwich out.

"Do you need all that mayonnaise? You're supposed to be watching your cholesterol."

"Can a man," her father says, "not get fat in peace? Even in his own house?"

"How do your patients take you seriously?" Her mother sounds spiteful. "You always have doughnut jelly on your collar."

Ava ducks her head to smile. Her father is barely taller than her and in recent years has sprouted an impressive spare tire.

"Avey!" Idris says suddenly. "I didn't tell you my other idea for this summer."

"You're selling the California house," she jokes, but her mother is too busy looking glumly into space to hear.

"I want to throw a memorial."

Ava frowns. "For Jiddo?" she asks carefully. It's been months.

"Yes, a ceremony to honor him. We can show old videos and give speeches, and the neighbors can all come by."

"The neighbors will think you're crazy," Mazna tells him. "There was already an *azza*. Nobody does memorials over there."

"We'll be trendsetters," he says, "and anyway, none of you were there the first time around." Finally — a direct accusation. "Only Naj."

"Naj lives there," Ava reminds him, though she still feels guilty.

"Be that as it may. We couldn't all make it," her father says archly.

"*We* had gallbladder surgery and were on bedrest," Mazna counters.

"*We* were cleared to travel."

"*We* didn't feel well enough!"

"Okay!" Ava interrupts. She peeks back in the bedroom. Nate has gotten dressed. The sight of him is confusing. It feels like he's the one hundreds of miles away; that's how consuming her parents can be. "Why don't I call you both tonight?"

"Wait, wait." Her mother stands. "Let's leave your father to his sandwich. I need some fresh air."

Ava sighs. This is code for more gossip. She obediently waves back at her father. "We'll talk more later, Baba."

"Nothing left to talk about," he says cheerily.

Mazna takes the phone and Ava sees a jumble of images — her mother's knee, the yellow couch. At the screen door, her mother slows — it always gets stuck — then she's outside. She sets the phone down, and all Ava can see is the blue, endless sky.

"Mama?"

"One second." Her mother reappears holding the phone too close to her, so only half her face is visible. "Can you believe your father? He's going to give me a stroke. I tried talking to him last night."

"What did he say?"

Mazna snorts. She gives a devastating pause. "He said one of his stupid hearts told him to sell."

"Mama, no." Ava chews the inside of her cheek to keep from joining in her mother's laughter, which feels like a betrayal of her father.

"Mama, yes. He said during his last surgery, he was holding one, and after he spoke to it, the thing apparently spoke back. Told him he had to sell his father's house! What a liar your father is."

Ava coughs to cover her laughter. "But Mama, you know that's part of his . . . his ritual. It's part of what makes him so good." At her father's hospital in Blythe, California, the nurses call him *the heart whisperer.* He is the only surgeon who bows his head and speaks to the hearts that have been pulled from splintered chests. Once, when Ava was a child, she'd asked him what he said. *I ask them to be good to their new humans,* he'd responded, a perfectly Idrisian answer.

"I don't know, Ava," Mazna says. "As far as I'm concerned, you speak to hearts, that makes you an interesting surgeon. The hearts speak back, that makes you a little loosey-goosey upstairs." Her mother ducks her head offscreen; a feather of smoke floats by.

"You're smoking!"

"Oh, for God's —"

"Mama! We talked about this. Does Baba know? I'm telling Baba." This is the family's default mode: tattling.

Her mother rapidly dives through the stages of negotiation, diplomacy, guilt, sweetness, and, finally, insult. "Ava, it's one cigarette. It's been a stressful week. Your father eats Kit Kats for breakfast — does anyone say anything to him? He's getting to be the size of a buffalo. Listen, I know you're a darling to care, I do. But do you think you're in a position to say anything? Don't you remember all those drugs you did at Harvard?"

Ava shuts her eyes briefly. "It was pot, Mama. I smoked pot. Like four times." Nate appears in the doorway. He has his THE NATIONAL shirt on. He mimes swinging a bat. Rayan's Little League practice. "Shit. Mama, I really do have to go. Thanks for the call. I'm sorry about Baba."

Her mother grunts. "We need to get there around June fourth. So find tickets for that weekend and let us know what flights you're on. The lawyer said it'll take a while to sort out the paperwork. They lost the original deed during the war."

"Wait, what? Why would we need tickets? What are you talking about?"

"Well." Another long exhale. "That's why we called, isn't it. Your names, all you children, are on the deed of the house. Your father can't sell without you there."

"Without us," Ava echoes faintly. Nate waves at her. *What?* he mouths.

"Yes, in Beirut. You all need to come to Beirut. I suppose we can do this memorial thing too, so Idris can stop complaining about the funeral. I'd had *surgery,* for God's sake. Anyway, the trip shouldn't take more than four, five weeks. Bring the children. Maybe we can make a holiday out of your father's godforsaken mission."

Ava hates the playdates of Park Slope — the organic unsalted almonds and white wine laid out for the mothers, the kindly barbs of *Oh, but of course you have to run to work,* to which Ava just smiles, never saying just how much she actually does *have to* work, that their modest one-floor apartment in a prewar brownstone, while partly paid for with Nate's family money, Upper East Side money, still has a crippling mortgage, and the children's school eats up nearly half her paycheck.

Several days have passed since her mother's phone call, and Ava's mood has lifted with each one. But even so, she is distracted with thoughts of her mother. She knows she needs to tell Nate. The problem is that to speak with Nate would be to splinter the fragile peace that has descended on their apartment in the past few weeks, after the marital logjam of nearly a decade together — their tiny discontents, Ava's long search for a professor position, disagreements about daycares and backsplash tiles and bank statements — had broken, Ava finally giving in to the oldest wifely impulse in the world: she snooped. And she found freckled cleavage. In an e-mail thread in Nate's Gmail account, a woman named Emily signed seemingly innocuous e-mails — *Loved the cake today. Meeting made me want to fall asleep* — with a series of *x*'s and *o*'s. In one e-mail, she'd included a selfie — copper hair, pale eyes, freckles all over. The cleavage underneath a black blazer, the camera obviously angled to capture as much of it as possible, was what had sent Ava over the edge.

She hadn't seen the rage coming. If anyone had asked her a year ago how she'd respond to finding slightly incriminating e-mails in Nate's mailbox, her best guess would've been with weepiness, self-hatred. Late-night recriminations. *What about our life? What have I done wrong?* Instead, she gave his laptop to the first homeless person she found in Prospect Park, a disgruntled Black man eating pumpkin seeds, who'd whistled and said, *Lady, this some sort of setup?* but eventually took it.

Nate was stunned.

"You realize, don't you," he'd said, panting, "that now some fucking *bum* has our family albums? Projects I worked on for years? Goddamn it, Ava, he has nude photos of *you.*"

"I don't care," she said, and she didn't. She was high on not caring, on the sheer irresponsibility of what she'd done; she was intoxicated with the way Nate looked at her for weeks after, a combination of fear and marvel; for the first time in her life she'd been neither responsible nor predictable, as crazy as a plot twist in a movie. She called him an asshole and a liar; she ended fights by kissing him unexpectedly, then bursting into tears. Entire days went by when she spoke to him only through Rayan (*Honey, can you ask your father . . .*), even when they were in the same room.

She was, for three weeks, her mother.

Of course, that level of caprice and rage is exhausting, and eventually Ava burned out. One evening when they were having the same argument for the fiftieth time, Nate telling her she had to stop this, that he'd made a mistake, that he was sorry and he loved her, she decided, abruptly, to forgive him.

It was a relief. She'd used up all her anger and self-pity; she was like a bonfire out of wood. She sank back into his arms wordlessly.

❖

The woman was an administrator at Sprout, the lifestyle-advertising firm Nate was a senior consultant at — she was *nothing,* he said, *a nobody,* just an office flirtation.

"Oh, I'm *so sure* he didn't fuck her. What an exquisite load of bullshit," her sister had said over the phone, her voice clipped and sarcastic. Ava regretted for the millionth time having told her. In a dark moment after the e-mail, she'd tried to call a friend, but, getting her voicemail, Ava had grown desperate. She wanted to call Mimi; she'd wanted to call Mimi ever since she'd found those e-mails. But she couldn't. Ava had fallen even more in love with Nate after they'd first visited California and Nate and Mimi had spent hours playing old Xbox games, their laughter tinkling throughout her childhood home. She still has a photo of them from that trip — Nate's arm loosely around Mimi's shoulder, the two men's smiles easy and open — tacked up at her desk at work. She knows that if Mimi ever found out about freckled cleavage, that smile would disappear for good.

And so, sobbing on her bedroom floor, Ava called Naj, even though it was four in the morning in Beirut. But she'd immediately wished she hadn't. Naj had the memory of an elephant. She didn't forget and she didn't let you forget either.

❖

Their marriage went limp with relief after those weeks passed. Nate took her to Atlantic City for their anniversary in March, an ironic honeymoon suite with champagne and rose petals. The months clicked by and now it's May and the truth is Ava likes all this; she likes their apartment, likes the Guatemalan lady — Cindy — who comes on Tuesday mornings, the thrilling scent of lemon polish and Windex that greets her after work on those days. As much as she complains about Brooklyn, it's partly because she can't believe it belongs to her, the same way she can't believe that Rayan and Zina belong to her; it's like she accidentally picked up the wrong life at the supermarket.

But her mother's call threatens to upend things. The summer has already been planned — a trip to the Finches' estate in Cape Cod, the children already enrolled in day camps — but also Nate has never quite relaxed into her parents. He is always too stiff around her father and too informal around her mother. Nate hoards his vacation days like Halloween candy, looks forward to Cape Cod all year. And she'd been looking forward to it as well after all those fights, a stretch of relaxing, endless days, the whole family lazy and tan.

It might be wrong, but more than wanting to be vindicated, Ava just wants to go back to how things were.

❊

"The lovely Finches!" Chloe trills out at the door. She promptly plops down to Zina's eye level and inquires, "Where can I get such *stylish* yellow buttons, Miss Zina?," then cocks her head and waits intently, as though Zina is a lady who lunches.

Zina gives Ava a mournful *Et tu?* look as Chloe leads her into the playroom with the other four- and five-year-olds, the ample-hipped Haitian Clarice running after them with cups of water and paintbrushes.

"Maybe I should —" The usual guilt pulses through Ava, a new limb she'd grown after Rayan's birth.

"Don't be silly, Eye-vah." Chloe's Georgian accent is at its most spectacular when she is in hosting mode. "You're here to relax, put your feet up. Parents these days are stuck on their kids like southern moss on brick. We have to let them *breathe*."

This last statement she delivers to the eight women gathered in her kitchen. Eight chins nod earnestly. The women greet Ava, kissing her cheek, getting her a glass of white wine. Female voices sweetly compete and gripe in the same breath.

"Can you believe summer's here? Is Maddie going to Camp Laurel again?"

"Not after what happened last year. Didn't you hear? One of the counselors was kicked out, something about drinking. I wouldn't send her there if you paid me . . . of course, that doesn't mean you should pull Beacon out, he's such a *hardy* kid. Maddie's an artist, you know. She just soaks all those things up."

"Ava, what do you think about Lake Bryn Mawr? I think it's too much. Don't you think it's too much? They're children, after all; the whole point is for them to have fun."

"Definitely," Ava says. "Definitely." She already feels tired.

"What about Nate?" Chloe asks. "He went to Trinity, didn't he? Or was it St. David's?"

"St. David's."

"Oh, right," says Susanna, a red-haired jeweler. "And then he went to Regis?"

"St. David's till ninth. Then Collegiate. Then Yale."

This is the real reason the mothers want her at their gatherings, the reason Zina and Rayan are always the first to receive bright-colored invitations to birthday parties: Nate. Or, rather, Nathaniel Tucker Finch IV, son of Lucy Babette Finch (née Washburn) and Nathaniel Tucker Finch III, a family that has its own crest, Upper East Siders by way of London — a cool three hundred years ago — a family that alternates between Maine and Cape Cod in August and owns estates older than Ava's family's infamous house in Beirut. They drink gimlets in the summer and cognac in the winter; they spend fortunes on beach houses and marry each other and have beautiful porcelain-skinned daughters and athletic sons; they call their children by animal nicknames — Bunny, Birdie — and vote Democrat every election. They are well read and can find Kabul on a map, but Ava knows it shocked them nonetheless when they met her and realized that Nate wasn't going to marry some typical Yale coed but *her,* a biologist, daughter of a Syrian actress turned housewife and a Lebanese heart surgeon. Marrying a woman with one foreign parent, they could understand. One foreign parent — preferably the mother so the daughter would have a pronounceable maiden name — would be exotic, but Ava was unavoidably entirely Arab, her bloodline cut with nothing else.

"St. David's," she repeats. "Although Lucy, his mother, says she always regretted not sending him to boarding school in Paris." This is simply untrue, one of the many lies she has fed the women over the years. Wealthy as they all are, their money *came from* somewhere — cotton farms or someone's great-grandfather writing a bestseller — and that ultimately sets them apart from the Finches, whose wealth had simply existed for as far back as the family tree went. Because of that, the Upper East Side of Ava's in-laws might as well be Prague; that's how unlikely it is that these women will ever meet her mother-in-law, Lucy.

"Paris," the women repeat with awe in their voices. For all their talk of eco-friendly diapers, their decidedly casual fashion choices — Kurt Cobain T-shirts, pigtails; they give the impression of children who have children — these mothers revere wealth as much as anyone. Or, rather, not *wealth* but what wealth leaves in its wake: veneration, respect, fear.

"God, I wish my mother-in-law wasn't such a bumpkin," Chloe declares. Several of the women laugh obediently. "The only advice she ever gives me is to buy burp cloths. You're so lucky to have Lucy, Ava."

"I am," Ava agrees. The truth is, of course, more complicated. Lucy and Tucker — to avoid confusion, all the Nathaniels go by different monikers — are always polite to her, but with an undertone of bewilderment, as though they're still surprised to see her. Occasionally, when Lucy has had too many drinks, she'll ask Ava to tell her about all that *unpleasantness happening in Syria,* as though Ava were a sixth-grader who'd written a term paper on it.

"Sometimes I think it's worth moving up to Park just for the schools."

"Good luck with that! My sister's friend Jane tried to get her daughter into Nightingale and there was a *four-year* waiting list."

"But just think of what the kids would get," Susanna says wistfully. She catches Ava's eye, and Ava tries to look neutral.

More exhausting than wealth is the appearance of wealth. The money, the money. Ava knows it isn't fair, but she's resentful of the money. The wealth that remains in the Finch clan is, as Nate likes to say, *mostly views and porch furniture,* concentrated in antique clocks and engagement rings, in houses that were erected in the eighteenth century and meant to be passed down to a few siblings but that are now, several generations later, used by dozens of cousins who time-share every summer. Nate's great-great-great-great-great-grandfather arrived from England and made his fortune centuries ago, and since then, his descendants had been drinking away the family's wealth, spending it on therapy, on trips to India, and on expensive tuitions, a lifestyle that wasn't sustainable because so many of them simply never worked. At this point, Zina and Rayan will be lucky to inherit a patio table.

"So, Ava, have you given any thought to the book club?" Sheila asks. She is plump and from the Midwest. Her husband works at Saks. She still has a pleasant honesty in her face that is incongruous with New York. Ava likes her, but the woman can be exhausting. She's always beginning sentences with *Back in Ohio* and organizing happy hours and get-togethers. In a city where effortlessness is currency, she tries too hard.

"It sounds so fun, it's just —"

"Back in Ohio, we'd do it once a month, with plenty of wine, and if the book had a movie, we'd watch it after the discussion. This month Chloe picked and we're reading —"

While Sheila is talking, a persistent chirp starts inside Ava's leather bag, slung over her chair.

"Oh, *sorry,* let me just put it on — oh, *shit.*" Ava glances up to see raised eyebrows. "Sorry, sorry. It's my mother. I should probably get this. Family stuff," she finishes enigmatically and Chloe waves her onto the deck, which overlooks a little tomato patch. Ava slides the door closed behind her and takes a breath, alone for a moment with the chirping.

"Mama?"

"Ava, do you not think, given my age, that it's an *unkindness* for you to worry me constantly? I've called you seven times. Seven times."

"I've been working and Rayan's school just ended. I'm actually at a play-date now."

"*Seven.* I've been trying to call your brother since yesterday. He's never able to speak. Najla just sent me a text with nothing but a question mark. A question mark, Ava! Does that seem like a reasonable way to respond to your mother's calls?"

"I'm not the one who sent it!"

"Well, I think you need to speak with her. She doesn't even know that we're coming to Beirut. You'll speak to her?"

"Why do I have to speak with her? She never answers and the reception is always shit —"

"*Your mouth,* Ava!"

Ava rolls her eyes. Her mother hates cursing. "The reception is always bad," Ava says. "Can't Mimi call her?"

"Your brother has a lot going on, Ava. He's got this new album to record." Ava swallows her irritation. Much as they like to bemoan Ava's siblings' careers, her mother and father understand them more than they do hers. They understand ambition, the hunger for the spotlight. Visibility. When Ava told her father during her sophomore year at Harvard that she wouldn't be taking all the premed classes and that her concentration would be molecular biology, Idris — beloved surgeon, saver of lives — had spluttered, *But, but . . . nobody will ever see your work!*

Molecular biology had already been a compromise for Ava; she preferred the dreamy, almost inventive world of theoretical mathematics, but she'd intuited during her freshman year that biology would be more impressive to her parents. (*My siblings are the free spirits,* she'd once joked to someone at a party and was confused by the look of pity he gave her.) But ultimately, academia was what Ava loved, the most familiar part of herself; she was a natural learner and had neither the ego nor the impatience that most students had. At Harvard, she marveled at the ancient tomes and at the small, hard biceps she got from toting them around. The biology texts could be impossible to read, but their very dreariness gave them a certain sanctity; somebody, Ava realized, had loved this enough to make it. Somewhere out there, somebody would always write more books on the radulae of gastropods or the function of S-layers and glycocalyces, and over the years, Ava began to see these folks — not their sexier counterparts, the studiers of chimpanzee mating habits or the Zika virus epidemic — as the true unsung heroes of the field. They devoted their lives to research so that Ava would know what made endospores survive.

And a few people had devoted their lives to those gastropods. So while her classmates complained about the tedium of classification tables, Ava perversely loved it more. She began to cast her professors in the same light. If no one taught microbiology, no one could practice it. The whole thing seemed honorable. When graduation saw her classmates capering off to the NIH and public-policy firms, Ava quietly submitted her résumés to teach. They couldn't all have the red hawks. Someone had to name the sea slugs.

Her mother's voice tugs Ava from her thoughts.

"So you'll call Najla, then," her mother says. "What day did you book your flights for?"

"I—wait, Mama. Wait." The abrupt change of topic takes Ava by surprise.

"What wait? I've been waiting two days. All I've been doing is waiting. Your father wants to book flights and I keep telling him we have to see what day you are arriving."

"Mama, I can't go," Ava says. But there's hesitation, and her mother hears it.

"Ava," she says, purring, her Vivien Leigh voice, "listen, *habibti*, you think I agree with what your father's doing? Selling the only thing on Arab soil that still belongs to us? My parents' house is gone. Much as I hate that goddamn city, Beirut's all we have left, and just because I'd rather never see it again doesn't mean I want that house gone."

"That's *exactly* what it means—"

"Not everything is a debate to be won, Ava," Mazna scolds. "In any case, Idris decides something needs to be sold, it must be sold. I swear that man will put me in an early grave. It's not my fault your names are on the deed! And anyway—" Here her mother gives a spectacular, theatrical sigh. "You're the only one I can count on."

There's a brief silence during which Ava, forty years old, is transported back to elementary school and the only time her mother chaperoned a field trip. How glamorous Mazna was, with her bobbed hair the color of a Hershey bar, her fur-lined pea coat, compared to the frumpy, ponytailed mothers. Mazna's presence had catapulted Ava, however briefly, into the orbit of the popular girls; this was her experience through childhood, at birthday parties and back-to-school nights—her mother made her own stock rise. Ava lets out an unconscious sigh, which her mother misinterprets as accusation.

"For God's sake, Ava!" Mazna snaps. "Fine. I lied. There is no deed."

Ava frowns at the azaleas tumbling their blue tails down the backyard fence. The petals are puffed out into little clouds, and there's a bee hovering over one of the stamens. Instinctively, Ava imagines her vantage point zooming in like a microscope, going past the bee to the invisible little hairs on each pistil, then even farther, to a host of mites wriggling across the stem.

"I mean, there *is* a deed. But your names aren't on it."

This is unusual for her mother. Mazna lies constantly, always has — *little whites,* she calls them — but never badly, and she never, ever takes them back.

"Mama," she finally says. "What's going on?"

Silence. "I don't want to go alone," her mother says. The Vivien Leigh purr is gone. She sounds small. "I've always had you children there with me. I told your father I had to stay here for work, but he said he needs me there — not that he deserves it or anything. He wants my help with this memorial of his. And — well." That *well* says it all, the decades of a marriage moored to umbrage and disagreements but also a shared history, hard and glinting, embroidering the years like a snake's backbone.

"But you've gone there without us before . . ." Ava says, confused, her voice trailing off as her mind counts back the summers — her father's trip two years ago to visit his father, then another trip for her aunt's surgery the year Rayan was born, then the funeral — and she realizes that, no, her mother hasn't been back to Beirut since Ava's adolescence. Even the one time Ava took Nate to Beirut, before the children were born, her mother had made excuses. Only Idris had gone; he'd played dutiful host, taking her and Nate to the grottoes and cedars, complaining about the roads the entire time. "Mama," she says, more gently now, "I'm sure he's not going to kick Merry out. And I'm not convinced Sara has no say. It's probably not even legal —"

"What legal? It's a country run by crooks and bandits."

"— and even if he gets Sara to agree, I don't think having us there will make a difference. What if I try speaking to him one-on-one? Maybe I can talk sense into him."

There's a long silence. "I don't want to go alone," her mother repeats quietly.

The bee has moved on to the dahlias. When Ava was in high school, she'd used a microscope from the biology lab to magnify an insect wing (she'd felt drunk then on the possibilities of magnification — hair! Saliva! Dandelion seeds!) and spent nearly half an hour scrutinizing its rivering ridges, the tiny hairs like cactus spines, coils at the edge of the wing.

"Ava?" Mazna's voice is a touch more imperious. She dislikes asking for things. "Are you going to make me beg?"

"Okay." The word tumbles out of Ava's mouth before she conjures it. "Okay, I'll come. We'll come."

"Oh, Ava!" She sounds as pleased as a child. "I knew you'd say yes. And you'll call Najla? And don't tell Mimi about the deeds. You're a darling," she adds, an obvious afterthought. "The best child."

The best child. Her mother's line, for years. After she hangs up, Ava feels dizzy with instantaneous regret and exhilaration. Her mother isn't the takesy-backsy type, as Rayan would say. A yes, in Mazna's world, is a yes. Her cell phone pings. *NateLove* appears across the screen, and Ava's pulse quickens as though she's been caught, as though Nate somehow heard the conversation with her mother. She presses a thumbprint onto the home button and the text message opens.

Honey, I have news. We need to talk, maybe on the way to the party?

"Yes, we do," Ava mumbles. What has she done? She walks back through the sliding doors and into the kitchen, and the women turn toward her all at once, reminding her of birds on a telephone wire.

"So, Ava," Sheila begins. "I was saying that —"

"I can't join the book club, Sheila." There is a relief in telling the truth, like ice water against hot skin. Ava wills her face into some expression of regret. "I wish I could, I really do, but — this is actually why my mom just called — something's come up with the family, and we won't be here this summer. I have to go to Beirut."

The day races quickly to its nucleus. When she gets home, Winnie, the babysitter, is already in the kitchen, removing the crusts from bread slices.

"Peanut butter?" she asks in her little-girl voice, which Ava finds annoying.

"And Nutella!" Zina says, gazing up at her adoringly. Zina loves Winnie's bobbed hair, her long necklaces. Even Rayan seems soothed by Winnie's presence.

Ava's almost excited about Beirut now. It's like jumping into a cold swimming pool; you dread it, but once you surrender, it's luscious. She and her siblings will talk their father out of selling the house, she knows they will. Zina and Rayan could play in the same courtyard she had, and she and Nate could go off on boozy lunches, leaving the kids with her mother. She's not teaching any courses at Fordham this summer; the three articles she needs to work on can be written anywhere. And Jiddo — her guilt has been gathering these past few months about missing the burial.

"Kiddos," she attempts as they eat the sandwiches, "would you like to go to Beirut this summer? We'll see Teta and Jiddo. And Auntie Naj. We're going to have a memorial for *my* jiddo. You remember I told you he died?"

"Jiddo's baba is in heaven now," Zina says confidently.

Rayan sighs in a world-weary fashion. "You're a moron," he tells her.

"Rayan!" Ava and Winnie say at the same time. Rayan has recently developed a coolness; on his seventh birthday, he informed her that *clowns are for pussies,* which resulted in a three-day fight between Ava and Nate — who were still barely speaking after the Emily incident — about whether they should've moved to Westchester when Rayan began kindergarten.

"My friend Selin spent a few months in Beirut," Winnie says more to Ava than the kids. "At some refugee NGO. It's really horrible what's happening." Winnie sounds truly mournful.

"It is." Ava shifts uncomfortably. She pretends to be distracted by Rayan. She doesn't want to hear Winnie's thoughts on Syrian refugees. "Honey, Teta really wants to see you."

"I like Teta," Rayan acknowledges grudgingly.

"Can Pippa come with us?" Zina asks.

Ava smiles. Pippa is Zina's bedraggled stuffed rabbit. *Such simple desires,* her mother had once commented while watching Zina entertain herself with a wisp of tissue paper. "Yes, Zinzin, Pippa can definitely come." She switches to Arabic. "What does Pippa want to see in Beirut?"

Zina rattles on in English about beaches and toy stores. Ava feels a ping of guilt. When she and Nate take the children to visit her parents in California, Mazna insists on speaking to them in Arabic and harasses Ava for being a "fake Arab."

It's one thing, Ava's mother has said many times, *to marry an* ajnabi, *live in an* ajnabi *city. But to deprive your children of their heritage? It's a tragedy.*

"And you can ride a roller coaster there. It's almost definitely not up to any building code, but we have to live a little, right?" Ava tells Rayan. He jumps from his chair, elbows Zina away, and stands on his tiptoes to speak in Ava's ear.

"I hope it's extra-creaky." He beams. His breath smells like Cheetos and peanut butter. He's a boy, Ava remembers, and she pulls him to her, smothers him in a trail of loud, smacking kisses from the top of his head to his ear until he wriggles away, saying, "Stop, gross, Mama, stop," but he's laughing.

"Listen," Ava says in a low voice to Winnie, straightening up. "Don't mention the Beirut stuff to Nate. I — we still have to sort some things out."

Winnie smiles with the condescension of a younger woman. *When I have a partner . . . when I have kids . . .* Sometimes Ava can practically hear her thinking these things. "Of course," Winnie says sweetly. "Not a word."

❈

For Nate's work party, Ava chooses a shift dress with flouncy, diaphanous sleeves that cover her upper arms. Her body is pear-shaped, and two pregnancies have only cemented that. She'd wept after Rayan's birth when she realized that her hips had irretrievably widened, like a cave chipped open. She pulls her hair back into a bun and sighs into the mirror. Her vanity seems to increase with age. *Shit luck,* as Naj would say. The front door opens. Ava can hear the children clucking over Nate with excitement.

"Ave!"

Her stomach knots before she remembers why: Beirut. After a minute, she calls back, "In here." The dress is a little short and she tugs at the hem. "Are we doing train or car?"

"Car's easier, I think. That way we don't have to worry about a cab at the station." Nate appears in the doorway. She watches him change into fresh clothes, notes the long parentheses around his mouth, deepened with age, the sandy hair with extra salt-and-pepper since he'd turned forty. He has longer eyelashes than she does, a stubborn set to his thin lips that Rayan inherited.

"Ready?"

Ava shakes her head. "I could stand here all day. Let's go."

❖

Ava met Nate when she was twenty-nine. It was an odd time to start a relationship; she'd already lived alone, had had two serious boyfriends, and felt both indulgent and wary of men. She was old enough that she'd begun to think about her ovaries but young enough that she still got blackout drunk. He was the roommate of her friend's cousin; they met at a poker table. It was a small game at an old roommate's house. Before that, she'd been at a girlfriend's birthday party on Ludlow. There'd been a row of cupcakes, each topped with a candy heart, a candle in the middle. After the singing, they'd all had to blow the candles out together.

Ava hadn't played poker for years — it had been her college job, instead of waiting tables or working at the library, an uncommon risk for her, which was why she loved it — but she'd always had a good head for numbers. She never counted cards. She didn't have to. The probabilities were spelled out on the table, clear as sunrise. She hadn't had a gambling problem *exactly,* but she came close, and there was one semester when she'd lost five thousand dollars, just like that, and then she *had* had to bus at a nearby diner for a full year. Now that she considered it a treat, she had rules: only with friends, only before two a.m., only if she was moderately sober.

That night, she'd cleaned the table out.

Afterward, Nate had come up to her in the kitchen. She was squeezing a lemon into her beer. "I don't usually play."

Ava smiled. "That's what they always say."

"I got distracted." He leaned in. "Your scent has been driving me crazy."

"What scent?" she'd said, flirting.

He considered. Finally, he snapped his fingers. "You smell like a birthday party." Ava had to swallow her laughter.

The first night they'd slept together had been in Ava's small studio, with low lovely windows and a bright kitchen, in Greenpoint. The landlady above her was a Polish grandmother who always invited Ava over for Christmas, and Ava had had the sense of doing something illicit as she and Nate tiptoed down the rickety hallway to her door. Ava lit the large Anthropologie candle on her windowsill for the first time. They drank whiskey from her water glasses and Nate teased her about the floral calendar above her desk. He told her about his private school in Manhattan, his parents, that long lineage of rich, white people, how he felt both gratitude and shame for their fortune. They talked in that deep, eager way of early love, when every thought feels new as snow, and you see yourself in another person, glowing and pretty and clever.

That was how Ava felt that night — incandescent with candle smoke and her winnings. She kissed him first and felt bold as she tossed her shirt to the side like a girl in a movie. Her body suddenly seemed miraculous, even with her heavy breasts, her broad hips. *I'm Rubenesque,* she thought when Nate nudged her against the wall and she caught a glimpse of her half-naked body in the mirror, her brown skin, even in midwinter, contrasting against his.

"Gotta pee," Nate mumbled into her neck. "It's gonna be hell with this." His erection poked comically into her thigh. "You're wild," he tossed over his shoulder.

Left alone, Ava had panted in the half dark. Her mind spun. She felt, for the first time, like an interloper in her own life. It was like betting everything on bum cards. She wanted to be wild. Suddenly, with a pang that she recognized as absurd, she wanted Nate, not just his long, whitish body, but his private school and upholstered family heirlooms and correct forks. She listened to the sound of his pissing and was seized by an idea. Over by the windowsill, the candle flickered. She blew it out, then ducked her hair — at the time, long and thick — over the wisps of smoke as they rose.

The drive to the Hamptons is long and filled with stretches of slow, maddening traffic. They chat about work, then fall into periods of silence. Ava likes being married. It suits her. Their life after children has taken on an inevitability that she finds lulling, working like a well-organized ecosystem — she'd realize Zina's hair needed washing, and he'd arrive soon after, bringing the strawberry shampoo Zina loved from the store. The scientist in her dislikes sloppy statistics — yes, fifty percent of marriages end, but that's only scary without context. That figure doesn't take into account length of courtship or socioeconomic status or the presence or absence of abuse. Nate sighs by her side, shading his eyes with his hand to block the sun. She's seen him do it a thousand times.

"You should put your visor down," she says, watching him squint.

"It cuts into my vision," he replies, as she knew he would. There's a pause, then he turns to her. "You knew I'd say that, didn't you?"

"I don't know what you mean." She grins, turning up the radio. It's a rap song from her twenties and she hums along. "Predictability is the bedrock of human behavior, *habibi*."

"*Inti habibi*," he says in his silly foreigner's accent. Ava holds her breath. This is the perfect moment. She'll tell him about the trip casually, like it's an afterthought. Like her mother would.

"Mama called again," she begins. Nate *hmm*s under his breath. She wants to buy herself more time. She remembers something. "Wait! Your text! I completely forgot. What were you going to tell me?"

He lets his head drop. "You're going to kill me, Ave."

"It might be mutual."

"What do you mean?"

"Nothing." She waves her hand. "Go on."

"You know how Alice wanted to talk to me this morning?"

"You're stalling. Yes."

"They've decided to go forward with the Portland office." Nate says it quickly.

"That's good news, isn't it?"

"Kind of." He doesn't sound like it is. "It'll mean fewer hours once they're up and running. But Alice needs someone to go out west for a few weeks this summer. There's going to be a whole training module. For, like, two months."

Ava's stomach drops. Nate is a senior consultant at the ad agency; he picks headlines, top seasonal products, determines which influencers on social media to back. "It's you," she says flatly.

"She hasn't decided yet. But it might be. They need someone senior enough to do this. I'm trying to get out of it, but I thought you should know."

Something occurs to Ava. "Two whole months," she says sharply, and he winces. His hand snakes behind the headrest and squeezes her shoulder.

"Alice said I'd be going alone," he says slowly, answering the question she hasn't asked.

"Just like a bachelor," she says meanly.

"Ava. Don't do that." His voice softens. He'd cried when she told him she'd found the e-mails. He'd said that he'd made *a mistake I can come back from.* "I was thinking maybe you and the kids could join me. That's what I wanted to talk to you about."

She knows he's telling the truth. That's the thing about Nate. She doesn't always know when he's lying, but the truth reeks off him like cologne. The rest of the car ride passes coolly. Ava's angry but it doesn't seem fair, which angers her further. Now the idea of Beirut seems like a prank, enormously unlikely. And maybe Portland wouldn't be so bad for the summer. Her mother would be fine. They arrive at Alice's house before she can give it much more thought and Nate turns into the driveway.

"I really just found out," he says. "It's not even for sure."

Her irritation deflates. If she tells him she's afraid that Freckles will be inside, Nate will turn the car around and drive home. He's good like that. "I know." They walk up the driveway together.

Alice has a gray bob, the personality of a hurricane, and a body that looks like it belongs to a twenty-year-old. She'd started the company in the nineties and rode the health-food wave to the top of magazine covers and TV slots. Sprout was a big deal. They consulted on international food budgets, had millions of followers on Instagram. There were Jungian psychologists on the strategy board who helped graphic designers find archetypal images that screamed well-being and vigor on a primal level. Having heard the gossip from Nate — apples, flowers mid-bud, hourglasses — Ava thrilled at sighting the logos in stores. It was all trickery, she came to understand. We are told what we want by people in suits. Alice herself has been divorced three times, most recently from a Finnish woman, and flirts outrageously with all her employees' spouses, both wives and husbands. Ava sees her only twice a year, at the Christmas party and this one. She loves her.

"You look like your goddamn namesake in that dress," Alice calls out as they approach the front door. She always says the same thing. Ava had once told her that her mother had named her after Ava Gardner and the older woman had literally stood up from her barstool and applauded.

"Oh, please," Ava protests. Attention discomfits her, especially when the bestower of that attention is in her mid-sixties and wearing a tangerine bikini. Alice has wrapped a lemon-colored sarong around her waist, which is much smaller than Ava's. "You're —" Ava doesn't even finish the sentence, just waves her arms at the hostess. Alice nods gracefully.

"Wear beige, they say. Hide your wrinkly knees with pants, they say." Alice tucks her hair behind her ears. "To hell with that."

"Amen," Nate cheers. He kisses Alice's cheek.

"No kids?"

"They're with the nanny," Ava explains as the woman hugs her. Alice smells like pepper and lemon.

"Better. Just the grownups. Nate, the sales department has already downed half the whiskey. Please don't feel obligated to catch up."

She ushers them into the massive house that's the opposite of its owner — muted, serene. It is a summer home, classically decorated in the manner of WASPs: woven baskets filled with flip-flops and sunscreen tastefully placed in corners of the otherwise white rooms. Not off-white but *white*-white, fluffy-cloud white, and in fact every part of the house — hardwood floors covered in white Persian rugs, velvet couches, cushioned window seat — looks like it could be lain upon at any moment.

"The place looks great," Nate says as they pause in the kitchen — even the refrigerator is painted a steely white — while Alice plucks two beers nimbly from the freezer.

"I'm getting tired of the white." Alice waves her hands. "Ava, I expect you absolutely loathe me over this Portland thing. I'm trying to avoid it, but he's the absolute best we've got. Portland is lovely in the summer. We can find a nice camp for the kids."

"We'll see," Ava says noncommittally, but Alice doesn't seem to mind. They follow her outside, and Ava feels a surprising fatigue as she stands at the French doors, a massive lawn beckoning them to a turquoise pool. All the younger women are taking laughing selfies. A few have kicked their shoes off. It reminds her of Winnie talking about refugees. She feels outside of life instead of in it, as though she's walking through a movie set. She wishes her mother would call her again. She could use Mazna's bracing voice, a reminder of who she is.

There are dozens of people milling around the exquisitely manicured lawn. The quiet elegance of the house continues in the backyard, where a row of holly hedges is trimmed into large rectangles. The men all wear similar outfits of neutral polos and khakis, while the women seem to be competing with the bright, vibrant flowers of the rhododendron bushes. But none, Ava notices with some satisfaction, come close to outdoing Alice herself, who moves her skinny body through the crowd, kissing guests on their cheeks and calling out names.

"Those ghastly deer," Alice cries, gesturing to a slightly dented bush. "They gobbled my poor hydrangeas up."

Only in the Hamptons, Ava thinks, would deer be worse than vermin.

They greet various people, then Nate slips into the crowd. Ava wanders over to the catered table, simple, high-quality foods with waiters in black-and-white uniforms serving them: unshucked oysters in buckets of ice, several trays of prosciutto, fruit salads in glass cups.

Colleen Winstead, whip-thin, another senior consultant, nods at the prosciutto. She lays a hand on Ava's arm. "Personally," she whispers, "I think it's disrespectful. It's the only meat option!" She raises her eyebrows. *"Not everyone eats pork."*

Ava smiles politely.

Sprout is a high-profile company, more prestigious than the startup du jour and less ridiculous than Goop. It has attracted a certain type of employee: smart, well read, religiously PC, often an East Coaster by choice or lineage. That didn't necessarily mean white — the director, Lynn, is Korean-American, though her fidelity seems more to social status than race — but it did mean white in a conceptual sense. There was a whiteness that seemed to transcend race in these spaces; they conferred whiteness upon anyone inhabiting them.

That's why Colleen's comment grates more than endears. An outcry in an echo chamber isn't much of an outcry.

"There's a nice bruschetta right there," Ava replies sweetly. Even though she has no taste for the salty meat, she takes two slices and walks over to Nate.

"Yeah, girl," Nate stage-whispers. "You eat that pork. Explode those stereotypes."

"Shut up," Ava says. She puts the prosciutto on his plate.

The yard is purring with dozens of different conversations; people are laughing or brow-furrowing. She doesn't see Freckles. Without Ava realizing it, her shoulders relax after the third wine as she's talking with one of the marketing consultants, Mary, about Instagram fitness models.

"That's the problem with the health industry in general," Mary is saying. "They co-opt the idea of health. It's another version of fat-shaming but dressed up better." Her words have the cadence of a well-rehearsed speech. Ava can imagine it not going over well in board meetings. Alice believed her brand — thin *was* better.

"It's kinda like all the Mommy Fittest bullshit," Ava says. She's borrowing from the Park Slope groups; they talk about this stuff all the time. "Like, *Love your post-baby body! Embrace your stretch marks! But also, here's a prescription for a sixty-dollar retinol cream.*"

"Speaking of," a large man booms from her side. He's vaguely familiar. Nate stands next to him. "How are the kiddos?" Ava and Mary exchange a brief, female peep of irritation.

"Yes, let's see them," Mary says gamely. "God, it's been like two years."

The group turns expectantly toward Ava even though Nate is right there. She understands. She's the mother. Ava pulls up photographs on her phone and obediently passes it around. They admire. Ava swipes her screen dark again, tucks it in her bag. The conversation moves on to real estate.

"They say Bushwick will triple," Mary is saying, "but I keep telling Peter, I don't want to have to tuck my debit card into my boots every time I walk home."

"Totally," Ava murmurs. Nate catches her eye and she has to suppress a laugh. There will be mimicking of this later in the car, an inside joke in the making. A hot little speck of joy sunflowers in her chest, for Nate and the sunshine and even Sprout, all these silly, rich people who have, after all — the realization dawning on her — known her for nearly a decade. Somehow they're her friends too.

Her phone buzzes.

"Win," she tells Nate and goes into the living room. "Hi, Winnie."

"Ava, I'm sorry, but Rayan *here*" — Winnie's voice rises in pitch — "is insisting that you said he could have Snickers ice cream for dinner. And I told him —"

"I absolutely did not."

"— I said, 'If that's the case, then I'll happily give it to you, but I need to check with your mother, Rayan,'" Winnie continues, barreling on like a patient, saintly train. Ava can hear her son protesting in the background.

Ava sighs. "Put him on, Winnie. Sorry."

"What." Rayan's sullen voice. "I don't want the lasagna! It's gross."

"Again, Rayan? Why are you giving Win such a hard time?"

"Because you're always *nagging* me," he shoots back and Ava is momentarily stunned. The phrasing sounds foreign and adult in his little voice, the product of copycatting. If he were in front of her, she might've slapped him.

"You —" She takes a breath so she doesn't curse. "You don't talk that way to me. Do you understand?"

"I don't want to talk anymore," he says flatly, and the line goes dead.

He sounds exactly like his father, Ava thinks — although that isn't entirely true; he just sounds like a man. She briefly feels an inexplicable, irrational despair, as though by channeling Nate, Rayan has negated her.

Her mood is ruined. The house is quiet save for some voices in the foyer. Ava walks to the living room, touches the velvet couch and perfectly white walls. Everything pulses with wealth; it reminds her of her in-laws' house, only Alice's rooms have the luster of something current, money in the present tense. Winnie texts her an apology, but Ava ignores it. She'll reply later. *Fuck Rayan.* Even the thought sends a little thrill through her, so clean and unmaternal: *Fuck Rayan and his shitty personality.* She's drunk and a little tired and she doesn't have to think about him right now.

When she gets near the front door, the voices become clearer. It's Alice talking to someone.

"So soon, dear! You barely made an appearance."

"I know, I'm sorry to jet like this. I have a thing on the Upper West Side. If I leave now, I'll get there, like, Tuesday."

Alice's laugh tinkles.

Ava peers around the corner to see two women hug. Alice steps back and there she is, in full view: Freckles. *Emily.* Barefoot and in shorts and a thin, red halter top. Her hair is less red than in the photograph, but it's still her most striking feature. Alice vanishes, and the girl bends over to put on her sandals, stepping on an ivory Moroccan-style ottoman near the door. Ava glances behind her. There's nobody else around.

"Hi," she says. Emily startles.

"Oh! Hi! Sorry, I was just — should I not be putting my feet on this, do you think?" She widens her eyes comically. "It probably cost a thousand dollars."

"More. I think that's horsehair."

"Oops! I'm Emily, by the way." She straightens. "Are you new at Sprout?"

"Yes," Ava fibs. "I'm Ana." The name on the fake ID she used in college. "I'm one of the Portland people."

"Oh, good," Emily says nicely. She's glancing at the front door. "Everyone's really great at Sprout. You'll meet loads of people soon."

"There are some cute guys too," Ava says desperately. "I'm single. Bad breakup."

Emily looks at her curiously. "Well, it was nice to meet you." Ava feels herself wilt against the wall. She can't think of anything else to say. Emily seems to take pity on her. "I might be in Portland," the younger woman shares kindly. "We can get a drink or something."

Ava's heart stops. "For the training," she says blandly.

"Alice was just telling me I might need to go help set up some administrative things. I'm in IT. Just for a week or so. The main guy's really nice; you'll be in good hands."

"Do you know who it is?" Ava waits. She wants to hear her say it.

"Um." They walk toward the living room, where the lawn is visible. Emily stands on her tiptoes, scanning the backyard from the French doors. Her sandals are flat, strappy and metallic. They look a little cheap. "I think Alice was saying it would be Nate. That guy over there, in the blue shirt? The tall one."

Ava can't tell if Emily's voice changes at his name. She seems nonchalant, even kind. She follows the woman's gaze to her husband. If this were a French novel, she thinks, Nate would look up right now. His face would fall. But instead, he tips a shucked oyster into his mouth. "He's *cuu*-ute," Ava says in a parody of a drunk woman. She lets out an ugly laugh. *I've lost my mind.* Emily takes a tiny step back.

"I think he'll be doing the training" is all she says. The woman's phone buzzes and she reaches for it like a lifeline, saying she really has to go. "See you on the West Coast."

"See you," Ava says. She waits a minute before going back outside. Her heart is pounding. She pours herself a glass of the Riesling and takes a quick gulp. The sun is strong. Across the lawn, Nate is telling a story. He's seen nothing. It's like it didn't happen.

The highway is surprisingly clear on the way back, and Ava pretends they're racing the setting sun, which flirts in and out behind the pines. Nate sings along to the radio. He's too drunk to be driving, Ava thinks, and for a second she imagines their car tumbled, Winnie getting the horrifying phone call. Their children orphans. *"La samah Allah,"* she mutters. She reaches out and touches Nate's wrist against the wheel.

"Mama wants us to go to Beirut this summer," she announces. After all that wine, the statement doesn't sound quite as ridiculous to her as it did. But Nate stops singing, lowers the volume on the radio.

"I thought she hated Beirut."

"She does. I think. I don't really know."

"I have a question." Nate pauses. She waits. "Does it matter if he sells? Your father. You all seem upset about it, but the house is — none of you live there. It's not going to be used."

Ava is surprised at the rush of blood to her ears. "It's —" She stops, swallows. "We went there all the time. My grandparents loved that house. *I* loved it." Saying it aloud makes it true. "And my dad wants to do a memorial for my grandfather. But she needs me to go and — I thought it would be nice. For the kids." Ava's slurring a bit. She can hear it.

"I mean." Nate rubs his jaw. "If you want to. Will it be safe? I'm a little worried about Portland, if Alice ends up asking me to —"

"She probably will," Ava says cautiously. "And it's okay. If my options are having the kids here solo for the summer or going somewhere else with them, I pick the latter. And in that case, I might as well do Beirut." Her logic is surprisingly clear. "I think it's safe enough?" Making it a question rather than statement doesn't seem to reassure Nate. People live in Beirut, raise children there; there are dog parks and vegan bakeries and DJ beach parties. But she knows what he's asking about — the kidnappings, the spillover violence from Syria. The country is always on the brink of some riot or assassination.

Nate wrinkles his brow, thinking. "Let's talk about it more later." He puts the volume back up. She already knows he can be swayed.

A flock of birds swoop against the fading sky. Nate flips the headlights on. In ten minutes, she won't be able to make out the trees anymore. It'll be too dark. She remembers something Naj told her months ago, when things were getting better with Nate.

I think, her sister said, *as long as things with that white girl are* over-*over, you'll be able to forgive him.*

Ava groaned under her breath. (This was the thing she most regretted telling Naj. Mid-sob, she'd blurted out, *It's that she's white, Najla. Do you understand? That's what makes it worse. Do you get that?* And her sister, uncommonly somber, had admitted, *I do.*)

How am I supposed to find out if it's really over? Ava asked. *I don't want to snoop.*

I don't know how you're going to find out, Naj said almost gently. *But you should.*

And then, like a bratty, punk-rock clairvoyant, her little sister hung up.

Almost Rock Star

MIMI STILL WEARS the eyeliner, although he has dispensed with the torn jeans, the leather wrap bracelet, even the shaggy Cobain hair. The last was the most difficult to give up, the barber finally saying, "Hey, man, *you* paid me to do this. What's with the Bambi eyes?" When it was over, his neck brushed off, a more-than-generous dollop of gel parting his hair to the side so that he resembled his elementary-school self more than a man about to turn thirty-three, Mimi's eyes pricked with tears and he'd had to pretend he'd gotten hair in them. The barber just shook his head.

Afterward, he'd gone over to Cordelia's apartment. *Happy?* he'd snapped when she opened the door, and she'd shrugged and gotten him a beer. Cordelia is his best friend, but also his boss, the owner of Olive, an Italian-Arab fusion restaurant that she'd convinced Mimi to work at a decade earlier after he'd graduated from college with no job prospects, just a string of cooking gigs and the stunned realization that there didn't seem to be a record deal waiting for him. He started as a line chef, coming up with seasonal menus, but he'd rapidly been promoted to manager, which he was grateful for, though he did feel estranged from the kitchen staff after being removed from the bustle of the line.

Your hair is the antithesis of the restaurant's ethos, she often said in that faux-Southern accent of hers — Cordelia, who was raised on a cattle ranch in Alpine, Texas, but liked to ape socialite Savannah. *Olive is supposed to be an elegant dining experience, and then you waltz in with that greasy mop on your head.*

Nobody's complained yet.

They will, she'd predicted and in the end she was right. One night, after seven years of working as the manager, the person who checked on important guests and brought out complimentary desserts and glasses of wine for celebrations, he'd served a chocolate–olive oil cake to an elderly couple celebrating their anniversary. Halfway back to the stand, he heard the woman's voice ring out across the restaurant: *Dis-gus-ting!*

It was a hair, one long curly strand, black as coal, undeniably Mimi's. Cordelia was more triumphant than pissed. Her *I told you* came in threes — once in front of the couple, once during the family meal the next day, and once alone, later that night, bouncing on the balls of her feet as they split a cigarette.

It's time, Samson.

But the eyeliner has stayed. Tonight, half an hour before his band's set time at Tulip, a tight, hip space usually filled with tough-looking women and their feminine boyfriends, Mimi changes into his band outfit — dark jeans, black T-shirt. Whereas youth was a time to stack on accessories, Mimi is starting to realize that as you get older, it's best to keep it simple. He pulls out the stubby eyeliner pencil, filched from his sister Naj a few years ago.

The eyeliner is old, flaking. Back in his twenties, he would draw thick circles around his eyes; now he barely brushes the pencil beneath his lower lashes, a trick he learned from Harper. *What a dream,* she'd quipped, *my boyfriend taking makeup tips from me.*

He fights Cordelia and Harper on it, the two women saying it makes him look *so adolescent,* but the truth is that's the point. His crow's-feet are more pronounced than ever, his hair slightly gray near the temples — if it were long, he'd pointed out to Cordelia, no one would notice — his thirty-five years plainly shown in certain lights. It's disconcerting. Certainly, *rock star* is preferable to *aging rock star.* But what about someone who was neither, someone who'd spent the past decade playing gigs in small basements at first, then in slightly less small basements, then finally graduating to South by Southwest last year, but only as the opening act for one of the first bands of the day to an audience of college kids who'd started drinking too early. Mimi's band, Dulcet — he's the lead singer and second guitarist — had played their hearts out but there simply weren't enough people watching.

❖

The band has four members: Mimi, Allie (bass), Jacob (drums, occasional vocals), and Diego (lead guitar). Jacob is a music snob, someone who spends his weekends browsing actual record stores in East Austin; if you don't recognize an esoteric song he mentions, he shakes his head and mutters things like *Music's dead, man, music's dead.* Diego and Allie are cousins, both slender and gray-eyed, their parents raised in San Miguel. They smoke a lot of pot and love Miracle Legion. Allie is darker, and she wears her hair loose and greasy over her shoulders. Mimi had known she was trouble from the second she walked into the audition, slung her studded bass strap around her neck, and played "Come as You Are" with her eyes shut.

Dulcet is on its fifth incarnation, the only original member Mimi himself, who'd started the band the year after he graduated. Back then, it was him and a group of smart, genial guys he'd known in the music department at college, all brown, their families hailing from Peru or Afghanistan, and they all shared in the songwriting. But one by one those guys had drifted off, answering a call louder than the band's, lost to women or jobs in accounting or relocations to California.

Mimi stayed on. His father started to make suggestions. *Mimi, of course I know how talented you are, how much you love music, but what if you . . . maybe it's time to . . .* He'd leave the sentence trailing for Mimi to finish. When Mimi went home to visit, Idris referred to him as the owner of Olive, a revision that spoke volumes. Only his mother spoke of the restaurant as his side job, e-mailing him articles about local bands that ended up on *SNL.* When he once confessed to her — a little drunk on the phone — that he thought he might quit the band, her outraged response startled him.

"You think Mozart quit? You don't *quit* music, Mimi. It's in your blood. I've been watching you play since you were five."

"I'm not Naj," Mimi had said sulkily, but the pep talk worked. The next morning, he was at practice at nine.

It was the restaurant that people — other than his mother — shifted their attention to over the years, his father framing a rave from *Time Out,* friends begging him to cook during holidays. He'd slowly stopped mentioning the band. It had been years since his parents had seen him play. His mother still calls him an artist and sends money whenever he asks, but he understands what's left unsaid — that Naj doesn't need any pep talks. His parents are fairly predictable; it isn't the dream of music they have an aversion to so much as failure.

He'd found all his current bandmates through the usual channels. He'd met Diego through a former classmate, and Allie through Diego. Jacob was the younger brother of an old bandmate circa 2012, when Dulcet briefly flirted with electronica and needed a keyboardist.

Mimi himself is loyal to Dulcet to a fault. When an old roommate had asked if Mimi wanted to join *his* band, Mimi said no, and now that old roommate's band has mildly blown up in Portland; they'd even played on *Conan.*

"I'm no sellout," he told Harper when she'd gingerly asked if it upset him. But he checks the roommate's band's Instagram page almost every day — twelve thousand followers and counting. In its current incarnation, Dulcet is strong and lush-sounding, a fusion of equally talented musicians. Jacob knows enough music theory to compensate for an occasional tin ear; Diego's superb with beat, and even when Allie fumbles, her fierce playing — and, frankly, stunning looks — make up for it. These three members got it in their heads somewhere along the way that Mimi doesn't care much about Dulcet, that the band is his side gig, that he's just there to mentor them or something. Mimi has no idea why they think this but also understands it's best not to correct them. Of the four of them, Mimi is the oldest by a decade.

Tulip is a short walk from the restaurant and he hates showing up early for gigs; it makes him feel like a kid at a school pageant, eager and obvious. It's a slow evening; about a third of the tables are empty, and the new hire Jenny is discreetly checking her phone at the hostess stand.

"I'm going to stop in the kitchen before I head out," he tells her.

Jenny straightens, her hand ducking into her pocket. "Sure thing. I've got it handled up here."

I don't care if you check your phone, he wants to say. The kitchen isn't visible from the dining room, which is a shame. Cordelia spent a fortune on the appliances. It's like entering a church, cavernous and imposing. Mimi feels a familiar spasm of nostalgia at the clanking of dishes, the intermixed voices of cooks and dishwashers and waiters. One of the dishwashers is playing a Spanish song on his phone, and every few seconds a new voice hums out a few words.

"Everything good, guys?" Mimi knows he isn't imagining the slight frowns in the chefs' foreheads, the glance one shoots another. When he worked back here, the thought of being out front was inconceivable. The kitchen was where everything started, a Wild West — stovetop fires, severed fingertips, grown men bursting into tears at a sunken cake. The chefs called themselves the alley cats; Mimi went and got himself domesticated.

"All quiet back here, boss," Deacon says. He's in his fifties, a former line cook at a Michelin-starred restaurant in Chicago. "Better than being in the weeds. Junior over there spoiled a nice batch of lentil soup, but he's not allowed to touch the salt anymore." The men snicker while the new hire blushes.

"I thought it was bland," he says earnestly. Someone is frying onions somewhere — the mujaddara dish comes with a sprinkling of them — and the smell is mouthwatering.

"That looks good," Mimi says, watching Deacon's chef's knife fly over a mound of carrots. Deacon looks at him like he's dumb.

"You can have one," he says.

"Thanks, I'm okay." Mimi meant the knife work but is too embarrassed to explain. "Sorry for the slow night," he says as though it's his fault.

"A breather's always nice."

"The extra time's good," one of the sous-chefs pipes up. He's brushing syrup on a row of raw balls of *awameh.* "Cordelia said she wants a new dessert menu by the end of the summer. We're thinking a kanafeh cannoli. With sweet cheese instead of ricotta."

He pronounces the word "ka-na-fee." Mimi wants to correct him but doesn't. He thinks of the kanafeh he grew up eating, sheets of syrup-smothered cheese and shredded phyllo. Once a year in California, for Eid, his mother would drive to an Arab supermarket two hours away and fill the car. They'd eat leftovers for weeks, until the pastries became so stale they wouldn't soften in the microwave anymore. He hates the idea of it rolled up in a crunchy shell. The textures will clash. He imagines a more elegant reimagining of the desert — attractive triangles of kanafeh topped with powdered sugar and a drizzle of Italian syrup.

"I love that," Mimi says instead. When he still worked in the kitchen, Cordelia would let him play around with entrées and desserts. But now she says it's too distracting. *You're just going to confuse the cooks. Let them do their job.* He clears his throat.

"I'll see you all tomorrow." A halfhearted chorus of goodbyes. Mimi avoids eye contact as he makes his way to the back door.

❖

It's a perfect Austin evening, the air warm but not too humid. When he was in high school, his screen saver was an aerial photograph of New York City at night. His friends would argue the perks of LA versus East Coast music scenes. It never occurred to him that he wouldn't end up in either, that Austin would gradually grow on him, a *place where it's actually about the music,* like he tells people. What he doesn't say: As he gets older, LA becomes more claustrophobic, and New York's subway makes him panicky. Like it or not, Austin is what he can manage.

As he nears the bar, his phone buzzes twice. The first text is from Allie. *Three minutes or I'm giving your guitar to the first guy that quotes Vonnegut.* Despite himself — and the inter-band politics, the age gap, Harper — Mimi smiles. *I'm sprinting,* he texts back.

He scrolls to the second text. It's from Ava, two sentences:

Mama-tiger wore me down. Guess who's going to Beirut?

"Shit," he mutters. "Shit, shit, *shit.*" He presses Call, puts the phone to his ear. His sister's voice is sheepish.

"I know," she answers.

"Ava! What the *fuck,* man. If you go, it'll make me look like shit. Naj's already there. I can't believe you did this!" He can only speak to Ava like this. The two of them were so inseparable as children that his parents finally forced them to spend afternoons with their respective classmates, a decree that led to weeping and a petition titled "Sibling Power." He can get as mad as he wants at her.

"I don't know what happened! She just assumed I was going, and then she brought up not wanting to be alone, and I'm not *you,* Marwan, okay? She immediately made me feel like shit." What Mimi has in temper, Ava has in guilt. Many of their arguments have started with Mimi yelling and ended with him apologizing.

"Okay, okay." Mimi takes a deep breath. "It's just . . . *fuck,* man."

"I know. I feel like a fucking idiot."

Harper had once observed dryly that whenever Mimi and Ava were in the same room, their vernacular devolved into frat-boy speak.

"Jesus, Avey."

A brief silence. Then: "I'm sorry, Mimi. United front and all that."

"It's okay. I'll figure something out."

"Actually, you might like to know . . ." Ava hesitates.

"What?"

"I need you to swear to God you won't tell her."

Mimi hears the telltale *ping* of a new message. "Ava, what is it?" he says impatiently.

"All the stuff with the deed. She made it up."

"Ah!" Of course. "I knew there was something off, remember? I mean, Naj opened a bank account all by herself there when she was eighteen. This changes everything!"

"You can't tell her I told you. Promise?"

"I promise, I promise."

"Look, she adores you. Just tell her you and Harper have something planned. She'll get over it. Or," Ava says slyly, "you can just say you need more recording time."

Fucking Mama. Of course she told Ava. Despite what Ava thinks, Mimi hates asking his mother for money. He does it sparingly, like for this studio time at a workspace usually booked up years in advance. When he was younger, asking for money didn't feel as shitty — he was still "figuring things out" — but the more years pass, the more it feels like shoplifting. And then Naj's band had exploded six years ago, and everything *really* went to shit. "I don't know what you're —"

Ava laughs. "It's fine, Mimi. I admire your initiative."

Mimi can't help but grin. It's an old inside joke, something their father once said in his stiff, strangely formal English after Ava had made a strong case to go on her senior trip in high school.

"Please, permit me, I admire *your* initiative."

"No, yours."

"Yours!"

Laughing, the siblings hang up.

⁕

After dashing into Tulip, saying a quick hello to the proprietors (two aging musicians from Denver), and checking out the space — attractive crowd, on the youngish side — Mimi heads to the backstage area, where the band's waiting for him.

"You got lucky, *aceituno,*" Allie says as she passes his guitar to him. "None of the other guys wanted this piece of shit." It's her nickname for him, a hybrid joke based on the restaurant and his skin tone.

"Not in front of her." He pretends to cover the guitar's ears. He never named his guitar but finds her clearly female — those curves, the tuning pegs like dainty ears — and although he has two newer ones, this is his favorite, a birthday gift from his parents when he turned sixteen. The instrument is worn out; the strings have snapped countless times, the neck's scuffed from restringing, the bridge twice replaced.

"But for real, the owners seemed a little pissed," Jacob says with the tiniest trace of haughtiness. Jacob has never been late to a single practice and possesses that undeniable superiority that comes with youth, that belief that there is a *right* way to be a musician. "I mean, no offense, Mimi, I totally get it, you're busy and all that, but we've got an audience, man, you know, it's a little *cheap,* showing up late."

Mimi ignores him. He nods at Diego. "'She's Not Mine' good for an opener?" Diego clears his throat, looks away.

"Actually," Jacob says, bristling—ignoring him was a mistake—"we already did the set list. 'If It's Not You' is first. We're closing with 'Downstairs.'"

Mimi groans. He hates "Downstairs." He'd written it when he was twenty, after a breakup with a red-haired econ major named Elsa, and the lyrics— *I'll meet you downstairs, downstairs, downstairs / I'll be looking for your hair, your hair, your hair*—are stupid and catchy, which of course makes it a crowd pleaser.

"I really think we should close with 'Simple.' Diego, you said you liked that ending, remember?"

"Yeah, man." Diego looks thoroughly miserable. "I think it's dope, only thing is it's a little, ah —"

"It's depressing," Jacob says bluntly. "That refrain, that whole *you was simple, I was simple, it was simple* thing, it's a little repetitive."

"It's supposed to be repetitive. It's restrained." Mimi's ears burn.

Allie coughs, does a stretch, her thin, braceleted arms above her head. Her Ramones T-shirt lifts to reveal her bellybutton. They all look, even Diego.

"We'll close with 'Simple' next time." She walks out toward the stage.

The three men glance at each other, then after her. Allie is the youngest of four brothers, inured to male egos and tempers. Sometimes she talks about moving to San Francisco, where her friend owns a music club. She'd wanted to be a booker when she was younger. The prospect of her leaving is terrifying to Mimi. It's partly Dulcet-related—she's a commodity, the hot girl playing the shit out of her bass, someone people in the crowds immediately want to fuck. Her presence sets Dulcet apart. But there's something else there that he doesn't like to acknowledge. The flirtatious texts. His eagerness at showing her a new song. The first time Harper saw Allie play, she'd been quiet all the way home. Mimi pretended he didn't notice. What could he say? There was nothing to tell her.

Allie waits at the stage's wing, the bass slung low. Diego and Jacob file out first. As Mimi passes by her, Allie sticks her hand out, stopping him, and brings her mouth very close to his ear. Her breath is a little sour; she's just smoked.

"Don't pout, *aceituno.* 'Simple' is my favorite."

❈

Their set goes smoothly, each of them working hard. When the band is at its strongest, it reminds Mimi of a machine he'd seen once during a school trip to a doughnut factory. The manager had shown the class how, when you flipped a switch, the thing rumbled to life like a long metal river, every part working to produce thousands of perfect golden doughnuts. If even a single coil broke, the entire machine became useless. It's the same with Dulcet; during a good set, Mimi feels part of something indomitable, more than he would ever be alone.

The audience is only relevant afterward, now, as they peer down from the lip of the stage, surrounded by applause, the stage lights brighter, Diego glistening with sweat, his shirt off and slung over one shoulder. Allie's mascara has melted into the corners of her eyes. The aftermath of a set always reminds Mimi of a drunken fuck, that same element of dazedness, musicians shyly smiling at one another, then laughing, rubbing their eyes, coming back to their senses.

❈

The others all went to Midnight Cowboy after the set; Mimi bowed out to go home to Harper. As he walks, his guitar comfortingly clunky against his back, his phone buzzes. Jacob. *You're missing out; happy hour extended.* Mimi can picture it: a round of Rolling Rocks, Allie stuffing a lime wedge into hers. He regrets not going, but he knows that if he had, Harp would have been hurt.

When Mimi was a kid, he'd been sleeping over at a friend's house and overheard the parents having an argument. The mother was saying something about wanting to go to Florida, and the father didn't want to. Mimi can't remember how it ended, but the father caught him eavesdropping outside the guest bathroom, toothbrush in hand. The father looked startled, then amused.

"Marriage is a racket, kiddo," he'd said, smiling ruefully. "You're stuck with the same radio station for the rest of your life."

His words never left Mimi. During fights with girlfriends, after breakups, during slow, stale phases with Harp — *the same radio station for the rest of your life.* Of course he loves Harper. Mimi is a romantic, the product of a generation suckled on *Buffy* and *Dawson's*, a generation that mocks commitment but secretly believes in soulmates and thinks that love is difficult to find but easy to keep. Unsurprisingly, Mimi is at his best in courtship (for his and Harper's first anniversary, he'd written adjectives like *authentic* and *sexy* on scraps of paper and put them in clear helium balloons to make *a word cloud of you,* as he'd told her) and during makeups. More than enduring the relationship, he loves *returning* to it — the first few days back after a tour, filling the sink with tea roses after a fight.

But the rest of it is wearing, more than he wants to admit, and a little boring. Brunch. Monthly haircuts at the neighborhood barber while Harper flips through the *GQ* magazines on the waiting-area chairs. Annual trips to a place like Playa del Carmen or Puerto Rico or Turks and Caicos, somewhere they'd get sunburned and day-drunk and have sex in the afternoon.

Lately, she's been touchy about some things — him being where he says he'll be, whether they get invited to certain parties — which he suspects has to do with poker night. Every other Thursday, Harper and her friends gather in their house, drink powdery margaritas, and talk shit about the men or, in the case of Harper's friend Dev, women in their lives.

When Mimi first met Harper's friends, it was the summer after junior year in college and they were all equally ambivalent about their lives. Harper would tell Mimi about how Dev wanted to travel to Peru, Colleen was thinking about med school, but nobody knew for sure. Harper herself agonized over her future with the painstaking dedication of a Tibetan monk on a sand mandala, spending months researching internships or law schools only to wipe everything clean and start again the following week.

"I can't make up my mind," she'd say as they sat on the balcony of their first apartment together, her bare feet up against the railing. Her voice would be bright, excited. "I mean, fortune favors the bold, blah-blah-blah, but can you actually see me doing a pottery internship in Sausalito? Or a year in that farming program in Tanzania?"

Here she'd pause and Mimi would say he could see her doing all of it — working at the orphanage in Chile, constructing the new school in Kenya, farming in Africa — and he *could*, never mind that Harper was five foot one and loved long, hot showers. They were still so young; everything had potential. Mimi could be magnanimous with encouragement because he was getting it as well, from his music professors at the university, from friends, from a club booker who'd recently told Mimi he was the next Jimmy Page. There was time. That's what everyone said when Mimi was twenty and then twenty-three and then twenty-seven, that's what he and his friends told one another, a refrain among their group, the phrase as soothing as an aperitif. *There's time,* they'd assure each other, he and Harp, *there's still so much time,* and it truly felt that way, time like a lake of water they strode toward, jauntily, certain it was bottomless.

But when Mimi turned twenty-eight, the language changed. *This is the time,* they'd say to one another at dinner parties. *If I don't move now, I'll never do it.* Friends started to leave Austin, a couple moving to Long Island to buy a house, Mimi's band members dropping out. After poker nights, Harper would offer him tidbits of gossip: Colleen was starting to *try;* Maisie's boyfriend had proposed while they were on vacation in Prague.

Then one day the temp company Harp worked for — there were never any orphans in Chile, no Fulbright in Paris — placed her at Slate Records, and everything changed. She happened to be there at the right moment; she was taking minutes for a demo meeting and the boss was about to pass on a young woman singing a ballad when Harp spoke up without thinking, saying, "It's too bad it's not faster. More like hip-hop? Over some snares and . . ."

She'd trailed off, embarrassed by the heads swiveling in her direction — she could hear them thinking the same thing: *Who is that girl and why is she speaking?* — but Dakota, the boss, was having a good day and indulged her. She asked Harper to explain, so Harper talked about the hip-hop groups in her native Dallas, how they often mixed edgy beats with unexpected singers, blending the traditional with the à la mode.

"I've got my hands full with the summer releases," Dakota had said. "Katie,

Jason, do you guys have openings?" They shook their heads. Dakota turned to Harper, narrowed her eyes for a second (she was thinking about how Harper reminded her of herself in a room like this one twenty years earlier, the CEO of Slate Records asking Dakota to take on a client), and nodded. "Okay. You. Your name?"

"Mine?"

"Yes, sweetie. What's your name?"

"Harper."

"Okay, Harper. How'd you like to take this artist, ah, what's her — 'Mabel Ray,'" Dakota read out. "How'd you like to take this Mabel girl to the studio upstairs and see what she can do with a faster track?"

Harper said yes before Dakota finished the question. Later — in the coming weeks — Mimi would listen to Harper tell the story to her parents, to their friends, about how she'd had an epiphany as Dakota spoke, how she'd suddenly seen everything clearer than ever before and she understood that, *duh,* of course she should be a music agent, a career that involved travel and music and helping people like poor Mabel Ray, who'd grown up in a trailer park in San Marcos, who would soon discover that she could sing a strange kind of song, and who would then sing those kinds of songs in front of thousands of people, people who would love her and buy every album she put out, each one outselling the last, and Mabel Ray would leave the trailer park and never return, breaking into the music industry with stratospheric success and taking Harper with her.

Meanwhile — Mimi kept deviling eggs at Olive. He kept booking gigs at the same clubs, gently but firmly refusing Harper's offers of help. He said he didn't need it, but that wasn't it at all. And the women at poker night, Mimi was told, started to talk about the best kindergartens in the city. They had long debates about the Ferber method. The mothers in the room talked about motherhood; the non-mothers talked about marriage and general contractors. Harper, Mimi was slowly beginning to understand, talked about nothing.

They call their little house the Igloo because of the sloping roof and the white brick exterior. It's at 1812 Pine Street in a distinctly Mexican neighborhood. Their street is residential, homes with grassless lawns and black-haired children playing hopscotch, but nearby there are several taco stands, a dollar store, and a large white church brimming with music and taffeta dresses on weekends for weddings and *quinceañeras*. The house itself is small but homey, with an old velvet couch and large windows that Harper has framed with twinkle lights instead of curtains. They have a small guest bedroom for visitors with a private door to the backyard.

For years, they'd lived in the same apartment complex with other students and young professionals. But two years ago, Harp got promoted from A and R scout to manager, a position that added a zero to her salary. So they bought a house. That's what was said to friends and family, to Harper's parents, to virtually everyone except Ava, whom Mimi had called drunk one night after a gig.

"*We* didn't buy a house, Ave. She bought it. My credit's so shit the bank didn't even want me on the mortgage."

His sister had let out a soft murmur of air. "I know," she finally said. "I figured."

But he never said a word to Harper, who was so happy about the house, showing off the buttery yellow guest room and walk-in closet during their housewarming party. The guests cooed over the bur oak in the backyard. "Harp, this house is a *dream*," Mimi heard over and over again.

In the driveway, Mimi pauses in front of the Igloo, checks the time — it's nearly ten p.m. — then shakes his head and enters. The foyer is warm, the sound of hip-hop trailing from the kitchen. Mimi follows the garlicky scent like a cartoon wolf lured by a cooling apple pie. He finds Harp wearing a Kiss the Chef apron, her fine blond hair sticking to her forehead as she spoons nests of pasta onto plates and tops them with meatballs.

"For me?"

"No, for the mailman." She kisses him briefly, her breath warm and sweet. "You want Parmesan or mozzarella?"

"Neither," he says. "I'm good with just sauce."

Harper rolls her eyes. "Trying to keep your girlish figure?"

"Lactose hurts my stomach." He can hear the churlishness in his voice.

"Fine." Harper pushes the plate toward him. It makes a scratching sound against the countertop. "Take this one." Mimi watches her grate Parmesan onto her own plate, a larger mound than she might have otherwise. Mimi knows he's being a little mean.

"I'll take a little, actually," he says, relenting. "The Parmesan looks good."

She smiles. In certain lights, Harp still looks as young as a college student. She sprinkles some onto his plate, then snakes her arms around his waist. "God," she groans into his shirt. "Your waist is half the size of mine. You can afford the cheese."

"Shut up." He pulls her chin up, covers her mouth with his. "I was just thinking that you still look like a teenager."

"That's right. I'm the pick of the litter, baby." Harper speaks sarcastically, but he sees her shoulders lift as she carries the plates into the dining room. He hates himself for noticing the sag of her breasts beneath the nightgown, the way her hair is a little greasy at the temples. He follows her with two beers.

"How were the girls?"

"Oh God, don't let Dev hear you say *girls*."

"'Girls have ribbons and prepubescent bodies. You're talking to women, Mimi. Women,'" Mimi says, mimicking Dev's bossy tone.

Harper giggles. She places a salad bowl on the oak dining table that cost them twenty dollars at a yard sale. "She's right, you know. How often do you get called a boy?"

Mimi holds up his hands in surrender. "Gendered norms! Gendered language! I'm an ally to all g—women." They eat in silence for a moment. "Anyways," Mimi says, chewing, "I'm pretty sure my entire family refers to me as a boy." Harper takes a swallow of beer. Her jaw is tense. Something is coming. "How was poker?"

"It was good. Fine. Leslie put Akron on a waiting list for some pre-K program. She got a little touchy with Dev for making fun of her." Harper rolls her neck around, releasing little crackles. "Sumi's pregnant."

"No way! That's great." Mimi can hear the falseness of his voice. "I should give Jason a call, say congrats."

"You should. They'd been trying for a year."

"Is she happy?" Mimi can tell from Harp's slight flinch that this is the wrong question.

"What do you mean? Is she happy she's having the baby that she's been wanting for months?" Harper's eyebrows furrow. "Of course she is."

Do you want a baby? he could ask. Should ask. It's the unasked question of the past few years, and, like a spider plant left in sunlight, it's growing more unruly the longer it is unasked, and so is the corollary question from Harper: *Do you* not *want a baby?*

"Right," he says instead. "That's great."

It isn't anyone's fault. That's how Mimi sees it. They hadn't discussed babies or mortgages or marriage during their twenties because it wasn't relevant. They were artists! They were living renegade lives! But the more time passes, the more difficult it is for Mimi to envision a different life. He knows his sisters would love a wedding, Ava organizing the bridal shower and matching the bridesmaids' flowers to boutonnières while Naj smokes pot with the caterers after the ceremony, but he can't imagine himself in the picture. Nor can he imagine his mother's reaction.

"At least Nate went to Yale," he'd once overheard Mazna saying on the phone. There was a pause, then his mother kissed her teeth. "She's a nice girl, but I believe she grew up on a *farm.*"

Mimi felt like he'd been slapped. He understood in that moment that Harper was not the kind of person Mazna wanted in the family, that Harper was even worse than Nate, whom his mother had disliked for a while before abruptly changing her mind. That shift had occurred suspiciously quickly after she'd received Nate's sixtieth-birthday gift to her, an original Edwardian perfume tray. Now Mazna occasionally compared Nate to the scions of certain families in Syria — old money, a status based on prestige and etiquette more than actual cash, but still, he used the right salad fork and spoke French and wore shoes that matched his belt. Privately, Mimi thought her approval smacked of colonial aftermath, the predictable — if subconscious — worship Arabs had for their countries' occupiers.

He'd never say this to Ava.

Harper has none of that regality. She grew up solidly middle class, the daughter of professors at the University of Dallas. She managed young artists who rapped the word *pussy* freely and she'd worked at a Dairy Queen in high school — *Dallas, Mama, Dallas! No farms for miles.*

"That's really *great,* Harp," he says, trying again now. He reaches over and strokes her forearm. "We should get them a car seat or something."

"That's a good idea," she says quietly. "How was the show?"

"The crowd at Tulip keeps getting younger."

They fall into the kind of silence that years together engender. "Your mom still pestering you about the Beirut thing?" Harp finally asks.

"She only called once," he lies. "I got back to her before the show."

Harper laughs. "Meaning you texted or e-mailed?"

Mimi grins. The tension scatters like fog. "Text. I told her I had a show in a few minutes but couldn't make the trip."

"What's Ave saying?"

"Oh! Get this, she's *going.*"

Harper lifts an eyebrow. "Are you surprised? Ava can't say no to your mother."

"I know, it's just, it's *disappointing,* you know?" Mimi feels a little bad for talking this way, but he knows it bonds him and Harper. It always has. She nods emphatically.

"Ava's got a mommy complex. She can't help it." Harper takes a swig of her beer. "It wouldn't be the worst thing in the world, you know. Going, I mean. I've got a ton of vacation days saved up and I've never been."

Mimi groans. "Not you too. Have you not looked at the paper this year? Hezbollah is ungovernable. There's a literal *garbage crisis.* Did you know that? There are piles of garbage high as buildings, Harp. Nobody picking them up. And besides, we'd have to run interference on Naj and my mom every minute."

"Okay, okay." Harper holds up her beer bottle. "It was just a thought."

"We'll go someday, alone," he says, more gently. "We can do Petra and all that." She rolls her eyes but drops it. He feels a sharp relief that he knows has nothing to do with Hezbollah.

Harper stands up. "Want another beer?" Mimi says yes. He thinks about his friend's father all those years ago.

"I mean, God, imagine having to put your kid on a *waiting list* for preschool," she says, sitting back down and talking as though they were in midconversation. "What a nuisance." But there's something unreadable in her tone, in her sidelong glance at Mimi as she hands him the open bottle.

"Yeah," he says. He stabs the last meatball with his fork. "It sounds like a pain in the ass."

✦

The following morning, Mimi's mother calls twice, that evening once more. A couple of days later, she slyly catches Harper at work and corners her into admitting that, yes, Mimi has seen his mother's texts and, yes, it is possible he's avoiding her calls. On Saturday morning, Mimi wakes with a pang of guilt, his dream fluttering bright as a parakeet: his mother swimming in his high-school pool, an oil spill rendering the water mucky and black.

The feeling persists through his morning coffee, and during a brief, unsatisfying tryst with Harper in the shower — both of them out of breath, the acrobatics of sex tiring after a while; Mimi finally holds the showerhead between her legs while she works on him. Finally, she pushes it away, panting.

"This isn't working," she says. Her hair is matted like a wet dog's, her face still puffy from sleep. He replaces the showerhead.

"I was getting close," he protests, though this is a lie.

Harper rotates her wrist in circles. "I'm getting carpal tunnel."

Mimi groans and submerges his head under the shower. The sound roars in his ears. When he opens his eyes, Harper is frowning.

"What?"

"This thing with your mom, Mimi," she begins.

"I know, Harp, I told you, I'm sorry she called, she'll let it go eventually —"

"She sounded different," Harper finally says. "It wasn't like it usually is with her. She sounded . . . lost."

This takes him aback. Mimi feels a surprising yearning for a world where Harper and Mazna are close, calling each other weekly to gossip about him. Everything would be different. Harp would call his mother and complain about wanting babies, and then his mother would call him and tell him to get his shit together. The fantasy always saddens him; it would make everything easier. He wouldn't be able to resist the two of them.

"I know it seems like I'm being an asshole," he says. "But trust me, there's a lot of nuance here. There always is with my family."

Harper lets out a snort. She puts her hand on her naked hip. *"Really?"* she says feistily. "Y'all aren't as complicated as you like to think. Ava's going because she never wants to let your mother down. Your mother *herself* is going because, despite complaining nonstop about your father, she either loves him or feels an obligation toward him, which after that many years" — she shrugs — "is basically the same thing. Naj is totally oblivious to all of this, which isn't an accident. She's been priming all of you for years not to expect anything from her. You're avoiding returning the call because you know how persuasive your mother can be, and you feel guilty because of the money she's given you. Yes —" She holds up a hand at his protesting. "I know how much studio time costs, Mimi. And, let's see, what's the missing piece here?" She drums her chin, pretending to think. "Oh yes! Your father. The person who set this whole thing in motion. He knows that the rest of you will clean up the mess for him." She gives him an impish grin. "But he's so endearing, y'all don't even notice it."

She waits. Mimi can't help himself — he laughs. She's completely right.

"Look," he says, changing tactics. "It's just a stressful time. And you know how my mother is. I've got the tour coming up, and Jacob said he's close to booking Longhorn, even though the guy's taking forever and a half to get back to us —"

Harper's hand falls from her hip. "Mimi," she says gently. "I've known Alfred for years. Let me just send an e-mail to him."

"Jacob's close." Mimi knows he sounds surly. He turns off the water. He can feel Harper deciding whether to push it or not. She snakes her arms through the sleeves of her bathrobe. Finally, she speaks.

"Just call your mother, Mimi."

Mimi is working the brunch shift at Olive, and the dining room is already set up when he arrives. Each table has an olive branch in a glass vase. Cordelia is standing on a chair writing specials on the chalkboard in her fanciful hand-writing. She's like a capricious mother when it comes to the restaurant — arriving on a whim, changing the menu, sometimes very involved, then unseen for weeks. It drives the staff crazy. He starts counting menus.

"Who pissed in your cornflakes?" Cordelia finally asks.

"Classic Southern belle."

"Fuck off," Cordelia says, flushing. "I can't afford your moody-Mimi shit today. We already had to cap brunch reservations."

Mimi doesn't argue. "Sorry." He swipes a heel of French bread from one of the baskets lined up. "It's my mother. She's not letting this Beirut shit go."

"Just tell her you've got stuff coming up."

"I did. She won't stop calling."

"I mean." Cordelia purses her lips.

"What?"

"I don't know, Mimi." She clearly does know. "I realize you have your summer plans. But, like — isn't there some compromise here? You and Harp could go for a week or something."

Mimi's neck feels hot. He doesn't want a compromise. "I've got gigs lined up all summer," he half-lies. "Harper's got two new acts. It's the busiest time of the year at Slate."

"She's got vacation saved up," Cordelia mutters. She frowns at herself. She's said too much.

"I *knew* it!" Mimi brings his hand down on the tabletop with a clatter. "What did Harp tell you?"

"What?" she says innocently.

"Since when do the two of you even speak to each other?"

Cordelia sighs like he's a child. "You're not being *conspired against,* Mimi. We text every now and then."

"All of a sudden, Harper wants to go to Beirut?"

"First, it's not all of a sudden. Second, you know how your family is. It's not like she gets to feel good about herself."

"She sees my parents like twice a year. She sees them as much as I do!"

"How much of that time does your mother spend either ignoring her or talking about conception?" Cordelia pretends to focus on the chalkboard. "I think a trip like this would mean a lot to Harper. It would show her that you're serious . . ." She lets her sentence trail off.

"About what?" There isn't a response. Mimi blurts out: "Cordelia, does she want to get married or something?"

Cordelia looks taken aback. Then she laughs. "Poor Harp."

"What?"

Cordelia observes him like a cat. Her eyes are always made up, heavy with fake lashes and liner, making her look more beautiful than she is. He's known her since he was eighteen. They never dated, never even kissed, though for one ill-fated semester in Mimi's sophomore year, he'd fallen briefly in love with her. The feeling never came back.

"I know you love her," she finally says. "And I know you don't want to hear this, but she needs more."

Mimi feels his heart sink with her words. His mind teeters between sadness and anger, and he chooses the latter. "Noted," he says tightly. "Thanks."

"I'm not saying *marry* her, Mimi, I'm just saying—"

"Forget it." He holds his hand up. "I'm calling my fucking mother. I'll be back in a few."

Olive has a back entrance that opens onto a small alleyway where garbage cans reek, no matter how many times Cordelia has the dishwashers spray them with disinfectant. Mimi kicks one. Then he calls his mother.

"I can't believe my ears." His mother's voice, deep and affected. "Is this a pocket-dial? It couldn't be the good boy I carried in my own body. It couldn't be my firstborn son."

"I'm sorry it took me so long to call you back. I've been very—"

"Busy. Yes, yes. Your sister tells me you're busy. Your little friend Harper tells me you're busy."

Mimi flinches at *little friend*. He thinks of Harp talking about Sumi the other night at dinner, of Cordelia laughing at his question.

"All anyone ever tells me is how busy my son is. So busy, apparently, that he can't call his mother and talk for two minutes."

"Mama, I'm not going to Beirut." He waits.

Mazna sighs. "Not even a hello. Not even a 'Hi, Mama, *keefik*, Mama, how's that awful California heat, Mama?'"

"That's what you've been calling me for!"

"Not even," Mazna continues to her invisible audience, "a single question about his mother's health."

"How's your health, Mama?" Mimi obliges.

"Not good! Not good, Mimi. Your father's going to put me in an early grave. 'Idris,' I tell him, 'Idris, your father just died. Your parents wouldn't want this. After so many years, suddenly there is a rush to sell the house? It *has* to be done this summer? What kind of man, tell me, what kind of man fixes strangers' hearts at work and breaks his wife's at home?'"

"Mm." This is an old favorite of his mother's: *A heart doctor who doesn't take care of his own wife's heart.* His parents have a strange, unconvincing marriage marked by testiness and droughts followed by capricious upticks where they seem young and playful again, giggling over old Egyptian films, his father begging his mother to re-create monologues from plays she'd starred in.

"Mimi," his mother says. "You think I like wasting my breath? It's out of our hands. The lawyer needs the three of you there."

Mimi clenches his jaw. "Why hasn't Baba called? Since the deed thing is so serious?" He knows it's wrong to set her up like this, but he can't help himself. "I can talk to Baba about it, and see if the lawyer will accept a notarized signature. I can mail everything from here."

"That won't work." He can practically hear her mind buzzing. "The lawyer needs you. They need you to sign the new deed in person."

"What about removing my name from the deed?"

"I already asked the lawyer. He said it's not an option."

Mimi can't control himself anymore. "I know there's no lawyer!" he explodes. "We're not even on the deed."

"*I knew it!*" His mother sounds furious. "I can't believe Ava told you. Your sister always does this to me. She just wants to paint me as a liar."

He immediately feels loyal to his sister. "It's not her fault. She wasn't trying to do anything. She just knows how stressed I've been."

"It must be so nice for you two, gossiping about me behind my back." She waits but Mimi doesn't take the bait. "What else did she tell you?" she demands.

"It wasn't like that!"

"Maybe I *have* to lie." There is a pause, and when his mother speaks again, her voice is quieter. "Because if I just ask you to come, you won't."

He retreats. "I don't understand why this is so important."

"Bah! Of course. It is *crucial* for Mimi to *understand*," she says. Then, unpredictably, "Never mind, *habibi*."

He remembers what Ava said about capitulating, Harper's comment about his mother sounding different.

"I'm sorry, Mama," he says. He means it. "When you guys get back, Harp and I will come to California for a few days. A week," he amends. "We'll come for a week."

"That would be nice," she says. "We can drive up to Long Beach." Her voice is softer now and Mimi thinks of his sisters, how they accuse Mazna of favoritism. He always pretends he doesn't know what they're talking about.

⁂

Seven o'clock that night, the streets in East Austin neighborhood are mostly empty, a few students walking to their evening classes. Mimi loves college towns. They have a certain amnesia about aging. He walks north, toward the space Dulcet has practice every week. The days are getting longer, and the flowering trees and shrubs casting their branches over the sidewalk remind Mimi, unexpectedly, of Beirut. He knows the city only in heat, he realizes. There were so many of his childhood summers when his entire family would pack up the absurd items requested — Slim Jims for the younger cousins, Tums for his grandfather — and set off on that unreasonably long trip across the Atlantic, stopping to spend a bleary-eyed layover in Munich or Stockholm or other cities that would forever remain to Mimi the amalgamation of their airports: hot sticky buns from the café, the glamour of heated toilet seats, rows of gift-store wooden clogs.

And then, miraculously, they would be *there,* standing in line at the Beirut airport, his father, so incongruous in a white Californian town, transforming into just another Arab man with a mustache arguing over luggage carts, Mimi's grandparents and second cousins and aunt all gathering at the arrivals gate, a comical number of people. The relatives never factored in the return trip with Mimi's family, so they'd all sit on each other's laps.

And the house. Their grandparents' house, perched a short walk from the Corniche, a long walk from the university, had been built in the 1800s — *Before the Ottomans let the French take over,* his grandmother used to say. Though Mimi hasn't seen it in nearly two decades, the house is etched in his memory, the mental blueprint as clear as the one he has of his parents' house in California. Bricks weathered and yellowed after a century of rain, the pale-tiled rooms. A small courtyard in the front, covered in July by almond blossoms, a pink carpet that the maid started sweeping every day after six-year-old Naj had slipped doing cartwheels and chipped a canine. Jiddo had taught him to drive on the road outside the house, whooping with laughter when Mimi accidentally hit a mailbox. Mimi's heart jerks at the memory. His grandfather had been lowered into the ground and he hadn't been there.

"Why'd you guys stop going?" Harper had asked. Sparrow's Pub. Their first date, Harper and Mimi sharing an order of mozzarella sticks, their fingers glittering with oil. This was before the Arab Spring, before the protests broke out, going from country to country as if transmitted along a chain of neurons, and he'd spoken casually of his mother's hometown, in northern Damascus, how they'd drive up through Lebanon and arrive in the late afternoon, Mimi and his sisters clapping at the sight of their favorite rock-candy vendor. He told her he'd started cooking because of the bakeries, where he'd stand transfixed as a kid watching the men knead little pockets of dough, sprinkle zaatar, drizzle olive oil.

"You sound wistful," she'd observed. "Why'd you guys stop going?"

He was surprised to find he didn't have an answer. The trips had ended suddenly, without any mention of why, his father taking them to Yosemite or the Bay Area during the summer instead. They were still young, he and his sisters, Mimi in high school during the last trip to Beirut. He'd asked Ava about it after that first date with Harp, wondering if their parents had had some fight, but she couldn't recall anything either. Not that they would have been paying attention. It was a time of crushes and trying to fit in, of hungering for their candy-colored iMac back home. There must have been adolescent relief when his parents stopped mentioning Beirut, but he can't remember any.

His phone buzzes just before he reaches the practice space. *Thanks, asshole.* Ava. His mother must have called her. He grimaces, taps out a response. *I'm sorry, Avey.* He sends it, then adds, *Was it bad?*

Ava's response is the middle-finger emoji. Brown skin tone. Mimi waits. Finally, the type bubbles reappear. Then:

You need to tell Naj we're coming. Mama told me to do it days ago. Naj isn't picking up her calls.

Mimi groans. *Why doesn't Mama just have Baba call?*

I don't know, Mimi. I didn't get a chance to ask, what with all the yelling.

Okay, okay. It's time to yield. *I'll call her.*

He hasn't seen Naj in nearly two years. The last time they spoke was months ago; she wanted to know what to get their father for his birthday. They text frequently, rarely in full sentences, just *You good?* and links to new groups. Before she started her band, they spoke more often, but then he couldn't anymore. And there's the other reason for his reluctance to visit Beirut — he can't imagine seeing her there, in a city where she is effectively a celebrity. It's unfair, but he avoids her. He's done it for so long it's become a way of life. She calls; he doesn't pick up. He arranges his holiday visits home to California to overlap only with the beginning or end of her trips. Even now, he feels a familiar ambivalence at the thought of her, her assortment of piercings and colorful tattoos. She has a mean streak, but so does he.

"Be done with it," he says aloud. He scrolls to the Viber icon and his younger sister's tiny pixelated photograph.

The phone rings three, four times. As Mimi waits, he does the arithmetic; it's three in the morning in Beirut, not a problem for his night-owl sister, who will be at a show or out drinking. But when Naj finally picks up, her voice is smoky, half asleep. "Is someone dead?"

"What?"

Mimi hears muffled sounds in the background, a bed squeaking. "Is some-one dead?" she repeats. "What's with the late-night call?"

"No," he says. "No one's dead. Hi."

"Hey. Mimi, no offense. It's great to hear from you and all, but it's kinda late."

"Mama and Baba are going to Beirut," he blurts out. "Ave too."

"Wait." Her voice rises. "Wait, wait, *wait*. What are you talking about? They're coming here?"

"Yes," he says, feeling a dark satisfaction at bearing the news. He pictures his sister upright in her bed, her hand tugging her short hair, a longtime habit. "They're going to Beirut. Around the beginning of June. Baba wants to sell the house."

"Fucking *excuse* me?" Naj whispers hotly. "He wants to sell my house?"

"*Your* house?"

"That's not what I said," she says, defiant. "Our house."

"You don't even live there." This has been a long-drawn-out battle in the family's history, beginning when Naj moved to Lebanon to study at the American University of Beirut. His mother had been furious. *We didn't leave a war zone so our children could go back.* But Naj wouldn't change her mind, not about moving there or about getting her own small apartment, a decision that caused uproar with the older generation — a girl, only eighteen, living alone *like some gypsy,* as his mother had said.

"Oh my God, how are we still having this conversation? I didn't want to live with Jiddo. Is that so *inexplicable?* A grown woman wanting to live alone? In the twenty-first century?" His sisters have this in common: when confronted, both go on the offensive.

"Wait." The question dawns on him. "Why are you whispering?"

"I —" Naj sounds uncharacteristically caught out. "Look, just tell Mama I got the message. They're coming, Ava's coming, the kiddos are coming. Noted. Fuck," she mumbles, "people just springing this shit on me."

"I think Mama's been trying to call you for a week, Naj."

"Why aren't *you* coming?" she asks.

It's Mimi's turn to change the subject. "I've got shit this summer."

"Shows?"

"Yeah, Naj," he says, sharper than he intended. "Shows. I've got shows. It may not be a *European tour,* but it's still —"

"Jesus, okay, sorry."

"—*something,* okay? We booked the East Room in Nashville. Cash played there." He hates how surly he sounds. He doesn't mean to be this way; he misses his little sister, their old relationship, with ferocity sometimes, but he just can't help it.

"Okay," she says. Her voice goes soft, and everything rustles up between them again. "That's cool, Mimi. That's really cool."

By the time Mimi gets off the elevator on the fifth floor, he is seven minutes late to practice. He finds Diego and Jacob leaning against the door, their instruments at their feet.

"The keys, man," Diego says.

"Shit. Sorry." Mimi fishes the lanyard from his pocket. He lets them into the room; the smell of sweat and takeout greets them like a ghost. The walls are covered in eggshell crates. Aside from a set of drums, the room is empty.

"Let's plug it in." Jacob begins to wind the amp wires, whistling something vaguely familiar. Mimi waits for either of them to mention Allie, but neither does.

Finally, he says, casually, "Where's the fourth?" They sometimes refer to her this way; she was the last to join this particular iteration of Dulcet.

Diego shrugs. "Dunno. I texted her — no response."

Mimi clears his throat. He can feel his pulse quicken. "Should we wait?"

"We've got the space for an hour and" — here Jacob raises his eyebrows meaningfully — "we're already getting a late start. She'll jump in when she shows up."

But the practice is jittery, sidetracked without their brashest member. Jacob's drums are too loud. Diego's strumming, without the steady, obstinate retort of Allie's bass, seems lonely and adrift, a dancer waiting for a partner.

Mimi sings okay, but as the hour ticks by, he realizes, with a sinking in his stomach, how much his act has become directed toward an audience of one.

They're all sulky by the time the practice is over.

"Flaky as *shit*," mutters Diego after the final chord of "Downstairs." He flicks his pick toward the floor. "She's probably stoned off her ass."

"We still have a few minutes left," Jacob says as Diego starts to pack his guitar.

"Today's a bust, man. Can't you hear it?"

"I can see if they'll let us book two hours next Saturday," Mimi says, feeling defeated.

"Let's just play 'Old Friend,'" Jacob says. "It's light on bass anyway. Then we'll go."

After the first few chords, Mimi has to admit the kid has good instincts; it's their nimblest song, spirited and crackly with energy. His mind swims in and out of images as they play; he envisions the music tipping over onto them like a glass of water, darkening their clothes.

"That's what I'm talking about!" Jacob yells after the last notes. He and Diego bump fists. Mimi puts away his guitar, then checks his phone. There's one new message. Allie. His heart races. He turns the screen away from the others even though he knows they can't see it.

Come to sally's saddle.

He admonishes himself for the commotion in his chest. Harper is taking her newest client out to dinner, but she'll be done early; they'd talked about having a quiet night. His fingers tap out a reply.

Where were you? Just finished practice. Can't come out tonight.

He busies himself with his guitar, trying to keep up with Jacob and Diego's banter as they argue about the merits of finishing the song with a fade-out versus ending it cold. His stomach leaps when the phone buzzes again.

The response is so plaintive, so un-Allie-like, that Mimi knows he'll go.

Please.

Mimi debates going home and putting on a different shirt — he can smell himself after an hour of playing in the airless room — but knows that if he does, he'll change his mind and cancel. If he sees Harp's bicycle, her assortment of scarves and tote bags in the foyer, something in him will wilt. He doesn't want that.

Sally's Saddle is a divey joint with a neon saddle flickering above the dirty windows. Mimi peeks through the glass. The bar is nearly empty. He wishes he still smoked. There's a couple sitting near the bar and a woman alone at the far end. Allie. Her shoulders are bare and slightly broad; she leans toward the basketball game on the television above the bar. A Tom Waits song is playing as he walks inside.

When he reaches Allie, he tugs her braid. Flirting isn't cheating. That's an understanding between him and Harp. Mimi has watched Harper laugh too loudly at other men's jokes, sometimes resting her small hand on a guy's arm. Their relationship is old enough to allow for play.

"Hey." She gives him a half-hug and he smells her, soap and something specific, like pencil shavings. "Want a drink?"

She holds up her beer and Mimi is relieved. He has two fives in his wallet, and his savings account has been in only the triple digits for months. Harp doesn't ask about his finances anymore, but he knows she does a lot to avoid talking about it — going to the grocery store alone, insisting it's easier for her to get the car fixed by herself.

"Put it on my tab, Mitch," Allie tells the bartender when Mimi orders a Stella. "How was rehearsal?"

"They were pretty pissed. You could've at least texted Diego." *Or me.*

"I had to finish something up. It took longer than I thought." She seems edgy somehow. He can feel her shoe bouncing on the foot rest below them. The bartender brings his beer, frothy and warm. He tries to sound casual. "What's with the secret meeting?"

She ignores the question. Instead, she wrinkles her nose. There's beer foam on the corner of her mouth. "You stink."

"Some of us just had a grueling practice."

"Right. I bet Jacob bitched the whole time." She rolls her eyes. "I can't wait to leave Austin. This city feels like milk gone bad."

"I thought you liked Dulcet." Mimi tries to keep the hurt out of his voice.

"It's not the band. The band's fine. It's just — I feel like I'm living everything on repeat. Every week's the same shit — practice, gigs, bullshit, work."

"Sounds like someone's midlife crisis came early."

"How have you not left already?" Allie suddenly looks serious. "You've been here for, what, ten years?" *Seventeen.* "The band is cool and all, but you can start one anywhere. Austin's where musicians peak at twenty. Anyone who's serious about their music —"

"Maybe I'm not serious." He means for it to come out light, but it doesn't. The bartender clears away Allie's glass. Mimi wishes he hadn't come. His ears are prickly and hot. "I'm not here for the band," he half-lies. "I've got a house. The restaurant."

"Harper," Allie says neutrally.

"Yes. Harp. I've got a life here," he says roughly. "If you hate Austin so much, why don't you just hit up your friend with the club?"

Allie sighs. "San Francisco fell through." She puts her elbows on the bar top, drops her chin into her open palm. "I didn't tell you guys — well, Diego knows — but I applied to USF to study music production. I got waitlisted in March. They e-mailed me today." She wrinkles her nose again. "I didn't get in."

Mimi's relieved — she's not going anywhere. Then he feels guilty. "A lot of people apply more than once," he says, trying to sound reassuring. "You should apply again in the fall."

Allie smiles thinly. "I want a cigarette. Do you have one?" Mimi shakes his head. She scans the room; there's a pack of Parliaments on the bar top in front of three men several stools over. "One sec."

Mimi watches her talk to the older white men. They seem enlivened by her presence. She tosses her hair at them. One of the men says something, and all three laugh. He nods toward the Parliaments and Allie shakes out two.

"Rednecks," she says sweetly when she returns. "I got you one." She grabs a book of matches from the bar top. Mimi starts to say something, but she's already moving toward the exit.

The air is cooler outside, welcome after the stuffy bar. The street is mostly empty, just a couple of lone smokers near the street lamp. Allie lights her cigarette, then passes the matches to Mimi. They smoke in silence for a minute.

He clears his throat. "So you're into music production?"

She ignores his question.

"You'd be good at it," he continues, nervous. Something has shifted in the air; it's crackling between them. Finally, she turns toward him. Her smile is cheerless. He envisions her opening the e-mail earlier today, her stomach dropping at the news. Her voice is low and vicious when she says, "Well?"

He swallows. He should've gone home. "Well what?"

"Well, aren't you tired of this?"

The question leaps at him. He knows what she means, probably better than she does herself. She's just in a mean mood, trying to nettle him. But it lands like a punch. It's what he always thinks before falling asleep after another day of pacifying customers at the restaurant, bickering with Cordelia, picking a film for movie night. Not making good music.

There are so many things he could do now. He could shake his head politely, kiss her on the cheek. He could stamp out the cigarette and explain that he loves Dulcet more than anything, and Harper even more than that, and that he was going to get better at both. He could be the adult, the one who recognizes, given the sheer number of years he's spent breathing and fucking and walking on this planet, that not all itches need to be scratched, that sometimes you have to look desire firmly in the eye and say, *Not today.*

Instead, he lunges for her.

Their teeth clang together as he kisses her, then her tongue darts against his, wet as a fish, pulling forth an intense desire; this is happening right now, Allie's beery breath in his mouth, her body curved beneath his, *her body,* his hand hesitating like a teenager's against her shirt, unsure of whether to go north or south, and so he takes the hand that is tangled in her hair and goes both directions at once, one hand slipping under the shirt, finding her nipple, pinching it, hard, until she lets out a little cry, the other hand pressing against the triangle of her jeans, rubbing up and down without any finesse.

Their lips break apart. He looks down at Allie, her head against the wall, her eyes half shut. He sees something there, in a split second under the yellow streetlight, that frightens him: an aloof expression, a knowing smile. She knew he'd do this, he realizes. She's known all along. She doesn't necessarily want him, and the realization cuffs him. She's just *letting* him do this.

Mimi rears his head back. Just as he's about to speak, Allie's face changes, her eyes widening. "Shit, hey," she says to someone behind him.

Harper, Mimi's stomach screams. He removes his hand from under Allie's shirt. He forces himself to turn around and feels such relief at the sight of three men, Jacob in the middle. Jacob looks at him with such disgust, he flinches. He can see himself in the younger man's eyes with sudden, nauseating clarity: an aging amateur with a potbelly. He's ruined something for Jacob, some idea the kid had about music and honor. Jacob says something low and rapid to his friends. They nod and the three of them turn to leave.

"Jacob!" Mimi holds his palm up uselessly. "Can you just come in for a second? One beer?"

Jacob turns back. He opens his mouth, and for a second Mimi thinks he will say yes; they'll go inside, drink a little, it'll become a secret that brings them closer together, but then Jacob shakes his head once, firmly, like he's clearing it. And there's something in that small gesture, the rigidity in his jaw, that writes itself into a eulogy. *There will be no Nashville,* that headshake says. *There will be no festival.* Mimi can see how everything will play out, plain as music, how Jacob will tell Diego, how Dulcet will crumble as the kids — because that's what they are, Mimi can suddenly see; tomorrow he'll just be some old guy Allie made out with, a story for her friends — leave him one by one.

And so he says nothing more, and Jacob's mouth twists into a sneer, and the men walk off, leaving Mimi and Allie alone under the yellow light, still out of breath from their stupid desire.

A couple walk past them, holding hands. The woman is wearing hoop earrings and sapphire-blue boots. They laugh as she holds the door open for him, gestures for him to go first.

"I'm gonna go," Allie says, breaking their silence. She looks at Mimi intently for a moment, like she might kiss him. But she doesn't. "I guess we shouldn't have done that," she finally says.

Mimi watches her walk to the corner, then pull her phone out before turning left. Maybe she's calling Diego herself. Fuck. Mimi looks at his own phone, the screen eagerly lighting at his touch. *Our electronic puppies,* Harper calls them. He wants to talk to his sister. Or Diego. Flirting isn't cheating. *But, you fucking asshat,* he hisses inwardly, *cheating is cheating.*

A man comes out and lights a cigarette. Mimi puts his phone back in his pocket.

"Can I?" Mimi gestures toward the cigarette. The man shrugs, hands him one. Mimi places it between his lips, then leans into the stranger's lighter. When it's lit, he nods and starts walking down Chavez Street toward home.

When Mimi was twelve, a fire alarm went off at his middle school and they were let out early. He'd walked home, the neighborhood quiet in the pre–rush hour of school pickups, expecting the house to be empty, his sisters at elementary and high school, respectively, his father at the hospital, his mother at the greenhouse she worked at despite his father's protests. *Mazna, we're not immigrant students anymore. I make a good salary. We live in a good house. You don't have to work there.* He'd gone on like that for years until Mazna finally replied, *I was never a student here. I will always be an immigrant.* His father never mentioned it again.

But that afternoon, Mimi found his mother's red Dodge in the driveway. He snuck into the house quietly, using the key they hid in a potted plant, with vague plans of jumping up behind her or something.

But she wasn't in the living room or the kitchen. He looked in his parents' bedroom. Empty. Finally, he heard laughter, tense and fake, the kind of laughter he recognized from when they had company over. He followed it to the spare room in the back of the house, ostensibly a study.

His mother was standing at the window next to the desk, her back to him. The window was open and she was leaning toward it, smoking a cigarette, the beige telephone cradled against her ear. Mimi took a step into the room. The desk was covered with highlighted papers and several headshots of his mother, headshots he'd never seen before. She was younger, her eyes thick with kohl, and she was smiling in a way that unsettled Mimi, a bright red scarf knotted at her throat.

"Of course," his mother was saying in her slightly British English, slow and careful, the tone she reserved for PTA meetings. "I just thought that . . . well, the call said for Persian features. I'd be happy to come to the audition on Saturday . . . I live — uh, I'm near LA, yes." There was a long pause. His mother's head drooped. "Yes, I go running every week. My measurements are thirty-seven, twenty-eight, thirty-four. People say I look like I'm thirty."

Later, the memory will haunt Mimi, returning to him whenever he's feeling particularly vulnerable — hungover, after fights with Harp, New Year's Day — forever an exposed nerve, a place of pain and embarrassment, the regret of having seen his mother so utterly laid bare. The shame of it, her forced lilt on the phone, the headshot of her younger face on the desk — it had broken his heart. He has wished many times that he'd never seen it.

This is what Mimi thinks of as he walks home toward the Igloo and Harper: that sensation of having miscalculated, of having done something that couldn't be undone. He knows Harp well enough to understand that she won't forgive infidelity, especially such indulgent, pointless cheating — Harp, who hates reality television and popcorn, *empty calories*, the sort of thing that's done just to show yourself that you can.

Their porch light is off. The dinner must have lasted longer than antici- pated. He knows he'll never tell her, has known from the moment he saw Allie at the bar tonight, even as he pressed against her crotch. He has done some- thing that doesn't warrant forgiveness, and so he won't ask for it.

The house is quiet and empty. Somewhere, a floorboard creaks. The house settling; he has always loved that expression. It makes him think of a gradu- ate student opening his first 401(k), doing his own taxes, settling into his life.

Mimi is suddenly hungry. There isn't much in the fridge; tomorrow is Trader Joe's day. He starts moving through the kitchen urgently, opening draw- ers and pulling out ingredients. A meal is starting to materialize for him — fava beans with chopped onions and tomatoes, fried slices of halloumi, a triangle of dough, large enough to share with Harp, stuffed with spinach and feta. He scrolls to an old Spotify playlist, and a Talking Heads song fills the kitchen. He used to make mixtapes for his girlfriends in high school and college, writing the titles in tiny letters. He'd make one every year for Naj's birthday as well; years later, he'd listen to her debut album and feel sick at the whispers of mu- sical influences he recognized — Fleetwood Mac and Janis and even NWA, all the ones *he'd* introduced her to. The last one he made was for Harp, their senior year; the only song he can remember is "Pink Triangle" by Weezer.

The thought of Allie threatens to wreck him, and so he dances around the kitchen like a boxer, pulling out the frying pan and spatula. His fingers know instinctively how to guide the knife over the tomato, halving it, then minc- ing. There's no halloumi — there's an Arab grocery store a few neighborhoods away, but he always forgets to go — so he uses mozzarella, easing the floppy slices onto the frying pan, humming along to the crackling sound. The first time he cooked was in high school when he took a home ec class because it was the only thing that fit into his schedule. He surprised himself by loving it — the perfect little madeleines they learned to bake that they dipped in almond milk before shaking powdered sugar on top. For his final project he'd made the class an elaborate *m'sakhan* — roast chicken with sumac flatbread — earning himself an A and a parking-lot blowjob from Caroline Greenburg, his cooking partner.

Harper keeps the fancy china on the top shelf, and Mimi takes down a couple of dishes. He plates the cheese, spoons fava beans on top. The spinach pie came out more rectangle than triangle, and he cuts it in half. He sets the table and waits. Just a couple of minutes later he hears the car in the driveway.

"That smells fucking . . ." he hears Harp saying. "Divine." She enters the kitchen. Her hair is in a ponytail and she's wearing her blue maxi dress, the one that's soft as a pet. Mimi feels his heart pound. He tries to make his face slacken.

"Sit."

"I just ate," she says, sitting down. "Although, actually, French portions are a joke." She whistles at the sight of the food. "Baby, this looks amazing."

Mimi goes behind her chair, kisses her head. She smells like her lilac perfume. He remembers Allie's coconut shampoo, and Harp's body stiffens beneath him.

Oh God.

"Nice try, Mimi." There's a pause. Harp laughs. "You know smoke sticks to you, right? You're not getting away with anything."

"I know." He tries to sound rueful. "I took one from Allie. You want a plate? I fried some mozzarella. Is that a thing?" Harp did a semester abroad in Rome.

She thinks. "*Mozzarella a carrozza.* No — *mozzarella en carrozza.*" Mimi puts her plate in front of her, puts down his own, and watches as she eats. She hates when he does this, so he pretends he's looking at his own food, stealing side glances.

"I'm throwing away these heels," she says. She kicks them off under the table, then groans. "My blisters have blisters."

Mimi pulls her feet onto his lap. *I'm so sorry,* he says silently to them. Her toenails are painted a pale pink, chipped in places. He kisses the arches. Her feet stink a little, something earthy, like pond scum. He doesn't mind it. Allie had bit his lower lip earlier, and he can feel it swelling. Without meaning to, he lets out a whimper. Harp looks up from her plate. He shakes his head. There are the beginnings of new wrinkles around her eyes, the same ones her mother has.

"You're acting a little Dahmer tonight, baby."

He laughs in spite of himself. He wants to tell her everything. Instead, he buries his face in her feet. *It was once,* he rehearses. *I've never done it before, I mean not really, not like this. I just wanted not to feel like myself for a few goddamn minutes.* He wonders if she's ever cheated on him, even a little, at one of her release parties and immediately feels terribly sad — it's not the sort of thought he would have had before. He's broken something; he has introduced suspicion. *It was only once, and anyway I think Dulcet is fucked now, so I won't see her again.*

"I want to go to Beirut," he mumbles into her feet. Immediately he scrunches his eyes shut. It's the cowardly thing to do, but he's relieved to hear himself say it.

Harp pulls her feet back. He can hear her breath. She lets out a sharp, amazed laugh. "Alone?"

He snaps his head up. "What? No — I mean both of us. We should go to Beirut."

"I thought you didn't want to miss the festival. What about Dulcet?"

"Fuck Dulcet," he says sadly.

"I can move around Laci's release. She'll be pissed, but late summer is better anyway. Shit! Is my passport about to expire? I have to check on that." Harp's cheeks are flushed, her tone eager. She sounds so happy, Mimi wants to punch himself in the dick.

"Hey." She nudges his thigh with her toe. "Is this some midlife thing? You've seemed off for days."

"You were right, Harp. It'll be good to go. We should've gone years ago."

Her smile is bright and guileless. "I'm going to get so fucking sunburned." She claps. "All that Rosetta Stone finally put to some use."

"Everyone speaks English there, baby."

"*Wayn el hammam?*" she says, ignoring him. "*Ana biddi aakol.*" She lifts her shoulders to her ears like a comic. "*Wayn el matta'am?*"

Mimi captures her hands with his own. He yanks her to him; they kiss for a long moment. He doesn't want to go to the bedroom. He pushes her down on the table, like they're in a movie. Her mouth tastes like spinach. They fumble with zippers and buttons, then Mimi's inside and it feels good; she's wet and sighing, her legs dangling off the sides like she's on a gynecologist's exam table. Her face is open beneath him; she digs into his neck with her fingers. He comes and she lets out a little cry, more for him than anything, he knows — she rarely comes from sex — and he can smell himself in the air.

Harp pulls herself up on her elbows. She looks happy. There's a draft in the room, some forgotten window left open; he can feel his erection softening.

"I'm sorry," he says. "That wasn't long enough."

"Oh, please." She rolls her eyes. When they first met, he thought her eyes were the exact color of gunmetal, but he now knows they're greener, soft and mossy.

There was a lyric he almost wrote once but didn't; he knew it would get him in trouble. It was about Harp's eyes, how sometimes they looked like the scales of a fish he should've returned to the water.

A Wolf in Wolf's Clothing

WHEN NAJ GETS off the phone with Mimi, she turns to the sleeping woman next to her. She opens her mouth in a silent scream. It's time to go.

She swings her legs from under the covers and holds her breath as she moves through the unfamiliar bedroom, the only light a nubby candle they'd lit a couple of hours ago. It's a one-bedroom apartment and Naj uses the glow from her cell screen as she makes her way down a short hallway to the bathroom. The overhead light is wincingly bright.

Her parents are coming. *Ava* is coming. Naj turns the faucet on and drinks straight from the tap even though she knows the water is dirty; it makes her feel hardy and powerful to drink it anyway, like her body is made for this place. Her head is pounding, the remnants of vodka martinis and a small but quality line of cocaine. The sleeping woman is Maggie, a coworker of Naj's friend. The damage will be minimal; they hadn't even exchanged numbers. Her friend will be annoyed about the Irish exit, but Naj needs to go somewhere she can think. Her mind, well versed in lying after nearly thirty years of secrets — girl-crushes in middle school, doctored report cards, the decision to move to Beirut — churns expertly through pretexts.

Mama, Baba, she rehearses, *I'd love to have you come but I'll actually be on tour.* Or: *There was another bombing last week, right next to downtown. I don't think it's a good time to come.* Or even — Naj is excited at the idea — telling them that *she* was planning on coming to America this summer, then waiting until last minute, after they'd canceled their trip, to tell them she couldn't come after all. She pees, the toilet seat cold to the touch. Her left forearm rests on her knee, the little red fox staring up at her with his pinprick eyes. Naj thinks of Maggie's lips parted in a moan, her teeth against Naj's nipple.

"Thanks for nothing," she whispers to the fox. She'd gotten the tattoo on New Year's Eve, adding to a collection of nearly a dozen. But this was the first one she'd gotten completely sober. She'd watched every line of red fur, the way the needle curled the fox's tail into itself.

What does it mean? the tattoo artist had asked, and Naj quoted from *The Little Prince:* "*You become responsible, forever, for what you have tamed.*" The artist seemed impressed, so Naj left it at that, not saying that when she'd read the line again, years after the first time, she'd thought not of an imaginary planet but of unfamiliar bedrooms and the countless cigarettes she'd smoked listening to women cry and tell her that she was ruining their lives while she tried to look understanding, explained that it wasn't them, it was her. There was just something about her.

The fox was a reminder. That you — that is, Naj — become responsible, forever, for what you have fucked. She got the tattoo thinking it would be a chaperone, a reminder not to pounce every time she saw a pretty face.

But when you've just done a sold-out show in Byblos, the stage surrounded by Phoenician ruins as old as dirt so that you feel like a conqueror staring out at the sea of dancing, screaming bodies, your violin bow moving like Zeus's lightning bolt, as though your arm is no longer your own because *it's not,* it belongs to the crowd, to the music; when you're screaming your own words into a microphone and then suddenly standing in blackness because the electricity has just been cut because *Fuck it, it's Beirut,* Naj had started screaming, and the audience echoed her words, magnifying them a thousand times over — when the show is over and you're at the lip of the stage with your bandmate, a large neon pink sign blazing over your heads (NOJA, a combination of your names), bowing over and over, the applause like the biggest love you'll ever know, all you'll want is a body to sign your name on.

Enter Maggie.

She had muscled her way into the circle of people surrounding Naj at Kayan, her favorite spot to hit after a show, a group of friends, her bandmate, Jo, and the crew, all good-looking men from Beirut, effeminate but straight, ordering rounds of kamikazes. Naj had felt someone's hand on her arm, heard a husky Australian voice in her ear: "You're phenomenal!" Maggie looked like a soccer mom — bobbed hair, plastic glasses — but she made frank eye contact as they spoke, clearly gay, and when they went outside to smoke, she'd stumbled into Naj, who'd laughed and held on a second longer than necessary.

"You've got the smile of a wolf, eh," Maggie said too loudly. Their ears were ringing after the loud show.

"It's my fucked-up tooth." Naj told her the well-rehearsed story of falling when she was a child. A couple of hours later, they were naked in Maggie's bed, the other woman licking the chipped bit and purring, "I love your fucked-up tooth."

Now Naj walks back to the bedroom and collects her bra, jeans, and purse, all strewn across the floor like a bread-crumb trail. One of the walls is covered with photographs. The room smells like vanilla and sex. Maggie sighs in her sleep and Naj hurriedly finds something to write on, a receipt on the dresser.

Thanks, she begins, then crosses it out.

Early flight today, had to go.

There. Simple, noncommittal. She adds a little heart, then goes. There is no flight, of course, but Beirut is a big city. Once outside the apartment building, Naj lets out a comical sigh. It's nearly four in the morning, late-early, as Jo likes to say. Some of the neighborhood uncles are already out for sunrise strolls; a tired-looking man is walking a beige Labrador.

Maggie lives in Gemmayzeh, ten minutes from Naj's apartment. Naj dislikes this neighborhood, with its fancy bars and overpriced teashops, the locals accommodating the influx of expats with yoga studios and European-style cafés. She cuts through rue Gouraud, humming one of her own songs, feeling better. The tattoo guilt dissolves like perfume in the warm air. Her T-shirt is torn and her rib cage is exposed. Nothing feels sexier than sex. Her underwear chafes in a slightly pleasant way. Everything will be all right. She'll call her father, convince him not to come; maybe she'll even see Maggie again in a week or two, after enough time has passed that there won't be any confusion about intentions.

At this hour, the city has a narcotic effect; ambient noise drifts from the passing cabs — a French song, the sound of a man coughing — and the few people on the street share a certain camaraderie, nodding and smiling wryly at each other. Beirut is an insomniac's city, unfocused, filled with half-finished buildings and impromptu crowds. There has been a high-rise under construction on Naj's block since she bought the apartment several years ago. She'd lived in this neighborhood longer, though, since her move from America. The newer houses live dissonantly among the older, plain ones. The city doesn't change from neighborhood to neighborhood but from building to building, and Naj is tired of remembering the former incarnations of places — the spa that was a fabric store, the health-food market that was once filled with antiques and toys.

Her own apartment building is similarly disjointed. The glass entrance has been cracked since December, but there's a stupidly ornate chandelier in the lobby, refracting light on guests like confetti. The elevator hasn't worked in months. Abu Nabil, the building's cranky, middle-aged super, lives in a small room next to the stairs. Someone decided to paint the stairwell a modern dark red but then apparently changed his mind on Naj's floor, where the walls of the stairwell become beige. Each floor has two apartments, and Naj likes her neighbors, an elderly pair of widowed sisters who go out every Sunday in matching dresses and honest-to-God church hats. There's a hand-painted sign on Naj's front door that reads *Abandon all   , ye who enter here,* the space intentionally left blank, and people have scrawled in things like *Wi-Fi* and *bras*. The sisters have never complained.

Naj's apartment smells stale, like something yeasty left out too long, with undertones of weed, even though she hasn't smoked in days. Near the window, an assortment of plants droop in various stages of dying. Naj always forgets them.

"One second," she promises them, then trots to the kitchen and fills a mug. She goes from plant to plant, watering the dusty soil. "You get water! You get water! You get water!" she sings out like Oprah. The water bubbles in the soil, then starts to drip onto the windowsill underneath. The plants remind her of her mother, of the swampy smell she'd bring home with her after a day at the greenhouse.

The apartment is a three-bedroom, too large for her, but over the years the rooms have filled of their own volition with guitars and clothes and hosted a succession of friends who'd left their exes. The electricity cuts off most afternoons — there isn't enough electricity generation to meet the country's needs — and the balcony rail squeaks anytime someone leans on it. The water runs hot for only a few minutes.

But she loves it, and more than that, she loves the idea of herself as loyal to modest living. The apartment represents her restraint; she could buy in one of the high-rises but she doesn't. Noja's ethos is folksy; Naj had once been called "The Proletariat's Duchess" on the cover of a European music magazine. The amount of money in her Credit Libanais account embarrasses her.

Her father was furious when she bought the apartment; she was only twenty-four, flush from the surprising success of their first album, *Proposal*. It hadn't reached the United States but sold well in Europe, taking off like a rocket in random cities: Amman, Kosovo, Athens, Riyadh. *What the audiences seem to have in common,* mused the *Guardian* article Naj had taped to the refrigerator, *are places of censorship, corruption, oppression. The musical duo Noja, fronted by Naj, née Najla, Nasr, creates an album of defiance, with guttural lyrics, powerhouse performances, and, most compellingly, a mixture of Arabic and English lyrics, so the listener might often be unsure of what is being said but is happy to sing along.*

"This is stupid, baba!" her father had thundered on the phone. "Stupid! First you say you want to study in Beirut — stupid number one. Then you say, *Baba, I can't live with Jiddo,* even though he is your *grandfather,* stupid number two, but okay, I pay for rent for an apartment *five minutes* away from our family house. Then — stupid number three — you make some money from your little band, okay, great, but instead of saving or investing, you want to buy your own apartment. Baba, for what! For what! Stupid number four!"

"I thought that was stupid number three," mocked Naj. The *little* had smarted.

"Baba," her father continued, "it is like the saying we have in Arabic —"

"Oh God," Naj grumbled. Her father had an irredeemable habit of quoting Arabic adages in English.

"A single mistake ensures a double misfortune —"

"Baba," Naj had interrupted. "I get it, okay? I'm making a mistake."

"A *stupid* mistake," he corrected.

"A stupid mistake, fine. Except I don't think so. I don't have to pay taxes over here, and my friend Jo knows a good real estate agent. It's going to be great. Can you try to be happy for me? Just practice it." She's the only one who can get away with talking to Idris like this. "It's not that hard. *Naj, congratulations,*" she said sotto voce. "Oh my gosh, thankyousomuch, Baba! Come on, your turn."

"A double misfortune," her father repeated.

But the grave prediction has not come true. No disaster has befallen the apartment. Sure, the bathroom leaks during rainstorms and she can't fully close one of the bedroom windows; twice the gas from the stove has leaked, the last time forcing the paltry fire department of Beirut to break her door open while the neighbors complained. But if Naj felt a slight unease when the doorknob literally fell out in her hand or when her bathroom mirror cracked, she pushed it out of her mind, scolding herself for being superstitious like Ava, who sprinkled salt on her children's heads when they were babies and always enters airplanes with her right foot.

She purchased the apartment five years ago; her father has visited once. He shrugged after walking around the rooms — she'd painted it with Jo the week before, had even arranged lilies in a water cup — and said aloud to the coat hanger, as though Naj weren't right there, *She overpaid for it.*

She would have paid double. She loves the apartment; it was the first place outside of the California house that became hers. She steps out of her sneakers now at the bedroom door, a vestigial holdover from her mother's reign — *No shoes in the house! What are we, Americans?* — the floor cool and dusty beneath her bare feet.

By the time she's gargled mouthwash, cursorily rinsed her face, and heaved a pile of clothes off her bed, the sun has begun to rise, pastel as a baby blanket. Naj falls onto the bed with a sigh. She'll deal with her parents later this morning, she'll come up with a story — the visit to California is a good one — everything will work out.

From the street below, the sounds of awakening: a car engine starting, someone talking to her child. A female neighbor's voice rises up — *Bonjour!* — and Naj falls asleep.

❖

Naj wakes up to find her bluster vanished. Her bed is soaked in sunlight; the clock reads 2:05 p.m. The thought of calling her father to lie is laughable; she feels too sorry for herself. Her head is pounding from all those kamikazes, and her mouth is sticky and sour. There's nothing in the fridge except a few cartons of yogurt. She forgot to plug in her phone; the screen is black.

"Why do you do this to me?" Naj asks it. As the phone charges, she eats the yogurt, licking the foil lid at the end, then pours herself orange juice and whiskey. It takes a few gags, but she forces it down.

There are ten unread texts. Her friend Tara; Mimi; the booker at Music Hall. Four from Jo. In a flash, Naj remembers a plan they'd made the night before to have lunch at the marina. He'll be pissed. Jo has a marathoner's body and is vexingly impervious to hangovers. They'd first met at freshman orientation, and ever since they'd been devoted to each other, coaxing each other through their twenties — her various romantic disasters, his father's slow surrender to pancreatic cancer, the setbacks of the band — an intimacy Naj couldn't replicate with any other friends, although they were usually more indulgent with her. Jo could be brutal. She'd said she'd meet him at the fried-fish stall at noon, and he'd expected her there. Naj shuts her eyes as she calls him.

"Asshole," he greets her. "Let me guess. Girl or drug? A memoir by Najla Nasr: *Girl or Drug.*"

Naj rubs her eyes with the heels of her hands. She should've waited another hour to call him. Her head would have been less achy.

"Can't it be both?" she offers in what she thinks of as her oh-Naj voice, like, *Listen, I know, aren't I a piece of work?* She waits, but Jo isn't charmed. "That

Maggie girl, you know her? She was cool. I think. I just did, like, two teeny lines, but I feel like death."

"Najla," Jo says dispassionately. "Do you know what is thought of men pushing thirty who stand alone at Abu Fady's fish stall for over an hour wearing the remnants of last night's eyeliner?"

"My phone died! I set an alarm and everything."

"And do you know," he continued, "what is thought of men wearing last night's eyeliner who stand in the parking lot and curse at someone's switched-off phone *eight separate times*? And —"

"Can you please," she interrupts, "stop?"

"In a minute. What do we say?"

Naj kisses her teeth. "It's not cute anymore."

"Not cute."

"Okay," she says. She grits her teeth. "I'm sorry, Jo. Okay?"

The tension slackens. "Abu Fady has a new harissa sauce," he says. "I had two plates. There's an exhibit tonight, some new show over at Art Factum."

"Who's the artist?"

"Not sure. This is her first one. Her husband works at the university. They're Syrian refugees. Well, not *refugee* refugees. But he was a professor at some college in Syria. Nobody knows much about her. She's the one who did that Skybar thing, with the Syrian children."

Naj feels her interest stir. She'd stayed in that weekend and was furious at what she'd missed: a mock dinner party set up in the parking lot of one of the fanciest nightclubs in town with Syrian refugee children serving socialites cigarettes and caviar on golden trays. The children were dressed in tiny tuxedos. There were opinion pieces about it for weeks, some calling it an exploitative ploy, others a brilliant juxtaposition of "the wealthy and the doomed, an incisive look at the treatment of Syrian refugees by Lebanon's elite class." The artist was referred to as Zizi, clearly a pseudonym.

She is already a little jealous of the artist. Beirut, like Amman and Dubai, is teeming with young trendy artists who admire Naj, but she knows success is whimsical; look what happened with her. People decided to love Naj, and her life changed overnight. She dislikes hearing of other female artists doing interesting things. It reminds her that she is always one *Jazeera* article away from being replaced.

"I was thinking of lying low," Naj says, already knowing she will go.

"Everyone is going to be there. There's even some reporter from the BBC."

A *Syrian* artist at that. Naj, half Syrian herself, had relegated that part of her heritage to second place her entire life, instead focusing on Beirut and hybridizing her California upbringing. In college, she'd drive into Damascus once a year, twice tops, to visit her grandparents, and she'd always forget to say she was Syrian at border patrol. It wasn't as though the two countries rarely interacted; the border between them sometimes seemed more decorative than factual. Syrian soldiers had entered the country in the seventies and *overstayed their welcome by about three decades,* as her father liked to say. Whenever Mazna overheard him say that, she'd snap, *As if we wanted to clean up your mess. We. Your.* Her parents rarely discussed politics with each other, instead preferring to complain about news reports to their children. Maybe you could blame Naj's allegiance to Lebanon on the patriarchy, the Arab tradition of lineage, selfhood siphoned from the father, but the truth was more shameful: she found Beirut sexier. And when the war started, it felt opportunistic to start claiming Syria as her own, so she never did. Naj, who has made a career out of screaming bracingly honest lyrics, who is known for appearing onstage in the clothes she'd worn the night before, feels most threatened by inauthenticity.

So, yes, Naj wants to see this clever artist.

"If I come," she says, "will you forgive the Abu Fady flake?"

"Abu Fady who?" Jo responds, and they hang up.

⁕

Naj meets Jo at Abou Elie, an old Communist bar near the university where a solemn Che glowers down at patrons sipping their watery whiskey sours. There is a group of old men at the bar, watching the news silently. At the other end is Jo. He has been growing his hair out again; she sees a tuft of curls behind one ear. His T-shirt is a touch too tight, and there are rope bracelets on his wrist. Jo has the kind of looks that endear him to people, and he knows it. He flirts with gay men, married women. Sometimes Naj wishes she could will herself straight and marry him. They'd slept together once during college, back when Naj was still sleeping with men, trying to convince herself she was bi. But the sex was unsurprisingly awful, and the two of them burst into laughter in the middle of it, giggling and clutching each other, then vowing, as they shook hands buck naked, never to do that again.

So she is left to admire Jo the way that gay men and elderly women do: from afar, with deference, aware that they are in the presence of beauty, but a beauty that has nothing to do with them.

"But do you know Maggie or not?" she asks as if they are in the middle of a conversation. She slides onto the stool next to him.

He squints. "I don't think so. The one with the glasses at the bar? She looked familiar."

"Well, she better not be there tonight. I said I was traveling."

"Nah. This won't be an *ajanib* crowd. You slipped out after she fell asleep?"

Naj lays her forehead against the cool bar top. She had another orange and whiskey; the ache is nearly gone. "I got some shit news. Mimi called."

"Oh no." Jo's eyes turn serious, and Naj remembers in a flash the day his father died, how he'd cried in her lap, *I had more to say, I had more to say.* When her grandfather died, Jo was at the *azza* all three days, staying until the last guests left each evening, then washing their plates and putting all the leftover food in Tupperware. He'd helped Merry clear out her grandfather's room when Naj and her father couldn't.

"Sorry! No, nothing like that. Nothing bad. Just — well, shit for me."

His face brightens. "What now? Has Ava discovered a new species of bacteria? Has your mother divorced your father?" Jo loves Naj's family despite the fact that he's met them only in bits and pieces, after a show in LA, during one of her father's trips to Beirut. The only child of a lonely mother following his father's death, he describes them wistfully to other people. He likes to claim he's half in love with Ava, whom he met during a show in Brooklyn last year; he called her an Arab Jane Austen character, earnest and underestimated.

"Shit news," Naj repeats. She signals the bartender, an aging grumpy man, and asks for a whiskey and Coke.

"Did something happen?"

"In a manner of speaking. I think my father might've lost his mind. He wants to sell my jiddo's house."

"Is it even his? What about your aunt?"

"I don't know. I think everything goes to the son. Mimi called me while I was at Maggie's last night. I haven't spoken to my parents yet. I need to come up with something good before they buy tickets."

Jo stills. His eyes narrow alertly. "Tickets?"

"They're fucking coming. All of them. Yes," she says to Jo's open mouth. "It's your wet dream come true. All the Nasrs in one place."

Jo holds up a finger to stop her talking. He keeps his finger up as he drains the remainder of his drink theatrically. He grimaces, burps, and shakes his head. He lets out a long exhale and stares at Naj for a moment.

"I honestly think," he says solemnly, "this is the best day of my life."

✤

They have two more whiskeys apiece at Abou Elie, and by the time they leave, Naj feels okay for the first time all day. Her headache is gone, her body pleasantly fuzzy. And sometime in the hourlong discussion with Jo about her father's motives, Naj finds herself rethinking the idea of lying to them. *I do kinda miss them,* she thinks to herself as they flag a cab. Ava's kids have never been to Beirut; she can take them to the water park, spend evenings on the Raouché. Also, Jo's excitement is infectious — her family is always a good diversion.

"But where were they a few months ago?" she demands suddenly when they're in the cab. "When Jiddo died. They couldn't come then, but suddenly their schedules have cleared up?" Her sharp words are met with silence.

"Everyone has their circumstances, Naj," Jo says, using the formal word in Arabic, like an old-school auntie. The rebuke works.

"It would be a change," she finally admits as the cab pulls up to the gallery.

"That's what I'm saying! I mean, no offense, Naj, but it might be good for you — something different."

Naj stops on the curb. Is it so obvious?

"No, no," Jo says in a rush, "I don't mean — it's just — with the women and everything." He drapes his arm around her shoulders. "Listen," he says, gentler, "not everyone has to get a warning tattooed on her arm."

Naj lets herself be tugged along. She rests her head against his arm as they walk toward the entrance. She knows what he means. Her career is fine. There's a satisfying archetype of the older rock starlet — Shirley Manson, Courtney Love — so she doesn't mind the thought of her thirties, forties, of strolling stages with her bright pink violin. Her brand allows for it. But there is something blank and yawning within her that's grown since Jiddo's passing; it's like she's been shaken loose from a safe branch. They'd seen each other weekly, had inside jokes about Lebanese politics and family anecdotes. She misses him. Since his death, everything feels painfully exposed. Her hungover afternoons and morose moods, the way she dislikes women after she sleeps with them — she is aware of it all, like a smell she can't identify the source of.

Enough. She hates being this neurotic. It reminds her of her sister. She turns her face into Jo's shoulder and bites him, hard. He yelps.

"Fucking *fuck*."

"I'm not stuck," she says, pushing him away. "I'm fine."

"You don't have to shoot the messenger," he mumbles, rubbing his arm.

The idea for the band had been Jo's. It was during their junior year, after a night with their friends on the grassy campus quad. They'd shared a bottle of cheap wine and Jo played guitar as the girls sang Tom Petty. Naj loved music and had an unusual voice, crackly and throaty, slightly off-key but with enough bravado that people overlooked it.

He'd known Naj played the violin, of course. She'd invited her friends to shows — formal recitals at the university amphitheater, but also small shows at interactive art galleries — where the music was unadorned, without vocals. But that night, one of their friends suggested Naj play along with Jo, and she had. The audience — for suddenly, their straggle of friends transformed into one — sang along, their thin voices rising into something more beautiful. Naj and Jo played together like they'd been doing it for decades, the high, flirty notes of the violin towing along the broodier strumming of his guitar. They braided into each other, faster, faster, until they were playing perfectly in pitch, the music suddenly bigger than any of the fragments.

It was fucking good.

That was Jo's first thought when the song ended. The quad around them erupted in applause. He looked over at Naj, whose face was shiny with perspiration. She gave him a victorious grin. *You felt that?* he asked silently. She nodded, laughing.

They talked about it for months, the idea delicious, returning to it on hungover mornings, between studying for midterms. They shared songs they wanted to play, e-mailed each other band profiles, had arguments about whether Naj should play the violin or sing. In the end, she did both. The logo for their band was a hot-pink circle; they named the band by putting the N, A, J, and O Scrabble tiles in a velvet bag, then picking them in random order. Noja was born.

There wasn't much of a struggling-artist phase; they started doing open-mics, then small pubs invited them, then bigger ones. They did their first festival within a year. Something about them — their attractiveness, the gritty but popular music, a bona fide chemistry — translated, and translated well. Privately, they were each other's lifeboats, seeing all the fault lines of daily life up close. But they become something else in front of an audience. Their fans loved their onstage flirting. They sold the *idea* of sex, which, as one early reviewer noted, was sexier than the real thing.

The art gallery is lit like a haunted house, with lamps blooming from unlikely corners. It is a large, open venue that Naj has seen before, but it's been completely transformed. The walls are painted a deep, outer-space black. The surface is shiny and Naj finds herself drawn to it, mesmerized. It reminds her of black-tar heroin, which she saw once in London when she and Jo went out with a group of teenage fans. There's a large sign near each wall admonishing DO NOT TOUCH.

People mill around the space, talking and laughing, and Naj says hello to the ones she knows. The art scene in Beirut is scrappy, divided into cliques: the expats; the French-educated elite; the university students, huddled tonight around the bar, glancing about in awe. This is mostly an urbanite Beiruti crowd, many of them architecture or fine arts majors at the American University who'd graduated but, for one reason or another, never left. They take unironic trips to the Cedars in the summer and write scathing articles on the garbage crisis.

"I swear," one woman is saying, "the day our prime minister's corruption is more shocking than a female orgasm, I'll finally sleep through the night." Nobody bats an eye. Unlike their more *Lebanese*-Lebanese contemporaries, these crowds have sex, and they talk about it; they argue about body politics and labor rights. Their families live nearby and fast for Ramadan but something — a summer in Paris, an internship with an American nonprofit — set them apart from their perfectly manicured peers in adolescence, and they've never looked back. Secretly Naj finds them obnoxious but not so much that she doesn't want to be liked by them.

"*After* an orgasm," the woman adds, and everyone laughs. Against each wall there are boxed displays with a photograph above each one. Naj makes more small talk, then excuses herself. There is a large placard on a stand describing the pieces.

> *The Queens of Aleppo series is an exploration of the debris of war. During the artist's final days in her hometown of Aleppo, before she fled to nearby Beirut for safety, she braved the streets of the Halab al-Jadida neighborhood in the south, which had recently been demolished by Assad's forces. Adib gathered lone cosmetic items from the rubble, finding them in places as unlikely as the burned back seat of a sedan and the collapsed remains of a nearby store. In a poignant and arresting commentary on the commodification of war, the Queens of Aleppo exhibition displays those cosmetics alongside images of Syrian women wearing them, an attempt to expose the capitalistic opportunism that emerges during times of war and occupation. The decision to display these photographs in Lebanon is a deliberate one — the new nations have coexisted in a delicate, forced ecosystem since Leba-*

non's independence from what had been known to the Ottomans as Greater Syria. The artist, Syrian-born but currently living in Beirut, goes by Zizi and describes the countries as "reluctant stepsisters . . . they didn't choose each other, and yet the survival of one depends on the other. When one nation is in war, it is my belief that the other is as well."

Naj wanders the room. Each glass box holds a single item on a velvet cushion: a half-burned eyeliner, a stub of red lipstick without the cap, the remnants of caked face powder. Above each object is a blown-up photograph of a different woman, a selfie from the top of her forehead down to her collarbones. The women all stare into the eye of the camera, adorned only with their assigned makeup. The burgundy lipstick is inexpertly smeared on one woman's lips; the kohl circles another's eyes.

"It feels like it's a bit manipulative, don't you think?" someone says to a friend, and Naj rolls her eyes. She walks around the room twice, hungry for the photographs. The effect against the pitch-black wall is hallucinatory; they're like glowing holographs. She looks over her shoulder, then surreptitiously grazes a finger against the wall.

It's wet.

"What the —" Naj's forefinger is tipped with a wet, obvious black.

"She couldn't resist" comes a voice behind her. It's one of the urbanites, clearly a friend of the artist. She speaks confidentially, pleased to know something about the show. "She wanted to catch people in the act," she continues. "You know, all our hands are dirty, et cetera."

Naj looks around and sees for the first time that some guests are gesturing with blackened fingertips.

"It's brilliant," Naj says. In spite of herself, she means it. "We're all complicit."

The woman nods. "Yes! Ugh. She'll be thrilled." She points to a woman — clearly the artist — who's talking to someone just a few feet away, her shoulder blades visible under her dress. Her friend nudges her as she passes and says in Arabic, "Fikriya, someone finally got your paint gag."

"At last!" Zizi claps her hands and turns to face Naj.

It's Fee.

Naj instinctively steps forward. They both freeze. Fee's hand goes to her throat, her face pale. Her hair is darker, her face a little thinner and longer, but it's definitely, unmistakably her.

"What are you doing here?" they both ask at once. There's a beat, then nervous laughter.

"I'm the one who —" Fee waves her hand. "Did this."

"You're Zizi," Naj says. "I didn't know you were into art." It's a ridiculous thing to say; ten years have passed. Fee could have become a zookeeper for all she knew.

Fee looks down. "I wasn't. I worked at a bank in Aleppo. But after the war, I started to take photographs."

"This is unreal. Since when do you live in *Beirut?*"

There is finally a flash of anger in Fee's eyes. "Maybe you heard about this, Naj? There was a *war* like fifty miles from here."

"You couldn't call?"

"*You* couldn't?" Fee parrots back.

"I tried," Naj mumbles. "After it started. But I couldn't find you anywhere. You're not on Facebook. And I couldn't call —"

"Because we'd both changed our numbers," Fee finishes for her. "I *am* on Facebook. I just use my married name." She looks hesitant saying this. Her accented English is exactly the same as it used to be, the care of someone who isn't a native speaker.

"Of course." A memory charges at Naj: Fee's mouth hot under hers, the two of them huddled under one coat, sharing a bottle of Jack. But she shakes her head against it.

"Is that Jo?" Fee points toward the bar, where Jo is speaking to a tall man in glasses.

"Yeah, he's the one who told me about this." Naj frowns. "We're in this band now."

"Naj." Fee's voice is sad. "I know. I have all your albums. Actually." She clears her throat. "We went to the Baalbek show last year, around Christmas."

"You were at that show." Naj tries to remember something distinct from that night, some omen, but there's nothing.

"So you and Jo are together now," Fee says. Her face is impossible to read.

There isn't a word for what Fee was for Naj; they were nineteen, practically children. The idea of calling another woman a girlfriend then had been unthinkable.

"We're not." Naj rolls her eyes. "We've never been."

The rumors have said otherwise for years. It's convenient, so Naj never corrects anyone, has been known to kiss him full on the lips after a good set. They once did a magazine photo shoot where they posed under bubbles in the same bathtub. Even her own mother slyly asks her from time to time how her *mate* is, her voice so suggestive it's clear Mazna believes that any day now, Naj will send her parents a photograph of a ring with accompanying exclamation marks.

The truth is that Naj'd had a fantasy when the band first started of being some sort of lesbian vanguard of the Arab world, a queer rock star, a lighthouse for the gay kiddos. But the closer she got to it, the more she shrank from the prospect. She couldn't tell her fans before she told her parents. Her mother and father were liberal enough, accepted that America was different, but some things couldn't be helped. It skulked in the house while Naj grew up — that time her mother called Madonna sick for kissing a fresh-faced Britney Spears on MTV, the way her father spoke of a gay patient with AIDS. It wasn't a matter of being pardoned; it couldn't be comprehended in the first place. Instead of queer, she projected sexy and hoped the little Arabi dykes would recognize it. (They did. There are hundreds of blog posts and social media tags about Naj's sexuality, her *quiet but ferocious nods toward queerness,* and Naj saves every single one in a Gmail folder.)

"He's my beard." Naj nods toward Jo.

"Your . . . beard," Fee says slowly. Naj remembers how Fee would discover new words in English all the time in college, thrilled at each one. They had come from different worlds. Naj was an American playing Arab. Fee was emphatically Arab, her parents agreeing to let her go away for college only because her brother lived in Beirut. She had a curfew, wore cardigans, dreamed in Arabic.

"It's like . . . it's what gay men call their wives."

"Why do gay men have wives?"

"Oh. Well, I guess before they accept that they're gay? Or when they accept that they're gay but can't come out?" Naj turns her sentences into questions when she's nervous.

"So you're a gay man now," Fee says, her voice amused. "And Jo is your wife."

"Basically." Naj gives her a sheepish smile.

"Well, your wife is talking to my husband."

Naj takes a second look at the tall man. He's vaguely handsome, with a goatee and a receding hairline. He looks positively pedantic.

"He used to work at the university in Aleppo," Fee says as though reading her mind. "He taught law and history." Something bitter flits in her voice. "Clearly, he was looking backward when he should've been looking forward."

"The photographs are great," Naj says, then feels a little stupid. She sounds like one of the moon-eyed art students.

"Do you really think so?" Fee's face lights up and Naj forgets everything. "I was interested in the idea of portraiture," Fee says, her tone immediately taking on a higher lilt, sounding almost as pedantic as her husband looks. "At first, it was going to be about having me photograph strangers, but then I started researching self-portraiture. Did you know it's been around for centuries?"

"Selfies?" Naj thinks of the idiotic duckfaces that flood her Instagram feed.

Fee nods, her cheeks flushed with excitement. "It's one of the oldest art forms. Cave paintings were often of the artists. And think of van Gogh. Frida. Self-portraits have existed since the beginning of time. Zen monks in Japan were painting themselves centuries ago."

"I never thought of it that way. All those self-portraits in museums. They're predecessors to the selfie."

"Now it's become more prevalent, because everyone has the tools for it. So we relabel it *narcissism*."

Pre-vale-*ant*. "Isn't it?"

"I suppose," Fee admits. "But I think it's more than that. Yes, we like to look at ourselves. Even the ancient Egyptians knew that. But modern self-portraiture has more to do with our cultural anxiety about representation."

Naj thinks back to their philosophy course in college, how after each class she and Fee would argue about soul theories for hours on the quad. "And representation during war is even faultier."

"It is!" Fee looks at her gratefully. "So I decided to have the women represent themselves. I guess I'm no less paranoid than those monks."

"But isn't their own representation as fallible as any other?"

"I'd rather be misunderstood by what I say than what someone says for me." Fee frowns, and Naj wonders if she asked the wrong question. "I think I got so sick of all the talking points. About Syria. People say it's cyclical, that what's happening in Aleppo today is what happened in Europe a hundred years ago. But I disagree. I think the Arabs have a particular sickness."

The room feels too hot. Fee is actually here. They are having a conversation. "Right." Naj tries to sound knowing, but she feels a brief panic, like she's taken bad mushrooms. This is too much. The last time she'd seen Fee, they'd both been nineteen, weeping on a bench in the university at night. Fee had been in her life fully and often, and then she was gone. Naj had a notebook of songs for an album entitled *Living Ghost*; she'd never released a single one.

As if on cue, Fee clears her throat, looking nervous. "It's about the war, yes. But also about being colonized."

Naj makes a noncommittal sound. *How is it possible,* Ava once asked her after she'd called to check in following a bombing in Beirut that Naj hadn't even heard about, *to be living in the heart of politics and know nothing about it?*

When in doubt, Naj thinks, *blame the whites.* "Yes, colonialism," she says. "It feeds on that internalized sense of inferiority. It sets people against one another. I guess in some places, representation becomes political," Naj concludes, a little impressed with herself.

"It starts wars," Fee says dryly. "You grow up being eyed through a certain lens, that's how you act. Women have learned to colonize themselves."

The conversation suddenly feels claustrophobic, the black room too small for Naj. She looks around at the happy, oblivious people and feels resentful toward Fee — the Artist — for standing there barely flustered, or at least hiding it well. Naj speaks a little harsher than necessary. "Is that what art does? Disrupt colonialism?"

"I don't know what art does anymore," Fee says quietly.

Fee wants to introduce Naj to her husband, so Naj follows her to the men. Jo has his back to them, and Naj pokes him harder than necessary.

"Look who it is," she sing-hisses.

Jo turns around and gasps. He keeps his mouth open for a moment before speaking. "Fee! What . . ." He trails off, looking back and forth between Fee and the man he's been talking to. "You're the artist?" he finally manages.

"She is," Naj replies for her. *Did you know about this?* she asks him silently. He shakes his head: *Of course not.* Jo had been the one to see Naj through that awful winter after Fee left.

"Jo, I see you've met my husband," Fee says. "Naj, this is Bilal."

Naj's fingertips are cold. She shakes the man's hand; the fox's face is tipped up toward everyone. She crosses her arms.

"You all know each other," Bilal says. It isn't a question. He smiles, and Naj can see his appeal. He reminds her of a nerdy guy in a movie.

"From university," Fee says quietly.

"They call you Fee," Bilal says to his wife.

"It's an old nickname."

"I like it," Bilal muses. "Fikriya is such a serious name."

The four of them look at their drinks in silence.

"I can't believe it was you all along," Jo finally says to Fee. "Bilal said you're working on a painting series next."

"Did he," Fee says sharply. "Yes." She's momentarily distracted by a couple of shy students who come over and praise the exhibit. When they leave, she seems unfocused. "I haven't worked much with oils. It's coming out quite messy so far."

"What are you painting?" Naj asks.

"Women," Bilal answers for her. "Syrian women. Old, young, even beggars." He places a hand on his wife's shoulder, ever so slightly proprietarily, and Naj decides once and for all that she dislikes him.

Fee seems to sense the shift. She moves almost imperceptibly to the left so that Bilal is forced to drop his arm. "The *subjects* are Syrian," she corrects. "But I'm dressing them up as characters in Arab folklore, then painting them. I'm focusing on Levantine figures. Princess Badoura, Scheherazade, that sort of thing."

"You're doing portraits?" Jo asks.

"Kinda. It's a little more complicated than that. I'm reimagining them once with the costumes and then a second time through painting them."

"You're representing a representation," Naj says.

"Exactly." Fee looks at her with that grateful expression and Naj remembers rather than notices the freckles spattered across her nose.

"It's a shame. You would've been good to paint," Bilal says to Naj, "but it's just Syrian women." That he seems to like her just intensifies her dislike.

"Her mother is Syrian," Jo says.

"I forgot that." Fee's face softens with memory. Naj wonders which one.

"Is she?" Bilal looks interested.

"Yes," Naj says, glaring at Jo. "From Damascus."

"I wonder if that would work," Bilal says. His tone is thoughtful. The quartet falls silent again, the three of them looking at Fee as she chews her lower lip, thinking.

"A mother would do," Fee says quietly.

❖

Jo walks Naj home after the show; they take the long way there. It rained while they were inside, and the streets glitter, the city subdued like a cat after its bath.

"I had no idea," Jo says the moment they're alone. "Naj, I swear to God."

"How can someone just appear like that?"

"You seemed" — Jo hesitates — "okay. In there. You were a lot better than I would've been."

"I think I just went on autopilot or something." Her face feels funny and a little numb, like she'd been given Novocain and it was wearing off.

"Did she *say* anything? Did you ask her anything?"

"Jo. I was trying not to freak out. What was I supposed to ask?"

"I don't know!" Jo ducks his head, and Naj can see he's angry, really angry. "How about 'Do you know that we filed a police report because we couldn't find you? Oh, also, is your scumbag brother finally in prison?'" He takes a deep breath. "And 'When the fuck did you start pretending to be an artist?'"

"I thought you liked her art."

"It's derivative and repetitive."

"Come on." They walk in silence for a moment. "It was weirdly good to see her."

Jo lets out an oomph of air. "I know," he says, defeated. "It was."

Naj's boots clack against the pavement in a way she finds satisfying. She remembers that there's a baggie of cocaine left over from last night in her purse. When they reach Naj's building, Jo seems reluctant to leave.

"Are you going to let her paint you?"

Naj doesn't answer.

"You're thinking about it," he says accusingly. "Naj, it's a terrible idea."

"I can't believe she has a *husband*."

"God," he mutters. "Your family can't get here fast enough."

"I didn't say yes to her."

Jo eyes her for a long moment. He'd sat with her in the police station, clasping her hand, as they waited for news. He had loved Fee as much as her back then. "But you will."

⁂

It's barely after midnight. Naj pauses at the landing of each staircase, out of breath. There had been a time, in high school, when she could've run up and down these flights seven, eight times without taking a break. She'd led her soccer team for four years straight, was the first freshman to be captain in the school's history. In those days, Naj was afraid of her body — of what it seemed to want, of the way she felt in the changing room watching the knobby spines and fleshy asses of the girls as they got dressed — and athletics was a way to transform that fear, to treat her body like a machine. She could run more sprints than anyone else, would practice dribbles with her teammates until the sun went down, their faces flushed and sweaty. Team sports bred a primal intimacy that Naj missed until she and Jo started the band. The girls slept two in a bed during tournaments, sometimes even took showers together. They all cried when someone's parents got divorced and they rubbed each other's backs when they drank too much.

I think that's why it took so long, Naj once told Jo, *to admit it.* The closeness of the team protected her from that sort of introspection. Yes, she looked forward to the moment at the end of the game when their girl arms and legs fell into a heap together. But so did everyone else. The nights they won, they'd

sneak their parents' schnapps and drink until the ceiling spun; there were predictable games of truth or dare, the soft lips against Naj's when she was dared
to kiss Jess or Samantha or Marissa. Who needed to dissect sexuality? They
clearly loved one another. They burned for one another.

She lets herself into the dark apartment, flips on the light switch. Nothing.
The electricity is out.

During one of the games of truth or dare, Naj drank too much, got carried
away by Sam's intoxicating watermelon ChapStick, and darted her tongue into
the other girl's mouth. The girls had erupted into giggles, then forgotten about
it. But Naj lay awake all that night, listening to their snoring, unable to calm
her heartbeat. *Here come the lezzies,* the football players would call out whenever they crossed paths with Naj's team on the field, and Naj would feel a specific, baffling panic at the word.

"Well," she says aloud now to the empty room, "I turned out to be the
queen of lezzies."

An idea strikes her. Naj picks up the bag she just dropped on the couch,
goes back outside, and bounds down the stairs. There's a lone cab driving toward her, and although the walk would take only fifteen, twenty minutes tops,
she flings her arm up.

"La wayn?" the cabdriver asks in a bored tone.

"Ain Al Mraiseh. Near the big pharmacy," she replies.

It's a quick ride, barely the length of the Najwa Karam song the driver is listening to. "Here," Naj calls out when the familiar sign appears. She walks the
rest of the way, going under the neon cross of the pharmacy and up a narrow
path that opens onto a residential street, a row of Moorish-style houses. She
stands in front of the fourth one for a second. There is a fence, framed by trees,
and the little courtyard is visible through the slats. Naj flings her bag over the
gate, then hoists herself up, feeling a satisfaction at the muscle memory, at how
reliably her arms hold her up, how she knows intuitively to jump down slightly
to the right to avoid the small jasmine bush.

Once inside, she's pleased to see that the almond trees have begun to
flower. The trees always make her think of her family. Everybody loves them,
even Mazna; she used to say they reminded her of a woman shaking her hair
out. They represented those summer trips, the trees — late-summer evenings

when the adults would let Naj stay up, afternoons in her adulthood playing cards with her grandfather. When Naj was a child, her grandmother told her people used to believe that flowers helped you enter another world; at the old woman's funeral, Naj — only nine years old — had thrown a temper tantrum until the adults agreed to bury a mound of the pink flowers with her grandmother. *This way, she'll be able to go to heaven,* Naj told them knowingly, then felt awful when her father began to cry. She thought often about the red flowers at her jiddo's funeral, but something kept her from asking her father if he remembered.

At the threshold of the house, Naj slips out of her sneakers. The doorknob turns easily. None of her friends lock their apartments in Beirut. The city is secure, even if it isn't always safe — car bombs, invasions, roads blocked by weeklong protests. Inside, the house is warm and still smells like her grandfather: baby powder and cinnamon and pickles. Of her grandparents, Naj had always felt closest to her jiddo, a calm man who ran a print shop near the university for forty years before retiring. *Even in war,* he told her once, *people take photographs.* He'd led a quiet, hermetic life after her grandmother's death; he played *tarneeb* with a couple of fellow widowers on Thursdays, went to the mosque on Fridays. Every afternoon he had lunch with his maid/nurse/confidante, a severe Ethiopian woman incongruously named Merry.

They buried him on a Thursday, after her father washed his body with some neighborhood men and a local imam. Naj wasn't allowed at the washing. She spent the *azza* alternating between bickering with everyone — her father, her aunt Sara, Merry — about minor things like when to put the food out and stupefied from grief and Oxys. She was angry the entire time. Her sister and brother texted questions about her father, and she responded with nonsensical emojis. At one point, her father had wept so hard, spittle ran down his chin, and Ava and Mimi were safely tucked away across an ocean; she hated them for it.

Merry still keeps the house spotless, as though guests might arrive at any second. Naj sees that she's arranged flowers in the doorway; she tucks one behind her ear. What's gotten into her father? How could he sell? Her mother is the one who scorns Beirut, who never visits, and her father bends to Mazna's will. Her brother must be mistaken; if her mother wanted the house, her father would come around.

Naj tiptoes down the front hallway, past the guest rooms and Merry's room. Merry has a proper bedroom, not the microscopic maid's room that most Arab houses have next to the kitchen (DISMANTLE ARCHITECTURAL OPPRESSION, Naj painted on signs during the labor protests she'd attended in college, although she still sat while Merry served her tea during her visits). Naj has glimpsed the inside of the room only once or twice, as Merry usually keeps the door firmly shut. Now that the house is empty, Merry could sleep in any of the rooms, and yet she remains in hers. If the house is sold, she will have to go.

The house is over a hundred years old, and the rooms are sunny and narrow, the courtyard visible from the kitchen and guest bathroom. Naj wanders through the living room picking things up and replacing them — her grandmother's candy dish, a pair of dice in a bowl, old sunglasses — then goes into the kitchen, where she filches a banana. In the foyer, a photograph of her grandparents printed at Jiddo's own shop hangs above an armchair. The room is dim, but Naj can make out her grandfather's young, mustached face, the velvety brown eyes Mimi inherited, framed with long lashes. He wore a suit; her grandmother was in a dark dress, her hair bobbed.

Naj meets her dead grandmother's gaze for a moment. It makes her uncomfortable to think about how old she was in this photo; she was likely younger than Naj is now. Her eyes are heavy from an already taxing life, hooded and dark; there's a weary set to her lips as she stares at the camera. By the time this photograph was taken, the woman had carried three children and buried one. Naj's father and her aunt Sara had grown up not knowing there had been a third child; when Naj's father was twelve, a relative's slip revealed the secret.

Naj continues down to the master bedroom. The door creaks as she pushes it open; her eyes have adjusted to the dark now, so she can make out the smooth, unslept-in bedcovers. She squints, conjuring the shape of a sleeping body; if he were still here, she would have gotten in next to him. He would have been startled in the morning, she knows, but not shocked. Her grandfather always treated Naj like a little girl perpetually on the verge of a tantrum. He offered her caramel candies when she came over, asked her to play "Au

Clair de la Lune" on the violin when she remembered to bring it. She often forgot. He didn't ask about her band, and sometimes Naj wondered if he even knew about it, if he realized how big Noja was. She could set the garden on fire and he'd smile tolerantly because, as she'd overheard him say to Merry once, at least Naj was here; the rest of the sentence went unspoken.

If Jiddo had wished that Naj would come over more, he never showed it. He was good-natured, used to being left, first by his son, then his wife. How strange, after a lifetime of that, to be the one doing the leaving. Even his daughter, Naj's aunt Sara, had left the house in her late twenties, not for husband but career, a lackluster job in the government's parliament, *wasting her life with those liars and crooks,* Jiddo said. Naj always watched her aunt's face when Jiddo talked about her life, but there was never any sign of irritation; Sara would just cheerfully kiss her father's forehead and sing out that yes, she'd lost her looks, but, let's be honest, she'd never had that many to begin with.

Plain, sensible Sara. The opposite of Naj's glamorous mother, Mazna. The two women's dislike for each other has always been a quiet, accepted thing. But Naj loves her aunt. The summer after Naj's freshman year, Sara had taken her shopping, and they happened upon a couple kissing, clearly hiding from the crowd, near the dressing rooms. It was two women.

Naj blushed so hard she felt incandescent, as though *she'd* been the one caught kissing a short-haired girl. Sara took a long, hard look at her niece's face, then ushered her out of the store and onto the bright, busy street, teeming with people.

"Well," she'd said in that firm voice of hers. "Nothing wrong with that."

Naj tried to speak but let out a squeak instead.

Sara reached over and squeezed Naj's hand without turning to face her. "Nothing wrong with that," she repeated slowly. They'd never spoken of it again.

Naj wanders back through the house to the courtyard. She tries to imagine everything buried under a bomb, then some artist finding the remains — the sunglasses, cologne bottles, spatulas — and making a show out of it. She'd be fucking furious with the artist, she has to admit. Fee has balls.

There's a porch swing in the yard, probably as old as Naj herself. It squawks at each thrust. The images flash through her tired mind — the burned cosmetics, her grandmother's heavy eyes, Sara's fingers against her wrist. Fee's face when she saw her. Mimi always wants to know why Naj stays in Beirut. She can be an orphan here, a fretted-over runaway, like in a fairy tale. Sara, her grandfather, Merry, Jo, the crowds at her shows — she's not their daughter, and yet it feels like she has a dozen parents here. Other artists speak of their fans like they're their children; Naj feels as if she's the child of her fans. With her grandfather gone, she has one fewer guardian.

Naj had tantrums all through childhood — although she herself has little memory of them. It was in an act of desperation one day that her father had sent her to one of Mimi's music lessons with him. They were in the teacher's large, ranch-style house; each of the bedrooms had been converted into a small practice room, and when Naj walked down the hallway, she caught wafts of the most wonderful cacophony. In one room, two older children were playing wooden instruments, their cheeks against them, moving what looked like magic wands back and forth. *I want that,* she'd told the teacher, who laughed and said she had expensive taste.

❖

The memory is clear as water. Naj is alone with the music teacher in a darkpaneled room, the afternoon sun yellow against the hardwood floors. Naj has on a plaid dress her mother forced her to wear, its collar white and itchy, and she has been standing for over an hour copying the movements of the music teacher, who is teaching her the alphabet. A new, strange alphabet. Two fingers against the neck of the instrument made E. A finger lightly wobbling against the second string made C.

Something is happening in the room. It started several minutes into the lesson, a look of bemusement on the teacher's face, the sharp line between her eyebrows softening. "This is D," she said, playing it on her own violin, then Naj nodded and played it on the smaller one the teacher had lent her. As the minutes ticked by, the music teacher seemed more alert, the room silent except for Naj's parroting notes.

"I want us to try something," the teacher says, her voice unusually light, almost mischievous. She plays a little ditty, first slowly, so that Naj can see her fingers, then quicker.

(It was hard to explain later to her parents and friends and, especially, Mimi. Even now, the rest of the memory is painful, how the teacher ushered her parents into her office, where Mimi was already sitting, and began to gush while Mimi stared at the scuffed benches. Mimi had been so excited to show his little sister the music school, but he'd quickly become distraught; later that evening, he'd pulled her into his bedroom and asked her to explain how she'd known what to do. The true answer—though it only upset him to hear it —was that it simply made sense. She'd watched the teacher's fingers moving across the neck of the violin and remembered what they did. Then she'd done the same with her own.)

Naj plays the ditty, then glances up at the teacher to see what's next. Her neck is itchy from the stupid dress and she is, truthfully, a little bored.

Mrs. McDonough is staring at Naj as though she's grown another head, a look of clear and decided awe on her face. "Well," she says when she can finally speak again, "who could've seen that coming?"

***

The violin changed everything. Suddenly the beating wings in Naj's chest didn't matter, nor did the rage that shook her wordless—she didn't need words anymore. She could play.

***

The dark feels like an animal, waiting and patient with its warm breath. The courtyard is sheltered from street lamps, and it seems impossible that in a few hours the sky will lighten, and people will curse their alarms. The memory of that first lesson has ruined Naj's mood. The more she tried to be like her brother, the more he pulled away from her. But she never stopped trying. Only her brother knows about her. Sometimes she wonders if he even remembers or if he'd heard her correctly. It was years ago, Naj visiting Austin for a few days, and they'd gotten too drunk at a college bar. She'd told him quickly *I-like-girls-I-always-have,* but everything is hazy after that. Sometimes she'll reference it lightly, testing him. She always mentions it as a what-if, a wacky joke. Telling him was an attempt at intimacy. She's never learned how to stop. She sends him a text now.

If I tell Mama I'm a lezzie will she cancel trip? Ha-ha.

Too late, she remembers the time difference; it's early evening in Texas. He'll be eating dinner or watching television in that small, lopsided house that Naj has visited only once, on a layover during a trip back home to see her parents. She can picture her brother next to Harper, whom Naj likes but always feels a little awkward around, as if one of them walked in on the other using the bathroom or something. Naj imagines a *ping* in her mind, like a slide projector, as the image shifts to Ava's brownstone in Brooklyn, which she's stayed at a few times. Finally, a *ping* back across America, to California, to the rosewood in front of her parents' house, the potted cacti near the back door, where her mother sneaks her cigarettes. The thought of her mother burying cigarette butts in the soil makes Naj's heart twinge.

Fee had touched her tonight. As they were leaving, Jo shaking Bilal's hand, Fee reached out and touched Naj's forearm, like they were at a dinner party. Naj pulled her arm back instinctively and Fee looked away. Naj doesn't want to think of it. She pulls the baggie out of her purse and taps its contents onto her cell phone's screen. She does the bump, but her heart isn't in it. The screen lights up.

Mimi. *Um, fairly certain she'd double down on the trip. Anyway I don't think Mama's the captain here.*

Is this the same woman? She's always the captain, Naj replies.

A text bubble appears. Then: *Dunno. It doesn't seem like that now. She told Ava it was wrong to sell the house.*

Naj frowns. *I don't get it,* she types out, *what's he doing?*

I know. Listen, I have to go but can call tomorrow. It's all weird as fuck, like even Mama seems pissed at Baba.

"Of course she is!" Naj exclaims aloud. Her father is out of control. Someone has to talk to him. Naj taps the remaining powder onto her tongue, then dials her father.

The phone rings six times before her father picks up. Whereas her mother would have greeted her with a predictable, self-assured stream of complaints, her father speaks easily, as though they've just had lunch.

"Hey, *irdeh*," he says, sounding happy to hear from her. *Irdeh* is the Arabic word for "monkey."

"What is going on with you?" she demands. "This is our house."

"Ah." There is some sound in the background. Beeping. He's still in the hospital. "I suppose your mother told you."

"What is Merry going to do? Does Sara even know? She's going to flip out, Baba. I don't understand how you could decide something like this. Mimi said that even Mama doesn't want you to! You can't just —"

"What is it, three in the morning there?" Idris's voice is emergency-room calm. "Are you on drugs, *irdeh*? Are you calling your old baba on drugs?"

"Of course I'm not *calling my father on drugs*." Naj spits out the words as sharply as she can to disguise the fact that she is, indeed, calling her father on drugs.

"That's good to hear, *habibti*," he says, continuing in his doctor voice, slow and a little smug. "So you're mad at me."

"Yup." Naj lays her head against the swing's armrest. If she squints, she can make the moon pirouette. "I was going to try to convince you guys not to come." Even a whisper of cocaine makes Naj irremediably honest.

Idris laughs. "You sound like your mother. She's positive I've finally lost my mind," he says sotto voce, as though it's a secret.

Naj feels her anger dissipate like a bad fog. "Have you?"

"*Irdeh,* do you think I'd make such a decision lightly?"

In spite of herself, Naj lets out a breath. Her father has a plan. Of course he does. "Then why?"

He sighs. "If I tell you, will you mock me like your mother does?"

"I won't," she promises.

"There was a heart that came in," he begins, his voice warmer now, conspiratorial. "A few weeks ago. It belonged to a young gentleman. There was an accident, but we didn't know that then. They just told us it was a donor. I have a patient who's been waiting for a heart for ten months. Blood type B negative.

This was a perfect fit. In the operating theater, I waited for the nurses to prep my patient, then I took the heart in my hands."

"And you talked to it," Naj finishes.

"I talked to it," he confirms. "I asked it to be strong, because my patient had had a rough few months. And then —"

Naj sits up. "Then what?"

"Well . . . it spoke back. The heart. It started to tell me something."

"Um. Baba. Are *you* on drugs?"

"I am not! I damn near dropped the thing on the floor right there. I asked the nurses if they'd heard anything. They hadn't, and then I realized it was only me."

"How did it talk? Like, did it have a heart mouth?"

"I'm glad I'm giving you something to laugh about, Najla. No, it didn't have a heart mouth. What is this, Nickelodeon?"

"Then how'd it talk?"

"It didn't *talk*-talk! But I could hear it. Like it was speaking just to me."

Naj laughs. "Baba, they have a psych ward in your hospital, right?" Her father lets out an indignant snort. "Okay, Ba, what did the heart say?"

"I really can't discuss it," he says formally.

She groans. "That's convenient. A magical heart tells you something you can't repeat."

"What magical? It was a regular heart. My patient is probably eating his first steak in years right now." He clears his throat. "How's the band?"

"Don't change the subject. It's fine. We just booked a UK tour for the winter."

"Ah!" His voice lifts. "My superstar girl. Oh, did I tell you? I'm investing in a tech company in India. I got an e-mail last week."

"Baba, that is one *hundred* percent a scam. Please tell me you didn't send them money." Her parents remind her of children sometimes.

"We'll see who's scamming when I become a Rockafellow."

"Rockefeller, Baba. You're never seeing a cent of that again."

He tsks. "Always so cynical. In Arabic, we say —"

"You must know," she interrupts, "that this isn't just your house."

"Baba, the house is empty except for Merry, and she will need to leave eventually anyway. For years, nobody's wanted the house — not you, not Sara, not your mother — and now suddenly everybody wants to protect it."

Naj is quiet for a moment. "You can't do this to Sara," she says.

Her father pauses, then says, "She'll understand once I talk to her."

"She won't."

"I hated the *azza,*" her father says out of nowhere. "I want to do something better. And we can clear the house out together. The hospital gave me the summer off."

"They're probably glad to see you go," Naj says meanly.

There's a delicate silence. She's hit a nerve. Her father was the only brown doctor in the hospital for a long time; when he was first hired, people had been awful to him.

"You should get some sleep," he says kindly.

"This is all because of Mama! Just say it. She finally got in your head about Beirut," Naj says suddenly, hotly, Mazna at last coming up.

"You don't speak about your mother that way, Najla," her father says casually but there's a finality in his tone.

Naj bites a hangnail in frustration; her parents' alliance is fickle and impossible to predict. "Fine," she says, switching tactics. "I'm just saying, Mama hates this country." Naj stops, realizing she can't even remember the last time her mother came to Beirut. Even before the war began in Syria, Mazna had visited her parents in Sweden, where they'd moved with her sister, Nawal. "I don't understand why *she's* upset all of a sudden."

"You'd be surprised, Baba." Idris's voice is almost mournful. "She used to love that house, back in the day."

"Ba." Naj snorts. "Honestly. Why do you want to sell a house you don't even live in?"

There's another pause. "Maybe it's haunted," he tries lightly. "A house can endure only so many deaths."

"It's been in the family for years!"

"*Irdeh*, sometimes we have to leave the past where it belongs."

"You're going to have to do better than that, Babs," she says gently.

"Okay, okay, Mr. Tough Guy." His voice is more mirthful; he's done with the topic. "Are you still going to try to convince me not to come?"

Naj dangles a leg out in front of her, rotates her ankle. She broke it years ago, and it still hurts sometimes. *That's because the body does a lot of remembering for us,* her father once told her. She feels the loneliness from earlier. She can picture her father perfectly, in his white lab coat, the blue thread spelling out his last name in cursive, tucking his chin down to his neck and peering out above his glasses as he spoke on the phone, a habit that often made passersby think he was talking to them.

"No." Naj sighs. "I'm not."

❧

After she hangs up, Naj curls her body on the swing. She'd meant to yell at her father, but she'd been disarmed. *He spat her from his mouth,* his mother often said when Naj was younger, meaning she was just like her father. And it was true; despite the fact that she looks more like her mother — alarmingly thick hair, bold eyebrows, thin physique — there has always been a kinship between the two of them. They both hook the left leg over the right when they sit. They hold spoons the same way; they have the same kind of gravelly singing voice. And she is the one her father can never say no to, which, Naj reflects now, is an indulgence that could be good or bad.

The cushion beneath her cheek smells gross. It's probably never been washed. She can't stop thinking about her mother waiting for her father to come home from the hospital. Naj wishes she'd told her father about the art show. She could've said that she ran into an old friend.

Without meaning to, she falls asleep.

❧

"Ai-*ya!*"

Naj wakes to a sharp poke in her midriff. Merry stands above her, the end of a broom pointed at her menacingly.

"I thought you were a burglar. What kind of girl sleeps outside like this?"

Naj sits up, yawning. She rubs her eyes. The first light has begun to creep around the edges of the sky like someone spilled pale beer. She thinks, *The azan should start soon,* and on cue, the air fills with the sound of a nearby muezzin.

"What would your jiddo — God keep him — think if he saw his son's daughter was homeless?"

"I'm not homeless." Naj groans. She rises; her neck has a crick in it. The cocaine was shit. She'd fallen asleep within thirty minutes.

"What kind —" Merry begins, but Naj holds up her hand for mercy.

"I just wanted some quiet. That's all. Anyway, I'm leaving now."

"Bad girl," Merry says softly. "Come all the way to Jiddo's house and not say hi."

Naj tugs her hair so she can roll her eyes without being seen. Merry still talks to Naj like she's seven.

"She comes all the way to Jiddo's house," Merry says to the tree above them, "and doesn't even ask if she can help with anything."

"Merry!"

"Or," she continues mischievously, "maybe Jiddo's son's daughter came all this way to help make breakfast."

Naj sighs. "Okay, okay."

She steps back into her sneakers and follows Merry across the courtyard. From the trees overhead, she can hear the chirps of those little red birds she'd loved as a child. For a second, she has the impulse to tell Merry about her father and the heart. But the moment passes. At the doorway, Merry steps aside to let Naj in first.

The pale light in the kitchen is exhausting to Naj. She wonders if Fee will paint her. Her father's words return to her, and Naj tries to envision her mother younger than her, eating a meal in this kitchen. Loving this house. It's still so early; Naj could slip into one of the guest rooms and sleep a little longer. But Merry has already started cracking open eggs, and she hands Naj a bowl of recently washed asparagus sticks.

"Snap off the ends," she instructs. And so Naj does, holding the pencil-thin necks still as she snaps them, one after another. Her mother sat at this table, she realizes. Doing what? Making polite conversation with Idris's parents. Laughing with Sara. They hate each other now, but maybe they didn't always.

"My parents are coming," she tells Merry. She can't bear to say the rest. "My whole family."

The other woman grunts. "Now they come?"

"My sentiments exactly." Naj smiles at the asparagus. "They want to do a memorial." Merry tilts her head quizzically. "It's like a ceremony," Naj explains. "When someone dies. People put up old photographs and tell stories."

Merry actually laughs. "Your parents really are Americans now, aren't they?" she sneers.

Part

II

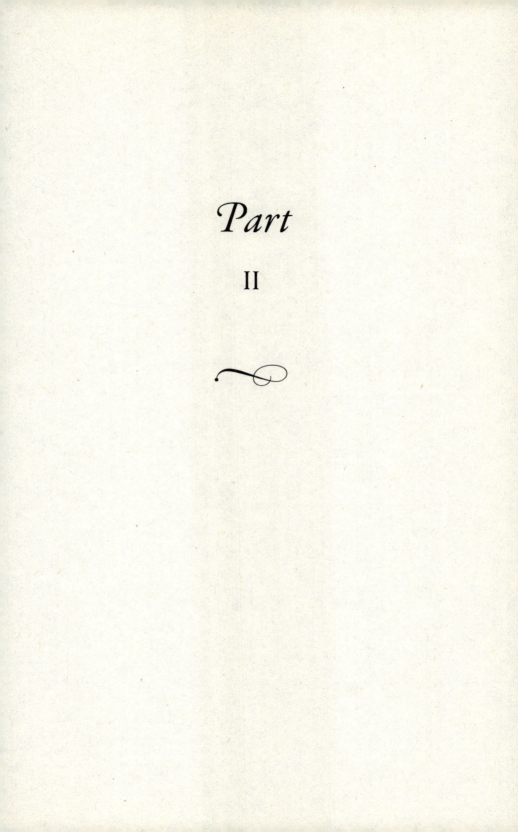

Liz Taylor in Damascus

1965

IT BEGAN WHEN Mazna's grandfather started talking to his brother. His brother, of course, had been dead for decades, but her grandfather seemed unperturbed by this. He scolded his brother for being late for dinner, told him jokes as he brushed his teeth, toothpaste flecking his lips.

"Well," Mazna's grandmother says with a sigh one night at dinner, "he's finally lost his mind."

Mazna waits for someone at the table to disagree, her mother or Great-Aunt Seham, but they only continue eating their eggplant and rice. She has just turned ten, her birthday two days after New Year's, a fact the elders always coo over, that she's entering a new year just as the world is.

"He's not," Mazna pipes up. "He told me a story last night and remembered all the good parts." Her father absently pats her hand; the other adults ignore her.

Mazna loves her grandfather Ghassan. He's tall and funny and bald as a baby, given to fits of anxious energy that translate into long walks or reorganizing the spice cabinet. *Your grandfather's done it again,* Mazna's mother will mutter, shaking her head over a completely reshuffled pantry. He used to write for a newspaper, but that was before Mazna was born. On the mantel, there's a photograph of him chewing the end of a pencil and smiling distractedly at someone off to the side. He looks like a movie star.

❖

The house, in the neighborhood of Abu Rummaneh, was built was built in the 1930s. The floors are marble with alternating black and white tiles; it's like living inside a chess game. In the summer, they leave the windows open at night to let in the breeze, and the trees that stand guard outside waft their pollen in.

Her grandparents raised their three sons in the house; Mazna's father was the youngest. Bassel had remained in the house while he attended Damascus University after his brothers moved into houses of their own with their new wives. While he was completing his master's degree, Bassel met Lulwa, a green-eyed literature student from a quiet, conservative family in Homs. She knocked over Bassel's mug in a café. They were married three months later. Abeer called Lulwa *the Homs girl* for years. She disapproved of Lulwa's family, her poor table manners, the old-fashioned headscarfs her relatives wore. Bassel's family wasn't well off, but they made do, and Lulwa was poorer. *It wasn't a necessary union,* Mazna once overheard her grandmother say to a guest, and she dug half-moons into her palms.

Mazna loves to imagine her parents meeting: her elfin mother with her hair swept back, eyes misty with distraction as she walks into the café; her father laughingly mopping up the coffee, offering her a croissant. There's one photograph of their wedding in the living room, next to the photo of her grandfather. Her mother is gathering the train of her dress, an anxious smile on her face. Her father is gazing directly into the camera, smirking, his hand gesturing to Lulwa as though to say, *Look at her.* Tiny pale grains dot the photograph: a rain of dry rice.

For a long time, Lulwa and Bassel and their two daughters lived in their own place, a tiny apartment near the university with a terrace painted watermelon pink. But six years ago Mazna's sister, Nawal, moved out to live with her new husband, and Bassel finally gave in to his mother's pestering. The three of them moved into his parents' house.

Mazna doesn't remember the watermelon-pink apartment, though she's seen photographs. Her sister was already gone by the time Mazna started school; she grew up the baby in a house of rapidly aging adults. Her father is nearly sixty. Nawal is kind to her, but distracted, her life filled with housework and a son only five years younger than Mazna. She gets the best desserts, the prettiest dresses, but she sometimes feels like an afterthought, like she was a pet her parents got impulsively and now pamper excessively to make up for their regret. Sometimes Mazna's life feels like a seat left slightly warm for her.

✦

One morning, her grandfather overturns his plate at breakfast; the olive oil darkens the tablecloth.

"I will *not* be spoken to this way in my own house."

The table falls silent. "This again," Mazna's father mutters, but her grandfather isn't staring off into space; he's looking directly at Abeer.

"Look at this mess, you crazy old man," she replies.

"I work until ten every night at the station, it *is* my business —"

Abeer rolls her eyes. "Eat your eggs," she tells Mazna, whose fork hovers anxiously over her plate. "Ignore him."

"— when you spend four *thousand* pounds on some trashy dress."

Abeer stiffens. Everyone at the table waits for her to react. "What?" Abeer raises her voice, urgent. "What did you say, Ghassan?"

"I said" — Ghassan brings both palms down, hard, on the table, his eyes strangely alert — "that I'm trying to save money for Istanbul and you're off shopping with your sister." He waves toward Khalto Seham.

"Mama," Bassel whispers, "what is he talking about?"

"It's just a fight," Khalto Seham says. "A fight he's imagining."

"No." Abeer's voice is frosty.

Mazna's parents exchange looks.

"We already had this fight," Abeer says quietly. For the first time, she looks alarmed. "Twenty years ago."

The doctors say his brain is beginning to atrophy. Mazna's father reads about it and translates the indecipherable terms. He explains that there's something in Ghassan's brain — Mazna imagines cotton candy, sticky and pink — that's keeping it from working, and so he is forgetting things that he should remember and remembering things that are gone and should be forgotten.

"He's living his life over again," Bassel says.

"*Ya* Allah, it wasn't tiresome enough the first time around?" Abeer is caustic during the doctor's visits, but Mazna can tell she's afraid.

Her grandfather spends his afternoons alone in his study. He picks fights with Abeer, topics from twenty, thirty years ago. He talks about his brother stealing his pencil case in school. He still seems to remember Mazna, but sometimes he has a milky look in his eyes, has to shake his head a couple of times before he can respond to her questions.

His illness is a match thrown into a powder keg. As if on cue, Mazna's own parents begin to bicker, about bills, vacations, where Mazna should buy her school bag. Abeer makes pointed remarks about Lulwa's makloubeh, and Lulwa sulks like a teenager. Mazna starts having stomachaches when she wakes up; she feels like the house is smothering her. When Nawal comes over, she mostly talks with their mother after asking Mazna to watch her son. She always pulls Mazna aside before she leaves and slips her some coins.

"Buy yourself some ice cream, baby," she says. Mazna forces herself to smile.

The peace nobody had realized was tenuous breaks. The women slam doors. The men draw out their silences. And at school, Mazna starts studying Shakespeare.

Mazna's school is called Lycée Charles de Gaulle and the classes are taught in both Arabic and French. She receives a quiet scholarship that none of the other girls know about; the headmaster knows the family well, and Mazna's clever enough. There's an all-boys school across the street and sometimes the girls will loiter around the gate during break and try to throw paper airplanes through the slats, doodles and hearts scrawled inside. They sing the French national anthem every morning, and the school uniform has a little rooster embroidered on the pocket. The girls are moderately catty with one another; alliances are fickle, dependent on who wears whose hair ribbon without asking or which girl went to Switzerland over the winter break. Mazna is mostly well liked because she can braid hair well and styles the hair of the more popular girls during recess, weaving in purple and yellow flowers from the schoolyard.

The English teacher is Madame Orla, a portly woman with bushy hair. She's half British and speaks in refined, clipped tones, scolding the students when they say *Yeah* or *Hip*.

"Open your throats," she admonishes. "You sound like Americans." It goes without saying that this is disastrous. They begin reading *Macbeth,* and Madame Orla flutters around the room, swooning over the dialogue. "*This* is English as God and the queen intended," she declares.

One morning, she bustles in with her customary muumuu fluttering behind her. "Ladies. *Ladies.* I have news. I have splendid news."

The girls stare at her, unfazed. Somewhere in the back, someone mutters, *"La belle cochonne,"* and titters break out. Madame Orla crosses her arms and waits.

"It's a trip."

This gets their attention. School trips are notoriously scrumptious — the sticky leather seats on the bus, the way freedom feels in their hair as they march past the school gate.

"Who here has heard of traveling theater troupes?"

Nobody speaks. The Shakespeare Revivalists, she continues, are a famous theater group in East London. They sometimes go on tours, and because she knew one of the actors from university, they're now coming to perform at a theater in downtown Damascus.

"And," she finishes, "they're doing our very own *Macbeth*."

The excitement grows the more she speaks and by the time the bell rings and the girls spill into the courtyard, alliances are momentarily forgotten as they chatter together. Not just a trip, but a theater show! They'll get to wear their own clothes, not the uniforms. It won't be over until after ten p.m. The girls buzz with anticipation.

(At home, Lulwa reads her daughter's permission slip and a vision of a beautiful performer dances momentarily in her mind — when Lulwa was fifteen years old, dirt poor, a kindly neighbor had taken her and her siblings to a show, the singers there splendid in sequins and gold necklaces, and she sneaked into the bathroom at night and mimicked their gestures and expressions in the mirror for months after, until her older brother walked in on her and laughed — but then she just shakes her head and says, "How wonderful, dear. You'll need a nice dress.")

✤

On the afternoon of the trip, Mazna stares at the pile of dresses on her bed in despair. Unlike some of her classmates, she is still flat as a horizon, despite the buttery rice the family doctor recommended to Lulwa. *How is it possible?* her mother sometimes mutters when Mazna steps on the scale. Lulwa no longer has the high cheekbones of her wedding day. Age has scrawled itself on her body in pouches beneath her eyes, in the breeder's gut over her belt.

Mazna finally calls for her mother to help, and Lulwa frowns at the pile as well. She picks up a white frock. "How did you fray a dress you've never worn?" she grumbles. She seems more nervous than Mazna.

Mazna hops on the tiles, the velvet of her Eid dress rising and falling in obedient waves around her.

"I think I like this one, Mama. Look, it's long and it feels so soft." Mazna proffers a swath of the skirt for her mother to touch, but Lulwa doesn't move.

"No," she says softly. "It's not right." She snaps her fingers. "Wait here."

Mazna twirls in the dress as her mother darts off. It feels nice to have Lulwa's attention on her, like a shot of balmy sunlight.

Lulwa returns with a garment bag, out of which she pulls a dusty-pink slip dress with a beaded bodice. Mazna stops twirling, transfixed.

"It was mine." Her mother answers the unasked question. "A long time ago."

I wore it to a party with your father once." She clears her throat. "In any case, it might fit you."

Mazna takes the dress mutely. It pools in her hand. She takes her clothes off self-consciously under her mother's eye, aware of her nipples hard as raisins, her oatmeal-colored underwear. Her mother does the zipper, and Mazna shivers at the metal against her bare back. She feels strangely ashamed as she meets her mother's eye and sees a dazed expression on Lulwa's face, like she's missed something monumental and now it's too late to stop it.

"Well," her mother says. "It looks better on you."

❊

The bus reeks of perfumes stolen from the girls' mothers and older sisters. They wear birthday dresses and ironed skirts, but Mazna knows from the narrowed eyes of the popular girls that her dress is best. She sits near the front of the bus with her back straight, listening to the others gossip.

"Walk in pairs," Madame Orla calls when the bus comes to a stop in front of an old, nondescript building. Mazna can see her own disappointment echoed on the other girls' faces. She'd envisioned gilded windows, Roman columns. Instead, there's a small food stand nearby, the oily smell of falafel thick in the air.

"Wait till you see inside," Madame Orla says, intuiting their thoughts. (*Brats,* she adds silently.)

The inside redeems the building; it's like a fantasy of what a theater should be. Midnight-blue carpet, dim lighting, a wallpapered hallway leading to two open doors. The auditorium is small but the seats are velvety and comfortable. The curtains on the stage are drawn closed. Mazna is pleased to see the lights make her dress sparkle. The students find their seats, the girls clamoring to sit next to friends. Mazna winds up between Madame Orla and Yara, a bookish, timorous girl. Yara's peppery perfume is so strong, Mazna has to breathe through her mouth.

The lights go down and the girls quiet. Around her, she can feel the audience settle.

The curtains are pulled back like a face breaking into a smile.

The audience begins to clap. Mazna can feel the suspended breath of the entire room as they wait; she squints to make out the dim shapes onstage. Suddenly, a spotlight is turned on — three women in dark robes and greasy hair, a bleak landscape painted on the backdrop.

"When shall we three meet again," one woman growls. It's like a fishhook in Mazna's lungs, something yanking her breath in quick, shallow bursts, moving her toward the spotlight, the stage's glossy floor, the woman's fierce gaze as she sweeps her eyes over the audience as though they aren't there, as though all that's in front of her is more rain and dirt. As though all of this is real.

Mazna believes her.

She believes the words from the actor's mouth, the moan of King Duncan as he clutches his gut and dies. She believes his death. She believes Lady Macbeth's tears as she sleepwalks. She believes the painted mountains on the backdrop, the sound of thunder played from a recorder.

The intermission comes. The lights snap on curtly; some of the girls yawn and talk. Mazna feels as if she's been woken from a dream.

"I know," Madame Orla whispers conspiratorially to her, a smile on her face. "It's like we're the sleepwalkers."

Mazna wants to say something about how it feels unfair that people can make such magic with the dead, boring words they'd studied in class, unfair that nobody had told her, but she can't manage to speak. She nods instead. When the lights go down again, she finds herself leaning forward instinctively, the actors' faces familiar to her now. At the scene of Lady Macbeth's death, Mazna hears a little gasp to her right. She sneaks a look at Madame Orla's face and is astonished to see how young the woman suddenly looks, her hand placed over her heart. (It's an image she will remember for the rest of her life, her teacher's radiant face, the light catching her damp eyelashes.)

The play finishes and it feels like summer ending for Mazna. The actors line up and laugh, then beckon to the director, a white-haired man who bounds onstage and kisses Lady Macbeth on the cheek. He lifts her arm and pulls her forward, gesturing for the audience to applaud harder, and they do.

Mazna's hands hurt from clapping. The actress beams and curtsies, a perfect modest smile on her face. The light catches the glitter on her cheek.

Mine, something inside Mazna screams. *Mine, mine, mine.*

❖

Mazna starts to notice things after the play. The way her mother rolls her neck when she's tired, pinching her earlobe with her forefinger and thumb. Her grandfather's half smile when he's lost in thought. She starts to watch how women rummage in their purses in the supermarket, how the neighborhood men clap each other on the back when they meet.

One night, Abeer is watching an old movie on the TV in the living room, and Mazna joins her. She looks at her grandmother, then the actress on the screen. The movie is about a girl whose family is moving to New York. Mazna feasts on the actress's millions of gestures, the way she tosses her curls, the tilt of her head when she sings. At the end of the film, the girl and her sisters go to a fair, rejoicing that they aren't moving; they're staying right where they are.

"Right here in St. Louis." The actress beams, and Mazna envisions a city of Ferris wheels and diners. The actress swallows. Mazna falls in love with that swallow, will watch the film dozens of times in the coming years just to see that tiny moment, that perfect touch from the actress.

❖

The following Monday at school, Madame Orla asks for volunteers to read Lady Macbeth's part in act 5, and Mazna raises her hand.

"Wonderful! I should tell you girls, I've been thinking of putting on a little play of our own for visitors' day. *Alice in Wonderland.* Some of you will have to wear mustaches, mind you. There will be enough parts for all of you, some bigger than others." Here her eyes flick over the front of the classroom, where the pretty, popular girls sit like flowers in a row.

Mazna makes her way to the front of the classroom as Dara and Lina, two of the popular girls, are reading the part of the doctor and the gentlewoman in bored tones. They go back and forth, then wait for Mazna. This is when they find Lady Macbeth sleepwalking.

Mazna clears her throat. She can feel her hands shaking and balls them into fists. She doesn't need the book. The words are emblazoned in her mind. This is her favorite scene.

"It's your turn, dear," Madam Orla says, not unkindly.

Mazna remembers how the actress who played Lady Macbeth had looked above the audience. Through them. She fixes her eyes on the window in front of her and thinks of her dolls. She thinks of how unhappy the house has felt lately. Her grandfather hasn't spoken with anyone in days, not since the fight. Mazna imagines she's in her bedroom, the door deliciously shut. She starts reciting.

When it's over, Madame Orla's mouth falls in a small, fat O.

"Mazna Adib." She says her name like she's speaking it for the first time. "Where have you been hiding *that?*"

❖

Mazna gets the part of Alice. Instead of being miffed, the popular girls seem impressed with her. They invite her to their lunch table and ask her to run lines with them. They offer to lend her makeup and pearls for the costume.

At home, the news of her part is met with halfhearted praise — *Wonderful,* habibti. *You hear that, Lulwa? We have ourselves a thespian* — but at school it transforms her. Madame Orla watches her attentively during rehearsals. She tells Mazna to watch old films to help her prepare for the part (this is how she says it, *Prepare for your part,* which makes Mazna feel important, like she's doing something as critical as God building Adam from clay), movies like *Gone with the Wind* and *Breakfast at Tiffany's* and *Streetcar Named Desire* and *Some Like It Hot.*

"I have to watch one of my films," Mazna tells her family importantly whenever an American movie is on television. "I'm doing research for my part." She isn't quite sure what that means, but it sounds adult.

To Mazna's surprise, Abeer often joins her. They turn off the lamps, and the television glows like an orb. Her grandmother works methodically through a bowl of pumpkin seeds, cracking and extracting the seed with her teeth and tongue, spitting out a clean, hollowed pair of shells. The films are all about pain in one way or another; Mazna studies Vivien Leigh's madness, Ava Gardner's glare, Lauren Bacall's spirited pout. The men are handsome props, but the films belong to the women. They drink too much at parties, weep in bathtubs over heartbreak. They get pregnant and run away. They marry. They divorce. They scream at their own reflections. It is, Mazna realizes, the most time she has ever spent with her grandmother.

Abeer always sighs at the perfect moments. She never seems shocked or outraged at any of the plot twists, instead nodding with recognition.

"You've seen this before," Mazna says aloud one night.

"Oh, *habibti*," Abeer says, smiling. "I've seen them all."

Films make people sad, Mazna is slowly understanding. They remind people of a time that is over or a time they've never been part of. Even the happier films, like *Sabrina* and *The Wizard of Oz,* sadden her; she will never go to those glossy dinner parties, see those Technicolor skies. Theater is the same. It's heartbreaking because it will end, because people will become a part of the story and then be abandoned by it. She's aware of this during rehearsals as she repeats the same lines dozens, hundreds, of times, learning to let her hands flutter naturally, playing with tone and volume. She's lying to a roomful of people. She is going to break their hearts.

On the day of the performance, her grandfather refuses to go, but the adults have prepared for this. Khalto Seham stays home with him, making his sage tea and biscuits. Mazna doesn't look back at him, sitting in his chair and grumbling.

The women let her sit in the front seat of the car, but Mazna can't enjoy this rare treat; her stomach's knotted with nerves. But as they walk toward the auditorium, Mazna spots the crowd of girls in the practice room, sees Madame Orla's face lighting up; her stomach unknots.

"I have to go get ready," she tells the adults and bounds off without waiting for a response.

The girls are already in their costumes, but Madame Orla and a couple of the older students are doing makeup. The air is thick with nervous sweat and perfume and powder. Madame Orla will do Mazna's makeup herself. She swipes a layer of lipstick on one of the bit actors, then eyes Mazna with great concentration.

"Big," she muses. "We need big."

Mazna keeps her eyes shut the entire time, feeling a sensual prickle at the brush across her face. Madame Orla blows the eyeliner dry; her breath smells of cinnamon and garlic. Mazna runs lines silently as fingers touch her — one of the older girls French-braiding her hair, Madame Orla rubbing rouge on her cheeks. (The sensation is so pleasurable that, years later, when she tries to remember her first sexual feeling as a child, this hot and pungent room will return to her.)

"Look at yourself," one of the girls instructs.

Mazna opens her eyes, her lashes unusually heavy beneath the mascara. It's as though she's seeing her face for the first time. She looks like her mother, like Lulwa as a teenager, but different somehow. Prettier. Madame Orla finally hustles her out of the room.

Two scenes in and, offstage, Mazna cannot breathe. It's her turn. Suddenly, everything she thinks she knows about this evening disappears. Her lines are gone; she doesn't know where to stand. The terror is quick and cold. The girls are standing in the dark wings of the theater; she hears the audience murmur, then fall silent when the curtains open again. A spear of light hits the stage. *Move,* Mazna tells her legs, and they do, clunkily. The light is blinding. She cannot see a single face. Dara walks out from the other wing in her White Rabbit outfit, a drooping mustache glued over her lips.

"That's her!" a voice in the audience says, followed by shushing. Her father. Mazna ducks her head to hide her smile.

The rest of the play is a blur, as future ones will be; time seems to be both suspended and scrambling by. Mazna sees herself from a distance, lifting her head, kissing Dara's cheek. The room is silent when she speaks. When she can't enter the garden, Mazna drops to her knees, surprised to find that she is, indeed, crying. She doesn't miss a single line. Finally, the curtain sweeps over the stage, taking the last of the light with it. For a second, there is nothing, just the uneven sound of Mazna's own breathing, then applause, miles of it, the girls charging at her from the wings, piling on top of her with joy.

Back in the school's lobby, Mazna blushes at the compliments. Madame Orla wraps her in a bear hug, the woman's bosom squishy against her cheek. Her family waits shyly to the side. She feels a flash of irritation at her mother's nervous smile.

"Girlie," her father says. "That was superb!"

Her grandmother hugs her. "You sneaky girl. You had us all in tears."

Lulwa says nothing. Mazna looks at her mother, feeling the mascara weighing down her eyelashes. "Mama?"

"You were good," she says slowly, "very good. Mazna, you reminded me of Hind Rostom."

She has no idea who Hind Rostom is — later she'll discover she's a famous Egyptian actress who resembles Marilyn Monroe — and doesn't care. Her family beams and she understands that she's given them something. People crowd around her, and as they praise her, thank her, she sees that she's conferred this same status on her family, like glitter rubbing off one hand and onto the other. The noise and chaos encircle her in an embrace, she the hot, shining heart.

Pretty Girls Belong to Us

1972

THE ROMEO MISSES his cue. It's soon after the curtain sweeps open, and Mazna — Juliet — stalks the stage in her heels, waiting for the familiar footsteps from the opposite side of the stage, for Hamad Nabulsi, a handsome, quiet boy from a nearby school, to appear. He was struck by a sudden, excruciating bout of nausea right before his cue and is at the moment hunched over the toilet, moaning and wanting to die, but Mazna knows none of this. All she knows is that the audience is silent, watching her, that the scene they've rehearsed hundreds of times hinges on a series of reactions to Madame Orla's *postmodern adaptation:* Juliet walks out, Romeo speaks, Juliet demurs and turns to the side. But now she is alone on the stage, the lights boring their burning eyes into her, and something must happen.

"I swear," she blurts, her mind whirring, "I will spend my life waiting for this man to show up." She pauses, gauging the audience like a thermometer; there are a few laughs, a companionable silence. Good. *There are a thousand kinds of silence,* Julie Andrews said in an interview Mazna read once. "How difficult is it to wear a watch?" she asks the dark in front of her. The audience never knows what is scripted and what is not.

"Last time," she continues conspiratorially, "he was two hours late. Two!"

She waits. Will Romeo arrive? In the backstage toilet, Hamad wipes tears from his face as his bowels empty. He will not.

"Well," she says, fake disappointment masking the true. "I guess some things never change." After a moment, she arranges her face into disenchantment, tilts it up toward the lights — the best angle, she knows, for the audience to see her — then walks slowly off the stage.

The applause erupts behind her, but she barely hears it. In the wings, a group of people gather, Madame Orla among them.

"What —" Mazna begins, but Madame Orla interrupts, her voice furious.

"I'm going to end that boy's life when I see him. Vanished. He vanished! What kind of professional does that?" No one answers, but everyone is thinking the same thing: a nonprofessional. They're high-school students, seventeen and eighteen years old. While the girls take the performances seriously, the boys are often forced into them, part of a recent interschool enrichment program.

"Miss?" a small voice pipes up. Ghaith. He's an overeager kid, small for his age, given the part of a servant because he was too slight and fair to play any of the other roles. (He's dreamed of this moment for weeks now; he's secretly memorized the entire play, every single line. If he'd thought of it, he would've poisoned Hamad himself.) "I could do it. I know all of Romeo's lines."

"You do?" Madame Orla frowns.

"Yes, miss." He nods eagerly. "We could just go straight into the family scene."

Madame Orla sighs. Romeo will be half a head shorter than Juliet. But the alternative is no play at all, and Madame Orla, who's served as the theater director for the past five years — once the headmaster saw the turnout at the plays, he created the job — knows that would be worse. She turns to Ghaith. "Someone get this boy a costume."

The rest of the play goes smoothly enough and everyone raves about Mazna's performance. Afterward, she goes to the Zaman café with a group of friends to gossip and smoke shisha. Her family no longer comes to every play, and she can stay out as late as she likes, since she told her parents that Madame Orla hosted after-show dinners for the actors.

The girls and boys sit on opposite sides of the table, each group pretending not to be interested in the other. But Mazna can see a few boys in her peripheral vision watching her, trying to catch her eye. She's popular enough now and has noticed over the past year a shift of the boys' attention from the richer and prettier girls to her.

Finally, one of the boys gestures with his shisha hose to interrupt her conversation. Omar is good-looking, but there's something else about him that lures the girls, something hardened and crafty, like he's already decided who he is.

"Mazna," he says. "You were good."

She tries not to smile too widely. There is a move she's been practicing, her head lowered, peering up through her lashes — very Vivien Leigh in *Streetcar.*

"It was all of us."

Omar's own grin is unedited. He scoots his chair closer, expertly blowing a river of smoke. "But you know you're the best one."

Something about his tone unnerves her. Her body has become a Body. It still feels new and risky, like a house pet that suddenly transformed into a coyote. She cups her breasts in the shower sometimes, unsure where they came from. The Body is like a borrowed dress, and though she struts in it and admires it in storefront windows, the truth is, it frightens her.

But male bodies frighten her more. She has no brothers; her father and grandfather are old, another species entirely, soft and familiar and a little smelly. But the boys her age are solid as red apples.

"Thank you," she murmurs to Omar, letting herself lean in for a beat, long enough to graze his knee with hers — the Body sometimes makes its own decisions — before pretending to be distracted by a nearby conversation. Her only kiss had taken place a few months earlier, with a neighborhood boy she's known since kindergarten. It was winter and the schools were shut for a snow day; they'd gone for a walk, and, at a neighbor's privacy hedge, he kissed her quickly; the only proof it happened was the little stamp of perspiration he left on her upper lip.

"My father said I can have his car this summer." Omar has turned to his friend but is talking loudly enough that she knows he's saying it to her.

After the shisha coals have faded to ash, the little group disperses, the girls slowly walking home, speaking of the play and the boys. Mazna parts ways with her friends Lara and Fatima near the post office; her house is farther up the street. The marketplace has closed, the men packing up the last of their bread and fruits. She wonders what they do with them. She imagines small kitchens, the vendors' wives and children eating mounds of overripe peaches. One of the vendors nods briefly at her as she walks past; the street is busier than usual. The week is over.

She can continue on the main road or cut through her favorite alley, and she chooses the latter, with its quiet, unlit windows, a white cat slipping around the fire escapes. She pretends she's in Europe, returning to her apartment in Lisbon or Paris after a long day of rehearsals. Maybe the white cat is hers. She has a little ashtray perched on her narrow balcony but pretends it's only for guests. She stands on her tiptoes to peer into one of the lower-level windows.

"I didn't take you for a burglar."

Mazna startles, spins around. Omar is standing behind her, fidgeting with something in his hands. He has a strange expression on his face. "I didn't mean to scare you," he says, smiling. "We didn't get to finish talking."

Mazna's heart thunders. She can make out the thing in his hands: a flower, white-petaled. A camellia.

"Did you follow me?" she asks before she can stop herself.

Omar laughs, his face relaxing. "No, no. I live near the marketplace. I was walking with some of the guys. I saw you ahead of me a few minutes ago."

Mazna isn't sure if he's telling the truth, but he doesn't seem to notice. "I like this little street," she says finally.

"This is for you."

She stares at his extended hand. A word fans out in her mind's eye, silky, red: *Don't.* But she takes the flower, bends her head to sniff it. That is her white cat. This is her husband, her anniversary flower. From one of the apartments above them, a woman laughs, either in life or on the television.

"Thank you," she says. "It's really pretty."

"I thought you'd like it." His tone is a smidge obnoxious. He takes a step toward her and Mazna stiffens.

"I told my mother I'd be home an hour ago," she lies. The stories her grandmother and Lulwa have told her fill her mind: girls found strangled on the outskirts of Damascus, girls stolen from their bedrooms and never returned. She knows they tell the stories to frighten her, and it works. "I'll see you after school next week maybe?"

To her surprise, he doesn't protest. "I'll see you." He still looks amused.

"Good." Her heart is still racing, but she tries to appear nonchalant walking past him. He reaches out and takes hold of her elbow.

"Listen." His grip isn't rough, but she's still afraid. She waits; he doesn't say anything. "Listen," he repeats, then leans in to kiss her. It's sudden, the force of it pushing her back against the wall, his mouth rough against hers as he darts his tongue out. Omar's breath is sour from the smoke, but Mazna is dismayed to feel something spark in her abdomen. She tries to move past him, shoving with both hands, but he captures each one in his fists, easily, lightly, like he's catching June bugs.

"No," he says soothingly.

Mazna feels her Body freeze as though she has left it. Her mind alights on a single, random image: Liz Taylor in *Cleopatra,* her bejeweled hand gesturing for more wine, the way her hair swayed when she lifted her chin.

Omar presses closer, covers her thigh with a meaty hand. Mazna thinks of Omar's uncle, a neighborhood butcher who cuts veal and lamb for her mother, tying the cold slabs of meat with twine. She shivers. Omar's fingers feel like spiders, finding her underwear, pushing up, up, up, as she stands still as a carving. His other hand is over her heart, cupping her breast like a lemon. There is something hard digging into her hip. His fingers push aside her underwear and find the part that only she's ever touched; she imagines the scene from the white cat's vantage, a girl in a yellow dress, a panting, sweaty boy shoving his finger inside her. Her body traitorously responds, something like pleasure rocking her. But then she shuts her eyes and sees cold red meat slabbed on the countertop.

She lets out a sob.

Omar stills against her. She opens her eyes. He pulls his head back, searches her face urgently. "Oh." He sounds scalded. (Later, she will wonder what he'd been expecting to see, what it was that felled his expression.) He stumbles back.

"Shit." The word is somehow more shocking than his finger; the boys never cursed in front of them. "I'm sorry, Mazna. I thought —"

But what he thought, she never finds out. She cries harder, and he steps toward her but stops at the sight of her flinching. Omar looks around the alleyway; there's something in the way he glances around that reminds her of when her father spills something, then waits for it to be wiped up. "I'll go," he finally says, as she knew he would.

It takes Mazna several minutes to calm her chattering teeth. The cat looks down at her intently, as though it understands. Suddenly, Mazna picks up a pebble and throws it at the cat. She misses, but the cat jumps and scampers up the fire escape anyway.

There are fewer people on the main street now, but it still comforts Mazna to hear them chat and laugh. When she gets to her house, she drops the keys twice before managing to let herself in. The house is mercifully dark when she enters, heavy with the smell of her family's supper. She moves easily through the rooms, past her grandparents' shut doors, her parents' bedroom, until she reaches her own. She doesn't turn the lights on. She doesn't take her dress off. She drops onto the bed like an object, tries to concentrate on a single thought, but everything is jumbled, equally dangerous: Omar's face, afraid; Liz Taylor's wrists; his fingers inside her underwear. Through it all, there is something she is beginning to understand.

Omar did something wrong, but so did she. Another girl would have screamed, clawed at his face. Another girl wouldn't have felt pleasure. And even though there's no one to ask, she has an inkling that, if she *were* to ask her mother or anyone else, they'd say the greater sin was hers.

The Road from Damascus

1978

THEATER HAS ITS own language. The crew calls the backdrops *flats* and
the front of the stage the *apron*; *cheating out* is facing the audience. If an actor
isn't hitting his mark, murmurs of *blocking* rise from the stage manager. The
traveler hides backstage, out of the audience's view. Then there's the language
of a specific theater — under Madame Orla, if the understudy got sick, they
called it a *collapse*. In college, Mazna's theater instructor was jokingly called the
maestro, the lead was the *philly*, and the whole class referred casually to empty
theater seats as *bodies*.

Mazna barely saw Omar again after starting at Damascus University, but
over the years she has had other similar encounters. During a performance
of *The Tempest* in her second semester, the Ferdinand playing opposite her
Miranda tilted his head during their fake kiss and pressed his lips full on hers
in front of a hundred people. And the night of her college graduation last year,
Garo, the faithful pianist who wrote the scores for all the university plays, had
slipped a hand over Mazna's ass during a hug.

College itself was a heap of quixotic false starts — meeting men for cappuccinos at canopy-covered cafés, falling in love with other girls' boyfriends. Mazna and her friends were a vibrant, well-known group, in some ways more so than she and her clique had been in high school; people often faded into anonymity in college, but the theater students' names were in the school paper, their faces recognizable from plays.

Men wanted them — men wanted *Mazna* — but Lulwa's vague fear-mongering about *girls who get themselves in trouble* became more real in college. These girls had names now: Meena from philosophy class, who got pregnant and was sent to live with her grandmother in Jordan; Tamara, who lost her virginity to a classmate, after which the boy ignored her; and Mazna's own friend Lara, who, thankfully, didn't have sex but gave enough to a boyfriend to start a rumor that haunted her throughout college.

In theater, a cursed union was *star-crossed*. And Mazna saw more of these than not. There were times she felt her sexuality hard as a rock between her legs, but she hid it. Only when she was onstage did it peek out, as she drawled over unlit cigarettes, dressed in low-cut gowns — once, she'd even let out a moan during a stage kiss, which caused quite a stir on campus — but the rest of the time she kept it primly folded away. She went for daytime coffees with classmates and tolerated her mother's talk of suitors. She had kissed exactly six boys, including Omar and the old, handsy Garo. None had made much of an impression.

* * *

Back at home, nobody dies. Not her grandfather, not Abeer. The house is like a museum exhibit of its former self. There aren't any new photographs for the mantel. Her grandfather speaks less frequently, his brain hardening with plaques, the doctors say. When Mazna enrolled in Damascus University, she spent several months trying to convince her parents to let her live in her own apartment, but she never succeeded.

"You want the neighbors to think we kicked you out?" her mother kept saying. Mazna knows that's not all of it; her mother doesn't want to be left alone. But for years Mazna has been distancing herself from her mother, a growing hardening mottled with pity between them.

"I'm moving to California," Mazna finally told Lulwa, spitefully, "sooner than you know, and I'm going to visit only once every couple of years, and even then, I'll sleep in a goddamn hotel."

Her mother looked almost impressed. She recovered quickly. "All your father's money goes to your grandfather, so I'd like to see you manage that," she said coolly.

It's true the money has dried up — Mazna hates that phrase, like a mangled apricot left in the sun. Her father's bad back, her grandfather's medical expenses, and the family money is, like anything, finite. After Mazna graduated from university, she took a job at a banking firm, doing administrative work. She saves a little and gives the rest to her father; she'd never admit how resentful it makes her, watching her salary go like that, but she can't bear not to do it. Madame Orla has put her in touch with a theater school in London, and that is the plan: save enough for a few months' rent in England, move there. She consoles herself with the idea that she'll be closer to California.

On the weekends, Mazna rehearses downtown at the theater she'd gone to on her school trip years before. She knows the space like her own palm now, has had the lead in five shows in the past few years. The first couple of years, the plays were predictable — Shakespeare, Miller — but since the war in Lebanon began, things have changed.

The war often feels farther away than it is. It started abruptly and rocketed, a flame to dry kindling: a gunman opened fire on a Maronite church, and, within hours, a bus full of Palestinians were killed as retribution. The newscasters are constantly reporting on what's going on, but in actuality, Syria feels untouched. When those first clashes broke out, during Mazna's sophomore year, she'd listened to reports of the massacres with a distant, sheltered unease, like she was watching a pileup from the window of her own intact vehicle. It was sad and violent and patently irrelevant to her life. Even after Syrian troops flooded Beirut — *This is how it starts,* her father warned the evening of the report, *this is how you get dragged into the troubles of others,* as though it were a small marital spat they were discussing — the changes in Damascus have been slight. The following year, there was an influx of Lebanese students at the university, fewer vacancy signs outside apartment buildings. There are now Lebanese beggars throughout the market, supplicating and holding out their babies like alms. Mazna herself feels affected in the silliest ways — no more shopping trips to Lebanon, a vague missing of the country her family had vacationed in a few times, a place she'd visit maybe once a year.

The old theater director retired after the war, replaced by a new émigré from Lebanon, Tarek Haddad.

"We don't need white men to teach us about war anymore," he said grimly on his first day. Under his direction, the theater has changed; now it features plays written by young Tunisian men, Beiruti playwrights. Mazna nearly always gets the lead, but Tarek can be aloof. He doesn't praise or prattle, and she gets the distinct sense that for him, words are the real heart of theater; actors are merely bodies. When she nails a performance, he simply says, "You did the script justice."

It's a different kind of theater, darker, grimier, with less glamour and admiration — her job is to execute, not to be lauded, and the task fills her with a cold satisfaction. The plays are about one-armed merchants who speak to animals or women who sneak across borders in the bellies of trucks. For the first time, Mazna performs in Arabic. The audiences are different too, not just the university and school crowds. There are older patrons, entire families from the south, Lebanese intellectuals, people who travel to watch their compatriots' plays. They all know Mazna by name, and sometimes she's stopped in the neighborhood by someone who recognizes her.

"We're putting on plays that aren't allowed in Beirut, in Libya," Tarek said once. "Of course, there are plays that wouldn't be allowed here —" His eyes flicked toward a framed photograph of the president on the wall, and the room got quiet. "Let's not forget we're under *Syrian occupation* in Beirut," he said a little mockingly. Mazna laughed uncomfortably along with the others but asked her father about it that night. He sighed deeply and explained that the Maronites were outnumbered, that the Lebanese parliament favored them, that there'd been an exodus that flooded the country with Palestinians but that the tiny country could not carry that many different people. Syria had sent in forces to control the Palestinian guerrillas, who in turn were controlling the leftists; by the time her father got to the Arab League, Mazna regretted ever asking anything. She preferred talking about acting, though even there, she and Tarek didn't always agree.

"Why on earth would you want to go to America?" he asked her when she told him about the school in London, her plan for California. He'd lived in New York for a year before the war and referred to that time as the Black Days. "They'll cast you as an exotic woman, a terrorist. Here, you get to play everything."

"That's because there's no competition," she retorted. She didn't say that she wanted to be on screens, that she would never stop wanting that.

But he shook his head sadly, like he heard her anyway. "They won't even see you there."

The latest play is about a couple in Beirut. The man lives in the eastern part of the city, the woman in the western, a wartime Romeo and Juliet, unfortunate, separated by God and checkpoints. This one was written by Tarek himself, and he's been touchier than usual, given to fits of irritated embarrassment if the actors forget their lines. It's a small cast, twelve total, most of the scenes going to Mazna and her lover, played by a Lebanese actor new to Damascus named Ralph. He's Christian, which lends an authentically scandalous air to the whole thing.

"You," Tarek barks at Hania, a shy newcomer playing a grocer, during their first rehearsal. "Explain the civil war in Lebanon. Quickly."

Hania looks terrified. "Ah." She clears her throat, her eyes darting around the room. "Well, there's a lot of different religions."

"Kill me," Tarek says to the ceiling. "Lara, let's hear it."

"I mean, my father says if Palestinians hadn't tried to kill Gemayel —" she starts.

"Nobody knows who tried to assassinate him," Nasser, a veteran actor, counters. He's playing Mazna's father. "They *wanted* it to be Palestinians, so they told everyone it was. Then the Phalangists slaughtered those poor people on that bus."

"Yes!" Tarek looks excited now. "Continue, people."

"The Syrians had to send in peacekeeping forces," Mazna says, repeating what her father had said.

"Interesting wording. But fine. What else?"

Ralph raises his hand tentatively. "I also think the Cold War played a part. The Christians became aligned with the West instead of the Soviets."

"Don't forget the Lebanese Forces — my father also says they're starting to fight each other."

Finally, Tarek holds his hands up and they all quiet down like children. "You're all right," he says softly. "And you're all a little wrong."

"Wrong how?" Nasser demands.

Tarek smiles thinly. "There's one thing nobody's mentioned. We've got the Christians, the Sunni, the Shi'ite, a strained economy, the Palestinian camps." He counts them off on his fingers. "What's missing?"

There's a long silence. It reminds Mazna of school, when the teacher asked the class a difficult question and everyone avoided eye contact, waiting for the right answer to drop from the sky like a bird.

Suddenly, it does.

"The Europeans," she cries out. Everyone turns to her. She remembers the pastel-colored maps in school, those harsh black borders. They'd reminded her of a woman's hairstyle, easily changed to match the current fashion. "The French. Well, the Europeans in general."

Tarek claps his hands together once, loudly. "Yes." He stares at her intently. She looks away first. "Yes, the colonizers. They're involved, however indirectly, in every single political thing that's happened since the Ottomans. Each country had its oppressor — the British in Palestine, the French in Lebanon. The Westerners drew the maps. They're the reason the streets in Beirut have French names; they're the ones who set up a parliamentary structure that distributed power unfairly. They're the reason Palestinians arrived here in the thousands in '48, then again in '67. I want you all to remember that as we rehearse: The biggest war criminals are always offstage. They're continents away."

"But why does that have anything to do with today?" Lara asks. "That was ages ago."

"Because," Tarek says, as though Lara is terminally stupid, "this war didn't happen in a vacuum. It was fashioned out of years of bad colonial decisions."

"What are you saying?" Lara asks. "That the war was *constructed?*"

"That." Tarek raises his eyebrows. "But also, as much as people hate to hear it, that it was inevitable."

⁂

The play is called *Meet Me in Ramleh*. Most of the scenes take place in the lovers' respective homes, as they write letters and talk animatedly in their bedrooms about their love and longing for each other. They're under curfew for days at a time, sometimes sleeping in makeshift bomb shelters. Tarek gave Mazna a stack of newspaper clippings and letters written by a woman — she suspects it's an ex-girlfriend of his — describing hot July nights spent in bomb shelters, tense neighborhoods, uninterrupted boredom. It's the most Mazna has thought about Beirut ever.

The pinnacle scene is on a deserted road, the sound of an ambulance playing on a backstage tape recorder. The lovers have taken advantage of holiday ceasefire to rush out and meet at the fruit stall where they'd met years earlier, before the war began. The scene is taut and crunching, Mazna's favorite, the lovers not bantering or kissing but exchanging realistic, painfully awkward dialogue.

"What they've been in love with is imaginary. It was invented by them," Mazna explains when Ralph complains about the lack of romance.

"Exactly!" Tarek points his pen at her like a crossbow. "War heightens everything. But it doesn't manufacture love."

"Wouldn't they at least, I don't know, try to kiss or something?" Ralph asks hopefully, avoiding Mazna's face. His ears turn red.

"They wouldn't," Tarek says firmly, and not for the first time, Mazna feels a wave of respect for him. "Let's do another run-through."

That evening as Mazna is getting ready to leave, Tarek asks for a word. Opening night is in a week, and she can feel the nerves vibrating off him. When they get to his office — spare and tidy, the only decoration an old travel poster of Jerusalem — he asks if she's ready for Friday.

"Of course," she says sharply, a little miffed. Mazna isn't a casual actor; she's always on time, runs her lines over and over until they're memorized.

Sometimes, she stress-dreams of plays from years earlier, and to calm herself upon waking, she runs the dialogue perfectly.

"I mean emotionally. Farida is a complex character. She requires openness."

Mazna tries not to roll her eyes. "I know."

"Opening night is already sold out," Tarek says, changing the subject. He squints at the Jerusalem poster. She notices he's hung it on the wall facing his desk; something to look at instead of his guests. This strikes her as eminently sensible. "I have people coming from Beirut."

"That's nice," she says, mildly interested. "Your parents?"

He shakes his head. It occurs to her that Tarek seems a bit lonely, that she knows very little about his life. "My cousin's coming. Some friends," he says. His eyes light up. "My friend Idris is studying medicine at the American University. He just finished some important exams, but he called me today to say he's coming."

Mazna senses he wants to talk more. She says nothing.

"We went to school together," he tells her gratefully. "Back when we were children. He's like my brother."

"As close as me and Lara," Mazna offers, then remembers that Tarek doesn't seem to like Lara. She's caught him pinching the bridge of his nose when she complains about her lines.

Tarek grunts. "Our good friend Zakaria can't come . . ." His voice trails off. "He lives in the camps," he says, as if that explains everything. Mazna tries to envision the trio he's describing, three little boys playing tag. She isn't sure what he means by the camps — poor? Palestinian? Her stomach rumbles; she always diets the week before opening night and her last meal had been around noon.

"I'll be happy to meet your friends," she says politely. Tarek grunts at her; she shakes her hair, and his face softens.

"He's always supported my work," he says. Mazna isn't sure which one he's referring to. "He's a good man," Tarek continues, as though that settles the matter.

Friday is sultry, the evening holding the promise of later rain. Mazna and Ralph are perfectly in sync, the production like a tightly played tennis match; all that rehearsing has paid off. Each scene ends to a smattering of applause, the audience generous with their laughter and reactions. The two hours pass briskly.

"You two!" Tarek roars after the final curtain drop, rushing to the stage. Ralph and Mazna freeze, glancing at each other. "*Fucking* marvelous." Mazna has never seen him look so happy. He nearly embraces her, then catches himself and pats her on the back instead. "They set up some wine and cheese in the lobby; the audience wants to meet the stars."

Mazna changes into a fresh dress in the back room while Lara washes the powder off her face. Their friend Fatima is waiting when they emerge.

"You both did well," she says equably, two similar-size bouquets in her arms. Of the three of them, Fatima is the most poised for adulthood; she's practical and mature, with a job as a junior banker. She comes to all the plays, but Mazna wonders if she secretly finds them silly.

"Thank you," they say in unison. The flowers, red roses, smell wonderfully of rain. "You didn't have to come," Mazna says. "I know you're busy."

"It's nothing." Fatima swats the comment away. "I need a little culture in my life. The play was quite political, wasn't it? In a sense. I like the way it uses love to talk about sectarian divides."

From the look on Lara's face, it's obvious she didn't catch that. She clears her throat. "Who is *that?*"

The girls follow Lara's gaze. Near the entrance, two men in plain khakis and dress shirts are talking and smoking, an air of money about them. Mazna knows intuitively which one Lara is referring to — the shorter one, with rumpled hair and a trimmed beard. His nose is too big and his eyes too wide for him to be handsome, but he's commanding nonetheless.

"I don't know," Mazna says, but a possibility springs to mind. The shorter man meets her eye and smiles, bows his head. She feels caught.

"Well, they're coming over," Fatima says, a little panicked. Her confidence falters around men.

Mazna clears her throat. She fluffs her hair discreetly. Lara notices and adjusts her dress straps, then moves forward to speak first to the men. "Did you enjoy the play?"

The taller man smiles at her. "You were great." Lara flushes. "I mean it," he assures her. "You nailed the timing."

"The play was excellent, really excellent," the shorter man says a little effusively, mostly to Mazna.

"Thank you."

"You're Lebanese," Fatima says unhelpfully. She seems flustered.

The shorter man laughs. "Beirut," he says, his palms up as though in guilt. The air around them changes. The very word, especially after the play, seems glitzy and dangerous, a kaleidoscope of snapshots from news reports — checkpoints, religious identification cards, soldiers looking in car trunks.

Lara holds out her hand to him even though it means leaning across Fatima. Mazna pretends not to notice. "I'm Lara."

"Idris." He gestures toward the taller man. "And this is Majed." The five of them shake hands, the girls giving their names.

"Are you in Damascus often?" Lara asks just as Mazna asks, "How'd you hear about the show?" The two girls look at each other and burst into annoyed laughter.

"That would be from me." Tarek appears. He looks transformed, happily draping an arm around Idris. "Mazna, I told you about my friends?"

"Oh, yes," Mazna remembers. "Tarek is the best director this theater's seen," she tells the men.

Tarek waves off the compliment. "The acting pulled it all together." Mazna turns to him, surprised at the praise. But he is saying to Idris, "One of the crew filmed it. I'll send it to Zakaria."

Idris nods. "And I saved him a program." He turns to Mazna. "We have theaters in Beirut, although nothing as organized as this, of course, not these days. But we're going to get someone to direct Tarek's play on the American University's stage."

Fatima looks confused. "Why wouldn't you direct it yourself?" she asks Tarek, but the question is the wrong one, and the men avoid one another's eyes. There's an awkward silence.

"I'm not spending much time in Lebanon lately," Tarek finally mumbles.

"So, would you ladies like to get dinner?" Idris asks the group, but Mazna can feel his eyes on her. It's not entirely unpleasant.

They choose a restaurant nearby and sit outside at a long wooden table under a yellow umbrella. The air is rambunctious and celebratory; Ralph and a few other cast members have tagged along. They order fried fish and too much coffee. Mazna is regretting her second cup, the headache she can already taste tomorrow morning, but it all feels so far away.

"I can't wait for Tarek's next play," Idris says, and she feels a distant warmth toward him. He reminds her of a Labrador, sweet and attentive. Most of the stories originate with him; his excited gesturing at one point knocks a glass over. Tarek and Majed seem used to this. Lara is clearly interested in Idris, giving her prettiest laugh when he speaks.

"You have to tell us all about Beirut," she trills, and Idris says he will, he will, but he says it to Mazna.

After that night, Mazna falls into a prickly, sour mood that lasts for a week. There won't be another performance for a while, as Tarek is finishing his latest script. The days are getting longer and hotter, and at the firm, Mazna feels like a cooped-up schoolgirl, glaring at the beautiful day outside the window while she makes phone calls, so when her line rings on a Tuesday afternoon weeks later, she's pleasantly surprised to hear Idris's voice.

"Majed and I were thinking of visiting this weekend," he says after saying hello. There's something in his eager voice — already familiar to her — that relieves her.

"You should," she says, and they plan to meet for lunch at the same restaurant. "I'll tell Fatima and Lara," she assures him; petty, but she'd rather not have him call Lara. It's ambiguous, this Idris situation, and until she figures it out, she prefers to keep the odds in her favor.

"Great," Lara says in a clipped tone when Mazna tells her, and there's a chill between them the following Saturday. The three girls arrive first and choose the same table as last time, but there's a different atmosphere, twitchy, nervous. The numbers are bad. Tarek isn't coming, so there will be five of them. Fatima seems resigned to her fate and busies herself ordering appetizers for everyone when the men arrive.

"It's so good to see you all again!" Idris exclaims, sweeping his arms around the table, and Mazna feels his stock plummet. He's wearing an overly starched shirt and she can smell his cologne from across the table. She tries to catch Lara's eye to give her some sort of tacit permission, but Lara is too busy ignoring her.

It's like a game of Ping-Pong. Idris acts keen and Mazna loses interest. Then he fills her glass without asking, and she finds herself soften again. Lara tosses her hair at him, and Mazna tosses hers harder. The lunch is surprisingly exhausting; Mazna's frustrated with herself for not having a clear reading. The men tell stories about their neighborhoods, and something within her goes off like a metal detector. They seem to realize it and they talk more, about the war and politics, their banter hard to keep up with.

"The problem with the south getting involved is that it's just going to alienate —"

"I know, but what alternative do they have? If they don't, we're going to lose the south."

"But we'll lose the south if they don't stop. I'd rather have thieves in my backyard than Israelis."

"Well, even so. This is really no country —"

"— for liars and cheats."

Only Fatima seems to have any understanding of the politics, asking questions about legislators and recent prisoner swaps. The men like her, it's clear, but there's something brotherly and academic in their admiration.

"We have a sea here too!" she says after Majed talks about the beach near his house, and the two men laugh pityingly.

"You can't compare!" Idris says. "Before the war, we'd go in the middle of the night just for a dip."

Before the war, before the war, before the war. Idris mentions his family's house lightly several times, and that night, Mazna dreams of it, of dancing in an unfamiliar bedroom. She dreams of Beirut, a fusion of the city she visited as a youth and the one the men described — milky-white beaches, glass cafés filled with smoking women. One night, her family watches a televised concert in Amman, and Mazna joins them, wiping tears as Fairuz blows kisses for her country. She knows it's wrong, but the war makes Beirut popular in a sick way, like a girl with a damaged reputation. In the following weeks, the men visit two, three more times, bringing with them more stories of recent skirmishes.

The delineations become clearer: Majed is interested in Lara, Idris in Mazna. Lara capitulates eventually and starts speaking of Majed as though he were the one she'd liked all along. Fatima continues joining their outings but doesn't bother with lipstick anymore. Sometimes Mazna sees their ragtag group as though from the outside, and the view is confusing.

What are we doing? she thinks. The whole thing smacks of a machine taking on a life of its own. What do the men want? They seem bored and a little restless. *We're probably different than the women they know in Lebanon,* Fatima once said, smartly.

But what do I want? Mazna sometimes puzzles. This is the biggest unknown of all. She finds Idris endearing but irritating. Her excitement at seeing the men has more to do with their stories than anything else. Her days feel like a dress that's too tight around the collar; she wants something that'll toss the men around like dice. Later, the answer to what she wants will become so clear it'll be embarrassing.

❖

Many years from now, she'll be grateful to the men for the way they made her pay attention to Damascus. Their talk of their city and how it had become irrevocably broken changes her understanding of her own. She doesn't know it at the time, but she is about to leave, and after that, there will be no real return. She begins to notice how dusk stains the pale roofs purple on her walks home, the way the city is always pulsing, like a person humming an ever-changing tune. She's not sure she loves the city, but she understands it, and that seems like a similar thing. There's always the sound of water running or azan or shouting. The city is largely unchanged from her childhood and it never before occurred to Mazna that there's something precious in this, that she once fought with Lara in front of the same downtown statue where she was briefly lost as a child while shopping with her mother. Damascus remains the same as it was for her grandmother and *her* grandmother, and Mazna knows it will always be. The truth is she can't unsee herself in relation to the city. No fantasy of leaving for California or London is complete without the fantasy of return; she can imagine herself returning transformed to the corner grocery store or the hair salon, a few years older and triumphant.

But at the moment, Mazna knows none of this. Damascus has actually begun to feel airless. It's late May and the days are almost startlingly long after winter. Mazna hates her job, truly hates it, hates the labeled Tupperware lunches in the staff refrigerator, the gossip among the receptionists, the way the analysts speak self-importantly to her. She has a phone interview set up with the theater in London. She's supposed to visit in late September to meet with everyone, and the position begins in October. When she speaks to the director, the woman's cool, lyrical voice is like an invitation to another life.

"I've known Orla for many years and she says you're the best she's seen. She tells me we'd be very fortunate to have you in our organization. Aside from participating in performances, you would teach a couple of basic theater courses. Have you spent much time in London?"

"A bit," Mazna lies.

"Well, you'll have to go through the formality of the interview, but Orla assures me you're just the person we want. Should the position capture your fancy, we'll find you a nice flat near the school. It's a short walk from the Tube."

Capture your fancy. Mazna wants to shout that she'll take the position, the flat, all of it, that she doesn't need to visit the theater, but of course they need to see *her,* so she bites her tongue and says thank you. She finally brings it up to her parents after dinner, when her grandparents and Khalto Seham are watching television, giving the details in a rush, as though to confuse them into saying yes. She leaves out the part about the job position, describes it instead as a temporary theater residency.

"And they'll help me find a flat," she concludes. Most of the speech has been delivered to the bowl of oranges in the middle of the dining table. "I would just need help with the ticket. I'm saving what I can, but it's peak season in September and tickets to London are pricey, so I was thinking—"

Her mother's sigh interrupts her. Her father keeps sneaking glances at his watch, clearly uninterested in the conversation, but her mother seems alert. "It doesn't make sense for you to go all the way to London just for an interview," she says. "What are you going to do about your job? They won't let you off for that long."

I'm quitting. "I'll see if they can manage some sort of leave."

"And if they can't?"

"Mama, I'm not performing brain surgery there. I'm sure I can find another low-level office job answering phones."

Her mother's nostrils flare. The job had been her doing; the head of administration was an old friend. "That is honest pay, Mazna. There's no need to mock. Anyway, your father's money is tight, we can't be flinging it away for ridiculous trips."

"I could see if . . ." her father starts cautiously.

"Money is tight," her mother repeats.

"What your mother is saying—" Her father hesitates. "Perhaps the theater here in Damascus can suffice. Your job should come first, and theater can be . . . a sort of . . . side project."

Mazna feels her hands clench. She finishes her tea in silence.

❖

The next day at breakfast, as though to echo Mazna's foul mood, her grandfather flies into a rage when Khalto Seham adjusts the table mat and spills some tea.

"You idiot!" her grandfather howls.

Mazna feels the other women at the table stiffen. Her aunt is sensitive and diffident; age has made her smaller than she used to be. Her lower lip quivers.

"What a mess," Khalto Seham manages. "I'm sorry."

"You stupid, stupid girl. How dare you threaten me?"

"Shut up, Ghassan," Abeer says wearily. She mostly ignores him at this point.

"You"—Ghassan points a crooked, trembling finger at Seham—"are the cause of all of this. I love Abeer. I love my children."

The women look up alertly.

"How dare you threaten me? If you tell Abeer, you think she'll believe you?" His tone turns beseeching. "We made a mistake, darling. Seham, think. Please think."

Mazna's hand freezes over her mug. She turns to the older women. Khalto Seham's lips are parted, an expression of terror on her face. After a moment, she lets out a squeak and rushes from the room. Abeer continues to spoon oatmeal into her mouth, but her lips are white as paper.

"Ghassan," Abeer finally whispers, more to herself than him, "why don't you just die already?"

❖

Spring turns into an early, muggy summer. Winds from Saudi Arabia become sluggish by the time they reach Damascus. Idris and Majed don't visit for the first two weekends in June after a bombing in Beirut. Mazna spends those afternoons holed up in her bedroom watching sad movies, taking spiteful pleasure in the protagonists' suffering.

The second week of June, Idris calls to say they're coming, and this time at the restaurant, they choose a table indoors, under the air conditioner. The men seem happier than usual, ordering food jauntily.

"Ladies," Majed finally says. "We had a thought."

The idea is simple. They have a car. The weather will be clear and warm next weekend, they say. The women stare at the men uncomprehendingly.

"Perfect for the beach," Idris clarifies. "If you want to visit Beirut."

"You're joking," Fatima says. "Five people were shot near Batroun last week!"

"Don't believe everything you read, Fatoum," Majed jokes with his easy smile. He drapes an arm around Fatima; she blushes and Lara pouts. "I promise it's safe. We'll stick to our neighborhood."

"We can do a day trip," Idris adds.

"My father would kill me."

"Don't tell him, Fatima."

"That's easy for you to say, Lara, your mother's half Lebanese."

"We'll get you back in time for dinner."

It's exactly what Mazna wants, she realizes with surprise. Something completely new. A little irresponsible, even.

"Yes," she says simply. Fatima shoots her an alarmed look — of the three of them, Lara is most impulsive; Fatima expects more from Mazna — but she just shrugs. "I'll go."

Majed applauds. "I knew you'd say yes."

Idris looks thrilled. "Back by dinner, I promise," he repeats. Mazna is too excited to be annoyed by his overzealous tone. He behaves like a caricature of a lovesick man, stammering around her, always cutting his gaze to her after telling a joke. He turns to Fatima and Lara. "What do you say? We could even go to my place!"

"Don't push it," Mazna says, laughing, although privately she likes the idea.

"I'm going too," Lara says, sounding bothered that Mazna beat her to it.

Fatima looks startled. "Well," she says shortly, "I suppose this is where we part ways."

Majed boos. Lara slips her hand in his, but he pats the table in front of Fatima with his other. "Come on! You have to join us."

Fatima looks around the table evenly. "I'm not," she says, not without humor, "going to a war-torn country to be a fifth wheel."

The table erupts in laughter. "There's no fifth wheel here," Mazna says firmly, and she sees the men exchange looks, Idris clearly crestfallen. "Like Idris said, it'll be a fun day trip."

But no amount of cajoling works. Fatima's mind is made up, and eventually the conversation drifts to the following weekend's logistics. Majed excitedly tells them about the restaurant they'll visit. The evening stretches on lazily, and after the men go, the women walk down the road. Fatima leaves them at her cross street, and Mazna and Lara continue on together.

At her corner, Lara murmurs, "Do you really think it's safe?"

"Of course," Mazna says with a nonchalance she doesn't actually feel. "People do it all the time. They wouldn't keep the borders open if it wasn't safe."

"Right," Lara says, sounding unconvinced.

They decide to tell their parents they're sleeping at each other's houses on Saturday so that they can return later in the evening. Mazna already knows what she'll say to her parents when they wake up to find her at home after all — some tepid lie about not feeling well, wanting her own bed. Mazna wears a whispery pale dress that reminds her of Mia Farrow in *The Great Gatsby* and Jackie O. sunglasses. She meets Lara outside her place and they walk toward the market together, mostly silent.

"I don't know about Majed," Lara says out of nowhere, and Mazna feels a pang of pity for her friend. She's being greedy, she knows. She doesn't even want Idris for herself.

"I find him hilarious."

Lara shoots her a poisonous look. "Oh, do you?"

I can't help that he likes me. But she can. For a second, she considers apologizing, but it would be strained and awkward. "Listen," Mazna says instead, "we're all just friends." Lara doesn't look at her. "I don't want Idris," she says quickly before she can change her mind, and she slips her hand in Lara's. They used to walk to school like this together, at seven, eight, nine years old, their hair in identical braids, holding hands and swinging them like adults did in movies.

To her surprise, this just seems to annoy Lara more. Her hand is stiff. "I'd like to see you tell *him* that," she mutters.

But their conversation is interrupted by the sound of their names being called out, Idris and Majed waving at them, and the disagreement is, if not forgotten, then deferred, replaced with the excitement of the drive.

They have no trouble at the border. Mazna and Lara had been worried, envisioning soldiers questioning them or demanding paperwork — neither has visited Beirut in years — but the Syrian officer is pleasant and young, asking only to see everyone's identification. He glances at Mazna and Lara a little curiously on seeing their Syrian residency cards but then just smiles.

"The reverse commute?" he jokes, and they all laugh.

The drive should be a little under two hours, but it takes longer because of all the checkpoints. They fall silent as they cross into Lebanon, the landscape initially unchanged, a striking terrain Mazna remembers from past trips, endless hills of greenery and terra-cotta-roofed houses. The villages connect to each other like bread crumbs, posters of solemn-eyed martyrs on buildings, mopeds zigzagging through the traffic. Many of the women are hijabis, their veils the color of summer fruits, laughing as they walk. Parts of the drive feel claustrophobic and then, suddenly, it's all highway again, a simple road flanked by rocks on one side and a cliff on the other. Idris sings the songs on the radio with comical exaggeration. Lara and Mazna catch each other's eye and exchange charitable smiles like they've seen their mothers do. Mazna takes Lara's hand, and this time she doesn't pull away.

Once they near Beirut, checkpoints mushroom up every few miles. The sea appears like a chaperone, the water lavender-blue in the late-morning light. The soldiers wear rifles and speak curtly to the men, smirk at Mazna and Lara.

"Have fun with your girlfriends," one of them says, his eyes on Mazna. They drive off. She's surprised to hear the anger shaking Idris's voice as he calls the soldier an asshole.

❖

They arrive in Beirut just before noon. Idris parks near the university and they follow him and Majed through the streets. It's hard for Mazna to pinpoint what's different. There are groups of men smoking and talking, girls walking by in shorter skirts than in Damascus. Several teenagers stand near the arched university entrance, heads bent over a flyer. The girls are wearing matching striped knee socks.

"Well, this is . . ." Lara says in an undertone, trailing off.

Mazna understands. She isn't sure what she was expecting — gun smoke in the streets? Women outfitted in black at every corner? Certainly not an elderly man grinning at her as they pass his fruit cart or a woman smoking a long, filtered cigarette in front of a *dikaneh*.

"It's nicer than Damascus," she mutters back to Lara. Dirtier, definitely, with a delicate, braced tension in the air, but also more spirited somehow. More alive. The people seem both alert and unhurried, and there are wafts of music from passing cars. It's like being in the midst of time-lapse photography.

Mazna and Lara sign in with a university security guard, then the four of them wander through campus. The men adopt a little swagger as they walk around, clearly comfortable on the grounds. "I wish you'd let us take you to my place; my parents are cool," Idris says, glancing at Mazna. She pretends to examine an inscribed plaque in front of the library. The buildings are clean and imposing. She feels as if she's on a film set — beautiful coeds lighting each other's cigarettes, flowering plants lush in pornographic displays of pinks and yellows. They walk until they reach a small clearing, the sea and coastline visible from the high vantage point. There is a massive, knotted tree surrounded by wildflowers and a bench with a perfect view of the water and green-locked firs.

They all sit down together, Idris and Majed telling the girls stories about the university. Idris talks about a time his class dissected a fresh cadaver.

"One thing they don't tell you," he says, laughing, "is that bodies can sigh. I make my first incision and I swear to *God,* the thing made a sound. I almost fainted."

"It did *not!*"

"Lara, on my mother's life, it *groaned.*"

"He wasn't dead?" Mazna envisions the scene like a film noir, with a swinging naked light bulb.

"Rigor mortis," he says. "The muscles stiffen and built-up gas gets released. The gas goes through the vocal cords too."

Mazna shudders. "I would die. A dead body."

"Don't forget the intestines." Idris grins. She can tell he's enjoying this, all the attention. He points toward a white building in the distance. "That's where the magic happens."

"When do you officially start working at the university hospital?" Lara asks.

"In September."

"If he doesn't leave us for America first," Majed says.

"I applied for a few residencies at hospitals in the United States," Idris explains to the girls. It's the first time Mazna has heard him mention America, and his voice changes. "I won't go, of course," he says quickly. "My mother would be devastated, and my life is here." He clears his throat. "Should we head toward the water? It's about a million stairs to get there, but at least we'll be going down. Up is murder."

"So why apply?" Mazna asks him quietly after the other two scamper off. It seems wasteful.

For the first time, he looks confused. "I don't know," he says finally. There's a long pause, and she remembers that she barely knows him. "Maybe I wanted to see if I'd get in?"

He sounds young and lost and melancholy. It's almost enough to make her want to kiss him. Almost.

They reach the beach sweaty and winded. It's surprisingly busy (*People get hot whether there's a war or not,* Mazna reasons), children chasing each other and a few women lazily spiking a volleyball around. The women who aren't in head-scarfs wear bikinis, and that includes some of the older, grandmotherly types, their skin wrinkled and brown as a walnut. A young man is dragging a cooler of Almazas and Popsicles through the rocks, and Majed buys them all beer.

"Wait." Idris covers the mouth of Mazna's Almaza. "You do drink, don't you?"

She laughs. During their group dinners, the girls stuck with tea and Cokes, a vestigial holdover in Damascus, where everyone knows everyone, and someone's neighbor's aunt might tell their mothers they were drinking. But she drinks with friends at cast parties. "This is my very first drink," she says demurely, then takes a long sip. The men laugh. The sun is very warm and very bright, and Mazna feels edible, stretched out in her red bikini.

The beer is cold and good, and she drinks it too fast. With her head enjoy-ably fuzzy, she tries to get Lara to come with her to the bathroom.

"I'm okay, Maz, I was going to take another dip." Lara is lying on Majed's towel, her head on his shoulder, their limbs entangled in a way that Mazna knows would send Lara's mother into a fit of prayer.

"Don't drown," Mazna says crossly and walks toward the small café near the strip. She's a little afraid of the water but wouldn't admit it to anyone. She's al-ready gone in twice, but only to her calves, the waves bucking against her like some mad, fickle horse, while Lara dived in easily.

The café is loud, with gritty floors and patrons wearing beach towels turban-style. Mazna goes to the bathroom, which is grimy with several stalls. There are two pretty women dabbing their dark hair with paper towels. One is wearing a caftan, the other a halter dress with bathing-suit straps visible underneath. Mazna listens in on their conversation while she pees.

"I like to leave the salt water in," one says. "Especially since I'm seeing Samir tonight."

"Again?" the other squeals.

There's a delicious pause. "He said he can't stay away. He told his wife he'll be working late tonight."

"You're terrible," the friend says, but her tone is admiring.

"I can't help it." Mazna envisions the woman shrugging. She stopped peeing a minute ago but is too embarrassed to flush. "I swear, he's like heroin."

"I'm pretty sure that's just the sex," the other girl deadpans, and they both giggle.

Mazna remains frozen in place for a few seconds after the girls clatter out. It feels like the word has been burned into the air. Mazna has kissed men, she has pressed her hips against theirs, been touched, but sex is something she's consigned herself to keeping bottled up, for theater and some vague, future man. Most of the women she knows haven't had sex, and even in their mid-twenties, they wouldn't think of it. And those who did — like poor Meena from sophomore year who, last Mazna heard, was working at her grandparents' restaurant in Amman — did so quietly and badly. They certainly didn't chatter about it in a public restroom, their curls dripping with salt water.

Girls in Beirut . . . Mazna thinks as she wads up toilet paper. But she doesn't know how to finish the thought. She doesn't know whether she's supposed to condemn them or judge them or want to be exactly like them.

❖

The four of them go back again the following Friday, and then once more the week after. Mazna's lies become simpler and more straightforward.

"I have rehearsal," she says innocently, although there is no play, although she's still not returning Tarek's calls about auditioning even though she'd told him she would. The more Mazna lied growing up, the less beholden to the truth she'd felt. She'd crossed a line long ago, and so, since her mind has been trained since childhood to split the world into *good* and *bad,* like removing dirt from rice, she accepts ruefully that she's already done wrong, so she might as well continue doing it.

It is the best summer of her life. The weeks of June are hot and sticky, and she returns from work during the weekdays famished, eating seconds in front of the television, then falling into easy sleep. Then, on Saturdays, she and Lara walk to the marketplace wearing their cutest outfits; in Idris's car, they roll the windows down on the highway and sing offkey. Idris tells stories about his and Majed's school days, so many in the backdrop of his house, where they'd play and have sleepovers; they all grew up in that house, Mazna realizes.

Before the second trip, there was a bombing near the post office, and Idris shuts off the radio as they drive by it, a somber plume of smoke rising from the building, firefighters huddled around it. The men don't speak. Mazna cranes her neck to watch the smoke until she can't see it anymore. That night, back at home, Mazna feels important watching the news report with her father.

Then, on the third trip, Majed and Lara get into an argument at lunch, Majed calling Lara's father a Jumblatt apologist. The rest of the day is tense; Lara sulks over her meal. When the men drop the girls off in Damascus, Lara says a perfunctory goodbye to Idris and slams the door extra-hard.

"Go back if you want," Lara snaps as she and Mazna watch the car drive off, her tone final. "I'm done with that sanctimonious shit."

No coaxing would change Lara's mind. Just like that, their little foursome is ruined.

Idris calls her at work a few days later.

"Hey," he says ruefully when she picks up. "Is Lara done?"

Mazna nods, though he can't see her. "Majed?"

"Yeah." They sit in silence. "I guess their thing is over."

She sighs. This is a perfect fork-in-the-road moment, one of a few that speckle every life, like knots in a fine metal chain. She isn't interested in Idris; Beirut is dangerous; she needs to call Tarek back and start preparing for London. It couldn't be clearer — their trips have come to an end. It's time to part ways.

"I could come next weekend," she says instead. "By myself."

Idris laughs with what she's sure is relief. "That would be nice," he says. She can tell he's trying to sound restrained. "And Zakaria! You can finally meet him. He's just back in the city."

Mazna feels a nagging regret for the rest of the day. This was a sign, she knows. Without Lara, she is just a woman visiting a man. The message is clear. That phone call was an opportunity to explain herself, to tell Idris that he's a friend of hers, a dear friend, really, but that this is mostly about Beirut. She wants to go to the bazaar. To see the Communist bar Majed told her about. To finally enter the house Idris has referenced dozens of times. *Idris, you're really very lovely, but this isn't about you at all.*

He must know, she finally tells herself firmly. He must.

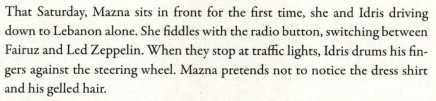

That Saturday, Mazna sits in front for the first time, she and Idris driving down to Lebanon alone. She fiddles with the radio button, switching between Fairuz and Led Zeppelin. When they stop at traffic lights, Idris drums his fingers against the steering wheel. Mazna pretends not to notice the dress shirt and his gelled hair.

"His mom was sick for a couple of months, so I was barely seeing him," he says into the silence as though they were in the middle of a conversation. "But now he's home until August." Mazna shrugs, unsure who he's referring to.

"Zakaria," he says, glancing over to her. "I already told you." He sounds wounded, and Mazna feels the familiar irritation bubble up.

"Your friend," she says, her tone a little more bored than necessary. "The one whose mother works for your family."

He brightens. *"Worked.* We still see her every now and then. But she left after her back gave out."

The song ends and "Smoke on the Water" comes on. Mazna turns up the volume slightly. She loves this song. It makes her think of California, the long-haired girls and beaches she's seen in photographs. "So, her son."

"Yes. He lives in the camps but usually stays with us for the summer. He works close by."

"He stays with your family? Why?"

There is a stillness and it takes Mazna a second to realize she's insulted him. "We grew up together," he says coolly.

So why does he live in the camps the rest of the time? Why not invite his mother as well? But it seems wise not to press it. There is something crackly and strained about the whole thing; whenever Zakaria comes up, Idris seems simultaneously happy and on edge, a combination she finds perplexing. She brings up the play Tarek is working on, and she can feel him relax. Mazna has forgotten all about Zakaria by the time they reach Beirut.

Idris says he wants to take her somewhere. They pass a checkpoint and Mazna arranges her face like an open window. Back home when she thinks of Beirut, it feels like a place she's fabricated, something fictitious, but each time she returns, it greets her anew, the car horns and coastline chiding her for doubting their existence. They park near the university and Idris leads her down an unfamiliar street, refusing to give details on where he's taking her.

"You'll see," he says, grinning.

This neighborhood is decidedly grungy. Many of the storefronts are graffitied with smiley faces and slurs, and a few barefoot children are playing marbles. At the end of the street, they turn left, and Idris stops.

Mazna looks up. They are standing in front of a tiny bakery, a sign in Arabic announcing DEEDEE'S SUGAR. "What's this?" she asks.

Idris smiles enigmatically. "There's someone I'd like you to meet." He pushes open the door. A bell tinkles, and Mazna sees that it's dangling from a dirty-looking rope. The store is roughly the size of her bedroom. The floor tiles are concrete gray and the ceiling is covered in water stains, but the glass display is sparklingly clean. There are rows of pink-iced éclairs and cream puffs and cakes; the smell is incredible. Nobody is behind the counter, though Mazna can hear someone in the back.

"This place was a famous bakery before the war," Idris whispers.

"Really?"

He nods. "My father is an old friend of the owner."

As if on cue, a large woman wearing a red apron appears from the back. Her arms jiggle with appealing girth. She has one of the prettiest faces Mazna has ever seen, round and unlined, with hazel eyes. There's a streak of flour in her salt-and-pepper hair.

"Good Allah in His plush purple chair!" she cries out at the sight of Idris. "What are you doing here?"

Idris vanishes in her embrace. "I missed you," he says, his voice muffled. "I've brought my friend. Mazna," he calls out, "meet Deedee."

Deedee releases Idris and smiles at Mazna. "Welcome, welcome," she says. "Éclair or mille-feuille?"

Mazna places a hand on her stomach. "I'm all right, thank you, I —"

"Nonsense! You're air and bones." Deedee slides an éclair onto a paper doily and hands it to Mazna.

"Nowhere in the world smells this good," Idris says appreciatively.

Deedee turns to Idris, fists on hips. "Just to see old Deedee, huh?" she says jokingly.

"Is he here?"

Deedee smiles. *"Zuzu!"* she hollers. "Some customers for you." She winks at Mazna, whose stomach, inexplicably, knots with nerves.

A door slamming, the sound of footsteps. A man emerges from the back room. The first person he sees is her and he smiles politely, thinking her a customer. Mazna feels her breath catch at her throat like a champagne bubble. He is tall and lithe and wearing a white apron. His beard is thicker than Idris's, and he looks unmistakably poor, though she feels awful at the thought. Idris says his name, and Zakaria turns away from her.

"Iddy!" he shouts. In three long-legged strides he's at Idris's side, bear-hugging him like Deedee (Mazna's mind hums with detective work: Idris doesn't visit often, there's something special about him dropping in), then the men kiss each other on the cheek. She catches Deedee's eye and the older woman winks.

Me, she's surprised to find herself silently urging Zakaria, *look at me.* And he does. He releases Idris with a final clap on the back and turns toward Mazna, a reserved smile on his lips.

"So," he says, like they're old friends.

Mazna smiles too, unnerved. She feels like she's about to go onstage. "I'm Mazna."

"I see that." He glances at Idris.

Her stomach sinks. That look between the men. She has been marked, she realizes, as Idris's.

"Let's sit for a minute." Idris gestures toward the only table, with long, hairpin legs. There's a goofy grin on his face, like a boy on his birthday. "I've wanted you two to meet for a million years."

"Please." Zakaria gestures for Mazna to sit first. He pulls the chair out for her, its legs scraping the floor below.

Deedee busies herself behind the counter, pretending she's arranging the cakes, but she keeps glancing at the threesome.

So Idris is dating a Syrian, she thinks.

In the corner, Idris tells a joke and Zakaria chuckles, but Deedee watches the girl watching Zakaria. He's not more handsome than Idris, but he's more *commanding,* even though he's often quiet, almost shy; the neighborhood women come in so regularly that Deedee's is one of the only businesses turning a profit in this war. Zakaria's voice rings out now: "You should've seen Idris!"

Deedee swallows a smile. She's used to being on the outside — youngest of five children, never married — and her years alone have granted her a near clairvoyance, the capacity to see things unsentimentally. Idris is clearly in love with the girl. Zakaria, loyal confederate, is puffing his friend up. Deedee feels a pang of sympathy for Idris. The Syrian girl laughs only when Zakaria does.

From the back, the oven with its rows of browning sticky buns lets out a bleat. Deedee forces herself to turn away from the laughing threesome, their youth heady and inviting and a little painful to bear.

Mazna is consumed. Never in her life has she felt so singularly fixated on anything; the closest she's come is preparing for a role, but even then, there's a skittish sort of interest, possibilities laid out in front of her like a feast —

accents, mannerisms, delivery. This is more determined, a laserlike focus on one person.

Zakaria.

He's always there — while she's shopping for new sandals with Lara, eating dinner with her family, answering endless phone calls at the firm. She rubs shampoo into her hair; she walks through her childhood neighborhood. And throughout, there's Zakaria, laughing at Mazna's stupid knock-knock joke — borrowed from Bassel — or tossing Idris a sweating Pepsi from a deli cooler. Now that he's staying with Idris again, they are suddenly, unceremoniously, a threesome, Zakaria joining them after his shift at the bakery. It reminds her of the first trip, when she and Lara stayed up all night going through every moment and conversation like loot, only now the loot is how Zakaria pronounces certain words with the broad, Palestinian *a*, how Zakaria's hair is a little long in the back, curling against the base of his neck. Every detail he mentions is preserved: his sisters, a love for mathematics, an old job as a mechanic.

Back home, nobody notices anything.

The idea of metamorphosis has always been unsettling to Mazna — as a child she dreaded caterpillars more than spiders — but never more so than this summer, when she feels like a traffic light blinking on and off everywhere she goes, only to realize that others see nothing. Even Lara and Fatima don't notice — Lara's still a little cool about Mazna's ongoing trips — and Mazna doesn't say anything at first, but after a couple of weeks she tells them about Zakaria briefly, keeping her tone casual.

"It sounds like trouble," Fatima says.

"And poor Idris," Lara says a little bitterly.

"I'm not sure it can end well," Fatima continues, ignoring Lara. "Eventually you're going to have to stop these trips. Just yesterday, there was another bombing in the south." She pauses grimly. "It's really not safe, Mazna."

She pretends to agree with them, but Mazna feels sulky and a little sorry for Fatima. In a spiteful moment, she remembers Madame Orla once saying of Fatima, *That girl has no imagination.*

It's July now, and Mazna can feel the summer scuttle toward her like an insect. It feels miraculous, how unaltered her life is. Only her mother seems to detect something; one morning, before work, she overhears Lulwa speaking to her aunt in the kitchen.

"... just not right. She seems preoccupied."

There is a pause, and then Mazna is shocked to hear Khalto Seham say, "I wonder if there's a man."

"From your lips to God's ears," her mother says back. "We should be so lucky. That'd take care of this London nonsense."

"A man," Khalto Seham says dreamily. "Our little one in love."

"Don't be ridiculous," Lulwa snaps. "If a man is not for marrying, he's for tossing."

Mazna waits until her mother's footsteps have faded before entering the kitchen. She tries to catch her aunt's eye, to see anything revealing, but Seham's expression is smooth as butter.

The next time Idris asks Mazna if she'd like to see his house, she doesn't say no right away. As though he can sense her hesitation, he presses on. "We have friends over constantly, and my sister's not that much younger than you. If you meet my parents, we can just say you're a classmate of hers."

"It's just a little unusual."

"This is Beirut." Idris grins. "My parents took a trip to Turkey together *when they were still dating.*"

"Really?" Mazna is scandalized.

"Oh yeah. Mama's friend mentioned it accidentally years ago. We've never let her live it down. Anyway, it's not that big of a deal here. Men and women are friends; they hang out all the time."

"That's nice," Mazna says honestly. "It's hard to befriend men in Damascus. At least it is in my neighborhood." She watches Idris realize his error in saying *friends;* his face falls.

"I think Zakaria's ending his shift early today. We could all barbecue or something."

Mazna's heart skips a beat. "Okay," she says before she can change her mind.

Idris lives in Ain Al Mraiseh, a fancy neighborhood near the sea with shops and cliff-side cafés. He parks in front of a pharmacy and they walk up a narrow alley and onto a residential street with a row of houses. At the fourth one, he pushes open a gate flanked by almond trees. The house isn't just a house — it's a House. After all of Beirut's grubby buildings, Mazna hadn't expected something so hidden, so pretty. This is like traveling back in time, the courtyard in front tiled, a canopy of branches overhead, the peaked roof.

It's still early, not yet eleven o'clock, and Idris has promised that his mother will be fine with the visit, and his father is already at work. He runs a print shop, an impressive-looking store they walked by once with large gleaming windows and elegant travel posters on display.

"This is it," Idris says when they walk through the gate. He seems casual about the House, which surprises her.

"It's lovely," she says honestly. The House rises elegantly against the blue sky, reminding her of the mansions in the nicer neighborhoods of Damascus, houses that have belonged to families for four, five generations, starting in the Ottoman time. Her mother loves Moorish architecture and for a brief, incongruous moment, Mazna wishes that Lulwa could be here.

She follows Idris into the foyer, an ornate evil eye hanging above the door. The Turkish blue stares at Mazna, and she's grasped by a fleeting anxiety. What is she doing here? She's about to enter a stranger's home and lie to the people in it.

But before she can hesitate, the door is open, and Idris is inside, stepping out of his sneakers; she has no choice but to follow. The House is unmistakably rich, with mustard-yellow velour couches and gleaming floors. Portraits and paintings of Ottoman souks hang on the walls. Every surface — the tables, the counters, the windows — looks recently cleaned. Even though Idris has been the one living here for twenty-five years, Mazna can imagine only Zakaria in the rooms. *He's sat on this couch,* she thinks, *run through these hallways.*

"Saroush," Idris calls. "Saroush!"

Mazna thinks he's calling for a cat. But a young woman appears and introduces herself as Sara, Idris's sister. She is surprisingly homely, with monkeyish ears and eyes, but she has clear, fair skin.

"God, you nearly gave me a heart attack. Why are you slinking around like a burglar?" She holds out her hand to Mazna. "My old friend!" she jokes. They shake hands.

"Thanks for . . ." Mazna trails off, unsure how to finish the sentence. "This," she concludes lamely.

"Where's Mama?" Idris asks.

"Baba's at the shop," she answers distractedly. "I'm running late. I was supposed to meet Fifi half an hour ago."

"Hang on," he says impatiently. "And Mama?"

"She's here," a voice trills behind them. *Her name is Hana,* Mazna remembers. Idris's mother is a perfect mixture of him and Sara; she has her daughter's long black hair, her son's sweet mouth. She glances at Mazna before saying, "Hi, honey," to Idris.

He looks simultaneously pleased and nervous. "This is—" He gestures toward Mazna, then freezes, realizing his mistake.

"My friend," Sara says, stepping in smoothly. "From university."

"I'm Mazna." She shakes their mother's hand. "Your house is beautiful, Auntie."

Hana cocks her head. She looks confused. "Your accent."

Mazna feels her cheeks flush. She's given herself away. *Stupid,* she chides herself. *Stupid idiot.* She'd *just* played a Lebanese woman in Tarek's play; her Beiruti accent is flawless.

"Mama!" Sara shoots her mother a look even though the woman had said it kindly. "I *told* you. We talked about this last week. Mazna's father is Syrian. Her mother's Lebanese."

Her mother contemplates this. It's evident to Mazna from Sara's bitten lip that she hasn't told her mother anything of the sort, but finally Hana shrugs.

"Ah, yes, yes. Your last name, dear?"

"Adib."

"Adib!" Her face brightens. "Why, one of my closest friends is Amira Adib, down the road, near the—"

"Mazna," Sara interrupts neatly, "you remember my brother? Idris." She gives Mazna a mischievous smile, and Mazna is filled with fondness for her. She and Idris shake hands.

"It's been ages," she lies.

"Too long," Idris agrees.

"What do you study, dear?" Hana asks.

Mazna freezes. Hana seems liberal enough. She takes a risk. "Theater," she hears herself say. "Well, English literature, but I'm minoring in theater."

Hana claps her hands. "Oh, how modern! I remember there was a little theater group when I was at AUB. Idris, does Tarek still do theater?"

"He does, Mama. In Damascus now."

"That's right, that's right. I need to call his mother, it's been months."

"I know Tarek," Mazna says, the perfect narrative unspooling in front of her like a bolt of fabric. "I acted in one of his plays."

"What a small world," Hana says distractedly. She reminds Mazna of Melanie Hamilton from *Gone with the Wind*. "I'm off now. I'm meeting some friends. Nice to meet you, dear. Please, make yourself at home." Her heels clack in her wake. Sara waits until her mother's car is gone, then she leaves as well, and it's just the two of them, Mazna and Idris, the House empty around them. He leaves her to wander while he brews some coffee. There are more rooms than she can count, many of them narrow and impractically built—they've got high ceilings but tight layouts—and there is a magazine-cover quality to the space. Lacy curtains. Expensive-looking knickknacks. Her favorite room is the guest bathroom, which is large and sunny, the window shaded by tree branches. There's a clawfoot tub and shelves with lotions and cotton balls. Someone—definitely Hana—has draped a blue and purple Moroccan rug across the tiles, and Mazna walks over it. Once she locks the door, she takes one of the shell-shaped soaps wrapped in French paper and slips it into her pocket. She'll use it every day back home, scrubbing her skin with it until only a sliver remains; the smell is floral and rich and perfectly Hana.

She's too afraid to do more than peek into the master bedroom—cream and blue rug, wood bed frame, a silky blouse on the bed—but she steps into the one next door, clearly Idris's. It's bright and smells like him. On the floor, there's a small cot with a folded blanket, sheets warm from the sun. Zakaria must sleep on it. In the hallway, there are framed photographs, many from when the children were younger. She finds Zakaria in five.

✤

It is impossible for Mazna to be alone with Zakaria. Idris picks her up. Idris drops her off. He follows her around like a starved dog, eager for her company, constantly talking about the future, where he'll practice medicine, how Mazna will become an actor. They spend more time at the House. Mazna's met Idris's father a couple of times as he rushes out to work; he's breezy, jovial. Idris's mother slips in and out of the living room, offering them snacks and then bustling off to do whatever she does. Whereas Mazna's mother rarely leaves the house, Idris's mother lunches with her friends and even goes to the beach alone. If she thinks it curious that Sara is often nowhere to be found when Mazna is over, she doesn't seem to mind.

But even when Zakaria is there, so is Idris.

He gets a letter from one of the university hospitals in California and waves it at her from the car like a flag: he is being considered for a residency there. He tells Mazna and Zakaria it isn't a big deal, that it isn't an acceptance, but she can tell how pleased he is.

"Do you think you'd actually go?" she asks him one afternoon as the three of them are sitting at the patio table in the House's courtyard sharing a bowl of pistachios. The shells are salty and hard to crack.

"He wouldn't do it." Zakaria groans.

"You don't know that."

"You won't," Zakaria says simply to Idris. "Don't misunderstand me — you *should,* you'd get better training there than here, plus you wouldn't need a bomb shelter there. But you won't."

"How do you know?" Mazna is seated between them, her body ever so slightly angled toward Zakaria. This is how it is now; every time the three of them enter a room, she does shrewd calculations to decide where to stand or sit. Her voice is husky, but not too husky. It's a tightrope — if she shows her hand, Idris will leave. If Idris leaves, Zakaria is gone. If she flirts with one, she has to flirt with the other. She playfully pushes Idris's shoulder. "I guess he knows you better than the rest of us."

"He doesn't know shit."

"I know you're *scared.*" Zakaria ducks as Idris throws a shell at him. "But if you *can* leave, you should. Even *she's* going to London."

Mazna looks up, startled at his mention of her. The word *she* is delicious as an ice cube, but she doesn't have much time to savor it.

"She's going for a month," Idris counters.

"I'm not! I'm going for a few months. I'll act and teach, and once that's done, I'm moving to California." She tries to keep her tone casual, but even as she's speaking, Mazna feels her stomach sink. She suddenly can't envision any of those things; it's like looking through a windshield filmy with fog.

"See?" Zakaria's smile is unreadable. "You two can meet in California."

Idris makes an impatient sound. "This is my *home*." He waves toward the beech trees overhead. They flutter their green hands back. "Would you leave?" The question is clearly directed at Zakaria.

"Yes," he answers without hesitation.

"You'd leave your *home*?" Mazna adopts Idris's exaggerated tone but neither of them laugh. Too late, she remembers: A homeland he was born outside of. The camps are where Zakaria has eaten and slept and lived his entire life, a place she's never seen.

"I bet they'll offer you a spot," Zakaria says, graciously changing the subject and sparing them his answer.

❈

Dozens of people have been killed in Beirut this month — this the latest tidbit from Fatima — and Mazna has been turning this fact over in her mind like a stone, trying to understand it. It seems fantastical. Idris whisks her around the city from place to place, the checkpoints like plot twists. The tanks and guns feel like props, so she pretends they are.

It's a little harder to pretend in certain neighborhoods. Like where the bakery is. The streets are grimier, and one of the neighbors was sweeping up broken glass during their last visit.

"Those motherfuckers shattered my window," the woman said. She was Abeer's age, her white hair in a loose bun.

Mazna and Idris tried not to look at each other. "Which motherfuckers, Tante?" Idris asked politely, but the woman snorted.

"Haven't you figured it out, sonny?" she asked, peering over her glasses. She stage-whispered, *"They're all motherfuckers."*

But in the House, she feels like she's in another world, far from the war and bickering parents and death. *The wealthy are different,* Mazna has heard Lulwa say, and she finally understands her mother. The wealthy *are* different. They aren't immune to things, exactly, but they've got another coating somehow. Idris's family wealth had seemed curious to Mazna, since his father ran a small shop, but once, after watching Mazna admire an engraved goblet, Hana had let her hold it and said, "It's lovely, isn't it? It was my great-grandmother's." And Mazna understood. The money came from Hana, from her family. This somehow made her love the House even more, this feminine money scented with lavender and face cream.

Outside, the world sputters on. A Christian couple are shot at a checkpoint in West Beirut, and in the House, Mazda and Idris and Zakaria bake orange-peel cookies, filling the whole place with heat and sugar.

"It smells like April in here!" Hana exclaims, walking into the kitchen. Zakaria is doing most of the work; Idris is in the doorway watching a World Cup match. Every time Idris hollers, Zakaria runs out, his hands covered in flour.

"What'd I miss? Scirea scored?"

Hana makes an exasperated sound and Mazna catches her eye. They smile at each other. Hana is the opposite of Deedee, who makes Mazna feel perpetually caught out, like her clothes are too thin.

"You like it?" Zakaria asks, and Mazna is startled to realize he's speaking to her. They are far enough away from Hana that she can't hear them, and Idris is preoccupied with the game. He's gesturing toward the tray of cookies. "They're a little crisp, I know."

"I prefer things burned," she confesses. "At home, I keep the toaster on high."

"Oh, Damascus." His nickname for her. He shakes his head, like she's an amusing child. "You're essentially eating carbon." His eyes meet hers for a quick second, then he looks away as though scalded. She has noticed more of these glances. Something is happening. He's catching up.

"Well —" She looks at Hana, who's peeling an apple. Mazna allows herself a small, flirtatious smile. "Carbon is delicious."

He smiles back. Leans forward infinitesimally. His shirtsleeves are rolled up, his forearms brown and ropy. Mazna wants more than life to run a fingernail down one of his milky-blue veins, to make him shiver.

Just then, Idris lets out a hoot. "Germany, baby! Zuzu, come take your boys home." Zakaria groans and rushes to the living room. Mazna wants to smack Idris. She has been feeling a little ashamed of her coldness toward him. In better moments, she can summon a tepid appreciation; he's gifted her two lofty things: Beirut and Zakaria. But beneath that is a fat, resounding nothing, an insincerity. Where once she'd looked upon him with gratitude for all he'd shown her, now there's only exasperation with him for spoiling the view.

❖

Tarek finally convinces her to meet him for coffee.

"Damn it, Mazna," he says. "I don't care if you move to London or Djibouti, you don't have to keep avoiding me."

She laughs it off, but it's true, she's been hiding from him, partly because of the play, but also because she has an uncomfortable feeling he'd disapprove of the Beirut trips.

This turns out to be correct. "I knew those idiots talked you into going a couple of times, but I can't believe you're still doing it!" He sets his mug down with a clatter. The other patrons in the café turn to stare. "Mazna, you can't *summer* in Beirut."

She avoids his eyes. He seems surly as ever, but there is a genuine note of concern in his voice. "I'm researching roles," she lies, but he just stares at her evenly.

"I never told you why I moved to Damascus," Tarek finally says. She shakes her head. "There was some political stuff. It wasn't anything major at first. Meetings, some military training. My friends and I policed a few checkpoints. My big brother was in the army when the war started, and he introduced us to some people. Don't look so surprised, Mazna. It's difficult to be a young man in Beirut and not get pulled into it."

"Is your brother still in the army?" she asks.

"He died," Tarek says flatly. "My brother. We stopped some Maronites, and one of them died. Then they came after him. They killed him in my mother's garden. She was watching from the kitchen window."

"Oh!" Mazna instinctively covers her mouth, nauseated. "Tarek, I —"

"Thanks," he says gruffly, cutting her off. "They told my mother I was next. I wanted to stay. She made me leave, and after what she'd been through, I couldn't say no. The men knew he was my brother, but they didn't know who else had been there that night. So I'm the only one involved who had to go." A note of bitterness enters his voice. Mazna thinks of Idris and Majed back in Beirut, drinking expensive wine by the sea.

"Idris is a good guy," he says. "But he's overzealous and impulsive. He doesn't always make the smartest decisions. None of us do."

"He's been fine," she says defensively. "It's not like we're touring bomb sites. Most of the time, we just hang out with Zakaria. He works a lot. But he's been moving his shifts around so we can see him." She feels a heat creep into her cheeks as she says Zakaria's name. All this time, she's forgotten there's someone in Damascus who knows him, and it's intoxicating speaking of him like they're all old friends.

To her surprise, Tarek takes her hand and squeezes it, hard. "Ouch!" She yanks it back. He looks out of the window and shakes his head. Finally, he turns to her. "For an actress," he says quietly, "you have a shitty poker face."

Mazna feels her cheeks get even warmer. "I'm sorry you never get to see your friends," she snaps.

He opens his mouth to respond, then changes his mind. She can see him weighing his next words. When he speaks, it's quiet and hurtful.

"Maybe it's a good thing you're going to London after all."

※

Tarek's words trail her for days, like a slug. The rest of the meeting was awful, and she'd finally accused him of punishing her for not acting in the summer play. He'd shaken his head as if she were a child.

"Idris and Zakaria have known each other for years," he'd said at last. "You don't know how things get between them."

"I don't know what you're suggesting," she said, opting for chilly. They'd left without ordering food.

Feeling spiteful after Tarek's words, during the next drive with Idris, she suggests a weekend trip. "I could stay in a hotel," she says, knowing he'll resist that. "These day trips are exhausting."

"Bullshit!" he says. Mazna holds her breath. "There's no way you're staying in a hotel. You'll stay with us."

Mazna hides a smile. "But your parents . . ."

"They adore you. There's plenty of space. They won't even notice. Zakaria's staying with us too these days, remember?"

"Oh," she says. "That's right." Her voice is breathy, like she's just remembered. She convinces herself she *has* just remembered. Is that all acting is, lying?

"They think you're Sara's classmate anyway. There's nothing strange about it."

"I guess it would be nice." She bites her lip, pretending to be unsure. In truth, her heart is pounding. She's never slept in the same house as a man she isn't related to. Her mother would faint on the spot if she ever found out.

"You're staying with us!" Idris declares. "It's decided."

"I don't know."

They meet Zakaria later that day at the bakery, and Mazna watches him intently while Idris talks about the plan. Zakaria seems politely interested, but when Idris goes to the back to make himself some coffee, he turns to Mazna with an impassive expression.

"Are you sure about this?" he asks.

She feels her temper rise. Why is everyone ruining everything? "What do you mean?"

There's a lock of hair on his forehead and he tugs it, avoiding her eyes. "I don't know. Won't it be awkward with Idris's parents? You and Idris already see each other a lot. And the electricity cuts off in the middle of the night."

Mazna feels her breath slow as she understands. There's a car driving by outside, blasting music, and she feels a mad urge to stand up and dance, to shriek with laughter. *He's trying to talk me out of being with Idris.* She turns to him so he can see her expression.

"Oh, I've already spent plenty of time with Idris. I want to spend more time in Beirut." Her voice goes soft on the last word. Zakaria's face opens. When Idris returns with their coffees, he looks at them quizzically but can't seem to pinpoint what to ask. Mazna waits until she's halfway done with her coffee before she tells them she's decided to do it.

�֎

They stay in the bakery longer than usual. Deedee and Zakaria are closing up the store, and Mazna tries to be helpful, tidying up. It's nearly six and they've agreed to get dinner before Idris and Mazna head back to Damascus; she's filled with that gloomy, familiar sadness that reminds her of Sunday afternoons as a child — the loom of something ending. Mazna has just finished stacking the last plate when the bell rings out. It's two soldiers, the same age as Zakaria and Idris, with rifles slung over their shoulders as casually as purses.

"Evening, brothers," Deedee says warily. "We're closed."

"Your door's open, Auntie," one of them says. He's decidedly uglier than the other one, with pockmarked skin and a weak chin.

"We were about to lock it."

"Sorry, Auntie," the more handsome one says, moving through the store carelessly. "I have an awful sweet tooth and we've been patrolling all day." He taps the glass display that Zakaria has just cleaned. "An éclair, please. The chocolate one."

"She said the store's closed," Idris says just as Zakaria asks, "Is that it?"

The handsome soldier cocks his head toward Zakaria, then looks at Deedee. "You hire Palestinians, Auntie? Plenty of honest Lebanese people looking for work." He speaks lightly, but there's something dark in his tone.

"I'll pack this up for you," Deedee says coldly. "And I'll hire whom I please."

"You hear that?" the soldier says to nobody in particular. "Some folks have a short memory."

"My memory's just fine," Deedee snaps.

"Deedee, don't," Zakaria says softly.

"Palestinian vultures," the soldier spits out. "Don't you have a bus to blow up somewhere, boy?" he asks Zakaria, who clenches his jaw. Idris moves as fast as a rattlesnake toward the man.

"Get the fuck," he says quietly, "out of my aunt's bakery."

The handsome soldier clutches his rifle, but the other one nudges him. "They want trash, let them deal with the flies." He turns back to Deedee. "A brioche as well. Two."

Deedee puts the baked goods in a white bakery box and slides it over wordlessly. Mazna is amazed to see the woman's hands are steady. She herself feels faint. When the soldiers reach the door, the handsome one turns, looks Deedee over, and murmurs, "I'd keep better company if I were you, sweetheart."

The door slams shut behind them, and Idris begins to curse. Deedee joins him, lamenting the deterioration of the neighborhood, the city, the country, wondering what her father would say, God rest him, if he were still around, seeing his darling homeland run by thugs, overgrown boys with guns, not just the ones on the other side, this whole country going straight to hell without stopping for air. Zakaria keeps polishing the display, not contributing a word to the conversation.

Eventually, Idris takes Deedee outside for a cigarette, leaving them alone. Mazna is still trembling. "I don't understand how all of this happened."

Zakaria nods. He doesn't seem to want to talk, but she's running on adrenaline from the soldiers, from the time alone with him; she presses on.

"It just makes no sense. How does a country turn like that overnight? My school had nuns too, you know. And Palestinians. We have a church in our neighborhood."

"You do know," he says intently, "that Syria has troops in every neighborhood in Lebanon, don't you? That they've been involved since the very beginning?"

"Of course I do," she says, flushing. She always forgets. "But *we're* not carrying around religious ID cards."

He sighs. "We all come from tribes, Damascus. Whether we want to admit it or not. It's just that in a tiny place like Beirut, like Lebanon, you can't help but notice differences. One family sees that another has a bigger olive tree. One village wants the other's water supply. Wars have been started over less."

"What about colonizers? If it weren't for the French —"

He shrugs. "People don't need much of a reason to hate each other. We're programmed to blame others for our unhappiness. And if your priest or imam or big brother tells you a whole group of people hates *you,* it's not like you're going to stop to ask them if it's true."

"Like Tarek's brother," she says, remembering. Zakaria looks taken aback; he must have forgotten she knows Tarek. *He's never seen me perform,* Mazna suddenly realizes.

"Like Ramzi, yes," he finally says. "We all did something stupid in the name of an allegiance, and now somebody's dead." He grimaces. "Many somebodies, actually."

"But the allegiance isn't even based on truth! Half the things the politicians say are lies."

"It's true to them. It's been said enough times to become true. I could stand out here and say, 'That tree over there is purple' thousands and thousands of times and refuse to listen to anybody, and eventually —"

"The tree would not become purple," she interrupts.

"No." He smiles. "But it would to me. And that's just as good."

⁂

One week later, Mazna packs a small overnight bag. She rolls her sexiest nightgown into a slinky ball. Her mother shoots the bag a look when Mazna walks into the living room and tells her family she'll be at Lara's.

"The show's in a few weeks," she says and holds her breath. But no one says anything, not even Lulwa. Mazna feels a lukewarm triumph; she almost misses arguing with her mother. Everyone in the house seems muted these days. The adults are distracted with Jiddo. Her grandfather had left the gas stove on the previous week.

Idris is waiting in their usual spot, but he looks a little nervous. On the road to Tripoli, he blasts American music, shimmying toward Mazna with his shoulders until she laughs, feeling silly and wonderful. She looks over at him as he butchers the lyrics and feels a sudden deep, sisterly love for him. He will forgive her, she knows. They'll become good friends, old friends; they'll know each other for the rest of their lives. She has a pleasant image of them in old age on a porch somewhere while Zakaria is inside, someone — perhaps a grand-child — asking when she and Zakaria met, and Idris smiling knowingly at her, a sad, accepting sort of smile that says he knew her first, but the right thing happened.

"I almost forgot!" Idris knocks her out of her reverie. "Look in the back. I just bought it yesterday."

Mazna rustles around in the back seat. There's a black bag and, inside, a fancy-looking contraption with a lens as big as her fist. "A camera?"

"A Super 8! I spent a tiny fortune on it. But it's the best kind. It even records sound."

Her heart quickens. She knows it's childish, but the camera makes her feel guilty; she thinks of all those movies she used to watch on television back home. It's like she discarded her closest friends. "Can I use it?"

"Yes. Like this." He shows her.

There's a cushion around the eyehole and Mazna presses her eye against it; the vista is suddenly compressed, narrow. She starts filming Idris, who grins and says, "Just point and shoot," and holds up a peace sign; she turns the lens to the blurry landscape outside the car window. It's strange to think of her future self watching these images; it's like she's part of a plot against herself.

When they arrive in Beirut they eat lunch at the Wimpy Café; Idris finishes Mazda's chicken burger. Her stomach feels jumpy. The whole car ride over, she kept nudging her overnight bag with her foot as if making sure it hadn't disappeared.

"Should we walk through campus?" Idris asks as they leave the restaurant.

Mazna hesitates. "Sure. Or, well, I was hoping we could get something sweet," she says slowly.

Idris glances at her. "You gave me the rest of your burger."

"Yes," Mazna says, smiling up at him, "but dessert's different, isn't it?"

Idris keeps his eyes on her. She can see him thinking. She needs *him* to say it, this much she knows. He always needs to be the one who says it. "What about the bakery?"

She exhales. "Perfect."

Before they go into the bakery, they look through the window. There are no customers, and Mazna's heart races when she sees Zakaria standing behind the counter in his dirty apron, reading a newspaper. His hair needs a trim, and as he leans over, a few curls fall into his eyes. There's a somber expression on his face as he reads; he looks older. Idris pushes the door open; the bell clinks. He's holding the camera up as he enters.

"Tell us something good!" Idris calls out, and Zakaria jumps, cursing; his hand comes down hard on the counter. "Whoa," Idris says. "Easy there, Zu." Idris laughs. "The natural Zakaria in the wild," he jokes to the camera like a commentator, "is a wild and restless creature, never to be snuck up on."

Zakaria glances at Mazna briefly, just enough to make her swallow. She can see him trying to brighten his expression. "Six hours and not a single customer. Puts a person on edge."

Idris frowns. "Where's Deedee?"

"Her mother's not feeling well."

"Say something for the camera."

Zakaria looks directly into the lens and lowers his voice like a newscaster. "From the bowels of this particular hell, local baker and lost soul has burned not one, not two, but three trays of madeleines."

Mazna laughs and Idris swings the camera around to her. She puts her hand up, crouches down. "No more," she begs.

The camera is put away, and the men start talking about soccer. Mazna pretends to be interested in the newspaper just to see what Zakaria was reading. The headline is stark: "Hostility Rises Toward Palestinian Camps." There's a grainy photograph of tires burning, a woman with her arms outstretched.

"If no one's coming in," Idris is saying, "just close up. I was thinking of taking Mazna down to the water."

Mazna tries to keep her tone even. "Yeah, you should come."

He looks torn, then undoes his apron. "Fuck it. If Damascus can come to us, I can let the petits fours babysit themselves."

They have a long dinner on the Raouché in a small, expensive restaurant overlooking the water. Idris orders a carafe of red wine, then another, and Mazna finishes two and a half glasses, a lot for her. She has drunk more this summer than in the rest of her life combined, and her body is warming to the sour, recognizable taste. Her guilt has grown smaller, like a phantom limb forgetting itself, but as the sun sets over the water and the azan starts, she finds herself setting the glass down. She's not the only one. Zakaria also pushes his glass to the side until the call to prayer is over.

"You're both ridiculous," Idris declares, taking a healthy swig. "You're telling me God wouldn't understand this—" Here he sweeps a hand toward the sea. "That He hasn't made this world to be enjoyed."

"Might be enjoying it a bit much yourself, Iddy," Zakaria says. It's true; Idris's speech is a little slurred.

"Oh, bullshit. I don't know if you've heard, friends, but"—here he drops his voice to a whisper—"there's a war going on. If you don't drink, you die."

"I'm fairly certain that isn't how it works."

"Who knows when the next bomb will drop?" Idris asks. "Who knows if there's a bullet with your name on it? Carpe diem."

"Yeah, well, there aren't many bombs in your neighborhood." There's a slight edge in Zakaria's tone, and Mazna notices his clasped knuckles whitened.

"Who knows what—ah!" Idris is distracted. He claps his hands. "The camera," he says delightedly. Mazna catches Zakaria's eyes and is glad to see him look annoyed; he gives her a quirk of the eyebrow as if to say, *Is this for real?* She rolls her eyes, then feels a little bad. Idris is so happy.

"One wish, Zuzu!" Idris is holding the camera a bit too close to Zakaria's face. "What would it be?"

Zakaria smiles tightly. Mazna can tell he's tired of the game. "For Italy to win the World Cup," he says, and Idris hoots. He swivels the camera.

"And you?"

The camera on her feels like an interrogator's light. She tries to think of something to say, a code to Zakaria but also her future self, watching this. An image of herself flashes in her mind, an actress, successful, Zakaria running his own restaurant in Los Angeles.

"I want this summer not to end."

The men cheer. She holds her empty glass out and laughs. "Oh," she adds, "and I want the wine. All the wine."

"Fruit, sir?" The waiter appears at their table and addresses Zakaria. Mazna sees color immediately rise in Idris's cheeks; she has noticed this happen often, in bars and restaurants—waiters and valets always speak to Zakaria as though he were the one in charge, ignoring Idris.

"Just the watermelon," Idris says sharply. Mazna looks at him, surprised. "And clear these plates."

The waiter bows slightly. "Right away, sir. We'll cut it as well."

"No need," Idris says in a tone Mazna finds a little imperious. "The rind is always cut sloppily. I'll carve it myself."

Zakaria frowns but says nothing. When the waiter brings the watermelon, the green shell is freshly washed. Idris waves away the waiter's hand and takes the large knife. He plunges it into the flesh and pink juice dribbles onto the plate. He cuts one slice, then another, then lets out a shriek.

"Aiiiii!"

Everyone freezes, including Idris, who holds his bleeding hand outstretched in front of him, staring at it in disbelief. The waiter covers his mouth.

"Oh," says Mazna. "Oh." She feels sick. She hates the sight of blood.

"I need to stanch it," Idris says faintly, and she remembers he's a doctor. But he seems too rattled to move.

Zakaria springs up. "Brother," he says to the waiter, who's turned white, "brother, could you get us a towel? A nice thick one?" He speaks kindly. The waiter nods and scuttles away. "Mazna," he says, and for an instant the restaurant fades — not *Damascus*, but her actual name in his mouth — "your water glass?"

She hands it to him and watches as he rinses the cut, the blood running onto the watermelon. The waiter returns with a small towel and Zakaria wraps Idris's hand. Mazna watches Idris's face relax, like a calmed cat, as Zakaria murmurs to him.

"It needs to be tight," Idris says.

Zakaria scans the restaurant. "Wait!" Mazna cries out. She pulls the elastic from her ponytail, and her hair tumbles onto her shoulders. The men look at her, and she feels their simultaneous admiration like an arrow. She holds out the red elastic. A few black strands are tangled in it.

Zakaria ties it twice, thrice around the towel. He clamps a hand on Idris's shoulder.

"Let's get out of here."

❈

The three of them return to the House. The route is familiar to her and she walks easily through the streets, but it's the first time she's been inside the House in the evening and it seems richer somehow, a little unfriendly.

"Sara already told Mama you're staying over," Idris says. He's regained some of his excitement, though his face is still a little pale.

"Oh, good." Mazna tries to sound unconcerned, but she has a bad feeling in the pit of her stomach. Before she can make sense of it, Sara appears in the doorway. She's wearing pajamas and her glasses. Despite seeing each other a fair amount, they've never been alone, and Mazna is still a little shy around her. "Hi, Sara."

She gives Mazna a mischievous smile. "There she is!" she says. "So glad we're finally doing a sleepover."

Mazna is embarrassed. Sara probably thinks she's a whore. "Th-thanks," she stammers.

"Where's Mama?" Idris asks.

"In her room, I think," Sara says to Idris. She hugs Zakaria easily and Mazna feels the usual flare of envy as he kisses her cheek. "Hi, Zuzu."

"Hi, *habibti*." Zakaria seems more confident around Sara. Mazna's stomach tightens. *She's basically his little sister,* she admonishes herself.

"What happened to you?" Sara asks Idris, noticing the towel around his hand.

Idris ignores the question. "And Baba?"

"He's right here," a voice booms from behind them. Salim looks worried. "Answer your sister."

"Just a little cut . . ." Idris mumbles. He looks younger all of a sudden.

His father peers at Mazna over his glasses and says, mock seriously, "I thought you were keeping these boys out of trouble, dear."

"I tried, Uncle. They're unmanageable," she says. He turns his attention back to Idris's hand.

"What happened, Iddy?" Hana says, coming into the room. She is wearing a long blue nightgown. "We've been waiting for Mazna."

"I told them you've been on campus," Sara says quickly.

"Yes, Auntie. Preparing for a role." Remembering that Idris's father saw them come in together, she amends, "I ran into the boys and we got some dinner."

"How nice, dear. Well, we're so happy you'll be staying with us this weekend." Hana turns her attention to Idris. "But Iddy, darling, what's happened here?"

His father nods toward the hand. "Let's see it."

Idris winces as they unwrap the towel. Sara lets out a thrilled squeal. Their father whistles. "It's a deep one. But this tourniquet is nicely done. Was it you, son?" He glances at Zakaria, who nods. Mazna notices something flicker among the three men, Zakaria smiling shyly at the older man's compliment, something shuttering in Idris's face.

"I told him how," Idris says flatly.

"Let's go to the bathroom," his father says. "It needs a little peroxide." Mazna remembers Idris telling her his father had done a year of medical school, then dropped out. She wonders if that's why Idris wanted to become a doctor; there's something oedipal about the thought. Suddenly it seems odd to her that she's never asked Idris about any of this but she knows plenty of details about Zakaria's life — the father that died young, the sisters that teach in the camps. She half listens when Idris talks but hooks desperately onto Zakaria's every word. "You too, Zuzu, you can help me."

"Don't forget the bandages, Salim, dear," Hana calls out. The three women make small talk in the living room as they wait. There's something distinct about Sara that makes Mazna a little uncomfortable. She reminds her of Fatima somehow — frank, unfeminine. When the men come back, they all seem a little relieved. They're strangely excited, whispering among themselves. Idris is holding something in his unbandaged hand.

"Looks like there won't be an amputation after all," Mazna jokes.

"No push-ups for a few days," Salim says. He swats the air. "He'll be fine."

"Well, thank God," Sara says. "Idris almost ruined the surprise."

"What surprise?" Mazna asks.

"Ah!" Salim glances at his son. "Well, we knew you were staying over tonight."

"And Idris told us about London! That you have some internship coming up." Hana clasps her hands over her heart, clearly thinking of London. "How wonderful for you, dear."

"I haven't gotten it yet," she says faintly. It feels like she's in a dream, her head already bleary from the wine earlier.

"We wanted to celebrate," Hana says, ignoring her comment.

"Voilà!" Idris holds something out, clearly thrilled. It's a videocassette.

"It was my idea!" Hana announces. "The cover, I mean."

"Tarek's crew filmed it," Idris says. "And we had it transferred to a video-cassette."

"I don't —" Mazna clears her throat. "I'm not sure what —"

Zakaria takes the cassette from Idris and holds it out to Mazna. "Look at the cover," he says quietly. Even he seems unusually excited. Mazna turns it over and finds her face looking back at her. In profile, glancing upward, sharply done red lipstick.

She looks up, dumbfounded. "How?" she manages.

They all just grin at her. Above the image of her face, the words *Meet Me in Ramleh* arch, like an honest-to-God film poster. Tears rise in her throat, and she blinks, her photographed face blurring into a splotch of color. Nobody has ever done anything like this for her.

"It's too much." She doesn't realize she's spoken aloud until she hears their laughter. Zakaria catches her eye for a second and sees her tears, her hard, desperate gratitude, she's sure of it, but then Sara is excitedly telling her to sit, sit, they've been waiting all week to watch.

"I have to tell you, dear," Hana says once they've settled down, Mazna discreetly wiping her eyes on her sleeve and clearing her throat, "I almost took a peek myself earlier today, but Salim caught me."

"Where did you even get it from?"

"It's the one Tarek filmed, remember? He did it for Zuzu, and we had it transferred to a videocassette so we could watch it on the VCR, but I kept forgetting to pick it up. And Baba did the cover in the shop."

"Thank you," she tells Salim. She can feel the tears dangerously close again, but he pats her shoulder and sets up the VHS player. He pats the machine as well, in a straightforward manner, and it reminds her of her father, as if she were in a parallel life. She tucks her legs beneath her, pretending she's their daughter. This is her couch. The family is settling in to watch her latest movie — but of course, they would've seen it live as well, so maybe this is a tradition, watching it twice — and afterward they will talk and laugh. Zakaria is her brother's best friend and she's in love with him.

Sara and Hana sit on either side of Mazna, and they share a plate of sliced strawberries. Mazna can see Zakaria only in profile from here. The recording is better than she would've expected, and the camera seeks out her face over and over. There she is, flouncing on her fake bed. Wiping her face. Running down a street in Beirut. She is a little embarrassed at the amateur set design, but the family seems to love it.

"That's exactly what Hamra Street is like," Salim muses.

"Tarek has outdone himself. He even remembered the grocer's broken sign!"

"War tells you who you are," Mazna's onscreen self says. She knows most people hate the sound of their own voices, but Mazna rather likes hers. She sounds like a smoker. She glances again at Zakaria; his expression is solemn, almost beatific.

"This is the best scene!" Idris pipes up, and Sara and Hana shush him. They all watch a costumed Mazna walk across the stage and embrace Ralph. Her onscreen self smokes a slim cigarette. The camera zooms in on her face, her eyes shining with tears. She feels turned on watching herself, the shape of her breasts visible against the thin material of her dress, her ankles flashing nakedly as she walks across the stage.

She thinks of the after-party, of Tarek saying he'd had a crew member film the show for Zakaria. This was for him. This was for him before she even knew him.

The family is full of compliments afterward; Hana calls her *an incontestable star.* Even Sara seems friendlier, with newfound admiration. Mazna waits, but Zakaria says nothing; he looks preoccupied and a little sad, and while Hana is showing her a print of the cover still they made her, he slips out of the room, unnoticed by all except Mazna.

"Thank you, Tante," she says distractedly. "And thank you, Amo, for this print. It's the best gift ever." She means it. But she wants to leave the gathering and follow Zakaria down the hallway.

"Mazna," Hana says in a low voice. She glances at her son — at his dopey smiling face — in a meaningful way that makes Mazna's stomach sink. "We're so happy to have you here."

Sara leads her to the bedroom. It's the one room Mazna has never seen; Sara always keeps the door shut. "Come on," she tells Mazna, "you'll be staying with me." They walk through a dark hallway. "Normally," she whispers, "we put visitors in the guest room, but that would be strange since you're my *classmate.*" There's a touchiness in her tone. "It'll be a little tight, but it's okay."

Mazna nearly laughs aloud when she walks in. *A little tight.* The room is probably twice the size of Mazna's, with a desk and an armoire. It's decorated in yellow and white; there's a canopy bed with a battered-looking stuffed bear on it. The bed is large enough for the two of them, but a mat has been rolled out next to it, a white cable-knit blanket on top. The mat reminds her of the cot she saw in Idris's room. She and Zakaria, beloved guests. *But nonfamily members,* she thinks, a little unfairly, *sleep on the floor.*

They take turns in the little bathroom adjacent to Sara's room, Mazna peeing and washing her face with the cleanser by the sink. She changes into the wispy nightgown she'd brought with her, and when she enters the bedroom, Sara claps.

"That's beautiful," she says appreciatively. Her own pajamas have cartoon birds printed on them. "Is it real silk?"

"Yes," Mazna lies.

Sara yawns, stretching her arms. Her pajamas are too small, and the top rides up to her bellybutton. She flicks the lamp off and they get into their respective beds. "Don't freak out if the electricity cuts off in the night. There's a little flashlight on the sink if you need to go."

"Do you ever hear bombs here?" Mazna asks. Her heartbeat accelerates at the thought. She tries to imagine what Lulwa would do if her body were found in the rubble of this girl's bathroom.

Sara hums. "Sometimes. We're far away from most of it. A lot of the apartment buildings have shelters in the basement. Here, we'll just sit in the bathtubs."

"The bathtubs?"

"It's the safest place," Sara explains. "And it's away from the windows."

"Ah."

They speak for another ten, fifteen minutes of predictable things — Mazna's work at the firm, Sara's university classes. Sara's voice becomes blurry with sleep and she says, in a simple, childlike way, "I'm going to sleep now. Good night."

"Good night."

The only illumination is a night-light near Sara's bed and the glow of the street lamps outside the window. Mazna listens to Sara's soft breathing punctuated by the occasional car honk from the street. She feels too riled up to sleep, her hands trembling. The image of Zakaria in bed or walking around, getting a glass of water, keeps her awake.

Suddenly she is plunged into complete darkness. Mazna blinks, disoriented, thinking herself asleep. But no, she's awake, and the room is black, no night-light, no street lamps glowing outside the window. She remembers a news report she watched with her father explaining Beirut's electricity grid, how there are blackouts across entire neighborhoods. She lies still for several moments, counting her breaths.

The decision is quick. Mazna kicks off the blanket, knowing swiftly what she's known all week — that she was always going to do this, move through the sleeping household to find Zakaria. If he's awake, she thinks, then he's awake for her. The bedroom door shuts obediently behind her. Tiptoeing in the absolute dark through the hallway, Mazna feels blindly with her fingers and bare feet, nearly tripping on the corner of a rug in the living room. There, past the bulky shape of the couch and coffee table, is the veranda, faint moonlight. A silhouette. Too tall for Idris.

Mazna's body is purring. She weaves between the furniture until she reaches the door. The swish of the door opening makes Zakaria jump. The night air is cool, and she feels her nipples harden in the breeze.

"You're awake," she says stupidly. He's smoking, but there's something in his other hand that he's absentmindedly fidgeting with. She tries to think of something smart to say. "Is Idris okay?"

Zakaria turns back to the yard. The cigarette glows as he inhales. "His father stitched him up. He'll be fine."

"Good." There's a long silence. "Sara's great. We talked a bit."

"Yeah, she's a strange little thing." He glances over at her. "Did the electricity cut scare you?"

"No," she says defensively. "I just wanted some . . . air." It isn't her best line, and now that she's outside, she's a little cold. She hopes he'll give her his flannel shirt. He's wearing an undershirt beneath. She feels an instinctive pang for theater — it's been years, it seems like, since she's performed. She crosses her arms under her breasts, channeling Vivian, channeling Audrey and Ava and Lauren Bacall, all those beautiful, ill-fated women.

Zakaria smiles as he shrugs off his shirt. "Dressed like that? How peculiar."

She bursts into laughter. The flannel is scratchy and smells like smoke. "I'm an impractical dresser," she admits.

"Well." Another glance. "It's a nice color. Like magnolias. My mother loves them."

There. Her first compliment from him. Mazna shuts her eyes briefly, soaking it up. "Those are the big white ones?"

"Big as your head, some of them. There was a tree in the camps a long time ago. Some white lady with an NGO had it brought over. But it's not the right climate. One winter and it was gone. My mother was a little crazy about the tree. She spent months trying to bring it back."

"That's terrible."

Zakaria looks at her sharply, like he thinks she might be teasing, but Mazna can so clearly see a heartbroken woman fighting to revive a dead plant. He relaxes. "She cried. I still remember it. I was five or six; my father had just died. I was playing in the house, and she came in with her hands all dirty and said, *Not a goddamn thing can be saved.*"

As Mazda listens to him, Damascus feels as far away as the moon. Her nightgown is embarrassing. Her cheap perfume is embarrassing. What a silly life she leads back in Syria.

"I'm sorry," she finally says.

"For my father or the tree?" A glint of humor returns to his face, though she notices he's still clenching his fist around whatever's in his hand.

Mazna takes a small step toward him. She imagines the tree scene in a movie: A tired woman returning to her tiny home, no state to belong to, her fingernails broken from the digging. She can hear Tarek demanding, *But why,*

Mazna, why would she want to save the tree? What's the character's motivation?
"It sounds like they were the same thing for her," she says quietly.

His face changes. Zakaria takes one last drag and puts the cigarette out on the sole of his shoe. She notices how carefully he extinguishes it, then how he pockets the butt, even though there are others in the garden, likely Idris's.

"That," he says, facing her, "is a very accurate way of putting it."

They turn away from each other and stand silently for a long time, thinking different thoughts, staring out at the dark, until suddenly, one by one, the lights of various buildings and street lamps come back on, an orchestra performing just for them.

"Oh," she whispers. Mazna imagines herself here every night, standing in this exact spot with Zakaria — a wedding, children. Never mind the war, she tells herself. Never mind that she'll be in London in less than two months. They can go to California together. Never mind the camps, the Palestinian visa, the matter of money. Her father had done this, hadn't he? Fallen in love with someone unsuited for him, chosen that person over everything else? Mazna has been a woman long enough to know — she would bet everything she has that Zakaria feels what she does.

"This house is like something out of a book," she says. She means it as a compliment but almost instantly senses something shift between them.

"It's not mine," he says, looking at her strangely.

Of course. She thinks of the mat next to Idris's bed. She'll never stand on this balcony night after night. It isn't Zakaria's. It isn't hers. She takes one last step toward him and he moves to pocket the item in his hand, but she sees the flash of red.

Her hair tie.

Zakaria sees her see. He clears his throat. "Here." He holds his hand out. "Idris left it in his father's study."

"You can keep it," Mazna says, her mouth so dry the words crack. But he continues holding his hand out until she reaches for it; he presses it into her palm, his own hot and dry.

✦

The next morning Mazna wakes late, her body stiff from the mat. The room is empty, Sara's bed unmade, her bird pajamas tossed in the middle of the pile of sheets. Mazna makes up the mat, then gets dressed.

She follows the sound of voices into the living room, then toward the kitchen. There's an appealing series of photographs in the hallway, close-ups of a spice market. She wonders if Idris's father printed them at his shop. The kitchen's a large, airy space, now with a strong smell of coffee and fried eggs. She hesitates at the sight of Zakaria sitting near the window, Sara at his side. He's wearing the same flannel shirt; she'd left it on the couch before returning to Sara's room last night. Sara is gesturing, telling a story, Zakaria nodding along. Idris stands at the sink with a thermometer sticking out of his mouth, looking pale and irritated. Hana, arms crossed next to him, is frowning.

"What's happened?" Mazna asks.

Idris grunts around the thermometer. "He's feverish," Zakaria says. "Morning." His voice is a little different, croaky from sleep.

"Morning," she manages. She feels the flush spread to her collarbone, her chest, belly, below.

Idris spits the thermometer out. "This thing is broken, I swear to God."

"Give it to me."

"Mama, I'm perfectly capable of reading a —"

"Give it to me."

Idris reluctantly hands it over; his mother whistles. "A hundred and one! Your father was right." She glances over at Mazna. "That fruit knife must've been dirty. He's been feverish all night. Can you imagine? Our doctor said if his temperature's above ninety-nine, it's antibiotics and bed for the day."

Mazna feels a sharp panic. She is suddenly unmoored. What will she do without him? How will she return to Damascus tomorrow? "That's too bad," she says faintly.

Idris catches her eye and mouths, *Sorry.*

"Why are you still here?" Hana says, turning back to her son. "Bed. Now."

After he leaves, Hana makes Mazna a plate of fried eggs and tomatoes and pita. Mazna sits, her stomach knotted.

Sara pats her hand sympathetically. "I was going to do a little shopping," she whispers. "You can come with me."

"Thanks." Mazna turns to look at Zakaria. Hana is rinsing a plate, out of earshot. She wills him to say something.

He clears his throat. "I'll be at the bakery all day," he says. "Don't get out until six. Otherwise . . ." He lets the sentence trail off.

❊

Sara takes Mazna to a nearby neighborhood, where they spend the morning window-shopping along the main street. They're the kind of stores that Mazna would've loved in high school—selling kitschy trinkets, cheap costume jewelry—but they depress her now, and she fakes enthusiasm each time Sara asks what she thinks of some necklace or skirt. The girl runs on chatter. She shares her brother's trait of assuming interest on the part of the other person. Every other sentence begins with *Isn't this* or *Don't you just love,* so Mazna needs only to half listen as they walk through the neighborhood, occasionally chiming in that she does indeed love the ghastly orange scarf and matching purse.

She knows she's being difficult, but the entire day feels soured by Idris's idiocy. The plan had been to spend time at the bakery, then convince Deedee to let Zakaria leave early so the three of them could go to the beach. But she has no telephone number for Deedee's bakery, nothing but those few seconds that morning in the kitchen, and now she's adrift in Beirut, trailing along with this prattling girl.

But eventually Sara tires of shopping and surprises Mazna by turning to her and asking thoughtfully, "Where should we go now?"

Mazna can't think of anywhere aside from the bakery, but she knows that'll sound peculiar, so she just says the beach, and Sara seems excited by the answer. She hails a stuffy cab. Neither of them has a bathing suit. "But we can just go in in our underwear," Sara says, then bursts into laughter at Mazna's shocked face. "Joking." She gives a sly smile. "Kind of."

At the beach, they rent chairs from the poor sweating uncle in a hat and lie out under the sun.

"So," Sara says. She's wearing round sunglasses that are a little big on her face. "You and my brother."

Mazna feels her stomach drop. Of course. "Your brother is" — Mazna hesitates — "a good friend."

Sara grins. "He's, like, *gravely* in love with you."

"Oh," Mazna says faintly.

"He talks about you constantly." Sara thinks. "You make him happy," she says simply.

Mazna feels sick. The sun is suddenly too hot. She wishes they'd gone for drinks in some dark, air-conditioned bar instead of coming here. "A good friend," she repeats weakly. "He and Zakaria both are."

Sara pushes her sunglasses onto her head and cuts her eyes to Mazna. Her expression changes. "I'm so glad Zakaria's back home for a while," she finally says quietly. "We missed him."

A couple on a nearby towel are arguing about something. The woman calls the man a dog. Mazna watches Sara warily from behind her own sunglasses. There's a slightly perceptible chill emanating from her. "I'm glad his mother is feeling better," she says.

"Oh, Auntie Hayat." Sara clasps her hands like a choirgirl. Her face relaxes. "She's my favorite. I haven't seen her in ages, but she, like, half raised me." She laughs, then stops abruptly. "Don't tell my mom I said that. When I was a kid, Auntie Hayat used to let me hang on to her back while she mopped. It was like a carnival ride!"

"How sweet," Mazna says, but she thinks it sounds bratty; Sara just made the poor woman work harder. No wonder her back gave out.

"She'd usually just bring Zakaria, but sometimes his sisters would come help with the cleaning." Sara laughs again, a pretty sound. "I was pretty much in love with them. I'd even comb my dolls' hair before they arrived to impress them."

"So you knew the whole family," Mazna says. She'd forgotten about the sisters and wants desperately to ask Sara for their names, but she knows it would be suspicious.

There's a loud shout, and they look over to see a couple of men arguing about something. Although it seems mild enough, some of the nearby sunbathers start packing up their things. A concerned-looking lifeguard walks over, speaks to them in hushed tones. One of the men is short, with a hairy belly hanging over his trunks. He's red in the face and shouting something at the other man. When the lifeguard places a hand on his shoulder, the shorter man shoves it off. Mazna can feel her heart rate quicken.

"Sometimes they have guns," Sara says casually. "There was a shooting a few weeks ago, near a school. Some guys from the east picked a fight and . . ." The sentence dangles.

A long silence settles over them. The lifeguard has given each man what looks like a drink ticket, and they seem pacified. The couple nearby are quiet now, the woman silently applying lotion on her legs. On the Corniche, a man goes jogging by in blue shorts that stop near his groin. He grins at them.

"What silly shorts." Sara giggles, and she's back to being a girl of nineteen again.

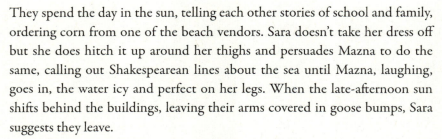

They spend the day in the sun, telling each other stories of school and family, ordering corn from one of the beach vendors. Sara doesn't take her dress off but she does hitch it up around her thighs and persuades Mazna to do the same, calling out Shakespearean lines about the sea until Mazna, laughing, goes in, the water icy and perfect on her legs. When the late-afternoon sun shifts behind the buildings, leaving their arms covered in goose bumps, Sara suggests they leave.

"I was thinking of visiting my friend Tamara. She's doing some work at the library on campus. Do you want to come?"

Mazna's heart soars with the opportunity. "I think," she says carefully, "I'd like to walk around."

Sara frowns. "There are a couple of checkpoints in this area."

Mazna has a map of the city in her mind. "I'll go along the Corniche."

"Are you sure? Do you know how to get back?"

She nods. "I have a good head for directions."

"Well." Sara looks reluctant but Mazna can tell she'd like to be alone. "The back door, near the big tree, is always unlocked," she says finally. "Whoever gets there first can just pretend the other has a headache and is lying down." Her face brightens. "That way we can stay out late."

The tricks of girls everywhere, Mazna thinks. She smiles and says she will. After Sara leaves, she wanders the beach for a while, a little stunned that she's alone in an unfamiliar country. The sun has taken most of the couples and sunbathers with it, but there are a few families eating sandwiches, some young boys kicking a ball around. Mazna slips her shoes off and walks barefoot, pretending she lives in one of the modish apartments overlooking the water, that she comes here every weekend.

The walk back toward the city is long and enjoyable. She sees only a couple of soldiers, eating shawarma outside a diner, and they just grin at her as she walks past. It's sixish, she can tell from the slanting sun, but a faint outline of the moon is visible, white as a girl's slip. She hadn't been lying about having a good head for directions. Her mind organizes streets and houses and signposts as neatly as a diagram. When she was younger, on family trips to the beach in Latakia, her father would always wink at her in the rearview and joke, "Make sure you pay attention, because I'm never going to get out of this town without that camera mind of yours."

Now she strolls easily between the peak-roofed houses, remembering that the small *dikaneh* with a broken sign means she should take a right, which leads her past the ivy-covered mosque to the garden plot, where she takes a final left.

There, between the hairdresser's and the shuttered storefront — the bakery.

She doesn't hesitate. Deedee is nowhere in sight, and the counter is empty. The bell tinkles when she pushes open the door. She doesn't call out his name, just waits, and after a moment, Zakaria walks out of the back room and sees her. His face startles and loosens at the same time; years later, she'll remember his expression as one of inevitability.

"We're closed" is all he says, reminding Mazna of the night the soldiers came. "Deedee's gone for the night."

"Then you should lock the door." She turns to click the lock shut. Her mind is racing. She moves closer to him. It feels like the first few seconds of a play, when everything freezes and she has to leave her body to become the role. There's an open newspaper on the counter. An image of bodies, grainy black-and-white. The headline reads "Beirut Split on Religious Lines."

"I don't understand," she says, "how in the same city you can have people going to the beach and also dying from bombs. How a place can let both those things happen at the same time."

He seems amused. "This country is honest. You have to give it that."

"But these men fighting each other — they were playing football together a few summers ago."

"They still are."

"It's like some part of their brains got flipped on."

"Like a sleeper cell."

Mazna sits at a table and looks at him blankly.

"They're like spies," he explains. "They're inactive until their commander decides to wake them up."

Mazna thinks suddenly of her grandfather. *Why don't you just die already?* Her grandfather is a sleeper cell, she thinks, a body that housed eight decades' worth of secrets and lies, an entire household's mistakes. He was a sleeper who'd been jostled awake and was now walking through the house, setting off tiny bombs wherever he went. She thinks of him so rarely, her jiddo, that he might as well be dead. For a moment, she's filled with such intense longing for her childhood, for her grandfather, that she blinks back tears.

"What is it?" Zakaria asks.

Mazna shrugs, looking down.

He sits next to her and rests his chin in his hand like a boy. "Tell me," he says.

"My grandfather's been sick for a long time. His mind . . . he lost it, and now he constantly reveals things he shouldn't. I know it's different, they're just family secrets, but, I don't know. It seems violent somehow."

The comparison feels stupid, but Zakaria just nods, so she keeps talking. She tells him about how she used to perform news reports with her grandfather when she was a child, then about her family, her sister who visits only every couple of weeks. Zakaria lets her talk, and before she knows it, she's crying, telling him about how she had planned to be in California by now but instead she's been doing small shows in the theater for years and how maybe it was all a delusion, but she's always wanted to be in films, to be famous, so much so that she was proud — here she buries her face in her hands in shame —

proud when that boy chose her in the alleyway all those years ago, and pretty soon she's crying so hard she can't gulp air fast enough and Zakaria reaches out, takes her hand, and holds it hard, firmly, and she calms down. There are sounds of cars from outside, and the street has darkened. Mazna's eyes fall on the open newspaper, and she feels bratty and childish, crying over her silly life.

She keeps her eyes down, too afraid to look at him.

"Mazna," he finally says. He waits for her to meet his gaze. "I've never seen anyone cry so messily in my life."

It is the perfect thing to say. They both laugh. She feels something in her release, a balloon slipping into the sky, and in that second the electricity cuts off.

The bakery is a foreign place in the dark; the back mirrors spray shards of moonlight across the walls. Mazna's mouth is bone-dry. She shuts her eyes and a life unspools in front of her, reverberating, splashing like film from a projector: a wedding in Damascus, her father's grim but accepting face, envelopes filled with money, jewelry she can pawn, a house in California, summers in Beirut, near the camps but not in them, maybe somewhere in the mountains, away from the war.

"You should see your face when you're lost in thought," Zakaria says, breaking up her reverie. "You give a lot away."

Mazna flushes. "You can barely even see me!" She pauses. "Tarek told me the same thing," she confesses. "He said that for an actress, I have a bad poker face."

Zakaria looks puzzled. "Does an actress need a poker face? Isn't the point to reveal feelings?"

Mazna thinks, then bursts into laughter. "You know, you're right. You're right!" She drops her voice. "So what am I thinking of, then?"

"You're thinking of the future," he says shyly.

Mazna looks at him, stunned.

Zakaria laughs. "Lucky guess," he admits. "Isn't that what most people are thinking of?"

"I wish I could see where you live." The words, inelegant, are out before Mazna planned to say them.

He tugs his right earlobe, a habit Mazna has memorized for a theater role. "You shouldn't romanticize the camps," he says in an empty tone.

"I don't." She's hurt.

He seems to sense her sincerity. "Nothing to see there, Damascus. Just four walls, like anywhere else. Smaller and dirtier, but it's just where people live. My mother always says the camps are where God forgets to visit."

"I'm not God," she says jokingly, but he doesn't laugh. She can just make out his eyelashes in the dim light. "I'm sorry." She means it.

"Mazna." Her name sits like a pet in his mouth. It sounds like what you'd call a woman. "I should walk you back."

She pitches herself at him.

It is a second, or a millisecond, and yet a cosmos unto itself, Mazna's body moving toward his, her hands reaching his shoulders, and then, as though that grants their bodies permission, their knees touching, the tip of her nose, the tip of his nose; there's the sound of a car honk several streets away, Zakaria's breath, shallow, audible, his eyelashes like black wings as Mazna leans into him, Mazna, *not* Liz Taylor, *not* Ava Gardner, but Mazna Adib, wanting and taking, performing for no one but herself.

The kiss is long and deep and lasts for approximately five seconds before Zakaria turns away.

"This is wrong," he begins. He shuts his eyes. "You know why."

Mazna feels a shock of despair. "Why?" She hurls the word at him. Then she answers her own question. "Because of Idris." Her fury is rapid and unreasonable and absolute. It doesn't matter what she feels; Idris has laid claim to her. "I don't want him! I never did!" She knows she sounds like a child, but she can't stop. "You pretend like you're brothers. Your family *worked for him.*"

Zakaria pulls away from her, a look of disgust in his eyes. "Don't," he says sharply, "do that. You're better than that."

"I'm not." Mazna feels her breath come fast and ragged.

"Idris is my bro —"

"God!" Mazna stands up. She wants to stamp her feet. The bottled-up lying and anger and lust of the summer is shaken loose like sand from hair. Her craving turns to bubbly rage; she wants to hurt both of them, these men who didn't even *exist* a few months ago and in whose lives she is now irrevocably caught. She wants to erase that look from Zakaria's face; she wants to break something that has existed longer than her. She leans down until her nose is nearly touching his. "You know what he said?" She can see flint in his eyes and wants to turn it into fire. "He said the camps are filled with trash, that people like your mother have more kids than they can feed." She straightens, panting, triumphant. Idris hadn't been talking about Zakaria's mother exactly, but he had said it, weeks ago, as they'd driven by the Nahr al-Bared camp. "He said it —ask him!"

Zakaria looks stunned. He lets out an ugly bark of a laugh. "You're so used to getting what you want," he says precisely.

Her rage collapses in on itself like a cake. She wishes she could take it back. "I didn't mean it." She starts to apologize more fervently. Her throat is prickly with tears, but she holds them back, stammering as she recants, says she's being a bitch, that she's wanted him since they first met. "Idris is a good friend," she says, then pauses, the words a déjà vu, and she remembers saying the same words to Sara earlier, though that feels like weeks ago. She knows what she's been doing with Idris, knows that he thinks she wants him the way he wants her. "But I kept coming back to see you. All this time. I didn't know if it was in my head, if I was the only one —"

"You're not."

Zakaria's words silence her. He looks stricken, yes, but also something else. Relieved. This time, he kisses her, stopping only to ask, "You're sure?" She nods, says yes once, twice, kisses him back harder. It's forceful and inelegant, their teeth clanking in the beginning, but like dancers they find a tempo, and he pushes her against the counter.

"The street," he mutters and goes to lower the steel gate outside the store. When he returns, Mazna has slipped her dress off, her first time naked in front of a man. He asks again if she's sure, and this time she doesn't answer, her ears are so filled with pounding, and it feels impossible that this is something she shouldn't do, that it would anger her mother or father or God, that anyone would want to deny someone this feeling. For once, her body feels tailored just for her, and she feels love for it, her housebroken animal, her breasts hardening for Zakaria, her legs knowing when to part like someone whispered the role to them.

They make love on the bakery floor, flour and lint rolling into their hair. It hurts but Mazna bleeds less than she thought she would. Even through the twinge, she feels a quiet shudder of something good, like she's meeting herself for the first time. Everything in the room is magnified, her sighs, noise from the street, the drip of a rain gutter somewhere, Zakaria's breath against her neck, the cold, square tiles beneath her bare back. They do it once, then two more times. At some point, Zakaria knocks a bag over, and the powdered sugar splatters on them, graying their hair, and they laugh and laugh like children cutting school, Mazna opening her mouth to catch the sugar like snow.

❈

They don't return to the House until late; every light is turned off. Mazna prays that Sara hasn't forgotten to tell Idris that she went to bed with a head-ache. But the House seems static with sleep. Zakaria keeps his finger to his lips as they sneak across the courtyard. Her underwear is still sticky, flecked with blood that won't wash out (not even later, when she scrubs it with salt back home in her bathtub). They haven't touched each other since they walked out of the bakery, but once they step into the dark foyer, he puts his hand on her shoulder. Mazna thinks she hears a tiny sound, footsteps, something coming from the living room, but when she turns, everything is dark, unmoving, the large, expensive furniture still as conspirators. She feels wrong returning to the House, like she's just cheated on the very bricks, on the couches and bathtubs, on Hana and Salim and Sara. And Idris. She can't think about Idris. Her joy is too greedy, a massive, resplendent snake, quick to eat any morsel of sadness or guilt. Zakaria leans over and kisses her, once, before slipping down the hallway. Mazna covers her mouth with steady fingers, as though memorizing the touch, then goes in the opposite direction.

❈

The week passes agonizingly slowly. The morning after her night with Za-karia, she'd woken too early and sat in the kitchen alone, waiting. But it was Idris who'd padded out first, looking truly awful, and told her he wasn't well enough to drive, that he'd asked Majed to drive Mazna back.

"He'll be here in fifteen," Idris said, and Mazna bit her lip with frustration.

She'd been hoping for some more time with Zakaria, but Majed was there before she could even say goodbye to him. She kissed Idris on the cheek, feeling her first pang of guilt since the night before; his skin was clammy and warm.

"Rest up," she told Idris kindly. "I had a fine time."

The car ride back with Majed was predictably awful. He kept the radio on a news channel, and a bored-sounding man droned on about the camps: "Palestinians in our country are a catastrophe. What kind of nation opens its doors when it doesn't have enough for its own?"

"Amen," Majed muttered, surprising Mazna.

Even though she knew it was best to keep her mouth shut, she couldn't help asking him, "How can you listen to that nonsense?"

Majed sighed like she was an incurably stupid. "Look, I'm an economist. It's basic supply and demand. A war changes the economy. There's little room for empathy when people are starving in the streets."

She chewed her lip. Outside the window, the water and the rocky coastline blurred by. The night before, Zakaria seemed to break open after they'd made love. Sex made him accessible; it cracked his shyness like an egg. She asked him about his mother, his sisters. He told her about watching his mother clean Hana's house year after year, about how he felt happiest in the early mornings, when everyone was still asleep and he was alone with the sun and trees and birds. He told her about his childhood, and when she asked about the camps again, he didn't scold her.

No one should have to see their family like that, he'd said. *If even one of your people is living in exile, then you all are. That's what Darwish always says.*

She shifted in the car's seat, a hot tremor suddenly shooting between her legs at the memory of Zakaria's bare chest, the buzz of his throat against her ear as he spoke. "But where would they go?"

Majed sent her a withering look. "How about Damascus?"

She shut up for the rest of the car ride.

❈

Idris calls her on Wednesday. Her nails are all bitten to the quick, but she feels happy. Whereas before, she'd spent the days distracted, preoccupied by Zakaria and what would happen, resentful of her stupid job and family dinners, now she feels liberated, answering the phones at work cheerfully, talking to her grandfather for the first time in a while, asking if he liked his soup, complimenting her mother on the pound cake. She sees her mother and Khalto Seham exchange looks, but she just smiles into her water glass.

"I'm so sorry about last weekend," Idris says. He sounds normal again. "Sara told me you had a nice time at the beach?"

"She's wonderful," Mazna tells him. "We had a great time."

"Would you want to come back Saturday? I'm sure you won't want to do another overnighter, but just for the day."

Mazna curses silently. It would be strange for her to contradict him. "Sure," she says lightly. "I'll see you at the market at ten."

On Saturday, Mazna puts on her favorite striped skirt and practically jogs to the market, excited even to see Idris. She'll be kind during the car ride. They'll break the news soon, her and Zakaria. In a few weeks. Before London, for sure. They'd spoken about it briefly that night, Zakaria shaking his head in awe.

"You're a madwoman. You do understand I'm the son of a housekeeper, don't you? A *retired* housekeeper at that. I share a room with roaches."

Mazna laughed. She felt light as air. "I don't care! My father barely has any money left either. We just have the house. It's all for show for the neighbors anyway. We'll move to London. We'll work and save money for America."

"And what about my laissez-passer travel papers?"

"You can apply for asylum." She wasn't entirely certain what that was, but she'd heard Fatima mention it. "And the theater pays well if I get the job."

Zakaria shook his head as though she were crazy, but he said, "I'm sure London has bakeries."

The marketplace is filled with families and tourists. A young boy is juggling three apples and when he catches her eye, he smiles shyly. Ten, twenty minutes pass. The juggling boy's mother scolds him when he drops the fruit, then pulls him away by the wrist. Mazna waves at him. More people come and go, some carrying ice cream cones, women laughing loudly in groups. Mazna's palms start to sweat. She wonders if Idris is still ill, if his infection has somehow gotten worse. What if he dies? Her mind flashes to an image of herself dressed in black, weeping, Zakaria putting his arm around her, telling her to be brave.

It's nearly three in the afternoon when she finally leaves, defeated. She is in a dark mood, angry at Idris. He determines whether she goes to Beirut or not, she realizes. For a few crazed minutes, she considers buying a bus ticket. But she's too scared of being molested. Eventually she forces herself to walk near the university. There's a Moroccan restaurant that she's passed hundreds of times, and she goes in. There are only a couple of other patrons, and the waiter brings her a pretty blue bowl filled with lentil soup. It's spicy but she eats the whole thing, then tips the bowl back to her mouth.

She walks east instead of north, all the way to the movie theater, and watches the same movie twice in a row, Olivia Newton-John's pretty face filling up the screen. The theater is cold and a little smelly. When Olivia appears in her skintight pants, she claps along with the other moviegoers.

It's late by the time she gets home, almost ten; she's spent nearly six hours out, and the effect is bracing, like she's taken a cold shower. The house is silent, and she makes herself a sugar-and-butter sandwich in the kitchen, thinking of Olivia's full breasts in the film. Licking crumbs from her fingertips, Mazna makes her way through the darkened rooms, the long hallway of bedrooms, hers beckoning like a comrade. She's halfway there when she hears her mother's voice.

"Mazna? Mazna!"

Her heart sinks. There is something about her mother lately that Mazna finds herself recoiling from. She seems a little desperate, asking her questions about her day as though relieved to have company.

"Mazna? Is that you?"

Mazna sighs. She follows the voice into her parents' bedroom, which is empty, past the bed with its mint bedspread, into the closet, where she finds her mother sitting cross-legged on the marble tiles.

"Where's Baba?" Suddenly Mazna feels exhausted. Hours of daydreaming, watching the film, worrying about Idris, have left her drained. "What are you doing?"

"You really get to do whatever you like." Her mother speaks neutrally. "Don't you."

"Mama?"

"No one says a word," Lulwa continues. "Your father is busy with work. He's at the university right now. Your grandparents are idiots. Even I don't say anything about it." She speaks in a murmur, as though to herself. "I could ask where you've been, where you're sleeping on the weekends, who you bought those whore dresses for. I could tell you no more rehearsals, that it's time to start thinking of marriage. That your sister had four suitors at your age. But I don't. I don't say any of that."

The silence is dreadful. Mazna's heart pounds in her throat. *How does she know? How does she know?* A terrible thought crosses her mind — maybe her mother is drunk for the first time in her life, or even stoned. But no, Lulwa's eyes are clear as water, the blue flashing.

"I've been sleeping at Lara's, Mama, you know that. We . . ." Her voice trails off at the sight of Lulwa shaking her head.

"Your father thinks I'm jealous. He says that I want to be going out all the time, doing God knows what with God knows who. Do you think I'm jealous, Mazna?"

Mazna shakes her head slowly. It had never occurred to her that her parents might talk about her, the two of them in that green bed speculating about her life. The thought is oddly flattering. Her mother holds out her hand, and Mazna helps her up.

"I know what you're doing, Mazna." Her tone is less severe, almost distant. "I don't know why or how, but I know you're doing something that's no good."

Mazna doesn't speak. She thinks of the bloodstained underwear tucked under her mattress. Of her bare back pressed against the tiles of the bakery floor.

"And this London nonsense," she continues. "Can you imagine what my mother, rest her soul, would have said if she knew her granddaughter was performing onstage in public like some commoner?"

Your mother was *a commoner,* Mazna hurls at her silently. London, she realizes, is the only thing the two of them have discussed about her acting. For years, no one has paid any attention to her. Why does her mother even care what she does with her time?

Mazna doesn't realize she's spoken the words aloud until her mother's expression changes. Lulwa deflates, sinks into herself; sixty years of living rush abruptly back into her pained, tired face.

"I care," Lulwa says, and her sad voice makes something twist inside Mazna, "because I'm your mother. I see you rattling around this city. No one looking after you." There's a silence and Lulwa walks over to the bed, sits down. Her shoulders slump. Several moments pass before she speaks again.

"I didn't think the years would be so short," she says simply.

The anger leaves Mazna in a single neat swoop. She suddenly remembers how her mother used to braid her hair after baths when she was a child, Lulwa's nails delicious against her scalp as she gathered strands.

"We should go to a movie sometime," Mazna says tentatively. She can think of no other thing to offer her mother. "There's a new John Travolta movie. I heard it's really good." She has an image of the two of them sharing a tub of popcorn, laughing at the songs.

"Maybe." There's a note of wistfulness in her voice. "You know who I always loved?" she asks suddenly. She doesn't wait for Mazna to answer. "Vivien Leigh. In *A Streetcar Named Desire*. When she firsts meets Stanley." Lulwa sighs. "With that perfect hair and beautiful dress."

"She was pretending. From the beginning." Mazna is surprised to hear her own voice.

"Mmm." Her mother looks pensive. "Do you have that scene memorized?"

"Um." Mazna shrugs. She does, of course, but the question is unsettling, makes something inside her squirm uncomfortably. She knows what her mother's going to say before she says it.

"Play her," Lulwa says. "Do that scene for me." She clasps her hands. "Please."

Mazna is shot through with resentment; she's not a circus monkey.

"Play her," Lulwa pleads.

Mazna sighs. Her fingers feel thick and clumsy as she unties her hair. She takes her place in front of an invisible mark near the bed and remembers Blanche's stricken face, the way she'd known that, in entering this house, she was entering something unknown and a little dangerous. She must have been tired. And hungry. Mazna says the lines exactly as she remembers them — *I'm afraid . . . I'm going to be sick* — and when it's over and she's crouching over an invisible desk, her head bent, her mother has tears in her eyes. She applauds quietly, her hands barely touching. It reminds her of Hana being excited about the videocassette, only this is small and sad and embarrassing.

"I guess that's why they let you do it" is all Lulwa says, then she tells Mazna to go to bed.

On Monday, Idris calls her. The second she hears his voice, she's so relieved it angers her, and she snaps, "So you're alive?"

"I'm sorry about last weekend," Idris says at the same time.

"I was worried." Mazna realizes as she speaks the words that they're true. She may not feel for him what she does for Zakaria, but still she loves Idris in a strange, tender way.

"I couldn't come in," he says. She waits for more, but he just starts talking about his exams. There's something different in his voice. A dreadful thought crosses her mind. Did Zakaria tell him something?

"How's your hand?" she asks.

"Oh, it's better. It scabbed over. Baba said there'll be a scar." He sounds more like himself at this last bit, a note of boyish pride. "Anyway, listen. I have to go."

"Oh. Okay." Idris has never ended a phone call first. She feels her mind sharpen.

"I thought I'd meet you Saturday?" he asks mildly. "For real this time."

Something still feels off and she doesn't like his tone, but she has no choice, she realizes, and so she says yes as cheerily as she can.

By Saturday, Mazna's convinced herself that she was imagining everything—*A guilty conscience punishes itself,* as her mother would say—and when she meets Idris, he does indeed look normal, and he gives her a big hug. But when she asks where he's parked, he smiles coyly.

"Actually." Idris flings his arms out: *Ta-da!* "I was thinking we'd do something different."

"What do you mean?"

"I want to see Damascus!" he says airily. "Well, with you. I want to see Damascus with you. I know we used to have dinner when we first met, but it was that same old restaurant every time, and now I'm always smuggling you into Lebanon."

"You're not *smuggling* me." Her stomach feels leaden.

"Like you're some kind of rug or something," he continues cheerfully, "and truth be told, I could use a little break from Beirut."

"Oh." Mazna's mind spins. This isn't what she expected. She's done her hair in a pretty French braid. She's painted her toes carefully. She needs — yes, that's the word, she doesn't care how ridiculous it sounds — to see Zakaria. She feels the same panic from the week before, like she's Idris's prisoner. She tries to speak lightly. "I was so looking forward to our little trip. It's just . . . I've been a little restless here. What if we spend time in Damascus next week?"

"Please, Mazna." His face turns strangely serious. His eyes search hers in an uncomfortable way. "I want to see your life here. It's important to me."

She's taken aback. Idris has never asked her for anything before. She thinks of the bakery floor and feels a beat of guilt. Zakaria will be there next week. And the week after that. Her pulse quickens with excitement, and she softens at the reminder of Idris's impending heartbreak.

"Okay," she agrees. "Let's stay here."

Idris lets out a whoop and hugs her again. He smells like cigarettes and soap. "Take me to your favorite restaurant. I'm starving."

They have a surprisingly pleasant morning. They go to Labidi, a restaurant she went to all the time during college. After they've eaten identical plates of poached eggs and fries, Mazna takes him to her favorite spot, a little garden sandwiched between a crumbling church and an auto-repair shop. They sit on a bench and she tells him about her mother taking her when she was younger and letting her pick a single flower, never more. She used to believe the fat bumblebees were filled with honey.

"I never understood why people were scared of getting stung. I thought you could just suck it out and it would be delicious."

Idris laughs. "Zakaria was stung when we were nine or eight. Right on the eyelid. Can you imagine?" His laughter stops unexpectedly.

"Poor thing," Mazna says carefully. "It must've been so painful."

Idris smiles. "He told everyone his imaginary friend had punched him."

Mazna recalls Zakaria shaking the powdered sugar from his head, joking that their lovemaking had aged him. "How is he doing?" she asks quietly, looking down.

"I was thinking we'd go see Tarek," Idris says, ignoring the question. "I called him yesterday. He said he'd be at the theater all day."

"You want to see him now?" she asks, surprised.

Idris is already standing. "Just for a bit."

But they end up staying at the theater for hours. On the walk over, Mazna points out her street, her family's gray gabled roof. She's a little embarrassed by the small size, but he just admires the tidy street, the trees pared into the shape of green lollipops. It's been months since Mazna was inside the theater, and she automatically rubs the silver dollar near the entrance; all the actors pat it for good luck before a show. There's a rehearsal going on, a pretty woman Mazna's age onstage, and it makes her jealous. She's grateful to follow Tarek to his office for coffee.

"If I have to explain enunciation again, they're going to be cleaning my brains from this carpet." He rubs his eyes. "That's what happens when my lead actress decides to bow out on me." He glowers at Mazna.

She groans. "God, can you forgive me already? It's been two months!"

"Well, the important thing is you're losing sleep over it." She and Idris sit on the sofa in his office and Tarek brings them matching cups. The window is slightly ajar and it's warm and sleepy, not unpleasant. The men talk about Beirut for a while, then Tarek turns his attention back to her. "Are you still thinking of London?"

She feels her neck get hot. This is her big news, what she wanted to tell Zakaria today. A few days ago, her father had given her a check. *For your trip,* he said. She'd started to protest, thinking of her mother, but as though he'd read her mind, her father told her that Lulwa had agreed. "I'm going," she says now.

Idris studies her warily. "I didn't know that."

"I've been saying it all summer," she says shortly.

"Well, yes, but not for certain —"

"Just because you're not going to America doesn't mean I'm staying here," she says, and her tone is harsher than she intends. She catches Tarek looking at her sharply.

"What is going on with you two?"

"Nothing," they both say sullenly.

"I see." Tarek looks like he regrets inviting them for coffee. "How's Zuzu, Idris?"

Mazna holds her breath.

"He's doing fine." Idris fiddles with the sugar spoon. "Fine," he repeats.

"He's back for the summer, right?"

"Actually." Idris glances toward the window. "He's been back at the camp for a few days now," he says nonchalantly.

"He's back at the camp?" Mazna says at the same time as Tarek asks, "Why?" Her mind flusters with fresh panic — she has no telephone number for Zakaria; she knows the name of the camp, nothing else. She racks her brain for ideas — she can ask Sara. She can beg Deedee for information. The bakery! Her breath calms. Of course. The bakery. She can always find him there.

"I don't know," Idris tells Tarek. "He just decided to go back early. You can ask him why yourself." There's a flash of anger in his eyes, but it's gone so quickly, Mazna is certain she imagined it. "Mazna!" He turns to her, all smiles. "Where are the famous Damascene sweets I hear so much about?"

She studies his face for a second. Then: relief. He knows nothing. It's the same Idris as always, distractible, eager. "Let's go get you that ice cream," she says.

He holds his arms above his head in mock victory.

❖

That evening, her grandfather falls asleep before dinner, so there isn't any of the usual tension around the table, all of them wondering what Ghassan will say next. Her mother tells a story about unwittingly repeating a curse word as a child and they all laugh, even her grandmother. Mazna bites back a smile when her father covers Lulwa's hand with his own.

"You know," Mazna's mother says to her, "this sleepy August weather reminds me of Latakia. Those summers before Nawal got married. You were so young. Do you remember those little hotels we'd stay in?"

"The pool was always covered in green muck."

"Egret droppings." Her father smiles at the memory. "They were migrating."

"Do you remember when Nawal got toothpaste in her ear?" Lulwa asks him, and they talk of finding a hospital in the middle of the night, laughing, speaking over each other, and Mazna can see the muscle of forty years of marriage, all the little signposts of love she's never noticed before. She's surprised to find that she wants to tell her mother about Zakaria, badly, that in fact, her mother is the only person she'd like to tell, more than Lara or Fatima.

They all help clear the table. Khalto Seham wants to henna her hair, and Lulwa surprises everyone by offering to help. They start gathering things, chattering about which shade to use.

"Keep a window open," Abeer says cheerfully, like they're schoolgirls, "or you'll choke on the fumes."

"Yes, Auntie," Lulwa replies, and on her way to the bathroom, Abeer touches her arm sweetly.

In the living room, her father has already settled into his favorite armchair, the newspaper held in front of his face like a fan. Mazna decides to join him rather than retreating to her bedroom. It occurs to her that she won't be living under this roof for much longer. The thought pleases and saddens her at once. There's a rerun of a soap playing on the English-language channel and Mazna tucks her legs beneath her on the couch, happy to catch the ending.

"Another dozen killed near Saida," her father says with a sigh, speaking to no one in particular.

The name tugs at Mazna. She remembers a woman who'd sold her tangerine ice cream weeks earlier. She'd told Mazna she was from Saida. *Poor people,* she thinks absently. She hopes the woman is still alive.

"And the camps again. A raid last night."

Every inch of Mazna stills, alert.

"So young."

"Can I see?" Mazna asks. She stands, holds her hand out. It feels like she's in a dream or underwater. Her body understands something her mind hasn't yet caught up with.

The paper is folded, the headline "Clashes in the South" screaming up at her. She unfolds it and sees the rows of grainy photographs; her eyes go from one to the other. *Slower,* her mind warns her. *Slower.* There, in the third row, second to last, the rest of her life stares back at her.

A school photograph.

Zakaria is looking unsmiling into the camera, but his eyebrows are raised, like he's just thought of a joke.

Bassel has returned to watching television, chuckling to himself as characters hit each other with lemon pies. He hears the thump before he realizes his daughter has fallen to the ground. She won't leave her bed again for twenty days.

❖

Friday. Saturday. Sunday. Mazna has never paid attention to time before, but now, it's all she thinks about, how it seems to freeze and sprint simultaneously, how the beat of her clock sweeps ruthlessly through the hours until she throws it against the wall; the hands peep through the broken glass like whiskers. Her mother comes running in, but Mazna sobs until she's left alone again, shivering under her comforter. She sleeps during the days and roams her bedroom at night, listening for sounds throughout rooms.

The nights bleed into each other. She steals every clock in the house. She fills a bathtub with water and drowns them all. In the morning, she hears a cry of surprise from Khalto Seham, but nobody asks her about it. She feels as though she can suddenly understand all the lessons in physics from school, the boring teacher who'd drone on about time and space existing only in people's imaginations. Time is a lie. She has been lied to. All these years, thinking it's something that can be measured and organized into days, hours, minutes. How peculiar to name it; it's like trying to arrest air.

On the third day, she uses a nail file to carve letters into her bedpost. *Please,* she writes. *Oh God. Za.* She doesn't finish.

Monday. Tuesday. She can hear the doorbell ring every now and then, the sounds of people talking, worried.

Mazna can't stop throwing up. Everything she eats promptly comes back up, like her body's chiding her for trying something as ordinary as eating. Abu Samira, their neighborhood doctor, comes in one evening to take her temperature. He gives her something bitter and warm to drink. But when he tries to talk to her, Mazna cries until he leaves the room. She tries to pray but halfway through *wudu,* as she's washing her wrists, her heart burns — his hand encircling her wrist the night at the bakery as he marveled, *Small as a bird* — and she crawls back into bed.

One morning she wakes to find a letter under her door. It was stamped days ago, a few days after the newspaper. In the corner, there's Sara's name, their address in Beirut. Mazna rips up the letter, without reading it, into sixteen neat squares. Then she flushes them one by one down the toilet. (Later, much later, after everything turned cold and stony between them, she'd regret doing this, wonder what Sara had written, but at the time, she felt only relief as the last slip was flushed away.)

On the eighth day, she hears familiar voices talking outside her hallway. Her mother and someone else.

"She won't speak to any of us."

"Let me try."

"I don't know what happened. It was out of nowhere. Bassel said she was sitting right there and suddenly —"

"I'll just try to see if she'll sit up. Talk a little." Nawal. Her sister. A second later, the door creaks open and Mazna shuts her eyes, holds her breath.

"Hey, kitten," her sister whispers. Her old pet name for Mazna.

Mazna keeps her eyes shut, but her sister sits next to her, puts a cool hand at her forehead. Neither one speaks for a long time. Seconds, Mazna thinks. Then minutes. Half an hour. She marvels at how, even in shunning time, she still needs it. Her sister keeps her hand at her forehead. Finally, Mazna opens her eyes.

Nawal slides her glasses onto the top of her head. She leans in, like she used to when Mazna was a child, until the tips of their noses touch, so that Mazna can see the pupils of her sister's eyes. *Let our eyes talk,* her sister used to say, and she loved the idea that there were conversations that could happen without speaking.

It feels like an hour. A year.

"Darling."

"Stop it." Mazna says. Her vision blurs. She blinks and leans back into the pillow, cries without wanting to, her cheeks wet, salt on her lips. She suddenly remembers a school event when she was seven or eight, how her sister had dressed her carefully in a frilly dress. Where had their mother been? Mazna wonders. Nawal had braided her hair. Mazna can still remember her sister's bright red lipstick, how she'd started to whine because she wanted some. Nawal had looked around, then cupped Mazna's face and kissed her very softly on the lips. *There we go, a little lipstick for kitten.*

"I know you don't want to talk to me. But there's something I think you should know. You've had visitors."

"I don't want to see anyone."

"I know."

"No one, Nawal. I can't." She turns to her side. An old *Romeo and Juliet* poster from a theater in England stares back at her. Madame Orla gave it to her years ago. The corners have faded over the years.

"I know, *habibti.* But I want to tell you about something. Yesterday, I was here for a bit in the morning. I didn't want to wake you; they said you were sleeping. There's a man that came over. He wasn't someone I'd seen before. Not one of your school friends. A Lebanese guy."

Mazna's brain feels sluggish. Each thought is taking too long.

"He said his name was Idris."

A distant emotion stirs within her. Curiosity. She remembers walking through her neighborhood on the way to the theater, pointing out the gray roof. "What did he want?"

Nawal gives her a sad smile. "He told Mama and Baba he was an old friend. But I walked him out after, and when we got to the porch —" She pauses. "He started to cry, Mazna. A lot. I couldn't understand what he was saying at first." She takes Mazna's hand, grips it hard. "Kitten, he told me. He told me about his friend. Your friend."

"He told you?" The poster blurs. Mazna buries her head in the pillow. She squeezes her sister's hand back.

"I liked him. He seemed a little lost. He wanted to see you, but I said he'd have to come back." She pauses. "He told me about Beirut. About your trips."

Mazna shoots her head back up. "You can't tell Mama."

"I didn't." Nawal nudges her to move over and lies down fully on the bed. She curves Mazna's body against hers so they're like two commas. Mazna remembers Zakaria's chest, his warm breath against her neck. She begins to cry silently. Nawal embraces her tighter.

"You don't have to say anything," she whispers. "I think I understand. He didn't seem to know himself, this Idris, but as soon as he explained about the friend, everything made sense. That—" A pause, and Nawal swallows. "I'm sorry, kitten. I'm so sorry."

Later, Mazna will be stunned when she pieces everything together—the timeline, how a mere three weeks had felt like years, entire realities that she'd lived and died in. Nawal came back every day, without her son or husband. She'd curl her body against Mazna's, play with her hair, whisper nonsensical stories, bedtime tales from Mazna's childhood. Mazna would keep her eyes shut.

Nawal feeds her clear soups, then holds her hair back while Mazna vomits into the trashcan that they've started leaving by her bedside. In a stroke of genius, her sister mixes ginger and boiled apples into a warm mash and feeds it to Mazna, spoonful by spoonful.

"I made it for Rami when he was a baby," she says, and miraculously, it works. It tastes warm and wonderful, a nothing food of salt and air. Mazna's surprised to find her mouth opening for more.

Another Saturday. Another Sunday. A whole day of rain. The following morning, Nawal comes by with a shopping bag. She pulls the curtains open, making Mazna wince. She can hear Nawal rustling around in the plastic bag.

"Please," she moans. "I'm asleep."

"I got you something."

"I'm asleep," Mazna repeats. But she lifts her head to see her sister holding out something silk and pretty. A dress.

"I figured you didn't want to wear color yet," Nawal says. Mazna is taken aback. She hasn't even considered the official process of mourning, but then, her sister has always been the practical one. Mazna realizes there must've been an *azza* at the camps, Zakaria's mother yanking at her hair, wailing. The sisters would be pressed against one another, dressed in black, holding each other up. Mazna's strangely hungry for human contact, longs to be hugged by these sisters she's never met. She remembers, with a jolt, that Zakaria's mother has now lost all her men. How can people bear it, she wonders, loss upon loss?

"What's it for?"

Her sister hesitates. "There's someone who wants to see you."

Mazna sits up. Her mind is like fog. "What are you talking about?"

"He came back, kitten." Nawal sits on the edge of the bed, the dress crumpled in her hands. "Idris. He actually—" She clears her throat. "He's come back a few times. He's been very sweet to Mama and Baba. They like him a lot. He admitted to them that he's from Beirut, that he saw you in a play a while ago and you've been friends since. But he hasn't said anything about the trips. The last time he came, I took him out for a coffee. Poor thing."

"You've been seeing him? You've been talking to him?" She feels irrationally angry. Betrayed. All this time, she's avoided thinking about Idris. Something about him makes her stomach turn.

Her sister touches her arm. "I think you should see him."

Nawal's cool hand infuriates Mazna. She shakes it off. "What are you talking about? What do you know about anything? You have no idea what's happened! No idea!"

Mazna isn't sure when she started screaming, when she kicked the sheets off and leaped to her feet. "Most of the time I barely even *see* you. And then, suddenly, you want to pretend you're part of my life? You want to tell me what to do? You don't know anything!"

"I know he loves you," Nawal says quietly, and the whole room stops.

Mazna feels the breath leave her in a punch. She slumps on the edge of the bed, and her sister sits next to her. Nawal smells of perspiration and cooking.

"When is he coming?" she mumbles.

"I told him to come at noon. He knows that you might not want to see him. But Mazna, my love, regardless of what you decide — I think it's time to take a shower." Mazna catches her sister's eye and smiles grimly. She lets Nawal lift her nightgown over her head. It's been weeks since she's worn anything else and the garment smells sour, or her body does.

"Mama put fresh shampoo in the bathroom for you. Gardenia. The one you like."

In the bathroom, Mazna avoids the mirror for as long as possible. All these days, she'd shuffle in and out of the bathroom like a ghost, never once looking up. But now she looks. It is extraordinary how quickly a body can change. She looks aged, ten years older than twenty-three. Her hipbones are visible, her breasts smaller.

The water is hot. It beats against her scalp until it hurts a little and she rubs the new shampoo under her arms, between her legs. A lush, floral smell fills the bathroom, like a wet rainforest. When she finishes, Mazna doesn't bother waiting for the water to pool on the bathmat. She wraps a towel around herself and walks into her bedroom.

Nawal is waiting, the dress laid out on her lap like a small child.

"You've lost weight." (There is a trace of wistfulness in her tone. Her own body has expanded with age, like a layer cake. Though Nawal knows it's wrong — her poor little sister, who's always seemed to Nawal on the edge of disaster, chasing after lofty, unlikely ideas — she cannot help but admire Mazna's flat stomach, the perch of her collarbones as her sister dresses.)

The dress is too loose. Mazna's arms are dark and thin against the black silk. She crosses them. All those weeks in Beirut have left her skin a deep, even brown, even after the recent days inside. There's something tacky about having a tan while mourning.

Mazna's brushing her hair when the doorbell rings. She flinches without meaning to.

"Take your time," Nawal says. "I'll go keep them company."

Mazna sits on the bed after her sister leaves; she tries to empty her mind. She counts the number of castle bricks on the poster. Somebody laughs in the living room. Mazna pulls at a cuticle so hard, it starts to bleed. She puts her thumb in her mouth; she tastes copper. How does she know it's copper? she wonders. She's only ever tasted blood.

I'll check on her, she hears someone — Nawal, her mother — saying, but nobody comes in.

Two minutes. Twenty. Forty. Time makes its cruel circles around her and she can only wait. She sits until something deep and unfamiliar in her whispers that it is time to get up. She rises.

There is the smell of baked bread in the hallway, a clatter of dishes in the kitchen. Mazna steps carefully into the living room as though onto a scaffold, and there, sitting on her mother's sofa, making polite conversation with her father, is Idris. There's a plate of baklava on the table in front of them. His hand is curved around a coffee cup and he's dressed in a black suit. If she looks older, Idris seems smaller somehow, as though he's a boy in his father's clothing. His tie is crooked.

She clears her throat and he looks up. She can see him swallow from across the room.

"Your mother made coffee," he says, as though that explains something.

"You should try one of those pastries. They're really good," Mazna replies. It's like they're reading from a badly written script. *Dialogue needs tension to make it realistic,* she could hear Tarek declaring. But there is nothing that could make this realistic, because she's wearing a new dress and Zakaria is dead and Idris is in her parents' living room.

It's clear that there had been some serious conversation before she entered. Her mother seems excessively cheerful as she bustles around, refilling cups and cutting brioche into thick slices. Mazna catches her father discreetly patting Idris's arm for reassurance, a strangely intimate gesture. They've met several times, she realizes. Her parents like Idris. Her mind tries to absorb these facts slowly, but it's like chewing on a piece of tough meat — it goes nowhere. They sit in stilted conversation, Nawal and their mother chattering on about the summer.

"Baba," her father finally says. The women quiet down. "Idris has come from Beirut to talk to you." Mazna finally looks up. She swings her head from her father to Idris.

Idris shoots her a pleading look. But she can't speak. Finally, he clears his throat. "I tried to come before," he begins. "Your family has been so kind."

"It's been a pleasure," Lulwa says rather gushingly, in a way that Mazna finds unappealing.

"I know this is a time of grief," Idris says, then falls silent. An awkward silence fills the room like a smell.

"Yes, yes," her mother says, too quickly, "we know all about that poor boy. The one that was your friend. I'm sure the theater will miss him as well."

There it is. Mazna looks at her sister, who avoids her eyes. Nawal and Idris had lied to her parents; of course they had. What had they told them — that Zakaria was an actor? A producer? That he was a close enough friend that his loss caused her grief, but not that he was Palestinian or that they met in Beirut. She knows she should feel relief; they'll never know anything. But it fills her with sorrow instead.

"Go ahead, son," Bassel says gently.

"I got accepted to the surgical-residency program." Idris speaks slowly. He busies himself with folding and unfolding his napkin. "In America. That university hospital in California. It's somewhere in the desert. A town called Blythe." He stumbles over the pronunciation. "They want me. Funding and everything."

Mazna stares at him, uncomprehending. She feels certain she's dreaming, as though a great big flock of flamingos could come crashing in any second. Had he come all this way to tell her this news? Was he expecting her to *congratulate* him? She opens her mouth, then shuts it. A long, uneasy silence drags on.

"I thought you were just applying as a joke." Her words come out shrill. She sees her mother and father exchange quick glances. Idris drops his eyes.

"I thought I was," he mumbles. "Then —" The rest of his sentence hangs there like a sharp cliff off which they've all fallen. "Everything is different now," he says quietly.

"Congratulations." She bites down on the word like an ice chip.

"I wasn't sure if I should come." Idris speaks with sudden vehemence, in a rush. "I didn't know if you'd want to see me. Your sister's been so kind. Your parents — I told them, but I didn't know if you'd want to hear it. I wanted to ask you, but I didn't know —" He takes a deep breath, fixing his eyes on the rug. The whole room holds its breath, waiting for Idris to speak again.

"I want to marry you," he whispers.

When Mazna was a little girl, she wanted only one superpower: the ability to stop time. She would fantasize about whistling and the entire world stopping, falling to a hush, people freezing like statues, forks midair, arms outstretched to catch keys. But she never wanted to move among the frozen people, cutting braids or stealing necklaces; she wanted to be still herself. She wanted to know what it would be like to be gone, briefly.

In the moments after Idris speaks, she feels it for the first time: the absence of herself. She finds herself twenty years younger, coloring on the floor of her grandfather's study. She can see the tips of his brown oxfords clear as day. She isn't coming back, she decides. She is going to stay in that long-dead room forever.

But the memory won't stay still for her. That room, this room, twenty years later, erupts in noise. Her father claps Idris on the back.

"He already asked us permission!" Lulwa says. "He did it the proper way."

"I asked your father," Idris repeats needlessly.

Her father nodded. "You've got yourself a good man here."

Mazna wants to scream at them to shut up, to give her a moment to think, she needs to think, but her mother's arm is around her shoulders, her overly sweet perfume like a cloud, then Nawal is hugging her, whispering in her ear, "He's a good man, Mazna, I promise your heart will open up to him." Mazna feels limp, like a flower someone else has plucked. When her father comes over to embrace her, something in her face must stop him, because he holds up his hand for silence.

"I think," he says, "that we should let the kids talk alone."

"Bassel —" her mother begins, but her father shakes his head, and, one by one, they leave the living room until Mazna and Idris are alone.

Nobody speaks. Mazna hates herself for breaking the silence first, but her anger is too painful, and she flings it toward him.

"What are you doing?" she snarls.

Idris shakes his head. "I don't know," he mumbles. "I know it's too soon. But I have to leave for California in two weeks, and —"

"Why are you doing this? Why are you going to *California?*"

"I can't stay there, Mazna," he says, and he begins to cry. "I just can't."

Her anger deserts her. She collapses back into her chair. "My sister bought me this stupid dress. You've all been planning this for days, haven't you?"

"Your mother got so excited," Idris says glumly. He wipes his face. "I didn't even know why I was coming the first time. I tried calling your work, but they said you hadn't been in. It was a few days after . . . I didn't know what to do. I remembered you pointing out the house on the way to the theater. And —" He clears his throat. "They just assumed I was a suitor. Which I was." His voice changes. "I am."

She thinks of her family. They're already gone, she realizes. Her crazy grandfather, her unhappy mother. A sister who's in the middle of her life. No one has asked anything of Mazna in years. These past few months, she's had a feeling of newness, waking her up like a pleasant electric shock. Beirut is lost to her, she understands. Zakaria. The future she'd glimpsed and let herself dip into like a stranger's pool.

"What happened?" She winces at her own question. The ending is already known; everything before seems cruel.

Something slackens in Idris's face; it's as though she struck him. He presses his lips together so tightly, they whiten. He speaks without moving his eyes from the rug.

"A couple of years ago, something happened with Tarek's brother. It — it's a long story." Mazna opens her mouth, then closes it. She doesn't tell him she knows. "I'm not sure how they figured it out, but some of the men found out where Zakaria lived in the camps. My mother saw his photograph in the newspaper. She fainted. Just dropped and cut her head on the countertop. There was blood everywhere. We thought there must've been a mistake. But when my father went to his mother . . . I'd just seen him at the bakery." His voice breaks. "I'd just seen him."

Mazna chokes back a sob. It's like drinking really foul medicine; she needs it, but it hurts. She can see Hana falling to the floor, Salim running over to her. They must know Idris is here, she realizes. They'll think nothing of it — Sara's friend spending more time around their son, a natural romance, albeit pressurized by tragedy. Idris seems roused by her crying, and he rushes to her, sits on the arm of her chair. She can feel his elbow against her shoulders, his familiar smell of mint gum and cigarettes. In spite of herself, she feels her body relax into his.

"Mazna," he whispers. "We could go far away together."

"Don't say that. You don't know what you're saying."

"They might come for me. The men."

She doesn't respond. The men didn't go after Zakaria just because of the checkpoint, the dead boy. A Palestinian life is worth less than a Lebanese one. Even she knows that.

"The hospital is a good one," he continues. "We'll be in California. You can drive up to Los Angeles whenever you want. You'd be just a couple of hours from *Hollywood*." He says the word with reverence. Even Mazna feels a chill. "You could audition for movies. You'd become a star." His voice throbs with need.

Mazna looks at him dully. She sees his want, how big and hungry it is, and it repulses her. She sees his receding hairline, the slight frogginess of his eyes. She tries to remember what it felt like to want something before Zakaria, and her mind thrashes about until it knocks against something solid. She remembers a film star she'd seen as a teenager at a premiere Madame Orla had taken the whole class to, an Egyptian actress who shook her black hair as she laughed and answered reporters' questions. She'd seemed like a god, someone above misery and damage.

"I can't go alone. Mazna, Mazna." Her name isn't hers anymore, said like that. Idris looks at her like a lifeboat. "Please. Let me give you a good life."

Grief will make you do crazy things. It will electrify the elegant, flower-stem neurons in the amygdala of your brain, will pluck them like an instrument. In ancient Rome, grief made men twirl in their thin, leather sandals and pirou-ette until their feet bled; in India, it walked widows onto pyres waiting for fire. The Persians gave the bodies of their deceased beloveds to dogs; the Egyptians buried them with servants. Grief will make you laugh at the funeral, weep over the cereal bowl; it will buzz your feet until they start dancing in the middle of the night. It's grief that inspires the unlikeliest of bedfellows. It will convince you, tugging at the hem of your ragged cotton robe — the one you've had since your father bought it for you in Latakia when you were fifteen, the one that will always smell hazily of summer — that the building is on fire, the world is on fire, and you'll find water in only one place: a city as far away from here as you can imagine. Grief will pack your bag, quit your job, buy a white dress. It will make you say yes.

Part
III

The Domestic in You

AVA WAKES IN her grandparents' house with a start. The dream feels like an animal chasing her. The road from Damascus to Beirut was blocked by dead buffalo, fruit flies feasting on their glassy, black eyes. Her mother was walking, stepping over the hulking carcasses; Ava was chasing after her, but she kept tripping in the dark as she called out her mother's name: *Mazna, Mazna.* Ava ran and ran; when she finally caught up to her mother, she yanked her sleeve so hard, fabric came away in her hand like a little flag. Mazna turned around, her profile regal. She opened her mouth, but she had no teeth. Even though Ava's awake the memory is unnerving.

The room is bright — she'd forgotten to lower the metal window shutters the night before — and the kids are curled on the other bed. This was the room she and Naj always shared, a fact that had felt deeply unjust to her as a teenager when her baby sister shook her awake in the middle of the night for water. Last night, she'd instinctively taken her old bed, the one near the window, and she regrets it now; the children are heavy sleepers, and there's the bleating of birds outside the window.

It is a sort of magic, waking up somewhere new. Yesterday was the length of a year — the morning in New York, the last-minute frenzy of packing, the long lines at JFK. Her parents met her in the Air France terminal; they'd arrived from Phoenix two hours earlier. Her mother had looked at her and said, "I read the most interesting article about keto diets the other day," and it was off to the races, Ava sulking as the children fought over pizza slices. She'd made a terrible mistake, she understood in the airport, a realization only underscored now in the heat of this old bedroom, in this godforsaken country where even the birds warred with one another.

Too late. She's here. Nate will be headed to Portland in a few days. At the thought of him, Ava rolls onto her stomach and scrunches her eyes shut. The memory of yesterday morning drifts across her mind like pond scum. The Uber that Nate ordered was early, the last few minutes in the house a whirl-wind. Zina was crying because she couldn't find Pippa, so Ava charged through the rooms while Nate took the suitcases to the car.

The stuffed rabbit was nestled under Zina's bed. On the way out, Ava stopped at the threshold of the foyer. She stood on her tiptoes, peering out the window to the street. The children were watching Nate and the driver strug-gle to close the trunk. Ava made a decision. She went into Nate's study — an old laundry room they'd converted years earlier — sat down and opened his laptop. Its blank, black face looked up at her eagerly. She pressed the power button.

His laptop password was Zivateyan, an amalgamation of all their names; he used it for everything. An internet browser was already open and signed in to his e-mail account. The second decision was made for her. Ava looked over her shoulder, then typed *Emily* in the inbox search bar. The search came up empty. She typed it again. Empty.

Ava blinked at the screen. She waited to feel relief. From the street, a car honk broke the silence and she jumped. In a moment, Nate would clatter into the apartment, asking where she was. She rose, started to leave, then paused at the doorway.

Another car honk.

She sat back down, hard. The laptop brightened again. This time, she clicked on the Trash folder. It was completely empty.

Ava let out a long breath the way her hot-yoga teacher had taught her to. In a minute, she'd move, go outside holding the stuffed animal over her head triumphantly. But for the moment, she just exhaled.

There are a million explanations. Nate could have just cleaned his inbox. Emily might have moved on. There could be someone else now, or nobody at all. Or there could be an actual movie affair, with hotels and burner phones.

Her texts to him after they landed yesterday were brisk, and she told him the children were asleep in the car on the drive to the house. They were awake, though, wired even, fascinated with the minivan Naj showed up in — "It's a friend's," she'd said airily — which of course had no seat belts in the back, so she and her mother each had to hold a child. They took turns berating Ava's little sister.

"What's that saying about good deeds?" Naj asked their father in the front seat, and he laughed as Ava and Mazna exchanged furious looks, an oddly warming moment between them. Fuck their husbands. Ava had learned to stop confiding her marital troubles to her mother — the news traveled like wildfire, and Mazna held grudges even longer than Naj — but it didn't tamp down her urge in that moment to lay her head on her mother's shoulder and whisper sleepily about Freckles and Portland as the nighttime cityscape of Beirut blurred by them like a sci-fi movie, the worn-down buildings hulking in the dark like massive animals, the highway trailed by the sea. Nate texted that he already missed them. She replied with a row of *x*'s.

❖

The house is quiet as a held breath; she's woken too early and the jet lag will be worse tonight. They hadn't reached the house until after midnight; Merry had appeared briefly in a nightgown and helped them with suitcases. Ava wandered around tired, the rooms both unchanged and unfamiliar. Her father was right. There is something peculiar about seeing an unlived-in house so clean and preserved, like a dog awaiting its dead owner.

"Smells like Windex in here," her father had called out jovially. Ava felt like a burglar, moving through the house in the dark, claiming bedrooms, putting the children's toothbrushes in the guest bathroom. Her last, delirious thought before falling asleep was whether Merry still washed her grandfather's clothes.

It's even more peculiar in daylight. She hasn't been here in nearly a decade, and yet she knows instinctively which chipped tile to avoid in the bath. The portrait of her grandparents above the armchair seems sad now; it always struck her as strange, a bit over the top, but now that they're gone, it's fitting. The living room is tidy, her grandfather's chessboard polished, the pieces standing at attention. She picks up a bishop and places it in the middle of the board. Her grandfather loved to play with her when she was younger. *You're the only one in your family who doesn't think she's too good to be taught something,* he'd once confided, and the compliment upset her. It felt like a spiritless thing to be.

There's a noise behind her.

"Merry!" Ava clutches her heart, then feels ridiculous. "You scared me."

The other woman half smiles. Her grandfather's affection for Ava always seemed shared by Merry. "You're not going to sleep tonight," she warns.

"I know." Ava sighs. "This always happens. Nate says my circadian rhythm is stubborn." She pauses. "You remember him? My husband." The word commands, like it or not. Merry pretends to think.

"The white one?"

Ava laughs. "Yes. The white husband. Not the other one. Mama and Baba are still asleep?"

"Sleeping or hiding." Merry kisses her teeth. "I know what your baba wants to do."

Ava sinks into the couch. She'd spilled cranberry juice on it when she was thirteen or so. Her grandmother had taught her how to blot it out with vinegar.

Merry stands closer but doesn't sit. "Your jiddo loved this house."

"I know he did, Merry," she says gently. "I think Baba's going through some existential crisis or something. You know how he gets."

"I do," Merry says grimly.

A thought comes to Ava, half formed. "Jiddo should've left *you* the house!" She immediately regrets saying it. Merry's face shuts and Ava feels her cheeks burn. She sounds like Nate's mother going on about pussy hats. *I'm the white feminist here,* she thinks. It's wildly uncomfortable; she's so used to being a minority in America, and it's chastening to have that reversed, to be talking to a family *servant* about inheritance.

There's a sound in the foyer and they both walk toward it, relieved. Naj is stepping out of her sneakers. Her face is flushed, and Ava studies it. She barely got to speak with her last night. Her sister looks older, undeniably beautiful but a little drained. The tank top she's wearing hangs loosely against her chest, and Ava looks away from the hollows of her clavicles. She has to pretend her sister's physique is separate from her or else she starts to hate her a little.

"Napping in the garden?" Merry says cryptically. Naj makes a *Very funny* face.

"I went out with Jo and some friends. We stayed out a little later than planned."

Ava kisses her cheek. "You smell pickled," she says, and Merry laughs like it's the funniest thing she's ever heard.

"Like *kabees!* It's true," she tells Naj, who rolls her eyes. Merry leaves the room.

"So far, loving this family-in-town thing." Naj flings herself dramatically onto the couch. She covers her face with a throw pillow. "Jo says hi. You know he's obsessed with you."

"I like Jo," Ava says, sitting down. "But he's, like, twelve."

"How's Mr. Finch?"

Ava tries not to look at her sister's arms. "He's fine. We're fine." Faced with Naj, she can't imagine confiding in her. She's tired suddenly, wishes Naj would move so she could lie down.

"It's weird being in this house," Ava says. She's glad Naj can't see her face. "I feel like Jiddo is going to appear any second. Ask me to play chess or something."

Naj removes the pillow. Her voice is sharp. "If you'd seen the body at the *azza,* you probably wouldn't have that problem."

"You don't have to be an asshole."

"I'm not."

"I'm just saying I miss our grandfather," Ava says. But she knows Naj is right, and her guilt throbs like a muscle. "Is that so bad?"

Naj shrugs. "I guess I don't really care about making you feel better," she says, and there it is, her little sister's meanness, that blunt part of her that Ava dislikes.

"Thanks, Najla." Ava rises. "This will be over soon anyway. Baba's already found a real estate agent."

"What the *fuck?*" Her sister punches the same pillow. "How is that possible?"

"It's some friend of a friend in California. She's coming over tomorrow." There's a petty satisfaction in ruining her sister's mood.

"At least Mimi will be here." Their brother and Harper arrive this evening. "There's strength in numbers. We need to strategize." She lies back down, losing steam. Looking at Ava, she asks, "What do we do, Ave?"

"I don't know." Ava sits down and hesitates, like she's about to utter a bad word. "Maybe we let him sell?"

"*Coward.*" Naj glares at her.

"I'm just saying, Naj, nobody's even living here."

"Merry's living here!"

"I'm not sure she even wants to be," Ava says tentatively.

"It's our inheritance!"

Ava shuts her eyes. She isn't going to be lectured about heritage by a twenty-nine-year-old wearing a bracelet engraved with the word BITCH. "We'll plan the memorial. And we'll talk Baba out of it. Okay?"

Naj considers, then nods. "Okay." She closes her eyes again. Ava watches her curl up for a nap, marveling at how easy it is to reassure her.

There are a few moments of quiet. Ava lies back on the couch but snaps up with a start at the sound of footsteps. Mazna pads out in her silky dressing robe. It's the same one she's had for years, pale blue lined with white, and it looks out of place in this house.

"The kids are still sleeping," she announces. "I just checked on them."

"Yeah, they're out."

"And this one? What no-good nonsense has she been up to?" Her mother nods toward Naj, who has fallen completely asleep. There's black smudged on her cheek, mascara or dirt. She looks like a movie urchin.

"The follies of youth," Ava says, trying for lightness. But there's a crackling tension around her mother; her fingers twist her wedding band, her eyes dart across the room, taking in the knickknacks, the portrait. She mutters something, but Ava doesn't hear it.

"This house," her mother repeats, but she doesn't say anything else.

"It's been years," Ava says. Mazna gives her a tight smile and walks over to the coffee table. There's a crystal paperweight shaped like a swan, and she holds it up to the light. Her face softens, and Ava is charged with a memory.

The day before, they'd sat in the first row of economy class, her parents in the two seats by the window, Ava and the children in the middle. The sky quickly darkened, and soon the passengers were asleep, a few seats here and there glowing with television screens. The plane was dim, tiny lights pinpricking through the ceiling like artificial stars. At some point, Ava fell asleep, then woke with her jaw aching and her arm, under Zina's head, numb.

Across the aisle, her mother was also awake. Mazna stared alertly out the window at the Atlantic. Ava watched her for a moment. Finally Mazna turned her head, and Ava was startled to see that her mother's cheeks were damp. Alone, in the darkness of the airplane hurtling toward Beirut, her mother was crying.

❖

When the kids and Idris wake up, they all have breakfast on the veranda; Naj is still asleep on the couch. Merry has boiled some eggs. Ava watches her parents like a hawk, but they seem normal — Mazna grumpy, if a bit more on edge than usual, and Idris cheerfully puppeteering pita bread with silly voices to make the children laugh.

"So when's the real estate agent coming?" Ava asks finally, a little bitterly. But her father seems unperturbed.

"Tomorrow, I think." He waves his hand. "She'll call."

"Do you like this house?" Mazna asks Zina, and the girl nods. She has jam on her chin.

"Zina," Ava says, "please use the napkin."

"I like the swing," Rayan says.

"Me too!" Zina echoes.

"Well, your jiddo is going to sell this house. Very soon. So don't get too at-tached."

"Jiddo." Zina sounds aghast. "Why?"

Idris glares at Mazna. "Because my father is dead." He speaks plainly. "And there's nobody living here anymore."

In that instant, Merry appears, her timing so flawless that Ava wonders if she's been eavesdropping. But she just starts watering some potted plants on the veranda.

"Merry," Mazna says imperiously in a tone that Ava hates, that makes her want to curl up under the table, a tone completely disconnected from the im-migrant woman who lives in California and mispronounces *salmon* and shows off rare strains of orchids to rich kids. "I'd like to make makloubeh for dinner tonight. It's Mimi's favorite. Do we have eggplant?"

Merry shrugs. "If we do, it'll be in the fridge." *I don't work for you.* Good for her.

"Well." Mazna is quietly furious. "I suppose we should get some. Mimi loves makloubeh."

Ava volunteers to get the eggplant, and toothpaste and conditioner and the dozen other things they've all forgotten and can't live without. "None of you would survive an hour on a deserted island," Idris says before adding that he needs antacids.

"Ava, remember to get a shower cap."

"Mama, I want to come!"

"Zina, baby, if you stay and be a good girl for Teta, I'll bring back some cookies."

"And Cheetos for me?"

"Yes, Rayan. Cheetos for you."

"Ava, can you make sure to get the fattest eggplants they have? Mimi loves them."

"Oh, does he?" Ava makes an exaggerated face and even Rayan laughs. "Does he love makloubeh? Does he love eggplants? I don't think I've heard that before."

Mazna swats her away. "Make fun, Ava, but I haven't seen your brother in months."

You hadn't seen me in months either. But Ava doesn't say anything. Instead, she stalks inside and kicks the side of the sofa Naj is sleeping on. Her sister startles, blinking. "Shift change," Ava hisses.

"What the —" Naj looks alarmed.

"I can't deal with your mother when she's like this," Ava hears Mazna saying to the children, and she has to force herself to keep walking.

❀

Ava takes her grandfather's car, a 2010 burgundy Mercedes that she hasn't seen before; he must've gotten it in the past few years. There's a medallion on the key chain. She feels like a trespasser as she starts the engine, as the car crawls toward downtown. She wonders when he last drove it. The radio is set to an Arabic station; she imagines him singing along, but it makes her feel uneasy and sad. She changes the station, and it's English and young and pure sex, the singer growling about touching her body. At a street corner, Ava sees a woman selling figs, her front tooth missing and a flower tucked behind her ear. Ava buys three packs of fruit through the window.

Ava will remember all of this perfectly later on, she knows. It's always like that — the first couple of days of a trip are a world of their own, everything rich and detailed, the clearest memory she'll have years from now: The man in front of a gas station eating a *man'oushe.* The brightly colored billboard that screams YOUR BEST SUMMER EVER. Her phone chimes and it's a text from Nate. *I cannot be left alone.* Below it, a photograph of a mountain of spilled cereal on the kitchen floor, a selfie of Nate looking contrite. She smiles.

When's your flight?

In a few hours. Portland, get ready. How's your mom and dad?

The same.

The light changes and Ava puts her phone away, although nobody would ticket her here; she once saw a child in his driving father's lap. The child was holding an ashtray. The trip to Spinneys, the market Merry directed her to, is short but she goes slowly enough to be honked at, taking in the new, expensive-looking skyscrapers, shiny as freshly frosted cakes. The water is an appealing blue, but she's seen the photographs, all the trash in it from the waste crisis.

A few years ago, there were protests that lasted weeks after the country's waste landfill shut down, leading to mountains of garbage; some of it was burned, some of it thrown into the sea, wrappers floating by like multicolored jellyfish. One day people woke up and nobody was collecting the trash anymore. She can't imagine living here. It seems impossible. What her sister did feels unnatural at times, reversing the immigration process. You don't go back once you've left.

The inside of the supermarket is frigid and unrecognizable; when she was a teenager, the shelves were grungy-looking, but since then, the store has been gutted and remade, a Beirut facelift. The women, old and young, scurry around in shorts and off-the-shoulder shirts with graphics, the latest fashion trend: PANCAKES AND CHILL. BUT FIRST — NAPS. Ava feels like she's dreaming, the fatigue cottoning her mind. It's imported. All of it. The smoked salmon and Slim Jims and humor. When she and her sister had visited as children, Ava had bemoaned the lack of Snickers and Lay's; now the sight of Hostess cupcakes makes her sad.

The eggplants are pleasantly plump, and Ava loads a bag with them, then fills another one with spring onions. Strawberries as large as Zina's fists. Pita bread. A drum of *labneh*. In the frozen section, she picks up two boxes of fish fingers and fries, a large tub of peppermint ice cream. Her mother's keto comment makes her vengeful. She takes another tub of ice cream.

The Lebanese man behind the olive counter is younger than Naj. "These are the color of your eyes," he says when she asks for Kalamata.

"Half a kilo," she says. She's forgotten about this, how sex froths every conversation between young people in Beirut. Everyone flirts with each other, strangers calling each other *habibi* as effortlessly as lovers. "Please." The Arabic feels strange in her mouth, immature.

The pharmacy section is near the cashiers, and Ava's mood lifts at the sight of the familiar rows of lotions, Band-Aids, shampoos. She stocks up on toiletries, her father's antacids. Her body moves instinctively, though she's never shopped here before; all pharmacies are organized the same — by ailment, by body part. During both pregnancies, she'd craved Duane Reades the way other women craved watermelon, their fluorescent lights and predictable shelves. She'd walk through the aisles and rub her lower back, sometimes crying a little, always soothed by the bright hair dyes, the seasonal ornaments, the medications, all those promises. She was afraid of having children, like most women, afraid of all the ways the world could wreck them. But those stores reminded her that there were myriad tools for repair. There were ointments for insect bites and minor burns and headaches; syrups for coughs; lipstick and hairspray for broken hearts. Everything had a remedy.

❖

The house is crackling when she walks in. Naj is in the living room, awake, typing energetically on her phone. "The kids are with Merry," she says without looking up. "They love her."

Ava waits, but her sister doesn't say anything else. "What happened?" she finally asks.

"They had a big fight," her sister says airily. "About the real estate agent, I think. I could hear Mama yelling about it."

"Great." Ava drops into the chair beside her sister. "That's really great."

"Oh, and then Sara called. She's coming for dinner tonight. So Mama's in a great mood."

"Does she seem —" Ava stops, not knowing how to finish the question, the image of her mother wiping her face on the dark plane in her mind.

"Sara?"

"No, Mama. Does she seem a little, I don't know, off to you?"

Naj smiles down at her phone. It takes her a second to respond. "Off how?" Her voice is distracted.

"Never mind," she says. "Can you help me with these bags?" Her sister sighs but uncrosses her legs. She takes all the bags into the kitchen herself, a Naj sort of protest. Ava peeks at the cell screen on the table. There are a bunch of short texts with someone called Fee. The last one received:

Flu is finally gone. Want to do the painting on thursday?

Fee. The name isn't familiar, but then again, her sister's life is foreign to her. When she pictures it, she imagines Instagram filters — sexy friends, neon-lit nightclubs, trips to Goa and Marrakech. She could ask, but she's spent so long not asking that it's become a habit.

"Ava!" She follows her mother's voice.

Mazna is peeling the eggplants in the kitchen. Naj gives Ava a look, then leaves. "Your sister is as useless as a box of rocks," her mother says. She picks up the quaintest expressions at the greenhouse. "And Merry's off *relaxing.*"

"She's with the kids, Mama."

"Well, I really think she could help with dinner. She's been in the house all this time."

Ava feels angry. "She's not a piece of furniture, Mama."

"Please do not begin with me, Ava. I am in a mood."

"I noticed." Nevertheless, when her mother gestures toward the table, Ava sits and starts peeling. It's a familiar sensation around her mother, recoiling and opening in the same instant. The bowl is pink with a little chip at the lip. Everything in the kitchen, she realizes, belongs to dead people. It's faintly nauseating. "I heard Sara's coming tonight."

Mazna waves her hand and makes an irritated sound. It would be impossible to ask her mother candidly, *What's the problem between you two?* Like asking her to solve an algebraic equation in Italian.

"She's as bad as your father."

"I'm pretty sure Sara would be furious with selling the house," Ava ventures, and her mother's expression hardens.

Mazna takes the rice off the stove and sits for a couple of moments before jumping up again to season it. She tastes a spoonful, shakes her head, adds more salt. The kitchen cabinets open and shut. There's a hissing tension from her that confuses Ava for a moment until she realizes that it's not confusing at all. It's familiar. She knows, more than remembers, that this is how her mother was during the Beirut summers, stiff around Ava's grandmother, taking long naps, retreating to bed early. Eventually, she'd book a taxi for Damascus, and, depending on the summer, she'd go alone or with the children. She was always uncomfortable in this house, and now, watching her mother scuttle around, Ava realizes that no one once asked her why.

Mimi and Harper arrive around eight, Naj picking them up at the airport in the minivan. All day, the lamb has been marinating, and the house smells like a holiday. Merry and the children fill water glasses with wildflowers, and Ava tries to take a nap but just tosses and turns, listening to Zina ask Merry questions in the other room. Her mother was in a rotten mood all afternoon; her father disappeared with the car for hours. By the time her brother arrives, she feels like she's been in Beirut for a year.

"Welcome," she says, greeting him with the weariness of a veteran prisoner talking to a newcomer. The children swarm him. Her mother dabs her eyes. Harper hugs everyone, looking a little uncomfortable.

"Ava!" she calls out in a slightly overdone voice, and Ava hears herself reply in kind. It can't be helped; theirs is a clumsiness based on laying claim to the same person.

"Let me see it," Ava says like a talk-show host, beckoning with her fingers. The engagement was a surprise, but also not. Her mother, in her defeat, has seemed halfhearted in her complaints. The usual reasons: Harper's age — the same as Mimi's but with the added albatross of possible childlessness — her career, her whiteness.

"It's a stunner," Harper says shyly. The ring is a solitaire, simple and sparkling against her pretty hand.

The energy changes with her around, the family a little politer with one another. Ava watches Mimi's pained expression as Harper relays their experience with passport control, and she knows the exact feeling. (She remembers Nate, at the first dinner with her parents, asking to take the rest of his meal to go.)

"It was amazing, I swear. They spoke English better than me." Harper, hearing herself, flushes. "I know, I know. White girl marvels at locals. I'm a cliché." Naj and Ava laugh, but they know the performance isn't for them. Mazna picks at her cuticles.

"Dinner will be ready in an hour," their mother says. "I suppose we have to wait for Sara." A small sigh, then Mazna vanishes into the kitchen.

They scatter before dinner. There's a plate of olives and crackers, and everyone grazes. Harper goes to take a shower. Her mother, Ava notices, is not really speaking to her father but puts out a plate of pickled radishes — his favorite — just the same.

"I asked Merry for photographs and stuff for the memorial," Naj says when she and Ava are alone in the living room. "She said there are boxes in the closet of the girls' room." *Girls' room.* The room Ava is now sleeping in.

"I saw those. I figured they were storage." She follows Naj into the bedroom, already strewn with the children's toys and clothes. A pair of Spanx are on the dresser, and Ava shoves them back into the suitcase. Naj lifts a heavy-looking box from the closet. Her biceps are small and hard. All that lugging of equipment, Ava thinks. The violin balanced for hours.

"It's weird." Her sister's voice is muffled, her head in the box; she looks like an ostrich. "I always forget about these." Leather-bound photo albums. "I don't think I've ever seen them," she muses, opening one.

"You have." Ava remembers the mind-numbing boredom of her early adolescence, listening to her grandmother, flipping through page after page of unfamiliar faces. There was the initial thrill of seeing her baby father, then it was just strangers. "Teta would explain who each person was."

Mimi strides through the door, barefoot, and flops face-down onto the first bed. His hair falls forward and he shakes it back. "Mama's furious, I can tell."

"She and Baba have been fighting," Ava says, which is a half-lie.

"Well, *he* seems like he's in a great mood. He's showing off the garden to Harp." He props himself up on his elbows. "What are you guys doing?"

"Memory-laning." Naj slouches a little more, Ava notices, an affectation. There's a tilt with their brother there. It's the nature of triads; something is always off. Mimi is the gravity hole of the room. "We have to pick out some things for the memorial."

"Pass me one of those." The leather books are different colors — navy, hunter green, red — and the year numbers are in Arabic. Naj passes each of them one. They rifle through the photographs, every few minutes interrupting the silence with exclamations of their grandparents' youth or a familiar face. There are several pages of the same event in Ava's album, 1969 to 1972, a birthday party of some sort. Everyone looks comically outdated, the men with their porn mustaches and tight pants. There's a shot of her grandmother wearing a short skirt, her hair teased big and full. Behind a large cake, her father grins; must have been his birthday, then. There's a trio of young men in many of the photographs, and she recognizes a couple of them — Uncle Tarek, still with a full head of hair, her father's old friend whom she's met a handful of times in Beirut, and another one, handsome and tall, whom she's seen in other photos but doesn't think she's ever met. In a couple of photographs, her father is being embraced by an older woman standing by her grandmother.

"Who's that?" she asks, but of course her siblings don't know.

"Remember when Jiddo was obsessed with *tarneeb*?" Mimi grins into his album. The collar of his T-shirt is damp from wet hair.

"Yeah, we still played every couple of weeks." There's an edge to Naj's *we*.

"You're lucky," Mimi says wistfully, and Ava shuts her eyes. "I wish I'd gotten to spend more time with him."

"*So lucky,*" Naj parrots sarcastically. The air tenses. Before anyone can speak further, there are voices, a *Hello* from within the house. Naj cocks her head like a dog. "It's Sara. Sara! We're in the girls' room."

Their aunt bounds into the room like a Labrador and jumps onto the bed, causing Mimi to yelp and laugh. "It's my babies!" she yells into his face.

"We're collectively like a hundred years old," Naj corrects her, but she holds her cheek out for her aunt's big kiss.

"Avey, baby, let's look at you." Sara is thinner and older than in Ava's memory, her skin papery. "I just saw those gorgeous children outside. I can't believe how big they are!" Sara made one trip to Brooklyn, years ago, when Zina was still a baby. Ava's memory of it is choppy, her aunt diminished by the city but gamely playing along, wearing a Yankees baseball cap every day and going all the way up the Empire State Building by herself. "I want to hear everything. Everything! You." She points an accusatory finger at Mimi. "I have to hear about your engagement from Uncle Facebook?"

Mimi hangs his head. "Again, I'm so sorry. There was a little miscommunication about publicizing."

"Well, she's a good girl. I almost knocked her over outside. Avey, what's new with you? How's Nate?"

Ava remembers Nate like a photocopy: His coffee mug shaped like a cactus.

The morning of her flight — *yesterday* — they'd had sex; he'd cradled her face after. For a moment she thought he might cry. "He's good," she says lamely. "He's in Portland. Or headed there right now, actually. Work stuff. I didn't want to drag him into this mess."

Naj's head shoots up. Mimi coughs.

"Ah." Sara looks intently at each of them. "I knew it. It's not just a memorial. Something's up, isn't it?"

"There's nothing." Mimi's voice is a little high. Ava catches his eye, and there's an old understanding in their silence, a loyalty to their father despite everything.

"Just the usual between Mama and Baba," Naj adds.

"I see." Sara smiles a little sadly. She shakes her hair. Her shirt tag is sticking out. "Well. My babies are home and I won't look gift horses in the mouth." She makes direct eye contact with Ava, who looks away first. "Even if they're lying to me."

"*Yalla!* Ava!"

She clatters to her feet, grateful for the distraction. She knows her silence has incriminated all of them, but she can't tell Sara outright. It would betray her father. "Mama, we're in the girls' room! Sara's here!" she warns.

"I heard." Their mother at the door, her face unreadable. "Well, Sara. It's been years." Mazna's tone is cinematic, like she's reading lines. It's a habit that Naj once pointed out — whenever their mother is flustered, she goes straight Audrey Hepburn, charming and calm.

"It has." Her aunt, by contrast, sounds emotional. "Oh, Mazna." Something collapses between the women and Ava's heart soars.

Her mother looks down. "I'm so sorry about your father. I loved him." They embrace lightly and her mother repeats the words into Sara's neck. It's odd, like she's defending herself against a crime she hasn't been accused of. "I loved him, Sara."

"I know you did," her aunt says. They hug for a few seconds, until her mother breaks away and tells them, her voice again all Hepburn, to wash up for dinner.

The next day, Ava takes Mimi to Spinneys for his what-we-forgot trip. They haven't seen each other since January, and their conversation is easy, moving quickly from their partners to Idris's motivations for selling to Beirut.

"I dreamed about Jiddo," Mimi confesses. "I was all wrapped up in this massive cobweb. I couldn't get to him."

"That cobweb's your guilt." Ava sighs. "I'm feeling it too. Naj doesn't make it easy."

"I don't know how weekly visits and getting high all the time makes her a dutiful granddaughter."

Ava snorts. "Don't let her hear you say that." A moment passes. "Harp said you canceled your shows."

Her brother shrugs, but she can see his jaw tense. "Yeah."

"That's it?" she pushes. "'Yeah'?"

His voice is flat. "I'm no rock star, Ava. I don't want people to think I don't know that."

"Oh." The sentence, so crisp and precise and brutal, startles the car into silence. They go on to talk about weather instead.

When they return to the house, the truck is parked in front. "Naj is back," Ava says. It's a bit of a surprise, her sister spending so much time with them. There's a woman standing in front of the house. She looks lost.

"The real estate agent," Ava says, remembering.

"Is he fucking kidding?" Mimi frowns. "She doesn't look like an agent."

"Don't be ageist." He's right, though. She's older, in her eighties. Her clothes are simple, a little worn. Mimi reaches her first. He greets her and the woman seems nervous. But when she turns and sees Ava, her eyes change.

"Hello," the woman says. She looks down. Ava tugs at her shorts. These conservative women. There's no middle ground in Beirut. "Oh, dear. This heat." She glances at Mimi. "I was just telling your . . . husband?"

"Brother," Ava says. Her hands feel strangely cold despite the humidity, the heat. Her mind flutters, whispery as a déjà vu.

"Brother." The woman repeats the word with wonder. "You're his grandchildren?"

Ava and Mimi glance at each other. "Issa Nasr's grandchildren?" Mimi says slowly, gently.

"Yes, Issa. I used to work for your grandparents. I only just heard about dear Issa's death. He was a good, good man. Good to me and to my boy." Ava finally places the woman's accent: Palestinian. A moped flies by, and the three of them watch it for a second.

"Do you want to come in?" Mimi asks kindly.

The woman steps back. "No, dear, I better go." She looks at the house as though afraid someone will come out. "You can tell them Hayat came by. I know the *azza* was months ago. I just heard. There was a message left for me, but I didn't get it until —" She seems reluctant to say more. "I would have come sooner."

"There's going to be a memorial," Mimi says. "Sometime this summer. We can call you when we know —"

"Bonjour!" A woman approaches, waving at them; her talon-like nails are painted lemon yellow. She's wearing a bright pink blazer, tight jeans, and a white tank top. Her hair is bleached. "I'm Mirabel. I'm looking for an Idris?" she trills in a strong Lebanese accent.

"Um." Ava can't think fast enough.

"Oh," Mirabel murmurs to herself as she scans the area, "is this the house? Very nice. Needs a little fixing up around the hedges, and this courtyard is a mess."

"Can we help you?" Mimi turns to Mirabel, and Hayat starts walking away, slowly at first, then quicker, surprisingly adroit; she's nearly at the end of the street before Ava notices she's left.

"Excuse me," Ava calls out. She jogs after her. "Auntie?" The woman vanishes around the corner. "Fuck." She rejoins Mimi, who's seething at Mirabel.

"We are *not* changing the courtyard," he's saying. The woman smiles at him. She seems undaunted.

"And you're Idris, then?" she asks sweetly.

"That's my father, but — oh, hey, Avey, meet the *real estate agent,*" he says, like he's introducing a unicorn handler.

"Nice to meet you." Before she can say more, Idris comes rushing out.

"You're early! What a gem in this city." He beams as though Mirabel's punctuality implies something deeper. "Please, please. Come this way. We'll start through here. Feel free to ignore my children." He grins his charming grin, and Mirabel smiles back.

"These are your children?" She makes a shocked face, though Mimi already told her. "Why, you must've been an *infant.*"

"Baba, she wants to rip up the courtyard!"

"Your son here seems a little upset." She lowers her voice as if discussing a child. "It happens all the time, families disagreeing about inheritance. I understand how difficult it is." Then her tone turns girlish. "The reality is that these houses often get completely redone anyway."

Ava puts a hand on Mimi's arm. "We'll leave you to it, then." She tries to glare at her father, but he's already leading Mirabel away.

"We'll figure something out," Ava tells Mimi, which was what she said to Naj last night, what she's been saying to her mother. It occurs to her suddenly that someone might hold her to that. "Listen." They reach the backyard, where the others are, and Mimi opens the door a little too roughly. "What about that other lady?"

Mimi frowns.

"What other lady?" Naj asks.

They're on the veranda now. Rayan is watering the plants with her mother, while Naj sits cross-legged on the ground like a yogi, her head straight and erect, a lit cigarette between her teeth and an ashtray on her lap. Zina is darting around her, fixing her hair in braids and adding flowers. The smoke swirls around Zina's face. "What other lady?" Naj repeats.

"The real estate agent is with Baba," Ava says, momentarily distracted. "Naj, can you get your goddamn cigarette away from my daughter's face?"

"Mama, look, I'm making Auntie Naj into a queen."

"I see that, baby." Ava's not sure why, but she doesn't want to mention the other lady yet; she tries to catch Mimi's eye, but he's already telling them. A flower falls from Naj's hair and she tosses it into the ashtray. "She said her name was Hayat," he finishes.

There's a loud crash.

They all turn to the source, where Rayan and their mother are standing. "Rayan," Ava begins, intending to scold him, but then she sees the mug, her mother's, in splinters on the ground, the strangest expression on Mazna's face. Her cheeks have gone a little pale.

"Hayat," she repeats, and the hairs on Ava's arm stand up.

"Mama, the glass!" Mimi rushes over. The veranda stills, everyone watching her.

"She's probably an old friend of your grandfather's," she finally says. "I'm going to toss this out." She scoops up some glass and walks inside.

"That was a *very* normal reaction," Naj says. Her cigarette is still hanging from her mouth.

"Put that out," Ava snaps. She rubs her arms. She can tell that her siblings are also unsettled. There's a long silence, all of them in their own thoughts, finally interrupted by Zina's small voice.

"Fire! Fire!"

They rush to look. There in the ashtray, that half-extinguished cigarette cherry is on the flower, and between layers of pinks and reds, the beginnings of a flame.

Homecoming

THE FAMILY QUICKLY settles into a routine that reminds Naj uncomfortably of her childhood. Idris spends his days with old friends or the real estate agent; her mother disappears for hours at a time, returning with freshly dyed hair or a manicure. Ava and Mimi take turns planning the days, trips to malls and the mountains and the beach.

Naj floats in and out.

She's already nocturnal, and her family's presence is pushing her to almost hallucinogenic heights of sleeplessness. She pulls all-nighters, then shows up at the house to take afternoon naps. Aware of how irritating Ava finds this, Naj convinces the children to nap with her one afternoon and it becomes a habit, the three of them sprawled on her grandfather's bed, curtains drawn, the room always a little too warm. Ava never complains again.

"I don't know why we'd ever get rid of naptime," she marvels at one point. "They're out for two hours, easy."

"You're welcome," Naj says, but she loves those hours, the only time in her days when everything is still, the sound of the children's breathing hypnotic. Everything slows and she can finally get the sleep that has somehow been eluding her.

Somehow is Fee.

Fee's large ears, pink as seashells. Fee's lips. Fee's hair. Fee's arm hairs. Fee's eyes. Each one of Fee's eyelashes, wiry and dark. The dozens of photographs that appear when she Googles Fee's name, opening one secret browser after the other. They've seen each other several times since the exhibit, always in groups. They text each other jokes, like they're old friends who have reconnected. It's going well except that it's not. There's something off about each encounter; they talk about the weather and art and politics but never the past.

"You know what I think," Jo had said to her last night as they walked home together after doing a show. It was a small one, a favor for a friend's new bar opening. They'd barely seen each other since her family arrived a few weeks ago. Fee and Bilal had been at the show. Naj made a point of not laughing at any of Bilal's jokes.

"What?"

Jo gave her an arch look. "I wasn't asking a question."

"She's painting me tomorrow," Naj said, because she couldn't think of anything else.

"I heard." Jo exhaled. "You were good tonight."

"Thanks."

"Better than usual, you know. Playing for her."

If only she could name what kept her wired awake at night. Nostalgia. Regret. "Jo, I'm not doing anything wrong. I'm up to my eyeballs in my parents' shit. Nobody's really speaking with anyone. Mimi's being weird with me, as usual. You saw how he was when you came over for dinner." The week before, Jo had visited and fawned over her parents.

"That thing about our Europe tour," Jo said, remembering. "Your brother's jealous as fuck."

"Anyway." The thought made her squirm. She tried not to mention Noja around Mimi. "It's been nice to see Fee." She sounded sadder than she'd intended. Jo gentled his tone.

"I loved Fee, Naj. You know that. And yes, it's been fun to see her. Even Bilal's growing on me. But there's a swamp of history there."

"I know. I guess it's just — the house and all that. I'm a little nostalgic, that's all." She pretended to look at her cell. "What about the painting? Should I cancel?"

Jo considered. "No," he finally said. "It'll be a killer promo for the band."

❈

For weeks, she's been envisioning an art-filled loft, one of those luxury apartments recently built with Gulf money. She's imagined Fee drinking a chilled gin, Bilal off at some academic circle jerk or, even better, watching his wife paint while Naj and Fee make occasional eye contact, illicit and charged. Fee would be the first to look away.

In reality, Naj is the skittish one. In college, she'd always been unruffled, but now she smokes four cigarettes on the car ride over. Fee and Bilal live in Bourj Hammoud. The neighborhood is a little scruffy, and as Naj passes the third broken window, she amends her vision of Fee's life. She finds parking right in front of the building. There is a dilapidated hair salon on the first floor, a peeling poster of an American model with bright blue hair taped to the window. The lobby is unlocked; someone's beat-up stroller is in the hallway. When Naj reaches the third floor, she hesitates at the two identical wooden doors across from each other. One has a silver cross above the eyehole. She knocks on the other.

"You made it!" Fee looks smaller barefoot. She is wearing a yellow kimono that dries Naj's mouth out. "Come in, please. We just ran out of Nescafé," she says over her shoulder. "Tea? Almaza? I wasn't sure what you'd want to drink so I made sure to have everything." Fee's nerves calm Naj. "Bilal says hi. He's at a meeting," Fee calls out from the kitchen. Circle jerk it is, then.

"Almaza, please." Naj clears her throat. "That's too bad." She steps out of her sneakers and into the living room. The apartment is ugly, peeling gray walls and water stains on the ceiling, almost a little industrial. Little has been done to enliven it — a cherry-red sofa, some framed photographs. They only make it seem sadder. There's a large easel and a wooden armoire next to the sofa, the door ajar to reveal colorful, tufted dresses, the focal point of the room. There is a stack of books on the floor towering as high as her. Down the hallway, Naj can make out a bedroom, the light fixture a naked bulb. It looks poor.

"It isn't attractive," Fee says, and Naj turns to find her staring. "Exile."

"No, no. I was just checking out this . . . book," Naj finishes lamely, tapping the top of the stack. She can barely read the Arabic title.

Fee straightens. "'The Society as Microcosm of God,'" she reads out. She lifts an eyebrow, waiting. "Why can't you just say it?" Her voice is quiet.

When Naj was six or seven, she'd been out shopping with her mother when someone called their names. It was Tia, their neighbor. Mazna had canceled a lunch with her that day; she'd lied, saying she had the flu. Tia had looked confused, then insulted, and she'd opened her mouth to ask the obvious question. Mazna struck first.

She talked in a flurry, asking about Tia's family, exclaiming that she must have the name of Tia's hairstylist, that the cut looked positively marvelous, and yes, she'd had the sniffles earlier, but how wonderful they'd run into each other, and wasn't it just destiny that they spend the afternoon together? And by the end of it, poor Tia was beaming as she fluffed her hair, nodding along, agreeing that, yes, they should get honeybuns at the food court.

As Tia bustled ahead of them, Naj had looked up at Mazna. Her mother winked at her. *When someone asks you something you can't answer,* she'd whispered, *change the subject.*

"Where'd you get these dresses from?" Naj asks now.

But Fee isn't Tia. Fee knows her. "You're lucky I'm excited about these costumes," she says wryly. She starts flicking through the rack. "I posted a request on Facebook asking for old clothes from Damascus, dresses that belonged to people's great-grandmothers, things like that. I have to be careful with them, though." She frowns. "The last girl, maybe you know her—Lina? Lina Mourtada? No? Anyway, I had her pose in this amazing old wedding dress. And of course she got lipstick all over the sleeve. It's at the dry cleaner's. I'm praying it comes out."

Naj watches the yellow kimono slip from Fee's shoulder. An inch of pale skin.

There's something unmistakably Arab in how she moves through the room, her hands arriving at places before she does. "I'm posing in a wedding dress?"

"No." There's something brief and flaring between them. "With your coloring, I wanted to go darker." She pulls out an enormous black gown. It is a black cupcake of a dress, all tulle and fluff, cinched at the waist, flaring into a half-moon at the floor. It looks to be a hundred pounds. Naj can't help herself; she laughs.

"Um. What. Is that?"

"It's too late to back out," Fee warns her. "I've already prepped my palette."

"Let's tame this beast."

It takes half an hour to set everything up; Fee is surprisingly fastidious and fusses about where the stool should be. Putting on the dress itself is a whole procedure, but Naj has learned to be nonchalant about nudity, perhaps because it's uncomfortable for others. In college, she read about censorship and queer bodies, the way nudity could be brandished as a weapon, but sometimes it feels more petty for her — it flusters people. So when Fee says Naj can use the bedroom, there's a victory in replying, "What are we, strangers?" Naj whips off her T-shirt, and Fee's face falls. It's mean and they both know it. Naj feels her heart quicken at the air between them, the scratchy dress in her hand, the apartment Fee sleeps and fucks in, although Fee is already turning around, her back a thin reproach.

※

The sitting takes nearly four hours. At first, each brushstroke feels personal, like spiders scuttling across her skin. The dress is a little big in the chest, and it sits stiffly, like a small, lacy monkey hanging from her shoulders. There's a quarter of an inch between Naj's breasts and the dress, and each time Fee comes over to fuss with a strand of hair or thread, her nipples rise dictatorially: *Look.* She tries to distract herself by watching Fee as she paints; she has a face like a Parisian window, opening and shuttering with the weather. In college, they used to get drunk on Johnnie Walker, and there's a similar dreaminess to her now, her face scrunched up in concentration.

Naj tries to talk, but Fee shushes her. "I'm doing your mouth now. It's the hardest part."

Fee's mouth, nineteen, parting. Their mouths moving hard against each other, the car honk from downstairs. It was in Naj's apartment, her first one, sophomore year at the American University, and Fee had given her brother the address to pick her up. *I'm studying at my friend's,* she'd told him. Neither of them had thought of that, how he'd then know where Naj lived.

Naj's ear begins to itch exquisitely. Fee starts to laugh.

"I've seen five-year-olds sit still longer than you." She taps the paintbrush. "Listen. It works best if you meditate or something. Try to empty your mind and focus on one thing. Shut your eyes."

Naj thinks of the concerts. The Nordic Rock Festival, Pitchfork, Gov Ball; the hotel beds in Tokyo, Arizona, Denmark. The flight delays and jet lag and hotel rooms. Once, Jo took a photograph of Naj completely naked in a tub with strategically placed CD covers floating in the water. It had hit twenty thousand likes by midnight.

The late nights. Day and night melting into one, Naj and Jo getting barely any sleep for weeks on end. The days always have an unwashed feel about them, the microphones stinking of years-old spittle. The beds she and Jo share, their feet smelly, their breath bad. Her hair starts to dreadlock on tour because she barely showers. The pills litter her backpack like jewels: Lunesta, Klonopin, Trazadone, Ambien. The names remind her of Caribbean islands. She keeps them in a box shaped like a genie's bottle, a joke that's worn out. The photographs from tours are always blurry, light-spattered and out of focus: a floral crown trampled after a show, some selfies, the audience a great blue smear behind her. Her own face is like a kaleidoscope, and Naj can see it now behind her eyelids, the silver streaks across her own eyebrows, bright orange lipstick or completely unadorned. She sometimes tosses glitter inside the violin so it'll shed as she plays.

The shows wait in her mind like patient dogs. They are exhilarating and loud and endless. They are bright pink logo tents and sweaty bras and unexpected rainstorms that only energize the crowds. Women screaming Naj's name. The entire audience going silent when she drops her voice and whispers the lyrics, the drums quieting and a thousand Egyptian or Danish faces looking up at her like expectant lilies, Naj's mouth so close to the microphone she can taste the metal. On the best nights, it's like someone has replaced the blood in her veins with Fanta, something sugary and fizzing. Afterward, backstage or in the hotel bar or the merch line, she'll sign albums or books or body parts with Jo, and the fans come up and talk to her. They'll hug her, cry, whisper about affairs and breakups and deaths. Their fans make sense only as an aggregate: queers, fat girls, lonely middle-aged men. *Your music got me through it. I don't know what I'd do.* Their eyes shine earnestly and it always makes Naj sad because it's not reciprocal, because they've given her nothing aside from a good show, and she can't thank them back, or she can, and does, but it rings hollow in her ears, so she says it again, then again.

In Europe, Peru, America, she's less careful than she is in Beirut. She wears men's suits with nothing under the jacket, flirts with the female tech crew. Once, a girl in Berlin tossed her panties at Naj, and she'd worn them like a necklace for the rest of the set. An article described the Noja mythology as *the idea of a sex that anyone can access,* but Naj knows that some people know. She didn't live in the closet as much as rent it, the truth peeking out beneath the fiction, a neon organ slightly visible under her skin. The secret is hers to keep or explode, like a warm gun beneath her pillow.

❧

After Fee is done painting her, they get a beer near the apartment. There's a surprising number of new bars in the neighborhood, with distressed-wood bar tops, intricate cocktails; they outshine the dated establishments like new puppies at a pound. Naj often chooses older bars out of loyalty; the one they're in has been around since their university days. They pick a corner table submerged in the setting sun's light, and a pretty girl brings over menus. She catches Naj's eye and holds it.

"Happy hour until six," she says, a Valley Girl accent imported from American sitcoms.

"Thanks." Naj hands a menu to Fee. Their fingers briefly touch. The silence during the painting had been a nice buffer. "My family's driving me crazy," she offers, but then it feels like the wrong thing to say, to bring up family. "I just mean," she amends, "I'm spending too much time in that house."

The girl comes back. They order fries and hummus and beer.

"I remember your brother," Fee says abstractedly, then her face changes. *I remember yours too.*

"That one time he visited. He'd just broken up with his girlfriend. Remember that? He had her photo in his wallet? Is she the one here?"

Naj laughs. She does remember. She wonders if Mimi remembers Fee. She'd told him nothing of her; they'd met for only a couple of hours. "Angela. Or Angelina! No, they never got back together. His fiancée's name is Harper."

"Harper." The name is bulky in Fee's mouth. Her *p*'s are a little blurred, nearly *b*'s.

The waitress brings their food and beer. The place is empty save for a couple of older men at the bar. There's a mounted television playing a nature documentary, and the women watch for a moment. A lioness is prowling the Saharan desert. "Many of their young will be lost come autumn. Each summer is more devastating than the last," drones the British commentator. "The lucky of the species will survive to see spring."

Fee leans forward. "The painting will come out nicely. I'll finish it in the next few days."

"When's the show?"

"I don't know." She sounds weary. "Maybe there won't be a show. Do you ever feel this, with your music — like maybe a little love-hate?" *Lahv-ayt.* Naj wants to tell her to speak Arabic, but they never did with each other.

"What do you mean?"

"Like I feel all I'm doing is working with a bad memory. I have an idea. Usually it feels very urgent. I want to bring my neighborhood back. I want to show my mother her city. But something happens when I make the work. It erases the intention." She looks expectantly at Naj.

"Right," she says.

"I get lost in the details. Then I realize I cannot remember very well. Or I am working with other people's memories. They are slippery, like fish. And so then you start to make little things up. Or you start to get distracted with the performance. Do the frames go with the wall paint? Should the chairs be in a row or a circle? Then it's opening night and you are distracted even more. *Did enough people come? Are people complimenting me? Are people upset?* Suddenly, it's not about the idea anymore. The idea has been lost for months. Now it's all about you." She stabs a fry into the hummus. "You feel like you're changing the world, but really all you did was get some paint on people's hands."

"That's a little harsh," Naj says. On the television screen, the lion cubs die of thirst. "But I guess it's different for me."

"How?" Fee looks eager to hear her answer. This irritates Naj. In college, she'd never heard Fee mention art, not once.

"I guess I'm less attached to my songs," she says tightly. "I just try to remember what something felt like and I sing."

"You're upset," Fee observes.

Naj tries to smile. "I'm not."

The waitress brings them fresh beers. Fee is chewing her lip, and finally she speaks, this time in Arabic. "I did write to you, Naj. Back then. But I never heard back, and I knew there wasn't anything I could say."

The abrupt shift in the conversation is less surprising than Naj would expect. She feels some relief. She leans back and Fee does as well, two boxers in their corners. Fee is blinking rapidly. The first time Naj saw her cry was on New Year's Eve, the two of them hiding on some house party's rooftop. She was telling Naj about her family, how burdened she'd felt in that house, what a relief it was to convince her brother and father to let her study in Beirut. Naj and Fee had sex later that night, and when Naj went down on her, she tasted salt everywhere.

"I'm sorry about Aleppo," she says, which is idiotic but also true, and Fee is wiping her eyes now. She whispers something, but Naj doesn't catch it and doesn't ask her to repeat it. Syria outside the window. Syria on the television screen. The children selling roses. The camps flooding in the winter. Naj wonders how many times she's said the word *Aleppo* in the past year. Mostly she avoids thinking about any of it. Her deliverance was unasked for and therefore particularly chastening.

"We left early on," Fee says. Her providence as well. Her apartment was small and drab but filled with books and a nice television and expensive oil paints. Even exile had tiers.

As though intuiting her thoughts, Fee leans across the table.

"Yes," she says to the unasked question with her perfect grin, the grin that

Naj thought was lost to the world, or at least her world, that reminds her of autumn and Hamra and the time they'd sung on the beach, alone, in the middle of the night. But also of Jo, telling her to be careful. She never really got over that grin; how could she?

And so as Fee grins, Naj swallows. "I'm the lucky of my species."

❖

When Naj returns to Jiddo's house, it's nearly seven, the children in front of the television. There's a mess of photographs spread out across the coffee table.

"What're these photographs?"

"Mimi brought them out. We're picking our favorites for the memorial. Harp was saying we should mount a little display."

"Thanks for asking me!"

"You can choose yours," Ava says patiently. Naj starts flipping through the photographs. It annoys her that they've already picked the good ones: her grandfather in front of the print shop, a birthday party, a family portrait. "What about that photo in the park?" she asks her sister. "With Teta in the red skirt?"

"That's a good one. I don't think Jiddo's in it, though. You can check." Ava shoots up from the couch. "I knew it!"

"What?"

"From the photograph! She was in the photograph!"

Naj frowns. "What —"

"Remember —" Ava lowers her voice. She glances over her shoulder. "Remember that lady that stopped by? The one Mama got so weird about?"

There were still pebbles of glass on the veranda. "Yeah."

"It's been driving me crazy. She seemed so — familiar or something. But I just realized, she's the woman in those birthday photographs. And some of the others, the older ones." She holds out a picture. "Here's another one! This lady, that's her. I'm sure of it."

"Really?" It's a photograph of her father and Jiddo, Idris seven or eight, dancing. The woman is stout and cheery, looking on, laughing; there's another little boy tucked to her side. "I think she's the housekeeper, Ave."

"You're right." Ava frowns intently at the photograph. "I remember Teta talking about her, they were old friends or something. I want to invite her to the memorial."

"The woman?"

"Yes." Ava sounds somber. "She was saying she didn't hear about the *azza* in time. Sara or someone must've left her a message. We can go back and look through the albums, but that lady, whoever she is, she was there for *years*. And she didn't even know Jiddo died."

"I don't know if that's a good idea. Maybe they had a falling-out. This was like forty years ago, Ava."

"You don't find it strange?" Ava shakes her head. "Baba wants to sell the house. Some lady shows up from ages ago, and Mama almost faints. You're seriously not curious about any of this?"

Naj is curious. About what Fee is doing tonight. What she'll tell Bilal about the painting. About the show they'd agreed to meet at in a couple of days. She feels bad for her sister. Nate and the white girl and her boring university job. She seems eager for distraction.

"How would we even get in touch with her?"

Ava drums her fingers on the door frame. There's an intensity about her when she locks onto an idea. Naj feels suddenly claustrophobic. She wishes her dead grandfather's younger face wasn't scattered all over the living room. She doesn't know who the woman is. She doesn't care. She wants to go home.

"We can find it." Ava sounds confident. "We'll find her."

✳

Naj avoids her family for a couple of days. She tells them she's ill, but really she spends the time with Jo, the two of them cuddled under a blanket on the sofa watching episodes of a murder documentary. It's disgusting outside, the humid, smothering days of early July in Beirut, steam everywhere, the streets filled with the smell of garbage. Everyone's cranky and the traffic is a disaster; people have been protesting the new parliament, which is really the old parliament, since nobody new ever gets elected, and posters of those men's faces, crossed out, decorate every corner. On the road to downtown, the protesters have set up a little headquarters; every few days, they burn tires and chant in the streets. They're protesting the piles of garbage, the old-new men, the corruption and high electricity bills. Naj always thinks about the fires — the protesters are unhappy with the city, and so they set fire to it. It makes no sense.

After several days Mazna calls her and says summarily, *See you at dinner tonight* — when Naj was in school, her mother always knew when she was faking illness — and Naj reluctantly kisses Jo and drives to the house. She takes the long way, through downtown, just to see the protests. There is a decent-size crowd, yelling and carrying signs. She can smell the smoke even in the closed car.

"Let's throw the real garbage out, sister," one of the men calls out at her as she drives past. He gestures to a sign that says PARLIAMENT IS GARBAGE. She throws up horns and honks.

The table is already set when she arrives. Merry has the children eating in the living room. Zina's head is in Merry's lap and she's combing her hair. "How's your flu?" Merry asks in a tone that reminds Naj of her mother.

"Much better, thanks." Naj sniffles in the most dignified manner she can muster. Merry rolls her eyes.

Her mother and Mimi have cooked up a storm, and the table is almost celebratory with favorites — mashed potatoes with extra butter, stuffed *koussa*, lamb chops. Harper coos over the spread and takes hearty portions but then salts it too much. Naj feels sorry for her, but she's also a little tired of her. She's tired of all of them. Her father clinks his glass.

"It's nice, finally all of us together." He raises his water glass to his right, Mazna sitting next to Mimi. "To the chefs!"

"That's enough," Mazna says, but her cheeks redden.

"Mrs. Nasr, this sauce is divine. I could just drink it up." Harp mimes tipping the plate like a bowl, and only Idris laughs.

"It's good of you to show up, Najla," Mazna says, and Naj knows she's been caught.

"The potatoes as well," Harp says. "Back home, my mama never cooked. My grandmother would make these delicious meat pies. I don't think I ever told y'all about her. She was the most wonderful woman." Harp's voice is a little higher.

"Is that so?" Idris says absently.

"Especially since," Mazna continues, spearing a tomato slice, "you are the one who lives the farthest away. And calls the least."

"I call you," Naj says unconvincingly.

"Her name was Ainsley. My grandmother." Harper is stabbing at her meat.

"Naj doesn't do phone calls," Ava mutters.

"Excuse me?" Naj feels her face get hot. "Last I checked, Brooklyn wasn't exactly a short drive away from California."

"Your sister visits enough."

"I'm not saying that." Ava is already backing down. "You're just far, that's all."

"It's not like Beirut is even a music hub," Mimi says. "You barely have internet here." Mazna nods.

"I do all right!" Naj fires back, which shuts Mimi up. She hates it when they gang up on her.

"Her name was Ainsley," Harp repeats. Her fork clatters to the plate. There's an uneasy silence. "She died from lung cancer," she says, louder now. "She loved her stupid Marlboros. Southern and sassy and super Christian, but also really smart and gentle. She voted for Clinton twice in the nineties." Nobody speaks.

"Who's this, dear?" Mazna says, sounding uncharacteristically kind, as though Harper has lost her mind.

"Just my dead goddamn grandmother." Harper stands. "Thanks for asking."

"Harper!" Mimi instinctively reaches for Mazna's hand, not Harper's, which everybody sees.

Harper pinches the bridge of her nose. She exhales. Her voice is calm again when she speaks. "I apologize, Mrs. Nasr. All of you. I must be catching whatever Naj has." She stalks into the kitchen.

"Well," Mazna says, loud enough for her voice to carry, "I'm not sure what that was all about. Clearly I can't even be thanked for making a nice meal."

"Mazna," Idris says.

"Thank you, Mama." Ava sounds exhausted.

Naj stands up, plate in hand. "Beirut *is* a music hub, for your information," she says. "The *Atlantic* did a whole article about it." Harper's anger is contagious. Naj finds her in the kitchen, scraping her plate into the trash.

"I really did like the potatoes," Harper says sadly.

There's a small groove in the counter and Naj digs her hip into it. "My mother . . ." she starts, then lets the sentence hang. Mimi comes in with his own plate.

"Harp," Mimi says just as Harper says, "Thanks for that."

"You know what?" Mimi sounds angry. "You knew what this trip was going to be like."

"This trip," Harper says sadly. "I'm talking about you." Naj sucks in her breath.

Her brother looks defeated. "What am I supposed to do, Harp?"

"Let's go out," Naj says, surprising herself. Her plan was to go home after dinner and watch more murders. But their misery is like a big, shedding cat in the kitchen. She wants it to go away. "The three of us." Ava's comment still rankles; she wouldn't join them even if asked, but the lack of an invitation will wound.

Harper glances at Naj. "You mean now? You really want to?"

She doesn't want to. She deeply doesn't want to. She and her brother have a family-time quota and it's already been met; she's on the penultimate episode of the documentary and feels a Pavlovian pang at the thought of her sofa. But even Mimi looks expectant; an excursion would kill this almost fight.

"Yeah," Naj says. "We can go to Loge. They always have good bands. It'll be fun."

❖

Loge has a line snaking out front, so she takes them to the Back Door instead, a small, hip space filled with twenty-somethings. Ava surprised her by apparently not noticing the lack of invite. At the doorway, she caught Naj's hand and said in a low voice, "I e-mailed this investigator guy. I asked if he could help me find somebody if I had only a first name and a photograph. He said he'd try."

"I mean, if I tell you to stop, are you even going to listen?"

"Naj." Her sister's voice was low. "I just have a feeling about this." As teenagers, Naj was the one who went to fortunetellers, collected the slips from fortune cookies. The reverse in dynamics was almost alarming.

Now, in the bar, she wishes she'd tried to get Ava to come. It's quieter than Loge would've been; they can hear themselves talk. The band's a mumblecore mess with lyrics about broken hearts and December. They sit at the bar and order Almazas with salt-rimmed tumblers. There's still tension between her brother and Harper. She's changed into a clingy red top, and it doesn't seem like a coincidence that her lips match the shirt. She leans toward the bartender when he brings their drinks.

"Thank you," she says ardently.

"So," Naj says lamely. "Ava's obsessed."

"With that old woman?" Harper pours her beer, glancing at the bartender. "It seems a little like she's looking for a distraction, no?"

"That's what I said!"

Her brother visibly prickles. "She just wants to invite her to the memorial."

"Harp's right," Naj says defensively. "It's not normal."

They order another round, this time lemon drops, the triple sec acidic and perfect. The bar is clammy. When one song ends, they clap louder than anyone.

"Name that plagiarism," Mimi says as the band starts another song, the first few strains familiar. Naj feels a flicker of irritation. They used to play the game back in California. For years, a song would come on, and Mimi would quiz her on the chords. If she got it wrong, he'd be condescending; if she was right, he'd become surly.

"No clue," Naj says tightly.

"So easy," he scoffs, but he takes a long sip of the beer. He hates this as much as she does, but he can't help himself. The year after she started music school, he'd wake her up an hour early so they could run scales together. She remembers the calluses that formed on her fingers, how she lied to the music teacher and said she wasn't overpracticing. Sometimes her fingers bled, but she never complained; there was only relief when he'd outpace her, learning a more difficult piece first. It was always fleeting, though, that outpacing, and then she'd go back to lying, pretending she was worse than she was.

In the end, it didn't matter. When Noja got signed, she'd called him and asked him to join the band, expecting joy. She'd offered him a European tour. A booked flight. But all it had done was extinguish whatever remained between them.

The memory hardens her. "'Wonderwall,'" she says. Her voice is cold. His face falls.

"That's it," he says glumly.

"I have an idea." Harper drains her glass. "Maybe we could skip the pissing contest for one night?" She turns to Naj, her expression light. "Let's dance. Can we dance?"

Naj can see her brother become annoyed, which is reason enough to do it. "Let's see those moves, baby."

The band seems to perk up at their dancing, and the playing improves a little, a singularity she knows from Noja — what the audience gives, you return. More people join them on the impromptu dance floor, and Naj catches a glimpse of her brother sulking at the bar.

"It's hard for him," Harp yells over the music. "And he doesn't know how to say that, so he just acts more like a dick, which makes it harder."

There isn't anything to say to this, so Naj spins Harp around, then pulls her closer, the other woman moving her hips in tandem. Fuck Mimi. She snaps her fingers coquettishly, the fox tattoo glaring at her. She wonders if her brother has told Harper about her queerness, and if so, whether Harp is uncomfortable about it or maybe a little pleased with herself, assuming Naj is attracted to her. She's not. Harp is pretty enough, but she's somehow both sharp and eager at the same time. They dance just long enough for Mimi to get jealous; he finally makes his way through the crowd to them.

"Harp, I'm sorry," he says, and the three of them stand awkwardly amid the dancing bodies.

Harper punches his arm. "I don't hate your mother, Mimi. I actually kind of love her."

"I know."

Naj's heart melts a little — her big, childish brother. She waves her arms around wildly. "She said yes! Everybody, she said yes!" People whistle and clap, and even Mimi laughs at her antics, finally kissing his fiancée until the cheering stops. They join the dancing crowd.

❈

Around eleven, Harper heads home, but Naj orders a fresh drink, and Mimi stays with her. The alcohol makes everything easier, and they joke about the geeky bassist, talk about their parents.

"They seem better," Mimi says. "They went out yesterday."

"I think he's keeping that Mirabel lady away on purpose. That's helping."

"Hey!" A college-age guy is at Naj's side. "I love your music. *Ladder* is a classic."

"Thanks," she says quickly, trying to wrap it up, but he's already extended his hand and keeps talking nonstop. Mimi won't look at her.

"I saw you in Byblos last year; it was a great show. I'm Kareem, by the way." His hand is warm. "You too," he says, turning to Mimi, then he does a double take. "Oh, shit, sorry. You kinda look like the other guy. Jo?"

"No," Naj says, her stomach dropping. "This is my brother. Mimi. He's actually got his own band back in Austin. America." She puts an emphasis on *America* and it works; the guy looks impressed.

"No shit. I have a cousin in Houston. What kind of band?"

"The defunct kind." There's an awful sort of silence. He smiles at their confused faces. "I quit the band. Right before my trip. So, actually, Kareem, I'm a restaurant manager."

"You quit Dulcet?"

"Cool, man. Can I buy you two a drink?" Kareem's eyes are on Naj now, avid.

"You quit Dulcet?" she repeats. To Kareem, "Sorry, we're in the middle of something."

"Must happen all the time," Mimi says viciously as Kareem walks off. "People coming up to you."

She ignores the comment. "What happened, Mimi?" He peels the label off his Almaza, bunches the wet paper. She does the same thing.

"It was time to retire the dream." Mimi's voice is studiously casual. "No big deal."

"It seems like a big—" But Kareem's been running his mouth, and now there's a pretty girl in white shorts at their side, introducing herself, gushing over Noja. This time, Mimi doesn't glare at Naj; he tosses his hair back.

"Hi." The girl eyes him. "Are you a musician too?"

"I used to be. I'm a restaurant manager now." There's almost a delight in how he's repeating it, but it's painful to watch, like seeing somebody pick at a scab. He slumps his shoulders slightly, and Naj can feel the molecules between him and the girl rearrange; she's leaning forward. Her brother's brand: gloom and morosity. Straight-girl catnip.

"I'd love to hear your stuff."

"I can send you some demos."

Naj rolls her eyes as obviously as she can. Neither of them is looking at her. "I'm going to the bathroom."

When she returns, the girl's legs are slung over the barstool, pressing against her brother's. Mimi's leaning so close to listen to her talk, their faces almost touch. Naj thinks of Harper beaming at him after they kissed. She storms toward them.

"Did you hear?" she shouts above the music. The girl shakes her head. "He's engaged!" She points to Mimi. "She said yes! Rhombus-shaped diamond or whatever the fuck."

"Square."

"Sorry, what's that?" She mockingly cups her hand around her ear. Mimi looks like he's going to kill her.

"Square, you idiot. Not rhombus."

"Congratulations." The girl is already gathering her bag.

"They're registered at Macy's," Naj calls after her. She turns to her brother. "You're the worst."

"What the hell is wrong with you? I'm just having a conversation."

"It's not just the girl. It's you and all your bullshit." She shakes her hair into her eyes and imitates his slouch. "It's so *tedious*."

"It's none of your business," he says furiously.

A thought strikes Naj, so simple it stuns her. "Do you cheat on Harper?"

The second she asks, she wishes she hadn't, not because she doesn't want to hear the answer but because she doesn't have to; her brother's always been a terrible liar and she can read his face like a script. They both freeze.

"You fucking twat," she growls, and she's already moving away. She stamps through the door, the outside air humid and disgusting and the opposite of relief. She makes it to the next street before he catches up to her, grabs her elbow, and whirls her around. "Get off me, you —"

He's crying.

"Once." He sucks in air. "I swear to God. Once. That's the only time." He wipes his eyes. "I kissed someone. The bassist in my band."

Naj was in third grade. She and Mimi were on a staircase. They'd just done the music school's annual recital, and Naj had closed the show. She'd worn a pink dress and played Chopin on the violin. He was behind her, carrying her violin, and somehow, somehow, the instrument ended up at the bottom of the stairs, the case flung open like a mouth — she remembered locking it — the violin's neck cracked like a woman's. Naj had started howling, but the expression on Mimi's face stopped her. It was wrecked, despairing. It was impossible to punish someone who looked like that.

"That's why you're engaged." It isn't a question.

"I had a come-to-Jesus moment." He wipes his face, laughs embarrassedly. "I couldn't tell her."

Naj is suddenly tired and drunk and sad. She drapes her arm around him. "Come on, Mimi." He hugs her back, briefly, hard; she knows in the morning he'll be sarcastic and cold again. "I'll walk you home."

⟡

The house is dark when they return, and her brother half stumbles in the entrance. She feels a little embarrassed when he kneels to untie his shoes — he is swaying. Her brother is a restaurant manager. In the dark foyer, she unlocks her phone, scrolls to Mimi's Instagram, and swipes until she finds a photograph of him playing onstage with Dulcet. The caption is *Dulcet in el paso,* and her heart aches. She taps on the bassist's profile, @alliezworld. It's mostly landscape photos and shots of her; she's sexy, tough. Naj taps on a selfie of Allie, her head tipped back, a silly expression on her face, standing under a sign that says DEAD END. She's prettier than Harper, which makes Naj even angrier.

Naj types, *@alliezworld, homewrecker extraordinaire,* sends it, then deletes it almost immediately. Fuck. Allie would still get the notification.

She wants her sister. Ava would understand, maybe yell at Mimi, which Naj desperately wants to do but can't. But her sister's door is closed, and she can't risk waking the children up, not when she's drunk enough for the walls to spin a little.

There is, however, a low light under her parents' door and she stands outside for a moment. It's past midnight. She can hear their muffled conversation, her mother's low tones. "Hey," she whispers. The voices fall silent.

"Ava?" her mother calls.

Naj pushes the door open. They're both in bed, facing each other. Only the table lamp is on, and they look younger in the soft light. "Not Ava," she says needlessly. "Me."

"Naji!" Her father seems delighted. "Come in."

She juts out her hip, surveying them. "Would you look at these lovebirds," she says to an imaginary audience.

"Shut up." Her mother pulls the comforter up to her chin.

"I feel like we've barely had a chance to talk," her father says. His face is shiny from the lotion he wears every night. He's a sucker for things like that. He stops a million times whenever they go to a mall.

"That's because she's always out doing God knows what," her mother says without missing a beat, but she moves over anyway, pats the mattress beside her. Naj gets in, curls against her mother. Mazna plays with Naj's hair, her fingernails sending pleasant chills down her back. "You reek of vodka."

"Gin."

"Oh, pardon me. Can you imagine telling your father that?" her mother asks Idris in Arabic. "God rest his soul. He'd be aghast."

Idris stretches. "We failed at raising children," he says conversationally.

"Heaven knows it." Mazna snorts.

"Jiddo drank," Naj counters. "Sometimes he'd have wine."

Her parents exchange a maddening look of placidity. "He didn't get fall-down drunk, dear." Her mother pets her hair like a dog.

"Who's falling down?" Naj mumbles. The bed is warm, and her eyelids are heavy. She can smell her parents' specific smells, Mazna's shampoo and baby powder, her father's minty toothpaste. "I thought you were mad at me." She hears her voice change, like a young girl's, charming, and it works, her mother folding her closer.

"You're a terrible daughter," her mother observes. "But I love you."

"How was the partying?" Idris asks.

"Ask your stupid son."

Her mother sighs into Naj's neck. "Your brother is going through a lot."

"Is he?" Naj asks. "Because it kinda seems like he's an asshole."

"Naji, now," her father admonishes mockingly. "Don't forget, your brother's an *artist*."

They both snicker quietly until Mazna yanks Naj's hair.

"Ow!"

"I hope you two idiots feel good about yourselves."

"Oh, come on, Mazna. We're joking." Idris ruffles Mazna's hair, an absent-minded gesture, one that travels through Mazna straight to Naj's heart. She might cry. She feels a childish urge to tell on her brother, report what he did with the stupid bassist. She did that often in her childhood, telling on Ava for staying out late and Mimi for hiding report cards. She was so little, she could sneak around and eavesdrop. They never figured out it was her, because her parents would lie about how they'd found out. She hated spending so much time alone in the house, and getting her siblings in trouble meant they got grounded, which made them hers again.

"Did you see the photos for Jiddo's memorial?" she asks instead. "Baba, the one of you dancing with Jiddo is adorable. There are some home movies in that closet as well. I think Ava wants to start watching them soon." Talking about Ava reminds her of the old lady, but she knows better than to ask about her.

"This isn't an American buffet," her mother says a little sharply. "We don't put on a show."

"The pictures are good, Naji. That night was the first time I saw my father dance. Or the first time I remember it." He dabs his eyes with the cover.

"He was a good man," her mother says quietly, and they all fall silent for a moment. In an uncharacteristic move, she speaks first. "He always called me Grace Kelly. Even though I look nothing like her."

"Because you were an actress," Naj supplies, cuddling closer. It occurs to her how infrequently her mother tells stories; they're like heroin to Naj.

"A marvelous actress." Her father sniffles.

"I don't know about all that. But it was always *Grace Kelly* this, *Grace Kelly* that. He once made me a videotape case that looked like a movie poster. I couldn't tell you where it went. It didn't make it to California." Mazna smooths the comforter, and Naj stares at her mother's hand. It looks older than Mazna does. She always forgets this, how being around her family means beholding their aging. Since Naj is the youngest, in her earliest memories, her parents are in their prime, attractive, already relaxed by a couple of children. Ava was curvy and arresting as a teenager, and Mimi the perennial heartthrob. But being the youngest means entering your prime while the rest of the family are leaving theirs. It isn't fair. She never got to dazzle with Ava.

"Maybe the videotape case is in the girls' room's closet. There are a lot of boxes in there."

"This isn't a yard sale, Naj," her mother says, but softly. "Those boxes belonged to people."

"I remember that case," her father says dreamily. "You were wearing a red scarf."

"No, that was the headshot. That red scarf." Her mother's laughter is rueful.

"You got the headshot when you moved to America?" Naj asks, but it's one question too many, and her mother is already turning away, settling into sleep.

"What a long day," she murmurs.

"That's right. The red scarf came later. And those dangly earrings. I remember. You know, on our wedding day, my father told me to look after you, to give you a good life." He leans over and turns the light off, the darkness enveloping them. Naj feels erased from the scene, no longer there. "He knew how sad I was, after Zakaria. He told me I owed it to him to live well. To live."

"Hush, Idris," her mother says, not unkindly. "We're all tired now."

"Who's Zakaria?" Naj asks, but her mother doesn't answer. Her father's voice is alone in the dark.

"My father would always want to know, when I visited here, if I had done what he asked."

Naj hears her mother rummage in the dark, then the sound of one hand patting another. "You did," Mazna says, her voice already blurred with sleep. "You gave me a good life."

❉

They've set a date for the memorial: August 12. A week before her thirtieth birthday. It's only four weeks away, and their father seems freshly energized. He's less focused on Mirabel now; clearly some truce has been reached with Mazna. The woman comes by every few days with her hawkish verve, trailing measuring tape out of her tote bag like a magician. She's meddling and annoying and has united the whole family — minus Idris — in their hatred of her; even Harper mimics her high tones behind her back.

"We have so much work to do," Mirabel often says with a sigh, gazing at the house as though it's a demo site. "And it might all get ripped up anyway."

Now that they have a date, Idris tells Mirabel often, "We get to knock out two birds with one stone. The house needs to be freshened up, and we need to get it ready for the memorial." Once he says pensively, "And you were saying the almond trees block the entrance?"

"Oh, yes. If we could trim them or —"

"Nobody touches the almond trees," Merry says, so sharply even Mirabel doesn't talk back. There's no more mention of the trees after that.

Merry's presence is like a pinball bumper they all keep knocking up against. Sara does some digging and discovers that her salary is paid through their grandfather's old account. *But the money will run out soon if it hasn't already,* Sara says. The topic makes them squirm. Merry reminds the family of themselves. Of their privilege. Of what they have. In America they are considered brown. You become attached to that. You are given a name and you respond to it. They are brown in America. There is something self-righteous that lives alongside that marginalization, the mispronounced names, the *Your English is so . . .* , the sideways glances in department stores. But there are browner bodies out there. There are women who take care of your grandfather while you're thousands of miles away — or ten minutes away — women whose own families are thousands of miles away, women who are washing your plates and washing vegetables for your dinner.

Naj can see it in her parents' faces, in her sister's and brother's, the same embarrassment she sometimes feels around Merry, what her presence tells her about their birthright. There are thousands of women like her, women from the Philippines, from Ethiopia, from Sri Lanka, who are brought to homes around the world and paid a few hundred dollars a month; their passports are locked away, and no matter what bedroom they sleep in, they are the *help.* Her family was tied to this truth like an anvil. Her family had maids. It doesn't matter that Merry has her passport, that she sleeps in a guest bedroom, that she comes and goes as she pleases. Naj's family, her beloved grandparents, had paid a woman a paltry amount to leave her country and life, and no amount of love for her, no legacy of two decades, of trips home for the holidays, of *she's like family,* can erase the reality that she is not, in fact, family, that Merry seems fortified by this truth, attached to it more than anyone, which Naj is both self-conscious of and grateful for. It holds them liable; it grants them no exit from the funhouse of their place in the order of things: they are moneyed. It's diluted money, perhaps. Money that is less than the neighbors' money. But it still sings loudly enough. Only one thing remains a mystery: why Merry chooses to stay. She ignores them if they ask.

"It's just that you don't *have* to stay," Ava tried one afternoon. "If you need to go home or something."

Merry frowned. "I'll leave when it's time for me to leave." She glared at Mimi and Naj, who were eavesdropping, then looked meaningfully around the house. "Maybe you and your siblings should worry more about your inheritance." That was that.

Mazna picks out somber gray invitations for the memorial, thick card stock, an homage to the print shop, but postal service in Beirut is essentially nonexistent, so they turn them into programs instead. The project pleases her mother;

it's a throwback to the crafty afternoons of their childhood. She hole-punches each program and weaves through a black ribbon; something about the precision of the motion reminds Naj of Fee, whom she realizes her mother would probably like.

"You need to call all of these people," their father tells them, giving them a list of old friends and relatives, and the siblings and Harper make an afternoon of it, sprawled in Ava's room. Sara joins them partway through with pizza, and the room fills with the smell of grease. The AC is unreliable, and they take turns complaining about the heat and calling these strangers they've never met, their grandfather's cousins, neighbors from the war, old colleagues. The invitees are gracious and puzzled and promise to come.

"We came to the *azza*," a few politely say, and the siblings have to explain that the family from America — this is their own description, *the family from America,* as though they are talking about some dimwits rather than themselves — wasn't able to come for the *azza* and that this will be a celebration of his life.

There are many jokes about America from the guests.

Afterward, the siblings and Harper play poker on the floor. Ava cleans them out, easily, maddeningly. She bluffs on twos and gets full houses on the river and can even shuffle the cards in that cool, easy manner of frat boys.

"How are you so good at this?" Harp asks, awestruck, after Ava sweeps another round. They are playing with Zina's barrettes; the blue ones are singles, the yellows are fives, and the reds are twenties.

"She's a shark," Naj says, a bite to her words. She usually wins when she plays poker with her friends. "A shark turned WASP."

"She cleaned me out when I visited New York." Sara smiles at the memory. She's counting the RSVPs, crossing names off the list. "I was thinking blue plates."

"With silver napkins," Harp adds. "Is it sick that I feel like I'm planning a party?"

"Yes," they all reply.

Harper shrugs.

"Sara," Ava says seriously, and Naj knows what's coming next. "I wanted to ask you something." She pulls the burgundy photo album from under her bed; it was clearly placed there for this moment. Ava flips expertly through the album, then stops. "Her." She holds up the photograph. "Who's that lady?"

Naj watches Sara interestedly herself. Ava's the eldest; her fixations have always had an infectious effect on her siblings. Sara looks at the photograph with a studied casualness. "She worked here," she says. She clears her throat. "Why?"

"She came by the house," Mimi explains. "She said she missed the *azza*. Ava here's been Nancy Drew ever since, trying to figure it out."

"Baba told me she was the housekeeper," Ava says, ignoring him. "But I mean, what's her story?"

"Ava has a lot of time on her hands here," Naj stage-whispers to Sara, but her aunt doesn't smile. She's looking at Ava intently.

"She was with us for a long time," Sara says quietly. "I loved her. Then she stopped working because of her back." There's an anticlimactic silence. Mimi clears his throat and they return to their game, Ava looking disappointed. They are halfway through a hand when Sara reaches for the photograph.

Later, Naj will wonder how things might've changed if the phone had rung that second or if the children had come running in. But it doesn't, and they don't, and Sara picks up the photograph. She speaks.

"She would bring her son with her. He and your father were inseparable."

"Uncle Tarek?" Naj asks, trying to remember her father's friends, but her aunt shakes her head.

"No. They lived in the camps. He went to a different school. But the two of them were always together. He was like a second brother for me."

Naj catches the past tense, but Mimi doesn't. "Should we invite him or something?"

"We can't." There's something approaching sorrow in Sara's voice. "He died a long time ago. During the war."

"What was his name?" Naj asks, but she knows the answer.

"Zakaria."

"They were talking about him," Naj tells her siblings. "Mama and Baba, a few nights ago. Baba was half asleep, and he was saying something about being sad during their wedding because Zakaria had just died."

"Your parents never mentioned him." Sara's voice is flat; it isn't a question.

"Mama knew him too?" Ava's cards are forgotten. She turns to her aunt. "You never mentioned him either."

"Honey," Sara says. "How many times have I seen you in the past twenty years?"

"When did he die?" Ava cocks her head. "Exactly."

"In August 1978."

"Right before Mama and Baba moved to California," Ava says.

"That makes sense." Mimi seems bored with the conversation. "I would leave too if people I knew started dying."

"Right before they moved," Ava repeats, quieter this time. She keeps looking at Sara, and it's starting to bug Naj; she wants them to stop.

"Yes," Sara says. Ava looks thoughtful but returns to the game. After a moment, she speaks again. "Sara?" she asks tentatively.

"Yes, honey?"

"Why don't you and Mama get along?"

The question detonates in the room. A creepy feeling crawls up Naj's back; it's as though Ava has taken out her tit or something. Even Harper looks shocked. Sara walks over and stands in front of the mirror, fixes her hair with that same nonchalance.

"I have to get these goddamn grays done," she says finally. The AC goes silent; the electricity has cut off. Sara looks at it. "This city is a mess. No wonder you all inherited your mother's hatred for it." She amends that. "Your father's too, actually."

"I didn't."

"No." She turns to Naj. There's a meaningful pause. "You might've overcorrected a little, honey."

"Mama —" Ava starts to say, but then silences herself. Sara turns around to face them. She's rubbing the pendant around her neck, a necklace of her mother's; it's a tic of hers.

"Make sure you put the boxes back when you're done. We have more than enough pictures for the memorial."

Fee invites Naj to see the painting, but not at the apartment; she texts another address. When Naj shows up at eight p.m., she finds a shuttered hospital clinic.

Wrong address, I think.

It's not, Fee responds. *The side door is unlocked.*

The waiting room is eerily empty. The lights are off; it's dark except for the exit signs. Fee is waiting in a radiologist's white apron. "You made it." She looks happy.

"Just in time for a little B and E." At Fee's confusion, she explains, "Breaking and entering. Like — trespassing? It doesn't matter. What are we doing here?"

"You'll see." Fee's clearly enjoying the secret. "But first!" She waves toward one side of the room, where, propped against the wall, is the painting of Naj. There's bubble wrap on the chair next to it.

"Oh," Naj says softly. She has seen hundreds of photographs and videos of herself, but never has she seen one that makes her want to cry — her face so naked, the dress billowing beneath her like dark water, as though she is half woman, half river. The glossy black of the dress is so mouthwatering, she wants to lick it. "Fee, look at this."

"I did look at it," Fee says, grinning. "I used a different myth."

"Which one?"

"It's a new one." She starts folding up the bubble wrap. The smell of anti-septic cleaner is making Naj's head hurt. "I wanted to make one up."

"What's the myth?"

"A woman that's left behind in an empty country all by herself. She builds a river with her own hands by gathering rain in tiny glasses. It carries her to the sea."

"What if she doesn't want to leave?" Naj swallows.

Fee doesn't answer. "I thought you'd like it."

"I do like it." There's an awkward silence. Naj looks down at the fox tattoo. She clears her throat. "What is this place?"

"My friend works here. She's a radiologist." Fee looks over her shoulder, though the place is clearly empty. "She's letting me use the machine."

"The machine?"

"I'll show you." They walk toward the back, a narrow hallway that forces their shoulders to brush. Fee keeps adjusting her apron. "I'd like to come to your show at the end of the summer. If we're here."

The *if* echoes, a red flag. "I tried to get out of it. My family will still be here. But Jo wouldn't let me." Nor would their agent. It was the biggest venue in Beirut, a smackingly large check. The tickets had started selling last year.

"You should let them come."

"You've lost your mind. Besides, Mimi's quit his band."

Fee considers this. "Still." She stops in front of a door marked AUTHORIZED PERSONNEL ONLY.

"Hey, Fee," Naj says casually.

"Yes?"

"What the fuck are we doing here?"

Fee laughs. "Through here." She steps back for Naj to enter first. The room is dark, with a large x-ray machine in the center. Fee's apron suddenly makes sense.

"What is this?"

Fee hands her a lead apron of her own. Naj can see stems of long, narrow yellow flowers on the tabletop. "We have to leave when the machine is on."

Naj laughs. "Fee. Are you x-raying flowers?"

They slip into an adjacent room. It's dark except for the radiant light from the light boxes on which x-rays eerily glow in the shapes of little plants, flowers, a couple of small, rat-like animals — skeletons of dead things. In one of the boxes, a note in Fee's handwriting is tucked in the corner: *You Don't Need Bones to Be Dead.* The entire room looks haunted.

"It's all native to Aleppo," Fee explains. "All the flowers and plants. Some men I know have been smuggling them in through Tripoli. Some animals too. It's for the painting series — for each live woman, a dead creature. We're so desensitized to images of bodies. Let them look at the carcasses of flowers. Let them feel something, anything, even if it's because of an insect."

The hairs on Naj's arms stand up.

"You're a genius," she says slowly. "A morbid little genius. People are used to looking at blown-up kids? Scale it back. Make them feel bad for orchids."

"Exactly. I thought you'd get it." In the ethereal light of the x-ray view boxes, Fee looks at Naj. "I have to tell you something."

Naj smiles. "You're not actually allowed to be in here."

"No." Fee looks away. "We're getting asylum," she says quietly.

The x-ray above Fee's head blooms — the bones of what looks like a frog. Naj wonders where the remains go after they've been photographed. They're probably outside at the bottom of a dumpster. Fucking Fee.

"You already have asylum," Naj says. She sounds ridiculous to her own ears. "Here."

There's a long silence. "My grandfather," Fee says in Arabic, "had a Lebanese housekeeper during the Civil War. Syria and Lebanon are like contentious siblings. We've poured people back and forth across the border like traded goods. I remember a time when the reverse, Syrians needing Lebanon, was unimaginable. Until it wasn't." She swallows. "There's no such thing as asylum in Beirut. This is the real thing. In Norway. There's a university in Oslo, and they've offered Bilal a position."

"Asylum takes a while," Naj says slowly. She is beginning to understand something. This whole summer — all those dinners. All those shows. Dozens of conversations, and Norway never came up in a single one. "You've known about this for a long time."

Fee won't look at her. "I didn't know how to tell you," she says simply. She is still speaking in Arabic. "It felt too delicate. To see you again. To have you talking to me again."

"When are you leaving?" Naj asks blankly.

"The end of the summer. The university is giving us an apartment, and the semester begins in September."

⁜

September. Or is it winter? Naj isn't in an x-ray room on a Tuesday night; she's nineteen and it's midnight, the grass beneath her legs damp from recent rainfall. She and Fee are lying down on a blanket, but the dew seeps through. They're careful not to kiss on campus even in the middle of the night, but they're holding hands and Fee is talking, then Naj is jumping up, pulling part of the blanket with her; she's yelling, they're both yelling and crying, and Fee is saying she's leaving, her brother found her cell phone, saw the dozens of texts between them. They've tried to be careful, but it's impossible; he's telling Fee's parents and they're pulling her out of the university. She's going back to Damascus.

You think I want this? Fee is sobbing, her face mottled.

But Naj is unmoved. She's shaking her by the shoulders, ignoring a couple of coeds walking by; she is speaking urgently about visas, saying that they can be in California by tomorrow evening, they can stay with her parents in Blythe. Naj can tell them, or not; it doesn't matter. She can say they're friends and something has happened, or she can call Ava — this she's forgotten over the years, that she'd wanted badly to call her sister, who had recently moved to Manhattan, and tell her everything — and so animatedly does Naj speak that it feels like they've already done it, that they're sharing a futon in the West Village, her sister's music in the background, living on a street named after flowers, two Chinese restaurants on the block.

It's working. *I can't,* Fee is saying weakly, but then she's crying less, something hardening in her face — Naj will mistake this for acquiescence — and calming down, letting Naj walk her back to her apartment; the two of them whisper about New York City as they fall asleep.

Later, Fee will be gone. Later, there will be the brother's car honking outside the building, and later still, him returning to wait for Naj outside her building. By then, Fee is in Damascus. Naj will spend weeks crying in Jo's lap. She will delete Fee's e-mail unanswered. She will scream Fee's name on stages across the world without ever saying it, not once.

"September."

"Naj." Fee's face is mournful. "He's my husband."

What was I? Naj wants to scream, only she actually is screaming it, and it feels far-fetched, surreal, Fee taking a step back, her face illuminated by all the dead things she's gathered. "And you just disappeared, Fee. You didn't even check in after your brother — after that piece of shit, after . . ." She cannot finish the sentence.

"I did! I did, Naj, that's not fair. You know I did."

"An e-mail. Two texts." Naj tries to snort. "You knew where I lived." She is running out of steam. "But no, you had fucked off back to Syria, too busy getting married to write more e-mails. You got to play queer and then go home."

It happens so quickly, Naj's words, Fee's face suddenly furious. "Play queer? I loved you, Najla. You know I love you." They both ignore the altered tense. "But that was never enough. You don't remember?" Her voice is rising now as well. "Do you remember how you'd make me hold your hand? Make fun of me if I didn't, call me scared. Like you forgot that it was different for me. That my family was different. It never mattered to you. *I* played?" Fee leans over like she's winded from running, her fists white. "Everything was a game to you. Or did you forget? You would try to sneak a kiss in front of our friends. You were always trying to make it more public."

"I didn't do that," Naj says, but even as she speaks, she remembers a party, some argument after a friend's dinner. The bold, reckless feeling. Kissing Fee's neck. Slipping a hand under a table.

"You did. And then you'd laugh at me for getting upset. It's in your music too. Everything for Najla is a big joke. Everything is reversible. But it's not like that for everybody. We don't all have family in California."

"My parents don't know," Naj says, stung.

"But if they did, Najla. Truly. Think for a second. You have gotten so used to not telling them. Maybe you can't see the situation clearly. What they'd actually do. What it would cost you if they knew. If they did, would they disown you?"

Naj thinks. Her mother would be frantic. There would be tears. Attempts to argue away her gayness. Something would break between her and her parents for a long, long time, Naj knows this in her bones. But they would never send her away.

"See?" Fee says quietly. She is watching her. "My parents." She lets out a shuddering sigh.

Naj doesn't want to apologize first, and so she doesn't. She just takes a step toward Fee and Fee takes one toward her, and they hug, and a second later Naj kisses her, or she doesn't kiss her, exactly, she kisses the soft spot between her earlobe and jawline, where the knobby bone juts out. She can feel Fee swallow; the exhale flutters onto Naj's neck. Fee is trembling, but she's the one who turns her head to the right so that they are actually kissing now, close-mouthed and sweet, and it's remarkable what the body remembers; Fee still tastes the same, has that slightly bitter, earthy smell that brings back basement bars and campus at midnight and everything about 2009, leaving Naj a little breathless. Still no tongue, and her mind flashes on Mimi crying in front of Back Door, then Ava's face as her aunt says, *Zakaria,* and the images all blur together, her mother's voice in the bed, her parents leaving for California at the end of a summer a long time ago, just as Fee will for Norway. They murmur as they kiss, just as they did that night years ago, their last time in bed together, only now they murmur remorse, confessions. But it doesn't matter. It won't change anything. The girls they're apologizing to don't exist anymore.

Despite the late hour, Naj wants to sleep in Jiddo's house. She drives through downtown. The fires have been gone for several days, but there are still discarded signs, litter. The protesters are gone for now, but they'll be back. When she reaches the dark foyer of the house, she stops. Her lips are chapped and dry. She wonders how many times Teta stood in this foyer, her grandfather, her mother and father. She wonders how many people have cried here in the middle of the night, not wanting to wake the others up. It breaks her heart. She thinks of the frog skeleton and Damascus, and for the first time in years, she really considers the house her mother grew up in. The rooms were small but always spotless, her grandmother constantly pouring fresh tea in everybody's cup. There was an ancient kettle, an engraving of a rose on the side. The entire country has vanished like a comet burning into nothingness. How had none of them said anything to Mazna, how had nobody really asked her about what she missed? How had they never held an *azza* for Damascus? How could she have kissed Fee in public, teased her about it after? Naj wants to whisper her mother awake and ask her about Syria, but of course it'll pass, it'll be over soon, and in the morning she won't be able to say any of this to her mother because that's just how it is in their family. It's what they've always made of the past.

"I don't think we've seen this one," Ava says. They are in the living room, Naj, Mazna, and Ava, her sister fiddling with old videos.

"When's it from?" Naj asks. She's playing Two Dots on her phone, the candy-colored balls spinning in a row.

Ava stills and Naj can see her sister's back tense as she holds up the spine. There's still a VCR in the house, a row of VHS tapes gathering dust in the TV stand. She glances meaningfully at Naj. "July 1978."

Naj sits up. They both glance at their mother, but she's reading something on her phone.

It feels like everything slows down. Ava puts the tape in, then rewinds it, which takes an agonizingly long time. Their mother puts her feet up. Her toenails are a perfect pink, and there are scraggly black hairs on her big toe. They remind Naj of the flower stems on Fee's x-rays, the night in the foyer.

"Do you miss Syria?" Naj asks her mother.

Mazna glances up. She is still so beautiful, but her beauty is more somber now, like the stepmother in a fairy tale. "What is this?" she asks. "The Spanish Inquisition? Am I doing a television interview?"

Naj drops it.

"It's ready." Ava's color is high, and she keeps putting her hair up in a ponytail and then taking it down. The screen fizzles to life and Ava leans back on her heels.

The first few minutes are a seascape blurring by on the screen. The camera is at an odd angle; there's something just out of frame — a car window. Then there's their father at the wheel, obnoxiously young, waving at the person holding the camera, looking so happy it's painful to watch. The picture keeps skipping, the sound lagging a little.

Just point and shoot, he's saying.

Their mother looks up. "What's this?" she asks warily.

"A videotape," Ava says, sounding unusually sarcastic.

"Where did you get this?"

"It was in one of the boxes." Ava is studiously watching the screen, and Naj sees that this wasn't a fluke; Ava had looked for a tape from this year.

The scene cuts out and there's static for a moment, but then the video comes back to life. Naj recognizes the Raouché, the two massive rock formations off the Corniche. It's twilight and the camera swings back to a table at a restaurant, the food on the plates half eaten. There's a wine carafe next to an overflowing ashtray. The person recording swings the camera and suddenly there's Mazna filling the screen, young and gorgeous, her black hair still long. She looks like she's sixteen, but Naj knows she's older, twenty-something. There's a man sitting to her side, and Ava lets out a tiny sound. It's the man from the photographs, the housekeeper's son.

One wish, Zuzu! a voice says off camera. It's their father, his voice a little higher. The man looks slightly weary, but smiles obediently. *What would it be?*

For Italy to win the World Cup. The man is humoring their father.

"Who's that?" Ava asks innocently, and Naj admires her sister's acting.

Mazna says nothing. Her face says everything for her. Ava sees it and her mother sees her see it, and Naj watches it all happen.

On the screen, the camera swivels to Mazna. She looks more blatantly annoyed.

And you?

Their mother — long before she was their mother — brushes her hair from her face and clears her throat. She lifts her chin theatrically, stares directly into the camera. Naj can see what her father fell in love with. She'd fall in love with a woman like that.

I want this summer not to end, she says. Then she speaks again, but Naj doesn't hear it because her real, actual mother is speaking louder.

"Turn it *off!*" she's saying to Ava, but she's not using her thespian voice or her injured voice but something different, throaty and girlish. Her cheeks are beet red. "Turn it off!"

"I'm trying!"

"Now!"

"Jesus. Mama, okay! Here." Ava ejects the tape; the screen stares blackly. "Can you calm—"

But Mazna is already up, flinging a throw pillow in the air. "Your father is selling a house that isn't his!" She starts stomping out of the room. "You three are poking through things that aren't yours! Everyone in this country is a goddamn vulture!" They hear a door slam.

"I guess she knew him," Naj says.

"Zakaria." Ava puts the tape in its case.

Sorry State

AFTER THE HOME video, Mimi loses Naj to Ava's cause. Sitting outside the next day with Ava and Harper, Naj gives a pitch-perfect impression of their mother's reaction to the video.

"Mimi, you don't get it," Naj says. "I had goose bumps. It was like she'd seen a ghost."

"Maybe he was an old boyfriend?" Even Harp seems captivated. She sounds uncharacteristically wistful. "The rich girl and the housekeeper's son. It's all very arthouse film."

"Oh my God, and maybe their families wouldn't let them get married," Ava says. The three women sigh in unison and Mimi wants to punch himself in the cock.

"Mama wasn't rich," he reminds them. "She grew up poor. And there's that little matter of *our father*. Whom she married? He was in the video too, but she wasn't even looking at him."

"So maybe not a full-blown love affair," Ava allows. "But there was something there. And his mother, this Hayat lady. She probably has some answers."

"Maybe Zakaria was in love with Sara, and Mama was helping them get together," Naj says excitedly and they're off to the races, talking about how a failed match would explain their mother's coolness toward Sara.

It's not that Mimi isn't curious. His mother has been an enigma his entire life, exacting and stunning, an impossible standard to hold women to but also fragile in a way his sisters don't see. But the love lives of people, dead or alive, forty years ago feel very, very far away when your own life is in flames.

His life's in flames.

What seemed manageable back in Austin is ruinous from a distance. The end of Dulcet wasn't even an actual end. That hadn't occurred to him as a possibility; he'd envisioned a final, tearful show, some rueful exchange with Allie. Instead, it was just him and Jacob in a bar booth. The younger man had regained some of his composure from the other night, and he kept cracking his knuckles, an affectation Mimi hadn't seen before.

"Diego didn't want to come," Jacob finally said, almost apologetically.

Mimi tried to seem unaffected. "I get it. I've texted him, but . . ." The truth was, Diego had responded. It was polite and cold and clearly final. Allie herself was absent; she'd replied to his texts, after several days, with incongruous emojis. Monkey covering his ears. Shopping bags. Umbrella. Penguin face.

"Yeah." Jacob untwisted his bottle cap. They clinked their beers awkwardly, talked about nothing until Jacob finally cleared his throat and said, "So I've already told Elliot about the changes. And I know you need your amp back. I've ordered a new one, but if I could use yours for the Friday show, that would be great."

It was like being slapped with ice water. Mimi gulped air. "The Friday show? Elliot?"

Jacob looked at him strangely. "Dulcet is still a band. I thought you knew that? There's no point in —" He didn't finish his sentence. "I mean, we're already booked through the fall."

"You can't use the name." Mimi's voice was hoarse.

"What?"

"You fucking heard me, Jacob. This is mutiny. You're kicking me out of my own band."

Jacob shut his eyes, as if Mimi were throwing a tantrum. "I got the sense you wanted to disband Dulcet."

"I can send Dulcet off to fucking sea if I want to!" The more ridiculous he got, the more he couldn't stop; it had always been a flaw of his. His stomach churned with shame at the idea of the others meeting behind his back, contacting bookers. He'd known fucking Elliot since he was a sophomore. "It's my fucking band, Jacob! It's been my band since you were in elementary school."

"I should go." Jacob got up, then hesitated. "You're a great guitar player, man," he said sadly.

Mimi laid his forehead on the table.

"These are on me." Jacob drained his beer.

"No." Mimi lifted his head. That would be the final insult. "I got it."

The younger man smiled sadly. "I already paid for them, Mimi." A pause. "Good luck, man." He tapped the table twice and then was gone.

❖

He'd told Harp it was no big deal, that he'd aged out of Dulcet. He'd pretended not to see her not believe him. Of course Beirut was a big fucking disappointment. He'd known it would be. The city seems like one long reminder of his transgressions; he'd never realized how much Beirut orbited around women and music. And the women all resemble Allie. Dark hair, dark eyes.

"Whatever it is you're going through," Harp finally says, "it's going to need to come to an end, Mimi. Because this summer has been —"

"I know," he says before she can finish. "I wouldn't blame you for leaving even earlier." She's set to travel the second week of August, a few days after the memorial. At the time, she'd been sad about leaving before him; now she seems relieved. Her Harpishness has followed her to Beirut — she's gone on solo trips to see the Phoenician ruins, tanned at a local beach with Sara. Still, she's reaching her limit, he knows, and it's not her fault.

The problem is his mother. She's pricklier than usual. There's a chill toward

Harp that's more and more palpable. At dinner, she passes Harp the first plate but says nothing. Whenever Harper asks a question, Mazna responds to Mimi.

"She's really keeping it up this time," Harp tells him.

"I've seen her do it to my father for months," he says.

"Your mother invented ghosting." Harp laughs at her own joke, and Mimi knows he should be grateful, but he can't help but feel a slight tetchiness when Harper says something about his mother. She catches it, and her face sobers. "Mimi, I'm doing what I can here." She speaks kindly, but there's a warning in her tone.

※

It comes to a head at breakfast two days later. Mimi has made the pancakes, lemon basil with blueberries in the batter. He is pleased every time someone takes another stack. "Mrs. Nasr," Harper says sweetly to Mazna in her starting-a-conversation voice. Mimi feels weary; the woman won't relent. "Did you ever do theater in America?"

"Why would I do theater in America?" His mother turns her attention to Rayan.

"You know," Harp says, and only Mimi can hear the steel in her voice. He doesn't blame her. It's been days of this. The whole house is going stir-crazy, as though his mother is bad weather. He touches her knee under the table. She moves it. "I've been meaning to ask."

Mazna scoops more scrambled eggs onto Rayan's plate. "It'll make you big like Popeye."

"Who's that?"

"Like Iron Man," Ava explains.

Harp sets her fork down. "Who is this Zakaria I keep hearing so much about?"

The table doesn't exactly go silent. The children continue their chatter. Idris methodically cuts his pancakes. Mimi catches Ava's eye. She looks astonished.

"He was an old friend, right?" Harp continues blithely, a perfect act, as though she's unaware of the tension in the room. For a second he does hate her, for the way she is laying claim to his family's history, for her Americanness, for tinkering with family dynamics she has no part in.

Mazna drinks her orange juice slowly. She doesn't speak. The silence among the adults stretches on, and Mimi would do anything to break it, but when he hears Harp inhale to speak again, he grabs her knee and squeezes hard, harder than he should, and she stops. His father finishes chewing.

"He was one of my dearest friends," he says breezily. "You must've seen him in the old videos?"

"We did," Mimi says quickly. "Him and your other friends. Uncle Tarek was in one. We just didn't recognize him, so we asked Sara. She told us he died."

"He died," their father repeats. "It was terrible." He spears a bite of pancake. "This is delicious, son."

"Are you sure you have enough syrup on that?" Mazna asks sarcastically. "I'd hate for you to die without a face full of food."

Idris blows her a kiss and keeps chewing.

✳

Mimi is surprised to find his sisters delighted with Harp. "Baba acted so calm about it," Ava says. The four of them are in the girls' room. The dresser is a mess of papers and textbooks. Just that moment, they hear their mother's raised voice, then their father's in return, a slammed door.

"This house is where relationships go to die," Harp says. She sounds almost amused.

Ava gives her a meaningful look. "I mean . . ." Harp gives her a sympathetic look in return, and Mimi wonders when the two of them started to talk. He thinks back to Ava's mentions of Nate this summer; they've been infrequent and somewhat edgy, but he can't pinpoint any specific problem, and with that comes the realization that he has barely spoken with her. Their gathering is large enough to get lost in.

"Amen," Naj pipes up.

"Even the matchless Najla Nasr has relationship issues?" Ava asks her sister.

Naj fluffs her hair. "I get mine, don't worry."

"Maybe Baba's right to sell," Ava's saying. "Name one good thing that's come from this trip."

"That's easy for you to say, that he's right to sell." Naj glares. "You all spring this on me out of nowhere, try to sell my house, and —"

"That's twice," Mimi says loudly.

"What?"

"That's twice you've referred to it as *your* house."

Naj looks at the ceiling. "I can see how difficult it must be for you, given how often you visit."

"The point —"

"The point," Harp says, cutting him off, "is that the house mattered to your grandfather. And that I need to keep my mouth shut around your mother." She turns to Ava. "On a scale of one to ten —"

"Twelve." Ava grins. "Would be my guess. But you'll find out soon enough."

"What do you mean?" Harp asks, but nobody answers her.

❖

She doesn't have to wait long. That afternoon, Mazna suggests taking the children to an amusement park in Zalqa. Idris stays behind to work on the house, which puts the siblings in the position — familiar from childhood — of having to neglect one parent to accommodate the other. The road is congested and Mimi, behind the wheel, curses every few minutes at the other drivers. There's a thin stream of smoke from the mountains.

"They're burning the trash again," Naj remarks.

Mazna makes a venomous sound. "Criminals," she says. Everyone knows better than to argue.

"Anyone want to go to a show tonight?" Naj asks. She has her head against the window like a child. Zina is on her lap and they're both leaving marks on the glass. "My friends are playing in Gemmayzeh."

"I think it's an improvement that she's starting to invite her family," Mazna says from the front as though Naj isn't five inches behind her.

"Hard pass," Ava says. "I've peaked. Haven't you heard?"

"Tell that to Jo." Naj snorts. "Mimi?"

He pretends to be preoccupied with his left turn. "Maybe next time," he says finally. He doesn't give a reason. Harp doesn't say anything, so he knows she must know what he's thinking—a small, smoky bar filled with excellent music and people who think his little sister is a god. Harder pass.

The amusement park smells bizarrely of America—caramel popcorn, children's socks, rubber, nachos. It reminds him of McDonald's play areas and Chuck E. Cheese. Zina and Rayan dart around like they've mainlined cocaine, Ava following them.

"I think I might get my fortune read," Mazna says. There's a small tent with an evil eye painted on it. Inside, a bored-looking woman in her fifties is smoking a cigarette. Mazna nods at Harp, who looks surprised at the attention.

"That sounds fun," Harp says. "You go ahead, and I'll do mine after."

Mazna smiles. They watch her enter the tent and hold her palm out. The woman speaks for a few minutes, then his mother glances back at them. She says something.

"She's probably telling the lady she got her fortune wrong," Naj says.

When Mazna finishes, she gestures for Harper to join her. "Don't leave me alone with the two of them," Harper jokes, but her eyes are serious. Mimi, Naj, and Harper all enter the tent.

"Christ." Naj wrinkles her nose. The space smells strongly of cigarettes and sandalwood; the offending stick of incense is burning in the corner. There are sheepskin rugs on the floor and a small animal skull on the table where the fortuneteller sits. She nods at Naj.

"Your aura is tired," she tells her. "A recent heartbreak."

Naj rolls her eyes. "Wrong mark, lady."

"It's me." Harp sits and extends both palms. The image is so incongruous that Mimi snaps a photo on his cell, Harper small and blond beside the portly woman.

"Please," the fortuneteller says to Mazna.

"Put your phone away," she tells him.

"Your health line is strong," the woman tells Harp approvingly. "Your communication is long and steady as well—see here?" There is a pause. The woman glances up at Mazna, then back at Harper. "But your love line, dear."

Mazna crosses her arms, her brow furrowed in exaggerated interest.

"It's fractured and uneven. You made a mistake in your, yes, early twenties. You started up with the wrong man. See all these lines to the side? That's where it went wrong. You're with someone who doesn't make you happy. You don't make him happy. You are pretending it works, but this whole time, you've been lying to yourselves."

"No fucking way," Mimi whispers to Naj. He notices his fists are clenched.

"You must break this love line, dear."

"Mama!" Naj says. Mazna ignores her.

Harp's face has paled. She smiles at Mimi, but it's pained and small, and he wants to scoop her up and run and not stop until the plane has landed in Austin. "You're a sociopath," he tells his mother.

"I don't know what you are referring to," Mazna says primly. "This woman is simply doing her job."

"Get up," Mimi tells Harp.

"My dear, I'm just getting to your line of fate."

"I think I've heard plenty, miss," Harp says politely, and she pulls her hands back. They hustle out of the tent, and Mimi turns to his mother furiously.

"You paid that sham to tell my wife she needs to leave me?" he roars.

"Girlfriend," Mazna says.

"Fiancée," Harp says. But she's smiling again.

"You've been a nightmare since we landed," he continues. He can see Ava approaching with the children, her face quizzical; Naj sends her a warning look, shaking her head. "I don't even know why you came here! All you've done is complain and nitpick and make Baba's life more difficult."

The metaphorical punch lands. His mother's face crumples. Her mouth twists in an ugly way, and he knows she's about to say something terrible, but she just turns to them, and only in that moment does he realize how they're standing: Harper off to the side, he and his sisters directly in a line opposite his mother. She shakes her head. Her voice trembles. "He's lucky to have you," she says. "Your precious father."

"Mimi," Ava warns.

But he's too angry. He loves his mother more than his sisters do — he *doesn't* agree with his father — and it's her mulishness that's forced him into this. That only makes him angrier, a body forcing you to stab it. He knows his mother, because he's like her. She made him in her image, the two failed artists. He knows how to hurt her.

"Just because your life is such a letdown," he says, "doesn't mean you get to control mine."

Then he grabs Harper's hand and stalks off; he can hear Harper saying something pleadingly, his sisters' voices behind him, but none of it is louder than the blood rushing in his ears. His throat's raw, already pulpy with regret.

His sisters know better than to argue with him. The car ride back is silent save for his mother's huffs and sniffles. Finally, she blasts the radio and stares moodily out the window. When they arrive at the house, the early evening stretches interminably long in front of him. He catches Naj's eye in the rear-view mirror.

"You got clean sheets in your guest bedroom?" he asks.

She nods.

"Let's go to your show," he snarls.

Everybody disperses without a word.

❖

He and Harp change into what Mimi thinks of as their show clothes, unofficial uniforms they've had since college for concerts and such. She wears black leggings and a stretchy Nirvana shirt, her hair in a low ponytail. He pulls on a U of T T-shirt, soft as paper from years of wear. There's a small hole near the armpit, and he's careful not to snag it. Naj is waiting in the courtyard, smoking and braiding a section of her punk hair. She grins when she sees them.

"Who says grunge is dead?"

"Shut up," Harp says, and Mimi laughs.

They run into their father and Mirabel in the driveway. She has a pen between her teeth and her cleavage is a sharp V. "I guess we can rebrand this worn façade as *character*," she's saying around the pen.

"Tell people it was built by the Phoenicians." Idris looks sweaty and miserable, and Mimi can tell he's struggling to suck his belly in.

"Was it?" Mirabel sounds delighted.

"Of course not," Naj says like the woman's a moron.

Idris ignores her. "In this country, dear, you can sell dirt to movie stars." Mirabel titters, and even Harper rolls her eyes.

"Good luck with that," Mimi says decisively. "See you."

"Have fun," he replies. "Also," he says softly as Mimi passes by, "you owe your mother an apology."

Mimi stops walking. He glares at Mirabel's cleavage pointedly, then at his father. "So do you."

His father tips his head back, as though Mimi has said something funny. "My son," he tells Mirabel, "doesn't think very highly of me. He finds me to be self-important."

"That can't be true," Mirabel says absently. She is framing the entrance with her fingers, like a fashion photographer.

Mimi smiles tightly. Once. He'd called Idris self-important once, during an argument in high school. His father has never forgotten.

❖

The club is larger than Back Door, and fancier. There are velvet couches the color of pomegranates, and there's metallic, figure-printed wallpaper in the bathroom. The stage is shaped like a horseshoe, with the crowd filling in the space between. They pass by the line outside; Naj takes them in through the side door, and a pretty waitress pecks her cheek.

"Which table?" she asks.

"I think we'll just hang out at the bar," Naj says, but Mimi knows she says it only because taking the table would be obnoxious. They order Tom Collinses at the bar, and Mimi insists on paying, but then the whole thing turns out to be on the house; the bartender knows Naj and showers her with kisses.

"How much money," he asks Mimi when she introduces him, "will it take to get your sister to play a song tonight?"

Mimi shrugs. "Do you have dimes here?" Everyone laughs, even Naj, who punches him in the shoulder, then kisses his cheek.

"I'm glad you came out." Naj's pupils are huge.

"How did you manage to find blow in the three minutes we've been here?"

She looks taken aback for a second, then laughs. "The waitress. She's an old friend." She smiles. "You want some?"

He surprises himself by saying yes, then Harp surprises both of them by also saying yes, and they go to their separate restrooms. He kisses Harp in the hallway afterward. "Are you too old to do coke," Harp says, giggling, "if you're worried about what it's cut with?"

There's an opening act onstage; Mimi didn't catch their name. The guitarist is better than the others, his fingers flying over the frets. Mimi's own fingers ache as he watches him. Harper is eyeing the guitarist with professional interest. "He's really good," she mutters, and Mimi hates himself for wincing. Harp clears her throat. "For a kid," she adds.

"You don't have to tiptoe around me," he says gruffly.

She eyes him steadily. "Then don't make me feel like I have to." She softens, snakes an arm around his waist. He dips his head toward hers and she bites his ear, then adds, "You're good too, Mim."

�֍

Back at the bar, they talk about Mazna and the fortuneteller again.

"I actually think it's pretty funny," Harp surprises him by saying.

"You can't mean that. She paid a woman to *lie about your fortune.*"

"I just mean it's ingenious." There is a look of admiration on her drug-flushed face.

"She's insane," he grumbles, but leaves it there.

"Your father, on the other hand . . ." Harp lets the sentence drop, which is just as well. The main act is now onstage, and their conversation is drowned out by the drumming. But Mimi finishes the sentence in his mind as the band begins a fast, angry song in Arabic. He and his father had done a science experiment together when Mimi was in middle school, putting droplets of canola oil in blue-dyed water. Ever since, it's the image that comes to him when someone asks about his father—iridescent beads skimming water. Untouched. He'd never known his father not to do what he wanted.

The singer hits the chorus hard and Mimi remembers being six or seven years old, holding his father's hand as they walked through the mall. There had been a fight, his mother yelling at Idris, and his father had taken him out. He'd gone reluctantly; it was perverse, but he almost liked it when his parents fought. His mother would get snippier with his sisters but softer with him, letting him trail her until he coaxed her into laughter, and she'd start to tell him stories about Syria. But that afternoon, he'd ended up with his father, who took him to get Dippin' Dots — it was Ava who liked them; they reminded Mimi of pastel-colored goat turds — and put on a jovial mood. As they walked back to the car, his father squeezed his hand. Mimi looked up.

"Your mother isn't easy," he said. "She can be a bitch." He smiled at his son. "Let's keep that between us boys, though."

Mimi hadn't waited a day. He'd told his mother that same afternoon, repeating every word when she asked, her eyes spitting fire as she listened. "Thank you, my darling," she'd said after. And they never spoke of it again. He never heard a fight about it; his father never said anything to him. But he must've known. That was their last boys' trip. His father was a little warier around him, and, truth be told, Mimi was relieved. It had felt embarrassing to watch his father trying to align with him. His father had his sisters. His mother had him. The gauntlet had been thrown down that afternoon, and after that, there was never any doubt about it again.

❖

Cocaine moves time along like a fast-forwarded vocal track. Before Mimi knows it, it's past midnight and he's on his third drink and he's having a *good* time. The crowd is different than in Austin, more careless, people smoking on the dance floor, screaming over the music in Arabic and French and English, the bartenders grinning like they're part of the crowd. Naj flits around like a moth, kissing people full on the mouth, her friend Jo appearing out of nowhere wearing purple eyeliner and a hoodie. The two of them pull Harper onto the dance floor, where she shrugs helplessly at him, though he can see how happy she is, pouting her lips as Jo dances with her.

Mimi flags the bartender down for another beer, and it's cold and perfect, and somebody leaves a pack of cigarettes on the bar top, and Mimi pockets them, then lights one, because everybody smokes in Beirut, and the music is really, really good, so good it's disrupting the part of his brain that automatically tries to dissect good music, to compare his own to it. This is so different, the lyrics in Arabic, the bass strong and lusty; it would be like comparing Dulcet to an Irish ballad. He feels a brief sorrow at the thought of Dulcet but churns past it, his synapses hooking on his mother's face in the amusement park that afternoon. It feels wrong to be on the outs with his mother. It's not the order of things.

"It was a little funny," he says to himself.

He fishes his phone out of his pocket. Before he can change his mind, he texts his mother the emoji of the monkey covering its ears. Almost immediately, she replies: the monkey covering its mouth.

The bartender catches his eye. Mimi laughs aloud, and the bartender laughs along, slapping his knee, which makes Mimi laugh harder. The band takes a break and incongruous seventies music blares from the speakers. The dance floor is thronged with people now; he can't make out Harper anymore, but Naj appears at his side, tugging his sleeve.

"Listen." She's chewing gum, and someone has drawn a grade-school daisy in black eyeliner on her cheek. One of the petals is smudged; she's sweaty. "Ramy asked me to go on for a song. I told him you could play backup guitar. We can do 'Her Back to the Rain.'"

It's the song title that catches him off guard. Naj, thirteen years old, right before Mimi went off to college. It was one of the songs they played back then. She was young enough that he could still boss her around; they'd formed a small band with his friend Jose and practiced in the garage. Naj sang and played violin, but really the experiment served to give Mimi a chance to treat her like shit. He could freely critique her playing or her off-key voice. She'd act tough, shrugging. He hasn't played "Her Back to the Rain" for years, but he could play it from memory, in a heartbeat.

"I can't," he says, but sorrowfully, and she's hesitating, deciding whether to push it, when a woman rushes up to Naj, clearly high.

"Jo's looking for you," she says, giggling, and Naj shrugs, just like she had all those years ago in the garage, and Mimi pretends to pull out another cigarette.

She and Jo play a Noja song and the audience sings along at the top of their lungs. Mimi catches a glimpse of Harper — her blond hair under the lights —

near the lip of the stage, shouting with everyone else. The manager had introduced Naj onstage to cheers, and even though she'd gone up with Jo, it was her
that everyone wanted, her name they were calling out from the crowd.

The pain of watching her perform is visceral, hot, sharp needles pricking
his skin from the inside; he almost cries in shame. After the second chorus, he
makes his way to the restroom — he doesn't want to hear the applause — and
gets bottlenecked next to two girls speaking animatedly about Naj.

"She's unreal. Unreal."

"I can't believe we got to see her tonight. I was in Larnaca during the last
Noja show." The second girl catches Mimi's eye and smiles. She nods at the
stage. "Amazing, right?"

Behind him, Naj is reaching the crescendo. "She never could carry a high
note," he says. He pushes past them and into the bathroom.

He can hear the roar of the audience even from inside the stall.

His sister's apartment smells terrifically of weed, and it takes him about three
seconds to figure out why, as she's already stuffing a fresh pipe. She and Harp
take two hits each, then start stretching out like cats.

"I lied earlier. I don't have any clean sheets," his sister announces, then
kisses Harp's cheek and goes to bed.

"You want one?" Mimi holds out the cigarette pack to Harper. She shakes
her head and nuzzles his scalp with her nose, an old habit from when they
first met.

"I love your scalp oil," she says as she's said a million times before. "It was
made for me."

"I know, baby."

"Good night."

"Good night."

After Harp goes to bed, Mimi lights a cigarette and props a kitchen window open. He looks out onto the street and wonders what it would take to
start a new life in South Dakota. The landscape has always appealed to him,
stark and rugged, alternating between wasteland and the plains and filled

with good, earthy people who couldn't care less about music scenes. He could learn to make hash browns and open a small diner, fill the plates with perfectly scrambled eggs and buttery brioche. It would be awful in the winters, but he'd make a few friends and they'd take turns playing poker at each other's houses in the darker months, sometimes jokingly throwing their wedding rings in the pot.

The breeze ruffles the dead plants on the sill. He can't find an ashtray, but there's a wastebasket, and he drags it to the sill and ashes into it. The cocaine is still drumming in his blood; he could stay up another hour or two. Naj's violin is on the kitchen counter and he lifts it, smelling the resin and chalk, and he's transported back to the music school's hallways, the intoxicating feeling of wanting to break the world open with his music.

His sister's laptop is next to the violin, and there's no password needed. He scrolls through some of her e-mails, mostly ads about stores or event invitations. There's one from Jo several weeks ago with the subject line *For end-of-summer show maybe?* Mimi opens it, clicks the audio link, then taps the volume down and leans toward the speaker to listen.

It's a new song, his sister's voice quiet and trembling, barely any lyrics, mostly the wailing he associates with Bedouin music. The sound is triumphant and mournful, a chilling contrast. Mimi lights another cigarette and listens to it again, then a third time. The cherry of the cigarette glows like an ornament and he listens and watches the red hypnotically. He's exhausted by the end. It's a perfect song.

"You're pretty," he says to the violin, then he puts the cigarette out in the wastebasket. He carries the instrument over to the couch and lies down, pressing against it like it's a child or a dog. He's asleep before he knows it.

❖

There's an alarm clock in his dream, but it's distant, more of a bell than a buzzer, and he doesn't want to wake up; he's finally arrived at the clearing in the forest and there is a long table set with pink mushrooms and meat. Somebody is barbecuing, and the smell is pure October, and his dream self is pleased with the thought. He can write it into a song, because he has a show in a week, at his grandfather's memorial, and his jiddo is coming, and his mother's parents, and Elliot from the Austin venue. They're already here! He can hear them crunching the leaves behind him, and he panics, because his songs aren't ready, but they're calling his name out; the trees have started to applaud.

"Jesus, fuck, wake up!"

Mimi opens his eyes to see his sister in a tank top and boxer shorts, her hair a mess. Harper is at his feet, yanking at him. Both women are carrying an armful of things, Naj's laptop, the violin, a small digital camera, and Mimi wants to ask if they heard about the show, but before he can, Naj is screaming again.

"Mimi, get up! You're going to pass out from the smoke."

Why do you have a halo? he wants to ask Naj, but then he notices that Harp has one, too, and so does the plant on the coffee table, and in that second, he wakes up completely, bolting upright. "What the *fuck?*"

The room is filled with smoke.

His first thought is the Lebanese soldiers have started burning trash inside. His second is that he needs to stop, drop, and roll. His third is *Can you can roll against a wall?* Then his sister is pulling him up, and there's no more time for thoughts.

"We woke up to the neighbors," Harp is saying. "Their alarm went off."

"You don't have one?" he asks Naj.

"Can you fucking move, please?"

The smoke is thickest in the kitchen, and something distant clicks in Mimi's head. "The kitchen," he says.

"It's that fucking gas oven," Naj yells.

They push their way out of the living room. Mimi's lungs are burning. There's a firefighter in the hallway, and he runs past them wordlessly with an extinguisher. The entryway outside the building is thronged with the neighbors in glasses and pajamas. A few are staring daggers at his sister. There is a fire truck and several men standing around looking up at the smoke as though waiting to be told what to do.

"I thought you were dead," Harper says, sobbing. "You weren't waking up."

He kisses her, then hugs his sister. He feels strangely heroic and pumped with adrenaline, as though they've climbed a mountain rather than walked down some stairs. A few more stragglers come out, and the doorman scribbles something into the notebook he's carrying.

"That's all of them," he says importantly to the fire chief by his side.

"You idiot!" a woman in her seventies yells. Everyone turns to her. She's pointing at Naj. "May God strike you with a fever. May He never forgive you. May you have no sons. You could've burned this entire building down."

"Come on, now," the fire chief says halfheartedly.

"May you have no luck."

Naj tugs her hair nervously and apologizes to the woman, to the neighbors, to the firemen. "Was it the oven? I could've sworn it wasn't on."

"Too early to tell." The chief brightens. "Maybe it's arson? You don't see much of that here, but there are certainly enough psychopaths with matches in this city."

"What?"

"He seems remarkably calm about this," Harper says in English. Her arms are wrapped around her torso tightly.

The fire chief chuckles and switches to English. "It's probably just the gas. It happens all the time. Maybe a cigarette or something."

"People could've died," Harp says and starts crying again, but Mimi doesn't comfort her; he is too busy remembering the red, hypnotic glow. The wastebasket. Full of wrappers. Full of paper.

"I swear I turned it off," his sister is saying, and she's crying as well, her voice muffled in Harp's T-shirt. Mimi hugs them both, and behind them the old lady starts up again, cursing the day their father decided to have children.

There is the predictable chaos when they get to his grandfather's house. Mimi can't find his keys — they'd fallen out in Naj's building and been kicked to the side of the second-floor landing — and they have to wake up Merry, who, upon hearing the story, says summarily to Naj, "This would never have happened if you lived with your jiddo," as though Jiddo is still alive, and then she makes them tea, which wakes up their parents. Their mother cries a little as well, which sets Harp and Naj off again, and the children wake up from the noise, which wakes Ava up, and they have to tell the story again. Everybody is angry with Naj, but their father intervenes, saying, "Let's just remember how lucky we are that nobody got hurt."

After Ava gets the kids back to sleep, Naj announces she is sleeping on the couch and nobody protests it. There's a camaraderie among her and Mimi and Harp, and they joke about fireproofing the living room. At the bedroom door, Mazna hugs Harp and says, "I'm glad you're not dead." Not exactly Shakespeare, Mimi thinks, but it's enough to make Harp cry again.

Later, he listens to Harp falling asleep. Her breathing evens. "Harp," he whispers.

"Mm."

"Harp."

"What?"

"I started the fire."

There's a stillness, then rustling around, and the lamp turns on. He blinks away the brightness. He can see each of Harp's pale eyelashes. Her mouth is quivering. "What are you talking about?"

"I smoked a cigarette before I went to sleep. I couldn't find an ashtray."

"Where'd you put it?"

"The trashcan. There was paper and stuff in there. I was half asleep. I don't know why she never takes her trash out —"

Harper smacks her forehead, such a cartoonish gesture that he almost laughs, but the look in her eyes sobers him.

"Your family has broken your mind," she says.

"I know."

"You've gone off the rails."

"I know, Harp." He thinks of Allie. "There's more."

She puts her hand up. "I don't think I want to hear more, Mimi. I think . . ." She pauses. "I think some things we can keep to ourselves. That's the core of a healthy relationship."

"Lying?"

"*Unburdening.* Yes. Sometimes keeping your mouth shut is, I don't know
— *kind.*"

"Okay." He wonders what she knows.

She sighs. "This has been the most stressful summer of my life."

"Your tan looks great, though."

"Stop." She bursts into laughter, and he laughs as well. "It does, doesn't it?"
She sobers. "I'll ask one last time. Do you want me to leave? Not *leave*-leave,"
she says at his stricken face. "I just mean move the flight up. I think your hands
are pretty full here."

He pulls her into his arms. There is a crack in the ceiling that is likely older
than he is. When he was a little boy, he'd sometimes think about how he'd
bring his own child to this house. He hasn't thought of that in years. He can
see Harp during a layover in Charles de Gaulle buying a *Vogue Paris*, then,
later, getting a cab from the Austin airport, unpacking her dirty laundry in the
Igloo. She'd be back in the office by the end of the week, Beirut a sandy dream.
She sighs and he hugs her tighter, tells her to stay.

Quarters are cramped. It's a big house, but they're a big crowd, and there's often
someone hopping in front of the guest bathroom or waiting by the coffee machine. Predictably, there's more bickering — Naj breaks Ava's hair straightener
and they have the sort of spat their age difference always prevented in childhood — but also, surprisingly, more fun. There are games of charades, where
Mazna beats everyone. Mimi cooks long, complicated feasts, Rayan helping
him in a too-large apron, washing vegetables. Harper and Naj record songs
with the children, and Ava spends an afternoon working on her paper while
Merry watches an Egyptian sitcom on the other end of the couch.

His aunt Sara comes over more frequently, and they organize the photographs on elegant boards. Sara and his mother bicker over the catering, but
their tastes are more similar than either woman would admit and often they
select the same appetizer or napkin color. The coffee table is covered with programs that Zina and Rayan have tied with adorable, lopsided ribbons, and no-

body mentions the old woman or Zakaria. In fact, the closer the memorial looms, the less anybody talks about the house being sold.

But the Friday before the memorial, they all wake to the sound of hammering. By the time Mimi gets outside, his sisters and parents are already gathered, their faces dazed. Everyone is yelling.

There are orange banners draped around the courtyard, and for a second he thinks it's for the memorial, the kids decorating the house with streamers, but then he sees they aren't streamers — it's a work zone, men in hard hats, one of them holding a massive saw that's embedded deep in the trunk of the largest almond tree.

"No," he says weakly.

Mirabel, wearing a hard hat and heels, is cowering as his sisters scream at her. His mother, for once, is speechless. Her hand covers her mouth. Mimi can't even look at his father. He runs to join his sisters.

"We'll sue you!" Ava is screaming.

"This fucking monster," Naj yells, seeing Mimi, "she murdered my tree."

This time, Mimi doesn't point out the possessive pronoun. "Stop," he says, but it's a whisper. "Stop!" he yells at the men — needlessly, because they've already stopped, nervous, the saw halfway through the tree.

"Listen, Uncle," a worker says to his father. "She just told us this was the job."

Mimi finally glances at his father. He is slumped next to one of the remaining trees. He looks bewildered. "We said we'd leave it alone," he says to nobody.

"I'd get your license number," Ava is saying to Mirabel, "but I'd be shocked if this stupid country even has licenses." Her Arabic is faltering and childlike, but she looks so angry that even the workers take a step back.

"You murdered my tree!" Naj wails.

"Ladies, please." Mirabel turns to Idris with what she clearly thinks is an appealing smile. "Almond trees have been out of style for years now. We'll plant some lovely bougainvillea."

His father says nothing. There's a terrible silence.

"After that —" Mirabel starts, and a dishrag flies by her face. "Ahh!"

"Shut up, you stupid girl." Mazna's eyes spit fire. She raises her hand menacingly again, though it's empty now.

"Madame Nasr, I really think —" Mirabel smooths her hair, trying to regain her composure.

"You have three seconds to get out. This is private property. One."

"Idris." Mirabel looks at their father, who shakes his head.

"We said we'd leave it alone."

"Two."

"My God, fine!" Mirabel grabs her bag and scrambles out of the courtyard. The construction workers turn to Mazna questioningly. She crosses her arms.

"We'll come back for the saw," the biggest worker says. They clear out within seconds. Naj goes to her mother and cries. Everyone waits for Mazna to say something, to yell at Idris, but she just pats Naj's shoulder. His father buries his face in his hands.

The door opens. It's Harp. She just woke up, her pajamas rumpled. Her hair sticks out like straw. She sees the tree, his crying father, Naj buried in her mother's arms.

"There's a saw in that tree," Harp says.

Mazna turns to her. "What's your people's expression," she asks, not unkindly, "about the cat with all the questions?"

Harp scans the yard, then does a quick salute. "Roger that, ma'am."

❈

The rest of the day is sad and dejected, the weather gray and rainy to match the mood. There isn't much talking, and even the children are well behaved. "We have to bury the tree now too," Mimi overhears Rayan whispering to Zina solemnly, and Mimi hugs both children so hard, they complain.

"You're not so bad," he tells Rayan, who grins.

"Yes, I am. I steal cookies from my friends' lunchboxes."

Mimi laughs; it feels good. He realizes the children have spent all summer in the house of a dead man they'd never met. It doesn't seem all that healthy. "I'm going to take y'all to Six Flags when we get back to the States."

"She's afraid of roller coasters." Rayan smirks.

"I am not!" Zina hesitates. "I like the teacup ride."

"Well, we'll do both."

Around dusk, he goes outside for a cigarette. He's been smoking more and more, but Beirut feels like a suspended reality, Peter Pan's attic. He'll stop when he gets to Austin, he knows. It'll suck for a few days, then it'll be fine. It isn't raining anymore; the sky is a deep rose pink. The air smells clean for once.

His grandfather used to smoke. He remembers his grandmother would tell him to do it outside, and there were often used matches on the veranda. One summer Mimi collected them, like baseball cards. Mimi goes over to the tree and touches the trunk, then the saw. He should finish the job; his family would be grateful. Surprised, but grateful. But he just touches the cold metal handle, then stops.

"I couldn't either," a voice says behind him.

Mimi nearly drops the cigarette. He turns. "Baba?"

His father is sitting on the little bench to the side, shielded from view, his knees pulled up to his chest like a child. "I couldn't bring it down."

"Yeah." He sits next to him. The bench is cold and wet, but it's almost nice to feel a sensation so specific. Rain feels the same everywhere. "I remember when I climbed it for the first time. Jiddo gave me some candy." He's surprised to hear his voice break, and his father pats him on the back.

"I talked to that tree the day of the funeral," his father says. He dabs his eyes.

"I'm sorry we didn't come," Mimi says. It's the first time he's said it, he realizes.

"Yes," his father says simply. It's been years since he's asked his father about the hearts he operates on. He can't imagine him dead. He can't imagine a day when he won't know where his father is, when he's not washing his scrubs, not sneaking a doughnut, not driving toward a Californian sunset. He starts to cry a little, and his father hugs him.

"I don't want you to die," he says idiotically and then realizes how terrible it sounds. "Oh."

"It's okay," his father replies. "I can report from the other side. As we say in Arabic, *Time doesn't change; time reveals.*" He turns to look at Mimi, and it's dark but he can see his father's eyes. "I'm here to tell you you'll survive it, son." Just like that, Mimi doesn't need to cry anymore, and it reminds him of his father carrying the heaviest bags himself, arguing with the examiner when Mimi failed his first driving test, giving dying people another life. When Mimi was a child, his father was a god, and he'd never forgiven him for it.

There's the sound of jingling keys. His father looks stricken.

"Sara. I forgot. She was coming by for dinner."

They hold their breath. Mimi can hear his aunt walking around the courtyard, but the two of them are shielded by the hedge. "What the —" they hear her mumble. A minute passes and she raises her voice as she enters the house. "Why is there a goddamn saw in my father's almond tree?" she yells.

Mimi catches his father's eye. Idris looks scared.

"You have to tell her at some point," Mimi says, trying to sound encouraging. His father shuts his eyes. He starts to rise.

His mother's voice drifts out to them.

"Oh, that. Terrible, isn't it," they hear her say. Idris freezes. "We had some men come out. The leaves were this strange color. It turns out it's tree rot. It's awful, but it has to come down." Idris sits again, breathing hard.

Sara has questions, and they talk for a few moments. Mimi and his father listen. Around them, the dark falls quickly, and the sounds of passing cars swell and fade, but his father keeps his head cocked to hear the women's voices, to hear the lies that Mazna tells for him.

When the children were younger, Rayan maybe four or five, Mimi had cooked a dozen tiny pizzas, and the event is hallowed in the boy's memory. He's brought it up all summer, and Mimi finally relents and goes to the nearby supermarket with his mother. It's not the best one, but it's a short walk, and the rain has finally broken the heat a bit. Mazna is in a good mood, merrily mocking the Lebanese eccentricities they see along the way.

"I mean, look at that electrical outlet," she says cheerfully in the grocery store. "I swear it's sparking. But I'm sure that puddle next to it isn't anything to worry about."

"I watched a video of a guy jet-skiing to work during the floods last year. Right through downtown," Mimi says and his mother laughs.

"We didn't have flooding back home even in the sixties. Here, they're still waiting to be washed out to sea."

He knows *home* isn't California. "Do you miss it?" he asks.

There's a slyness to her glance. "Your sister asked the same thing. So curious all of a sudden."

"I miss it." He realizes as he speaks the words that they're true. "But that doesn't seem fair. I didn't spend much time there."

"You can miss it," his mother says sharply. He waits for more, but she busies herself with bagging vegetables. A minute passes before she speaks again. "I pretend it never happened," she says in a conspiratorial tone.

"What?"

"All of it. The war. If you can call it that. The way this entire country — all these restaurants and cities and mosques and *people* — just went up in flames. It's too much. So I just . . . I pretend I just can't leave the greenhouse and that's why I haven't visited in so long." Her tone is nonchalant, but her cheeks are red and he knows this is a secret.

"Huh."

"What 'huh'?"

"So you just pretend there's no war?"

"I'm lucky enough," she muses, almost to herself, "to be able to pretend."

"I'm pretty sure there are therapists in California who wouldn't exactly call that healthy."

Mazna holds up a plum, considering. She sniffs it. "California isn't a real place."

He starts bagging the tomatoes. The vegetables feel more like themselves here. Misshapen. Prone to rotting. They still smell like dirt. "Why did you bail Baba out? With Sara?"

She snorts. "Because I am always getting him out of trouble. That man will be the death of —"

"So why not just let him get in trouble?" Mimi interrupts.

She knocks on a latticed melon like a door. "Your father," Mazna says, "thinks he knows how to fix everything. He doesn't, of course. Everything he touches multiplies into more problems. He is the biggest buffalo in the china shop."

"Bull."

"But he doesn't mean to be."

"That's why you haven't divorced him."

"Yet," his mother says crisply. "Life is long."

There's a line at the meat counter, but his mother flirts with the butcher, younger than Mimi himself, and he gives her the best cut of lamb. "Syrian!" the young man says in delight when Mazna speaks, like he's on a game show. When he hands her the twined package, he says, "You're welcome here, madame. You're welcome a thousand times over."

"Be sure to tell your government," Mazna says sweetly.

"Jesus, Mama." As they walk away, Mimi says, "I don't think you'll ever divorce him."

His mother looks at him archly. "Is this the part of the conversation where we talk about each other's relationships?"

Mimi holds his palms up. "Forget it."

But a minute later, she speaks again. "Did you think we would get divorced? As a child?"

The question surprises him. He thinks back. He remembers hearing the word dozens of times, each parent hurling it at the other during arguments — at amusement parks, family dinners, road trips. "Only once for real, I think."

"When was that?"

"We called it the Cold War. Ave and me. It was the year Teta died, and the Olympics were on. I remember because we'd watch the gymnastics and you wouldn't say a word to Baba."

"The Cold War." Mazna sounds amused.

"Do you remember?"

"I do."

"What happened?"

Mazna sighs like he's bothering her. "I sometimes did auditions after I had you kids," she says. "You remember. I had one that went well when you were very young. But your father ruined it for me and — I found out that summer."

"What did he do?"

But his mother is done talking. "It was a long time ago." She points toward the bakery. "Let's get some *manakish*."

The bakery is set up like an old-fashioned *khabaz,* with a man working the globe-shaped oven, tossing dough and hammering it with his hands on the counter. Once one is finished, he slides it onto a cooling rack with a wooden peel and starts working on more dough. Mimi watches the man's blackened fingers kneading expertly.

"Are you going to tell me why you quit the band?" His mother's voice interrupts his reverie.

"Naj needs to keep her mouth shut," Mimi says, annoyed.

"Harper told me." He turns to her in surprise. Mazna shrugs. "I asked. You haven't mentioned it all summer."

He's suddenly angry at all of them. Talking about his failure. Worrying about him. "Maybe I just realized I wasn't good enough," he says viciously.

To his surprise, his mother just shrugs. "You are good, Mimi. You must've heard that enough by now." He remembers Harper at the club saying, *Then don't make me feel like I have to.* "But you're also allowed to let the band go."

She touches his arm, but it hurts too much, her sentence, the finality of it. She speaks like she understands. Like there's something inevitable in him leaving Dulcet. He tries to imagine his mother on a movie screen, but it's impossible. If you live a life long enough, it becomes yours. The man is pummeling the dough again, sprinkling flour over it, and Mimi watches all of it, soothed by its familiarity. He could be in California. Austin. Damascus. There's only one way to make bread.

"Look how he's doing that," he says conciliatorily. "Punching the dough."

His mother looks. "What's it for?"

"It's for the air bubbles." He can almost feel the dough in his own hands, the satisfaction of each knead, how it would yield and change for him.

They barely speak again until they reach their street. His mother stops. There's a strand of hair in her eyes and she tucks it behind her ear. "You know," she says, a quiet anger to her words, "Naj should've asked you to be in her band."

There's nothing to say to this. Naj *had* asked him. The summer after Noja was born, after their first show in New York, when they were about to do a European tour. She'd had a layover in Austin for a couple of days; she and Jo had slept in the guest room. The night before their flight, she'd asked him if they could talk. He was in the kitchen alone, slicing vegetables for dinner.

"You could be the lead guitarist. Jo could play bass." She'd been thinking about it for a while, he could tell. She'd talked about splitting their time between America and Beirut. "I could even come here for a few months out of the year," he remembered her saying. Her hair had been long then, and she'd kept twisting the ends, nervous. He was angry and hadn't hidden it. Dulcet had never played in Europe. And besides, he had a house and a girlfriend; Beirut was a nonstarter.

"I already have a band," he said, and the conversation ended. But she had asked him, and he'd never told anybody, not even to correct their assumptions.

The following morning, they eat the pizzas for breakfast. He'd baked them in different shapes and with an array of toppings, and he chooses a star-shaped one with figs and mozzarella. The memorial is tomorrow, and everyone is restless, alternating between cleaning the house and snacking over the sink. There is a large board of the photographs in the living room. When they finish cleaning, he and Harp take a walk to Raouché. This turns into lunch, which they eat on the pier overlooking the wrinkled brown sunbathers and children playing at the water's edge, after which they wander through the streets, stopping at random stores.

It's nearly seven when they make their way back to the house; the sky is darkening. Harp is talking about Laci's upcoming release, but she stops at the sight of a woman in front of the gate.

"Who's that?" he says.

"Mimi. It's her," Harp hisses.

Her means a thousand things and his first thought — absurdly — is Allie, but then his eyes adjust. The woman is old, wearing a plain buttoned shirt. "The housekeeper," he breathes. They walk gingerly toward her, like she might disappear, but when she sees them, she just smiles politely and says hello.

"I'm Idris's son," he says. "Marwan."

She shakes his hand, then Harper's, nodding at the younger woman's greeting, though it's clear that she doesn't speak English.

"Are you here to see my father? I think he's inside."

The woman's eyes dart around. "I'm not," she says finally.

There's an awkward silence. The woman's mouth lifts in a polite half smile, and there's something recognizable about the expression, a familiarity bred from seeing her in so many photographs. "The memorial," Harp whispers.

"Oh yes!" Mimi says in Arabic, "The memorial is tomorrow. But you should come inside, my parents would love —" He thinks of his mother dropping her mug. "To see you."

"You're very kind," the woman says. Once more, she glances around. "But I should leave. I'll try to come tomorrow. Issa was a good man. May the remainder be in your life."

"And yours," Mimi says automatically. "Wait! Your address. Could I get your address?" The woman looks at him curiously. "We'll be mailing out programs," he lies.

"We don't get mail, dear," she says, but still, she scrawls some Arabic words and a number on a receipt.

"Wow," Harp says after the woman is gone. "Your sisters aren't going to believe it." She looks at Mimi squinting at the paper. "Are you not coming in?"

"You go ahead," he says. "I can't tell if this is a five or a zero. I'll try to catch her." He jogs to the street corner, but she's gone, probably already in a taxi. It doesn't matter. He'll try five *and* zero. His heart is still hammering, but the piece of paper feels triumphant in his hand. He's nearly back at the house when he sees someone running toward it.

"Sara?"

"Mimi!" His aunt is flushed and frenzied-looking, glancing at her watch. "I'm — ah, I was just meeting—" She glances around, but the street is empty.

"Meeting who?" he says.

Again, she looks helplessly toward the street, then back at the house. She rearranges her expression. "Nothing, nothing. I was just late for dinner." She looks at him hard for a second. "What?"

Mimi shakes his head. "Nothing, Sara. I'd just love to know what the fuck is going on with this family."

"Don't curse," she says automatically. She starts walking the other way.

"I thought you were late for dinner!" he yells after her.

She waves without turning. "Turns out I'm not hungry. *Bisoux!*" He watches her for a long moment, then curses and goes inside the house.

❊

He finds his sisters and Harp on Ava's bed. "Guess what?" he singsongs.

Harper shakes her head. She and Naj are on either side of Ava, who has her head bowed.

"What happened?"

"I'm calling him again," Ava is saying. "Is that crazy?"

"Call him," Naj says.

"Let's just take a minute." Harper tells Mimi, "Ava called Nate's hotel room and some woman picked up."

"I know her voice," Ava says stridently.

"Fuck him, Avey." Naj smooths her sister's hair.

"Wait. What? Nate's with a woman in a hotel?"

"The Portland hotel," Ava says miserably. "This whole summer, things have been off between us. He talks with the kids and then there's, like, nothing to say between us. He gave me the Portland hotel number in case there was an emergency. The past two days, he hasn't been responding to texts. So I got worried and called —"

"That motherless piece of gum-shit," Naj supplies.

"And he wasn't the one that picked up."

"I'm calling." Ava dials and puts the phone on speaker. "It's the middle of the day there," she says. "Remember."

The line is picked up. "Hello?"

A woman's voice. Harp gasps aloud, then clamps her hand over her mouth. Ava ends the call. She hangs her head in such defeat that Mimi wants to book a flight to Portland and feed Nate his own testicles.

His murderous thoughts are echoed in Naj's face. "I already have ideas," she says to Mimi's unasked question. "I'll call his HR department and file a misconduct complaint. I'll take out an ad in the newspaper."

"Please stop," Ava says miserably. Harp puts her arm around her, and it looks awkward, but his sister leans against it. "I fucking knew it." She turns to Mimi. "There's this woman. This *Emily*."

"We'll tell HR that he tried to sell you drugs," he says to Naj.

"Good idea."

Ava covers her face with a pillow and lets out a muffled scream. "What do I do now?" she says.

Harp touches her arm. "We got the address."

The pillow stills. Ava throws it off and sits up. "You didn't."

"We did!" Mimi brandishes the slip of paper. "She was outside the house." He considers telling them about Sara but changes his mind. "Her number too. You can call her."

"We could even go there," Naj says. "The memorial's tomorrow, but —"

"I told her about it," Mimi says.

"We'll call tomorrow morning to remind her," Harp adds.

"I love you guys." Ava wipes her face. She folds up the paper and puts it in her pocket.

"I have something as well." Naj glances mischievously over her shoulder. "I was going to save it for Jo, but —" She rummages around in her bag, pulls out a little baggie of pastel-colored pills.

"Naj, I have children." Ava sighs.

His little sister considers this. She cups her hands around her mouth. "Mama!" she hollers at the top of her lungs.

"*What?*"

"Come here! Please!"

Their mother pads into the room and takes in the foursome. "When I was your age," she informs them, "I didn't have time to lounge around like I had servants."

"Mama," Naj says, ignoring the comment, "I'm taking Avey out. Can you watch the kids?"

Mazna starts to say something but then catches sight of Ava's face. She shuts her mouth. "I will," she says finally. To Naj: "But I pray Allah will forgive your drinking and drugging and parties."

"And may He forgive you your miniskirts," Naj responds. She ducks expertly from the hanger their mother throws at her head.

✵

They wait until they are all gathered outside in the courtyard. They'll go dancing, Naj says. Ava has washed her face and changed into one of Mimi's band shirts, and the effect is transforming, like she's back in high school. Naj presses a small pink pill into each person's palm. Harp glances at Mimi anxiously.

"I felt that coke for days after. Maybe one of us should stay sober."

"I'm insulted," Naj says. "My dealer is top-notch." She throws the pill back like an aspirin. "Okay, babies. Your turn. One, two, three."

They swallow.

Part

IV

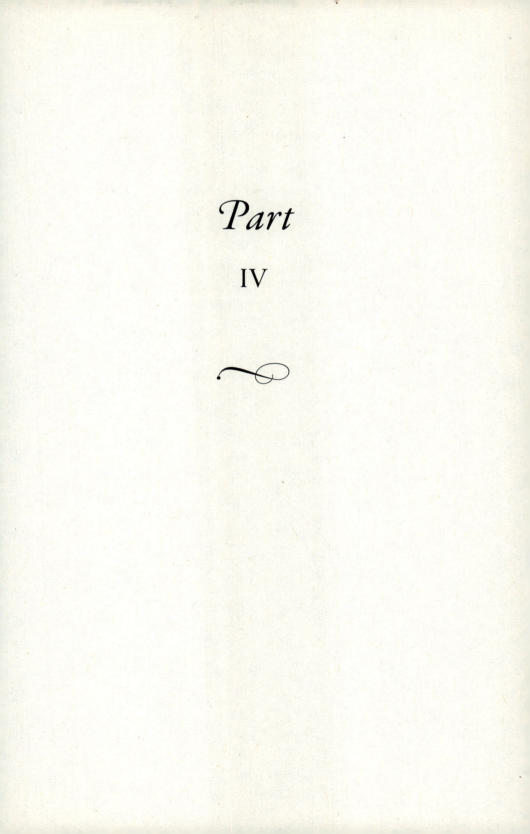

Amrika

1978

THEY ARRIVE IN California on a hot, unremarkable day. It's a week after their wedding, and Mazna still has some fake lashes glued on from the party. Somewhere above the Baltics, she started peeling them off, one by one, then hid the furry nest under the seat. A uniformed man at the John F. Kennedy Airport directs them to a separate line, and they wait forty-five minutes for the older couple in front of them to finish their argument about visas.

"Lebanon?" the officer says when it's their turn, frowning over the large packet of papers Idris's father's cousin, a lawyer, had prepared for them. His asylum case changed at the last minute — now it's built on Zakaria. The men would come looking for him. Sectarian violence. Death due to religious affiliation.

Idris nods. "I am here to study medicine," he says proudly, though the airport and officers and long flight have had a shrinking effect on him. His English is accented; his dress shirt rumpled from the flight.

"Sounds good, bud." The officer speaks like a character in *High Noon,* not what she'd expect in New York. "Lot of fireworks over there, huh?"

Idris looks confused. "Yes."

"Well," the man says, "we keep guns in the right hands here. Both from Lebanon, then?" *Leb-nun.*

"No." Mazna is surprised to hear her voice. She hasn't spoken since takeoff. When the flight attendants asked her questions, she nodded. Idris and the officer look at her with mild interest. "I am from the Syria." Her English, she realizes, sounds as bad as Idris's.

He gives her a second look. "Doesn't sound like you're overjoyed to be here, ma'am."

There's a long silence. The night before the wedding, she'd sobbed so hard, she'd soaked her pillowcase. In the morning, she'd stuffed it into the wastebasket. Her body aches like she's been awake for days. "I think," she says quietly, "you are correct." Idris says nothing at her side.

The officer considers this. He stamps both their passports.

"Welcome to the United States, ma'am."

�֍

From JFK they fly to Phoenix. Their baggage is waiting for them next to the carousel, a little reproach. They are oversize, wrapped in plastic, bulging in the wrong places. She had packed with detachment, her room dismayingly strewn with flung sweaters and cassettes and toiletries. *This is my life,* she'd thought with surprise when her father piled the luggage in his car to drive to Beirut. Her life could fit in a bag. Her life could be closed in a trunk. Her life could be flown across the Atlantic.

Arrangements have been made to get them from the airport to their new town. This reminds her of Hana — her mother-in-law, she realizes — who'd murmured those words again and again these past few weeks. The wedding dress, the apartment in Blythe through the university, the reception: *Arrangements have been made.* During the *katb el kitab,* she'd cupped Mazna's face and said, "It took me a year to feel happiness after my wedding." That was it. Nothing further. There was a visible scar on Hana's forehead from where she'd fainted after the news of Zakaria, and Mazna constantly wanted to touch it. For the wedding, Hana had styled her hair to cover the mark, and Mazna felt strangely angry at that.

"If I pile them sideways . . ." Idris murmurs to himself as he struggles with the baggage cart. She makes a halfhearted attempt to help. The top suitcase is going to fall, she can tell, and it does, a few steps in, and Idris drags it instead, pushing the cart with one hand.

"I can do that," Mazna says.

He smiles at her. "Can you believe we're here?" he asks. "Look at that!" There's an automatic drinking fountain to their side.

"Stop ogling," she says in a voice that reminds her of Lulwa. She thinks of the customs officer. "They already think we're peasants."

"This isn't Syria; Americans don't think that way," he corrects her. He speaks like he's been in the country longer than an hour. "It's the land of opportunity."

Mazna doesn't answer.

❧

A fellow resident from the hospital is meant to pick them up. The drive from Phoenix will be a little over two hours. As they walk through the automated doors and down the arrivals hall, see the hundreds of people carrying signs and balloons, Mazna has the perverse wish for the man not to show, as though that would settle it. She imagines them returning to the same customs officer. *Our car never came,* she'd say. *We have to go back now.*

But near the airport exit, Idris lets out a delighted sound. A balding, stout man with blue eyes is holding a sign reading DR. IDRIS NASR.

"That's me," Idris says pointlessly to Mazna.

"I see that," she replies, then turns to roll her eyes before remembering that there is nobody else there. She's used to dealing with Idris in groups — with his parents, Zakaria, Tarek. The two of them facing a lifetime in the middle of the desert is tolerable in theory, alarming in practice. She reimagines her conversation with the customs officer. *I have to go back alone,* she tells him.

But the colleague has extended his arm, and it's too late. "Mrs. Nasr, a pleasure. I'm Eddie. I'm in the same surgery residency as Idris here."

She shakes his hand. Idris reads her face. "It's Mazna Adib," he tells Eddie.

"You don't say. My wife kept her last name as well." He elbows Idris. "Guess they're keeping their options open."

Idris elbows the man back, looking pleased with the gesture. "I guess so."

The men chuckle, and this time Mazna does roll her eyes, to a blond girl holding a balloon. The balloon is silver and has blue lettering: WELCOME HOME! The girl smiles as though she understands everything.

✧

The flight had been long. They'd left in the middle of the night, their parents seeing them off bleary-eyed and tearful. In her exhaustion, Mazna slept as soon as the airplane rose and woke up to Idris shaking her and saying they'd arrived in Paris. He'd wanted to do a honeymoon there, but she'd said they'd go somewhere in America once they were settled. She knew there would never be a honeymoon.

She was wide awake for the next leg of their trip, sitting next to the window, crying, looking out at all that blackness, thinking of her mother's bedroom. Lulwa had seemed afraid in the airport, kissing her daughter's forehead, then cheek, then eyelid.

"I will pray for your happiness," she'd said, and Mazna had to chew her lip to keep from crying.

But in the dark airplane, the stewardesses huddled in the service area like flamingos, everyone around her asleep, Mazna cried and cried, for her mother and father and, most of all, herself. She remembered the little neighborhood cat she used to feed when she was a child and cried — the cat must be dead now. Zakaria. This was how her mind worked these days — every thought took her back to him, a maze in reverse. She cried and clutched the little purse that had her wedding gold in it. Even when she went to the bathroom to vomit — somewhere over Iceland — she took the purse. There were over ten pieces in it, coins and earrings and necklaces and even a sapphire pendant that Idris's great-aunt had given her. Before this, she'd owned only a single piece of gold jewelry — a pair of gold-drop earrings, a graduation gift — but at the wedding, strangers had lined up with gold.

They were her mother's friends, Hana's sisters, Idris's family's friends. Her parents' side gave her simple gold coins. Mazna took each piece like a bribe, folding it in her hands, and kissed the giver on the cheek. *And blessings upon you,* she recited to everyone, saying it so many times it started to blur into one alien word. *Andblessingsuponyou.* She didn't cry once all night. When there was music, she danced with her friends, Lara and Fatima cooing over her. If Lara was mad at her, she didn't say a word, and Mazna wondered absently about that until she went to the bathroom and, thinking her mirror reflection a wedding guest, reflexively smiled. She looked unhinged, her color high, her eyes blazing, brittle and beautiful, like she might set the building on fire.

Sara entered the bathroom. She seemed surprised at the sight of Mazna. "Oh." Her face stretched into its own false smile. They hadn't spent any time alone since that afternoon on the beach before Mazna had gone to see Zakaria.

"You look beautiful," Mazna said, because that's what she'd been saying to everyone, even the men. Sara looked down at her dress, gray with a white-trimmed collar.

"My mother bought it for me," she said. The girl appeared exhausted. She ducked her head for a second, then lifted it suddenly. "I sent you a letter."

Mazna wanted to hug her. She wanted to tell her she'd never read the letter. That she'd wrecked it beyond saving. She wanted to fix the ribbon on the side of Sara's dress; it was trailing on the floor. But she was tired. The stupor of grief had started to wear off earlier that week when Hana had showed her candle arrangements and she'd thought distantly, *What ugly colors,* then realized with a jolt that these were *her* wedding candles, that for the rest of her life, she would remember having blue and peach centerpieces at her wedding. Now there was peach and blue everywhere, and she was coming to, and she had no time for Sara, who was as good as a stranger, and so she said only, "I know," then pushed past the girl to the door.

❖

Eddie is a talker. Idris sits in the front with him and they interrupt each other. The other man is in awe of Idris, who loves a devotee, and Mazna can see their dynamic will work well. They're discussing the residency. His surgical training will be a byzantine and incomprehensible process, one that Idris has gone over with her many times but that she keeps forgetting. He will attend lectures at a university in San Bernardino, a few hours away, on Mondays and Wednesdays, but his clinical rotations are at a small hospital in their new town, Blythe. Mazna isn't sure if the *h* is pronounced.

From what she can understand, most residents are finished with their coursework, but the American system is different, and Idris must catch up. It isn't ideal to be that far from the university, but he says he doesn't mind. She figures they arranged his training this way because of his late enrollment, his asylum, but she wonders why Eddie has to do the same thing. He also lives in their new town.

"I used to think I'd do neurosurgery, but now I'm thinking cardiothoracic," Eddie is saying.

"I've always known I'd do cardiac surgery," Idris says. Mazna wants to interrupt, ask him why, but the moment for those sorts of questions has come and gone. She is supposed to know all that already. She looks out of the window instead.

The asphalt is the same as it is in Syria. So are the light poles. The desert even looks like the Palmyra region, in the east. But there's something unmistakably different about the whole. Everything is cleaner, more organized, and somehow sharper, as though she's just put on eyeglasses. She'd envisioned skyscrapers, neon signs, but instead it's all *sahra*. Desert for miles, flat reddish soil with the occasional cactus like an unmatched earring. The sky is ultra-blue and large, and if she crosses her eyes, the landscape is like an upside-down bowl of water on a rosy tablecloth.

"But it's faster if you take the interstate," Eddie is saying. "Cut straight through Joshua Tree."

"You hear that, Mazna? Four hours to Los Angeles."

You said two, she wants to spit back, but the name of the city has done its magic and she straightens.

"She's an actress," Idris says proudly.

"That a fact?" Eddie glances at her in the rearview. "I bet they'll be clamoring for you in Hollywood," he says shyly.

She smiles at him. "Four hours is a little far," she says. She wants to kick Idris's seat.

"I thought it was two," Idris tells Eddie. "I told her it was two." He turns around to give her a sheepish smile. He's beaming. He's finally in America. She looks blankly back at him. She's in the wrong play, doesn't have the words.

"I have some friends who do community theater," Eddie offers. "They put on shows a couple of times a year." He starts talking about the neighboring towns, the merits of different highways. He pronounces the town "Bly-the," stretching out the *y*.

"That's good to know," Idris says to him. He glances back at Mazna. "He talks like he's swallowed a radio," he says in Arabic, and she laughs, honestly and without meaning to, feeling that swell of reluctant affection she'd had in her father's living room when he'd taken her hands in his and begged. He looks grateful for her laughter.

"First thing we'll do," he announces, "is get ourselves a car."

⁂

When they arrive at the town, she's shocked by how small it is. Every landmark Eddie points out is prefaced by *the*.

"That's the movie theater," he says. "And over there's the high school." They drive down a main street dotted with palm trees. There's a woman wearing enormous sunglasses and pushing a baby stroller. Her dress is a little loose, but she looks serene and comfortable, one hand holding a cup of coffee, and Mazna envies her deeply because she's not Mazna. The woman crosses the street, and Eddie turns left and pulls up in front of an apartment building.

"A lot of the doctors live here," Eddie says. "The hospital bought the building." Idris had already told her about the housing, that it would be paid for. She wasn't sure what she'd expected, but the building is beige and ugly, with no lobby, just apartments stacked on top of each other. "There's a playground in the back. They have a little party at Halloween."

The men carry the suitcases up to the second floor. The hallways are empty. Their apartment number is 8 and Eddie gives them each a set of keys.

Inside, the floors are clean, and she steps out of her shoes automatically, her socks damp from sweat. The apartment is small, two bedrooms, a kitchen, and a little balcony overlooking the parking lot. Eddie carries her suitcase to the larger bedroom. Her life can fit in the corner of a room she's never seen before. After Eddie leaves, first shaking Idris's hand and writing his phone number on a notepad someone left in the kitchen — the housekeeper? The previous tenant? — they wander through the rooms like strangers.

"There's no shower curtain in the bathroom," Idris reports.

Their bedroom has a full-size bed with a white comforter. The couch is white as well. "We'll buy new sheets," Idris says. "Maybe even a new couch — this one sags a little." He bounces his knee on it. But Mazna doesn't want new furniture; she wants the uniform, standardized couch, the bed. The apartment wasn't theirs and it wasn't pretending to be.

"I like it," she says. Idris stops bouncing and comes over to her.

"We made it." He wraps his arms around her and she lets him. "As our mothers would say, 'May this house be filled with blessings.'"

"And blessings upon you," she replies.

***

She has made a mistake. The knowledge of this somehow eases it, like naming an illness. The fog she'd felt in Syria after Zakaria's death, the fog that has protected her through the past six weeks, up until the wedding, has broken like a fairy godmother's spell. She's awake now. Every morning, she wakes up in the little white room, looks across at the closet, and counts her mistakes. The biggest is the one that follows her from room to room like a shaggy dog: she's in a town in the middle of the desert married to Idris.

Idris, who begged her to get married. Idris, who chews with his mouth open, who brings home medical textbooks with USED stickers on them. When Mazna said yes to him, she'd assumed certain things. She put the truth together later, much later, after the wedding, after they arrived in California. He has gone to America against the wishes of his parents; his mother calls every couple of days and asks them to return. After the first time Hana did this, Mazna got into a huge fight with Idris. *It doesn't matter,* he'd said, his face reddening. *They want me to stay in that dead-end country. She's upset now, but it'll pass.*

Then there was the money — Idris didn't have much of it. Wealthy in Lebanon wasn't wealthy here. They have to live in America on the hospital's meager stipend. When Idris confessed his actual income — including what his father sent him — it made her want to weep. She thought of Hana's silk scarves, the bar of soap she stole. Their wealth, she realized, was purely ornamental. It existed in stationary ways: the House, fine clothes, inherited jewelry. It wasn't liquid. This was the word Idris used, *liquid,* and she imagined money boiled into a pulpy soup.

She'd thought they'd have a life of affluence and comfort, luxury apartments overlooking the water, her grief eased by money. Nonsensically, she'd said yes to Hana and Issa and even Sara, to the courtyard of the House in Beirut — crying herself to sleep in Zakaria's childhood bed, eating at his place in the table — and now she's thousands of miles away from all of it.

Every Monday, Idris counts out bills and leaves them in an envelope so she can go grocery shopping. "Buy anything else you want," he tells her. "Clothes. Get your nails done." But the reality is that the money just about covers their food and maybe a restaurant meal or two, and she doesn't have the heart to tell him. Idris is displaced too, although he's more cheerful about it, sheltered by his busyness and fellow residents and the hospital lab coat that has his name stitched onto it. He's in his new life. Mazna is in the produce aisle, picking the cheapest apricots.

She can almost pretend she's in Damascus in the supermarket. She wishes she could go shopping every day. The rest of the time, she smokes in their apartment or watches television. At least shopping day gives her some purpose, but there's always something uncomfortable. On the crosstown bus, the driver gets impatient with her counting out coins. Another shopper asks her something, but she speaks too quickly and when Mazna doesn't say anything in return, the woman giving her a concerned look. In school, she was one of the best in English class, but hers is an English of movies and theater, not everyday conversation. She freezes when a cashier says, *Have a good one.*

But food doesn't speak English. It is recognizable by sight alone. She spends hours pushing the cart up and down the aisles, examining the produce.

She starts leaving things in the wrong places. Leaving them where they don't belong. She stuffs frozen waffles on the potato-chip shelf; a frozen steak to thaw among canned foods. She puts tomatoes with the blueberries, saltines near the milk cartons. Her third shopping trip, she is caught. A pissy teenage boy in an apron approaches her, holding out a bag of frozen shrimp. She'd put it in the cereal aisle.

"Ma'am? Ma'am? I'm sorry, I just saw you put this over there. You can't do that." He's pimply, and there's mustard on his apron.

She smiles politely. "I changed my mind," she says in Arabic. The man looks stricken.

"Ma'am, I don't —"

"How does an elephant get out of water?" she continues in Arabic. She deepens her voice as though saying something important.

"Fuck," the boy mutters. "Ma'am?"

"Wet! He gets out wet!" It's her father's favorite riddle, and she laughs. Even her laughter is in Arabic, she thinks. The man looks scared now.

"I'm sorry, I have to ask you to leave." He gestures toward the door. "You! Leave! Now! Please!"

She laughs harder, then stops. She leans over the top of her cart and crooks her finger for him to get closer. He does. She whispers, in English this time, "Sparkly water and salt. For the mustard stain." She leaves the cart in the middle of the aisle.

***

In the afternoons, she walks to the post office to watch people. She misses Syria with a violence that wakes her up in the middle of the night. This is unexpected and also, she realizes, perfect. If it were a movie, this is how they'd write it: The heroine spends months obsessed with Beirut, hating her poor, boring Damascus. But then when she leaves, it's not Beirut she misses but Syria. In fact, Beirut now seems irrelevant, a burned-out fling.

Beirut is the cause of her sorrow. Without Beirut, no Idris. No Blythe. No Zakaria. The last always gives her pause, but she cannot imagine that he would be dead if she hadn't entered the picture, so it's a necessary sacrifice.

"Are you eating well?" her mother asks on the telephone. "Are you praying before bed?"

She and Idris ask Eddie to take a photograph of them in front of the apartment building, and they make copies and mail one to each set of parents, *Blythe, 1978* written on the back. When Idris has time off, they go to the mall and wander around the stores, avoiding the expensive ones. There is a Thai restaurant there that Idris loves, and they always order the same thing — coconut soup and fried rice. Mazna buries hers in chili pepper. Resignation is a kind of miracle, and her appetite returns with a vengeance.

"Do you miss Beirut?" she asks Idris once. At a neighboring table there are several young women, teenagers. They remind her of Lara and Fatima.

"It's been a month," he says.

"Is that an answer?" she asks the saltshaker.

"I don't know if I miss Beirut." He sighs. "I work every day. And I like Eddie and the others. Anyway — Beirut feels dead. Doesn't it? After everything."

She knows what *everything* means. This is the most they've said about the summer since arriving. They talk every day, about bills and America and a thousand stupid things, but nothing more. Nothing that could unravel them.

"You should start auditioning," Idris says. Mazna adds more chili pepper. The food hurts now. It's not even good anymore.

She'd tried to break into acting here. She'd found a yellow book that was called the Yellow Pages, and inside, there were thousands of phone numbers, including dozens of talent agencies. She'd mailed her headshot — a photograph her father had taken of her at graduation — along with a letter to one of them, and the agents had written back saying they weren't taking new clients at the moment, but they'd send her a monthly list of open audition calls. She hadn't received any yet.

"You could take the car. I can ride along with Eddie."

She looks at him. He's grown his beard out, and there's something stuck in the wiry hairs. He's good-looking enough — women glance at him when the two of them are out, and she senses that he's somehow more handsome in America, even with the accent, that there's some unearned air of exile about him that white women find attractive — and he is wearing a new shirt, one that they'd bought at the mall last week, on sale. It's blue with white buttons on it.

He's in America and he believes in it, believes his wife will become a star, that the hospital will support him. That they will have a long, good life here.

*

Her visa paperwork necessitates a physical, and so she goes to the community college health center the following day. The space is cheery and yellow, and there are brochures in the waiting room displaying cartoon hearts doubled over and instructions for healthy diets. There is a television mounted on the wall, a news report on Afghanistan. Mazna watches the women filling the streets, an explosion playing in a loop. The week after they arrived, a bomb hit the street next to Dee's bakery. She had been away at the time, but her store was ruined, and Mazna had envisioned the powdered sugar — her hair, Zakaria's hair — speckled across the street like the contents of a dropped eyeshadow case.

"May-za?" A woman in scrubs holding a clipboard appears.

"Yes." Mazna rises and follows the nurse down an antiseptic-looking hallway and into an examination room. There is something reassuring about the clinic. There's the same sterile gloves, the same model organs, an examination table covered in a wisp of paper. She could be in Damascus.

The nurse takes her blood pressure and sticks a thermometer under her tongue. "All normal," she says. Mazna takes her shoes off and steps on the scale in the corner, and she is surprised by the number. She's gained back the weight and then some. She mentally swears off coconut soup.

"Are you sexually active?"

The question surprises her. "Um."

The nurse seems annoyed by her diffidence. She gives her a cup and she goes to the bathroom and pees in it, then carries it back to the room like a child.

"The doctor will be in to see you in a few minutes." The nurse leaves with the cup. "Please change into that robe."

The robe is mint green and papery. It's impossible to close and so she just clutches it to her body. The doctor arrives ten minutes later, a woman wearing large, metal-rimmed eyeglasses.

"Mrs. Adib?" She smiles kindly. "Let's have a look." The doctor holds a stethoscope against her chest, listens to Mazna breathe.

"Have you been feeling all right?" she asks afterward. "Any cough or fever? There's a nasty flu that's been going around."

Mazna shakes her head. "No." She remembers the vomiting. "I had some sick in my stomach." She hears the mistake. "Some stomach sickness," she corrects. "But it's been better the last few weeks."

The doctor cocks her head. "Vomiting?"

Mazna nods.

"There have been some reports of a respiratory illness, not a gastrointestinal one," the doctor says. She looks at her clipboard. "From the Middle East. Why don't we run some extra tests? I'll get them to draw some blood." She leaves the room.

Mazna imagines her blood turning bad. She can picture the scene perfectly, her in a hospital bed, her family flying to California to be with her. Her mother would blame America; Idris would blame himself. One morning she'd shut her eyes and never open them again. She's not as sad at the thought as she might once have been.

The door opens and Mazna startles. The doctor is frowning. She strides over to her side and says without preamble, "You're pregnant."

Mazna stares at her. She's still thinking of the hospital bed, her mother crying over her body.

"The urine test," the doctor explains. "It came back positive. You're pregnant."

Her first thought is *That's not fair.* Distantly, like watching a sport where somebody cheats. *Well, that's not fair.* They've slept together only a few times, her and Idris, and she's tried to be careful. There was the night of the wedding — she wasn't paying attention to her cycle then. She'd drunk too much wine — out of sight from Lulwa, taking sips when her parents weren't looking — and the memory is splintered and messy, his breath loud and hot in her ear as he murmured things about her and her body until she finally asked him to stop talking.

If this were a movie, the woman would start crying, and so Mazna does.

"Oh," the doctor says. "Oh, dear." She explains the pregnancy test and the hormones it measures. Mazna stops crying. She lies down so the doctor can examine her. Her mind races. There are things women can do. She's heard about them. In Syria, they were haram and difficult to find, but America was where haram things were invented, wasn't it? The doctor's hands are cold and she palpates Mazna's breasts, performs a pelvic exam. "Excellent," she says. "I'd say you're about ten weeks along."

Mazna sits up so abruptly she nearly kicks the other woman. Something terrible and final dawns on her. She begins to cry in earnest.

The doctor clasps her gloved hands. "I'm not sure what to say, dear."

"I got married a little less than a month ago," she says. The doctor hands her Kleenex, and Mazna blows her nose like a child. Like somebody about to have a child.

Returning to the clipboard, the doctor reads something, then looks at her hard for a moment. "I see you're new to the country." She frowns, and in that frown, Mazna can see everything—the headlines about Arabs, the oil crisis, Beirut in flames, the pity for veiled women—and she doesn't care, she wants to soak in it, she wants the doctor to believe what she's believing, something about premarital sex with her husband, a disapproving culture. The assumptions mean she won't ask the right questions.

The doctor's face clears. She smiles. "You know," she says, "they say it's nine months, but it's actually closer to ten." There's a pause. "Babies are often born a little early." She can just tell people it's early, the doctor says. Nobody will know.

"You'll even tell my husband it's early?" It's a risky question, but the doctor doesn't catch it and she says yes, of course.

Afterward, Mazna wipes off the jelly between her legs with the wadded-up hospital gown. She washes her hands in the doctor's sink and stands in the room alone for several moments. There's a cheery wall calendar that's still on August, the photograph a field of daffodils. She changes it to September: a half-moon above a dark lake. She counts the Mondays.

It's September 25. The date of the London interview. The realization detonates, but distantly, in a room she's no longer in.

She'd never called the school. The day of her intended arrival came and went. They'd had only Madame Orla's address, since Mazna had no post office box in Damascus, but the wedding was so quick, then the departure, that even Orla hadn't known she was leaving. For all anyone knew, she'd disappeared.

❊

There's a church near the hospital. So close, in fact, that it must be by design. A house of science propped up by a house of God. It's appropriate, Mazna thinks. One needs the other to flourish. She's never entered a church before and is a little disappointed by the plainness. The mosque near her house, the one her father went to weekly, was a swirl of gold and hunter green, but the church has plain floors and a small cross at a marble altar. The windows dazzle, however, stained with images of crying women. Mary must've been so mad when she'd found out she was pregnant, Mazna thinks. Her whole life interrupted, and the worst of it was the father. Had it been some neighborhood boy or friend's son, she might've gotten rid of it, but instead, she must have felt beholden. Obligated. She couldn't do that to God.

Just as Mazna couldn't do it to Zakaria. Zakaria, whose grave she'd visited with Idris a few days before the wedding. He'd balked, but she'd insisted. They'd stood on the plot of land in the camps, a cemetery for refugees. There was no headstone, just a small plaque with his full name. Zakaria under the soil, the powdered sugar long washed from his hair. She had leaned down to the ground, tried to put her face on the soil to see if it would feel like his hands, but Idris had lifted her, made her leave. What was worse, having a piece of Zakaria or not? At the doctor's news, there had been a morsel of elation nestled in with her sorrow and shock, like a raisin. What they had done, she and Zakaria, it had meant something. It had created.

A couple is sitting in the front pew. The man is silent while the woman prays, her voice low and urgent. There are candles on a stand, and Mazna lights one. She wants to sound like the woman, but she can't. The last thing she wants is to speak to another man, much less one who did that to Mary. But the light is fading, and this is her role, so she lights another, then another. She touches her wrist bone like a prayer bead. She prays, but her heart isn't in it.

❊

The dean of the university throws a back-to-school party for the faculty and some students and residents. Idris hangs the invitation on the fridge — cream paper with blue lettering, a blue tassel hanging from the corner — and more than once, Mazna catches him adjusting it. She wonders why Idris got invited when some of the other residents didn't.

The house is a few miles outside of San Bernardino; its winding driveway is packed with nicer cars than their used one. But walking along the gravel in her heels, Mazna feels attractive. She is wearing a feathery light dress the color of pomegranates, and her hair is loose and riotous down her back. She hasn't told Idris about the baby yet. It's been two weeks since the doctor's visit and she's counting by two clocks, the real one and the fake one. According to either clock, the days are running out. She's already up a dress size and her breasts are swelling. The dean's wife, an older lady with perfectly dyed hair, greets them at the door, music and voices behind her.

"Idris, you say?" she asks. "You must be one of our international residents. We're *so* pleased to have students from around the world." She shuts her eyes briefly, as though in despair. "My heart breaks for your country," she says in her breathy voice.

"You have a lovely home," Mazna says, jumping in before Idris can speak. When the woman walks away with their coats, he turns to her with a questioning look, and she says, "Don't thank her."

"She's nice."

"No, she's not," Mazna says. She thinks of Tarek and his speeches about maps. "She's condescending. Don't thank her for that."

"You're such a cynic."

The house is understated, airy, and beautiful. The light fixtures are geometric, copper the exact shade of the chair legs. The rooms are filled with tiny details: paint colors that match flower vases, perfectly stitched pillowcases. It's a different wealth than Hana's, newer, shinier. People drift around with champagne flutes; a few couples sway to the music. Everyone is dressed up, and she can immediately tell who the international students are by their ill-fitting suits, their wives in overly fancy dresses. Idris falls into conversation with an Iranian physics student, and his wife talks to Mazna.

"Aram's family was related to Pahlavi," the woman, Amira, says. She is tall and pretty, wearing a thin hijab. Mazna can tell she's eager to make friends. "But after everything—" She sighs, and Mazna sees the protests in Tehran, the men rounded up and shot in the ear. "Imagine, the telephones are down in Iran sometimes for weeks. I don't speak with my mother for months at a time."

"That's terrible." Mazna asks the right questions and Amira talks about missing Iran, her baby brother, but Mazna feels her attention wandering around the room. She catches the gaze of an older man, in his forties or fifties, near the doorway. He lifts his glass to her. She turns back to Amira, but she can feel her shoulders straighten.

"We should get lunch sometime," Amira says hopefully. Her face falls when she discovers Mazna lives in Blythe, not San Bernardino, but the truth is Mazna feels no allegiance to the woman. Idris's asylum is different. Yes—Zakaria. Days without electricity. The city cracked in two like a plate. But there was the House. The university. She could return to Damascus anytime she wanted. Waiters come around with small plates of clams. Mazna doesn't know how to eat them. She talks with Amira a little longer, then excuses herself.

There are two white women having a conversation near the kitchen. "Isn't it so wonderful of William, inviting these poor students? Why, I was talking to this lovely young woman, the one with that pretty headscarf. She told me her neighbors were shot in the ear!"

Mazna picks at the clams grimly. She imagines playing one of these women onstage, affecting the accent and lifted chins. She'd have to channel pure privilege. Tennis courts and sparkling water and clean glasses. A belonging as effortless as air. It wouldn't be easy, but she could do it, she knows, lowering her voice to a blithe nothingness, moving her body like it had been built for her. At the thought of an audience, she lays a hand on her abdomen. The first list of open auditions just arrived, and she hasn't looked at it. Tarek, those rehearsals—it all feels like a thousand years ago. She wishes she'd listened to him more. She wishes she'd paid attention to every instruction, every moment on the stage.

"I've never seen someone eat clams so glumly."

Mazna looks up to see the man from earlier by her side, holding a glass of wine. He looks wry, in that perennial manner of men of a certain age. She doesn't know what to say. She's not sure what *glumly* means. She takes a guess.

"I was just thinking about their fates." It's a good response, a perfect English sentence, and she is pleased with herself, even more pleased with his returning laughter.

"Think like that and you'll have to survive on air and daffodils." His eyes flick over her so quickly, it's like it doesn't happen. "You certainly seem to."

Mazna arranges her plate to cover her stomach. She looks at him helplessly. She feels like she's run out of banter, all these days spent alone.

"I'm Cal," he says. He has a strong, warm handshake, and she decides she likes him. He looks a little like Cary Grant with a bigger nose. "You're a student at the university?"

Across the room, she can see Idris laughing with the Iranian student. People like her husband. He's bossy and sensitive and gregarious, and the combination has a gravitational pull. "My husband" — she waves — "in the blue suit. He works at the hospital."

"Ah." If he's disappointed, Cal doesn't show it. "Is he one of the postdocs?"

"Surgical residency," she says. "He has asylum from Beirut." It feels less unpleasant saying it to him for some reason. She explains their story briefly. Cal nods as she talks, resting his hand on the wall above her head. She wonders what the hand would feel like against her breast, then winces at the thought. It's a betrayal, but she's not sure of whom.

"What did you study?" He takes her plate when she's done, the glum clams cleared away.

Mazna thinks of the warm jelly between her legs. "I acted. I act." She clears her throat. "I'm an actress."

Cal smacks the wall. "I knew it!"

"You did?"

"Called it from a mile away. Either a model or an actress. It's how you watch people," he explains. "Like you're studying them." He smiles. "I'm cheating a bit. I'm the head of Film Studies at the university."

"No," Mazna says faintly. Cal reads her mind.

"Not making films myself anymore, I'm afraid. I was a bit of a one-hit wonder. And you know what they say — those who can't do . . ." He shrugs.

She doesn't know what they say. What comes after doing? "But you made a movie?" The thought is astonishing, like someone saying he's harvested plants on the moon.

"I did." He tells her the name of it and she almost faints, because she's heard of it; it had a good actress in it. That was before she was famous, but still, and now she's speaking to someone whom that actress knows. She wonders if they had an amazing affair. She envisions Cal's hands against her porcelain-white skin, fluffy hotel beds and big sunglasses and redeye flights.

A tall, brown woman makes her way to them. She half waves. "Hello," she says. Her voice is gravelly.

"Hello." Mazna is still thinking of the famous actress, and she wants to tell the woman about Cal's movie, but before she can, Cal slips an arm around her.

"This is my wife, Kit," Cal says, and it's Mazna who's upset, a jolt of envy.

"Oh." Mazna rearranges her face, but she sees Cal noticing and flushes at his discreet smile. "It's nice to meet you."

"You as well," Kit says. "I believe I talked to your husband earlier. He's a riot!"

"Mazna's an actress," Cal tells his wife, and the other woman smiles tolerantly.

"Of course she is. Look at that face." She speaks with the generosity of someone who is beautiful herself. She is older, fortyish, but her skin is unlined.

They talk for several minutes, then Cal goes to the bathroom. Kit lights a cigarette and offers Mazna one. It's slim and burns nicely.

"Are you an actress?" Mazna asks. This might be more than she can bear, though she can picture it easily. Kit looks like one of those French or Italian arthouse actresses, the ones who perform whole scenes entirely nude.

Kit is a therapist. She does hypnotherapy. She says it plainly, like it's any other job. She explains that hypnosis puts people in a different state, one where it's easier to face certain things. Or stop bad habits, Kit adds. The thought makes Mazna unexpectedly shy, as though Kit can read her mind.

"I used to sing," Kit admits. "That's how I met Cal. He had a bar scene in one of his films and I was the lounge singer. But when I turned thirty, I got tired of it. The performing. The always wanting more. I went back to school."

Mazna nods curiously. She'd guess European, maybe Turkish. It's difficult to read people in America; everyone dresses the same, speaks the same.

"I'm part Native," Kit says. "On my father's side. My mother was a white woman."

"I'm sorry," Mazna says helplessly. "My English — it's like it's gotten worse since our move."

"Native American," Kit explains. "My father's father is Hupa. Have you ever heard people talk about how this land was discovered?" She laughs a little angrily. "*Discovered*. As though they found it empty."

"Of course," Mazna says, embarrassed. Faraway history lessons float back to her. Ships crowding coastlines. Buffalo and an offering of squash and yams. A spread in a well-worn 1960s *Vogue* showing white women in moccasins and feathered headdresses. She's so used to the history of Europeans taking over Arab land, she'd forgotten they'd taken over this one as well.

"My father's people have been here for thousands of years." Kit speaks patiently. "I think he moved away from his heritage when he met my mother. Maybe it's not fair to say, but I was raised with the same people whose ancestors had displaced him." Her face darkens. "Cal used to say the anger was bad for me. How could he understand?"

Zakaria. His face when he spoke of the camps. She remembers how she thought of them as tents until Zakaria explained the telephone poles and concrete buildings. This was months ago. A laughable amount of time. She'd assumed there'd be so much more of it, so much they wouldn't know what to do with it, time to be bored and quarrel and sulk. She hadn't known to pay attention.

"I'm sure you understand," Kit says as though intuiting her thoughts. "I'm sure you've seen your share of it."

"I haven't told my husband this," Mazna begins, and as she speaks, she knows she shouldn't. She doesn't know this woman, and yet she wants something that will bind her to Kit and, by extension, Cal; she wants to feel connected to someone, someone she can tell everything to. "But I'm pregnant."

"Oh, wonderful!" She kisses Mazna's cheek and for a moment the air is expensive perfume. "No wonder you're radiant." She frowns. "You shouldn't smoke. They're saying it's bad for the baby."

Mazna takes in a last lungful before putting out the cigarette. She stares longingly at Kit's. "I can't seem to tell Idris." There is a pause, but she can't bring herself to say more.

Kit looks at her evenly, takes another puff. Right before Cal rejoins them, she says, "He might already know."

The words are sinister, although that's not Kit's intent. Before she can reply, Cal is placing an arm around Kit's shoulder, asking Mazna to describe her plays in Damascus. He talks about his department. His students make films all the time.

"Don't get your hopes up," he warns. These are starter films, artsy little nonsenses about angst and nothing. "But I'll keep you in mind."

Mazna feels a wave of nausea, or excitement, and thanks them both.

❀

During the next appointment at the clinic, the doctor does an ultrasound and gives her a printout of the sonogram. The gel is cold and gooey on her belly as the doctor moves the probe in circles. "You hear that?" she asks. Mazna listens. It's a quick, rhythmic thumping, like a muffled knocking. "That's the heartbeat."

She'd stolen one of Idris's textbooks titled *Maternal Cardiac Care*. There was a chapter on pregnancy, and she'd stared at the different photographs of fetuses at one, two, seven months of development, at their weird webbed fingers and eyelids, marveling over their smallness until she realized that they were all dead, and then she'd stuffed the book back on the shelf and hadn't slept well for a week.

"Would we like to know the gender?" This is how the doctor always speaks, as though there are three people in the room. Idris still doesn't know. Mazna has learned to strategically drape the hand-me-down shawls given to her by Kit, who drove to Blythe the previous weekend while Idris was at work and took Mazna out for dinner.

Mazna thinks about the question. She can see her mother's face clearly. *The Homs girl.* Her sister's eyelashes against hers. The schoolgirls she grew up with. It would be too cruel to have to raise his son, Zakaria in miniature. She already knows the answer. "It's a girl," she says.

The doctor claps, pleased. She tucks the sonogram in an envelope, and, later, Mazna hides it in a kitchen drawer.

❖

Cal calls one afternoon. She's in the middle of washing a pot and her hands are sudsy. The voice is not yet familiar to her, and for a disorienting beat, she thinks it's Eddie.

"Clearly I've made an impression." He laughs.

"I'm sorry," she says. She wipes her hands on her skirt, then regrets it. It's one of her nicer ones. She's taken to dressing up around the house. It makes the days feel less empty. "How are you?"

"I'm well. It's nice to hear your voice," he says, and she feels something hot and startling shoot between her legs. She sits as though to chide them. "I have a student that's doing a short film. His last one had terrible writing and the most incomprehensible dialogue, but they're shooting in the desert, not too far from you. I told him you might like to audition?"

She thanks him so profusely, she embarrasses them both. When she hangs up, she does a little shimmy, then goes to the hallway mirror and looks at her profile. "Ava Gardner was pregnant in *Mogambo*," she tells her stomach. "Did you know that?" The actress had had an abortion. Mazna doesn't say this part aloud.

The following week, she takes the car and drives twenty minutes east. She meets the student in a little town bordered by smokestacks. It's remarkably ugly, but the man is excited about it, chattering on about urban aesthetics and Hegel and lighting while they sip coffee in a diner. She thinks longingly of Tarek. There's a map of New York City on the student's T-shirt and he has a habit of tapping his lips before he talks as though barely able to control his anticipation. He can't be more than nineteen.

"I want to tell the story of decay, you know?"

She doesn't know. She nods.

"But, like, not in an existential way. None of that French bullshit. I want to show a world through the eyes of a broken woman —"

"What's broken her?" she interrupts. He looks a little annoyed.

"She did it to herself." He stares at her severely. His name is Pen. "This town is perfect, because it's, like, choking on its own fumes. And Professor Wilkinson was right, you totally have what I'm going for. The perfect look. A little 1920s, old Hollywood."

She sips her coffee, feeling her blush spread. "Professor Wilkinson said that?" she asks casually.

Pen is rummaging in his bag for a camera. "So we're gonna do some test shots today. Nothing formal, just a little audition. There's a lot outside and you can run your lines there."

"Okay." She ran her lines all week with Idris, memorized them. But as Pen sets up the tripod, she starts to feel lightheaded. There's a dumpster near the lot and the smell is ripe, like trashed fruit. It's almost mid-October, but the heat is stronger than it is most summers in Damascus. He nods at her to begin, but she looks directly into the camera and has to start over almost immediately.

"Take your time," Pen says impatiently.

Mazna inhales. She pretends Tarek's in front of her, but it's different without a stage or scene partner. She can feel her body freeze. The camera lens glares at her like an eye. The lines feel stilted and lifeless; she can picture them spray-painted on the sidewalk. It reminds her of the dead fetuses. By the time it's over, she wants to cry.

"That was great," he says unconvincingly. He keeps glancing at her as they walk to their cars. "The perfect look," she hears him mutter to himself.

She gets the part. Pen calls her the next day, and she has a sense Cal had something to do with it. "Professor Wilkinson said you did theater work," Pen says. "So you just need some practice with the camera. We'll shoot over four days, starting the fifteenth."

To Idris she tells only this news, nothing of how she crumpled up the script in the car and tossed it out somewhere on I-10, played classical music the whole way home. The roads are still new to her and she missed her exit twice, ultimately pulling into a Burger King for fries. There were a bunch of children screaming in the pit of brightly colored balls. She'd gone to the bathroom and locked the door. There was graffiti on the wall, hearts and love equations and a few penis drawings. While she peed, Mazna counted the *fuck*s.

❖

The days of shooting go by in a blur. There's a lot of waiting around for things like lighting and passing cars. She walks when she's told to walk, lifts her chin to the right, then to the left. Pen whispers directions like they're in a church: *Now with the left hand. Take a sip. Another time.*

Everywhere she goes, the camera follows, like a stray cat. She hates the glossy eye, a black so absolute, it swallows her.

"This town is so small I can't breathe," she says. She can hear the woodenness of her tone. "I keep trying to leave." She repeats the lines so often, they wilt, like rubbed denim.

On the fourth and final day, they shoot a scene of her walking along the road, the smokestacks in the background. The pretty, thin girl who dressed Mazna lights one cigarette after the other for her, and they film her smoking moodily as she walks, then crushing the butt under her heel. With every puff, she imagines a kitten in her belly wrinkling its nose at the smoke.

The girl drives her back to Blythe, as Idris has the car. She plays country music and smokes her own cigarette greedily through the cracked car window. "You've got the perfect look," she says. "The camera couldn't get enough."

Mazna smiles thinly. Her hands haven't stopped shaking all day. She's jittery from all the nicotine. She feels sick, nauseated, and wants to see Idris and tell him everything, never do this again. When they pass the hospital he works at, Mazna asks the girl to drop her off. Idris will take her home.

"See you," the girl calls out before driving off.

It's Mazna's first time inside, and she follows the signs for the surgical ward. She catches sight of Idris almost immediately, talking to the receptionist.

"And put her in for next Tuesday?" he asks. The receptionist nods, but Idris looks young and tentative in his scrubs. He's shaved his beard and now looks exposed, like a plucked bird. His English is not good; she's always embarrassed to hear him speak to waiters, but this is somehow worse.

She waves at him, but as she does another doctor walks past the front desk.

There's something unpleasant about his smile, and Idris shrinks a little at the sight of him.

"Hi, Abdul." The doctor snickers.

Idris's shoulders slump. A couple of the patients look on curiously, their conversations quieting. The man continues walking, and before Idris can see her, Mazna darts back down the hallway and runs out of the hospital. Her breath is uneven, as though she's just gotten caught doing something bad, and it occurs to her for the first time that Idris has a life she knows nothing about. It makes her sad, which is surprising. Idris is all she has in this country. She finds their car and leans on the hood. She waits there until he comes out.

The film shows at the university's auditorium, a nice enough room with plush seats and a large screen. There are maybe twenty or so people in the audience, scattered around the first few rows. Cal and Kit arrive, both dressed smartly in pale blazers, and Cal hands her an extravagant bouquet that clashes with the smaller bundle of pale flowers from Idris. There is something doubly embarrassing about the niceness of the auditorium, the engraved plaque outside, juxtaposed with the small audience and Pen's long, boring speech introducing the film.

Finally, he sits down, and the lights dim. Mazna imagines a yawning, pimpled teenager in the projector booth. The words *A Second Tedium* appear on the screen and then: her. On a thirty-foot-wide screen, her face smiling and grimacing and crying. Her voice filling the room. A specific, ancient thrill runs through her, almost orgasmic; it's like watching that tape with Idris's family, with Zakaria. Two truths unfold over the next twenty-one minutes:

Every fiber of her body wants more.

She is bad.

Deeply, spectacularly bad. Her acting is wooden and unnatural, nothing at all like it was in Tarek's play. Her face seems slack and bare. It's like watching a doll emptied of stuffing. For the first time in months, she feels a grief not related to Zakaria. She's losing something again. When the final credits roll, she realizes she's been digging her nails into her belly. She'll have left marks.

There's applause. Pen gestures for her to join him onstage and invites people to ask questions, but in the end, there are only three, two of them clearly
from Pen's friends, who ask about his inspiration and vision. After them, Cal
raises his hand.

"My question is for the actress," he says, and once more she feels that flare
between her legs. He smiles like he knows. "How did you prepare for this
role?"

She remembers something Tarek once told her. "I entered the character
from the flesh in."

Everyone migrates into a little room down the hall, where wine and snacks
are set up. People compliment her, and Kit hooks her arm through Mazna's
and leads her around the room like a debutante. "You look thoroughly miserable," Kit says neutrally.

Mazna smiles tightly.

Kit sighs. "The first time I played a big venue, it was like trying to sing underwater. You're theater-trained. It'll take a while." She pauses. "Hypnotherapy
might help. If there's something you're having trouble accessing or working
through. It can help you sort it out." She looks like she wants to say more, but
doesn't.

"You're very kind," Mazna finally says. "Excuse me." She gestures vaguely at
her belly. "I just need a moment." As she leaves the room, she catches Cal's eye.
She can't read his face.

The bathroom is empty, the porcelain sinks glistening in a row. She runs
her hands under the faucet, then pats down her hair. She doesn't look in the
mirror.

Idris is standing to the side of the bathroom door when she exits.

"I was worried about you," he says. He's carrying his papery flowers, and
she remembers him in the theater in Damascus. How could that have been less
than a year ago? It feels like two lifetimes ago.

She sniffles. Her makeup is ruined, she knows. She wants to sneak off into
the parking lot without any goodbyes, drive back to Blythe, to their white
apartment. "It was terrible," she says. "The film. Me."

Idris hesitates. "It was different," he says, "than seeing you onstage."

She wants to scream. She wants to hit him and ask where Hollywood is now, where London is, where the rest of her life is. "I'm not doing that again."

"Don't say that." Idris moves toward her earnestly. His face looks very focused, like it does when he discusses his work. "It wasn't you. It was the writing. This was some shitty student project. Cal shouldn't have involved you. You should be preparing for auditions."

"I can't."

He smiles. "Of course you can."

"No," she says sharply. "I can't." This is the moment. The only way to do it is to do it. "Because I'm pregnant. I found out when we first got here, when I was doing the visa physical."

"You what." The color has drained from his face. "That was months ago," he says.

Mazna sweeps her arms to her side like she's onstage and waits defiantly. *Encore?*

"You didn't say anything all this time. You fucking liar," he says quietly.

Of course there won't be an encore. She can't say the rest of it, Zakaria's name. She can't envision a future without Idris — can't imagine returning to Damascus alone or begging the London theater school to take her after all. That is the true panic — since that first doctor's appointment, the future hasn't expanded; it's telescoped. It barely contains their shitty apartment complex and the dusty highway and a single, awful student film.

"I'm sorry," she whispers. If the day ever comes, she thinks, the true confrontation, she'll tell him she apologized from the very beginning. Even if he didn't know what for. She raises her voice. "I'm sorry."

He's begun to cry and he hands her the bouquet and doubles over while she holds the flowers. Finally, he lifts his head pathetically. "I don't know why I get to live. When he doesn't."

Mazna lets out air like she's been punched. It isn't that Zakaria is never mentioned. Idris had given a little speech about him during their wedding. Sometimes, they'll remind each other of places in Beirut, and inevitably, his name appears; he was always there.

"I want to call him," Idris whispers. "I want to tell him." A garbled, ugly sound rises in his throat and he punches the water fountain, once, twice.

"Stop," she tells him. "You'll get kicked out if anyone sees you."

He groans. There's a little groove in the wall and he leans against it. "We don't have enough money."

Somewhere down the hallway, a door closes and voices rise. Mazna laughs. Money. Of all the things to worry about. "I'll get a job."

"No." He frowns. "I can find somewhere to moonlight." He straightens. "They're freesias," he says and it takes her a second to realize he's talking about the flowers. "The lady said they're for celebrations."

The flowers have buttery, drooping petals. "They're pretty," she lies.

"It's a good thing," he says slowly. He wipes his face. "Our chance to start things right. To have a life here."

What life, she thinks.

"You're right," she says.

The next day, she wakes up well after Idris has left for work and stays in bed for a while. She feels strangely lighter. She has told the worst lie a person can tell by not telling a lie at all. She fries two eggs and eats over the sink, sopping the yolk up with bread. For the first time, she walks past the end of their neighborhood, keeps walking until the streets get a little fancier. There's a WAITRESS WANTED sign in the window of a coffee shop.

"Have you waitressed before?" the fat man at the counter asks when she's inside.

She has not. In Damascus, the waitstaff are all men, many from Palestine or Lebanon. "I like to cook," she offers.

The man stacks five dishes and a glass onto a tray. "Why don't you walk this around?"

Within a second, the plan dies in its tracks. Mazna lifts the tray with both hands, then tries navigating it onto her right palm, flat, too flat, so that everything starts to slide. She tries to balance it, but it's too late, and a plate crashes onto the floor. A couple of men in trucker hats start clapping.

"Give her the job, Beck," one of them drawls. "She'll learn."

"Look at that face," the other says quietly, but not quietly enough.

Beck considers this. But Mazna has already put the tray down, her heart thudding furiously in her chest. "Never mind," she says quickly. She rushes out, and though the men are calling after her, she doesn't slow down. She passes a sign that reads LEWIS PARK AND GREENHOUSE. Trees flank a path that winds toward a small, strange-looking building, all glass and angles, the panes fogged up.

It's hot inside. Dewy. There's a sweet, coarse smell that reminds Mazna of the city gardens in Damascus, freshly cut flowers, soil and rain and salt. She's missed it. There are leafy bundles of an olive-green plant, several slender trees, cacti. Every now and then, a bright flower jumps out among all the green. There's a sign in front of each plant, little cartoon renderings with the plant's name in Latin, English, and Spanish, along with a little paragraph about its origin. Mazna glimpses them as she walks through the greenhouse. *Native to Latin America. Used by Aztecs for salve. This plant loves sunlight.*

The whole greenhouse is less than a thousand square feet, but there are three separate spaces, each with a sign announcing a different climate: RAIN-FOREST, DESERT, and AQUATIC. She gasps aloud when she enters the last one. There is a greenish pond, dappled with the bright sunlight filtering through the glass, mossy plants and flowers growing out of the water. There's a tree with candy-colored flowers the size of her head.

"Are you here about the position?" The words, disembodied, seem to come from the very plant she's staring at. An older woman with frizzy gray hair appears, carrying a brass plant mister. "I'm Janet."

"I just walked in," Mazna says apologetically.

"Oh! I'm sorry. I just — you didn't have a child with you. I assumed. Well, welcome. It's ten dollars. Seven if you'd like a membership."

"There's a job?"

The woman looks at her suspiciously. "You're looking for one?"

Mazna nods.

"Are you a botanist?"

"I worked at a bank — back home."

"Where are you from?" The question is suspended between them like a rope. *This is redneck country,* Kit likes to say cheerfully. Once, turning serious, she'd told Mazna, *They're the worst kinds of racists — they don't realize they are.*

Be careful. In the supermarket, the neighborhood, the mall, Mazna can feel others eyeing her curiously when she speaks, not hostile, exactly, but attentive. It's different with Idris — America can't abide Arab men — but with her, the re-action almost borders on pity. Mazna can't explain why it's worse.

"Istanbul," she says. It's what Idris sometimes says. *Far enough, but it doesn't sound like a threat to them.*

The woman nods. "My daughter went there on her honeymoon. She brought me the most beautiful throw blanket."

Mazna smiles. She has never been to Istanbul, but she envisions the mar-ketplace in Damascus. Rows of shawls and spices and fruits. Nailed at every stall, an evil eye. "I'm not a botanist, Janet."

"No," Janet muses. She waters a plant, and for a moment Mazna thinks she should leave, but then the woman speaks again. "It's a lot of watering," she says. "Preparing the beds. I can teach you how to prune and weed. We get some school trips through the spring. I'd need you to keep an eye on the children. Make sure they don't pull up any of the plants. You'd be surprised how many of them do."

⚜

Mazna starts working every Monday, Tuesday, and Thursday. The money is meager, but Janet pays her under the table, and it's about what she was making in Syria. Every month, she deposits the cash into her bank account with pride. She hides the audition lists under one of Idris's textbooks. On Thursdays, she drives him to the hospital, then parks the car at the library near the greenhouse. There's a sense of accomplishment in parking. In buying the cheese sandwich from the grocer. In walking to the library during her lunch break. The librarian is a sweet younger woman, about her age, and she carefully writes down Maz-na's name on a library card. The paper is heavy and Mazna keeps it in her wallet.

"I don't know," she admits when the librarian asks what she likes to read. She was never a reader back in Damascus. The librarian asks about her inter-ests and Mazna tells her about theater, Hollywood, the greenhouse, and the woman picks out books about botany and flowers, biographies of Liz Taylor, Hedy Lamarr, and Ava Gardner.

She reads them all. In the greenhouse, she waters, plants seedlings, and then curls up on the rattan chair by the ferns, her belly increasingly larger and firmer — this is the one unsurprising thing about pregnancy, how taut the skin becomes, like a watermelon to be knocked upon — and reads. The busiest hours are midday, during school field trips, but the rest of the time it's mostly empty, an occasional retiree wanting to sketch the needle palms or road-trippers stopping on their way to Los Angeles.

It never fully cools down. The evenings are nippy by January, but the days continue to be hot, the mugginess of the greenhouse lending the heat moisture; she sometimes falls asleep on the chair and wakes up wondering if she passed out. Everything is amplified in pregnancy. She lies in bed at night sometimes, unable to bear the ache of her nipples. The sound of chewing sets her teeth on edge. When Kit visits her in the greenhouse, which she does every month or so, Mazda finds her perfume nauseating.

"This is starting to hurt my feelings," Kit says wryly on her next visit.

"I'm sorry. It's everything," Mazna says. "Yesterday I made Idris shower twice."

Kit pats Mazna's knees. She's sitting opposite her, and she has to slouch to fit in the child-size chair, but she still somehow looks perfect, thin and tall and fresh-eyed. Mazna feels like an elephant.

"How are you doing?" Kit asks with concern.

Her touch is warm and Mazna almost cries. Kit has that effect on her. Sometimes she mentions the possibility of hypnotherapy again, but Mazna always changes the subject. She already feels enough of the other woman's pull, like a strong undertow. She drives the three hours from San Bernardino for no reason other than to see her, although Mazna hasn't seen Cal since the screening. There's always a breeziness to her visits, but she helps her water the plants, and she brings groceries that she claims are too much to take home. It nicks Mazna's pride, but the smoked meats are good and expensive, the gourmet cookies mouthwatering, and beyond that, there's something sincere about Kit; she reminds her of her friend Fatima, smart and open and astute. Sometimes Mazna wonders if Kit's a little lonely herself, if maybe the visits are a gift for both of them.

"Try the shortbread cookies. They're lemon. It's good for the nausea," Kit says. She's wearing an eggshell-colored dress and her legs are brown and long beneath. Her skin is perfect. Mazna didn't notice skin before America. Back home, she never thought of her own, save when she heard the occasional admonishing from her mother to avoid the sun—her complexion darkened easily. But here, she gawks in wonder at the black skin of the highway toll collector, the pale forearms of her doctor. Neighborhoods are arranged by skin. Jobs. Schools. Here, her skin is darker than many, but not the darkest. Most people think her Mexican, and she often has to apologize when flustered strangers speak to her in Spanish.

Mazna hadn't known how much she didn't know. Especially about this country. Sometimes Kit tells her about the history. The tribes. The land before reservations, the men that arrived with their Christianity and warfare. How they renamed everything: the children, the land. They slaughtered millions. The number is astounding and yet Kit says it plainly, accustomed to it. She is patient with Mazna's questions.

"They handed out blankets teeming with lice and smallpox, diseases the body didn't know how to fight against," Kit explains. "They raped the women. Then they changed the history of it."

It reminds Mazna of Zakaria, of his mother and Palestine. He'd told her that his family was from Jaffa, that sometimes his mother whispered the name. If she forgot it, she would die. Kit's aunts do the same thing, call the land by the old names, teach them to the children.

"I had a friend," she tells Kit. "Zakaria." It's the first time since moving to America that she's said his name aloud, except to Idris; it feels sacrilegious. "He was Idris's friend, actually. He was Palestinian and lived in this camp. A refugee camp in Lebanon. He told me that if you forget the name of your land, that's when it's really lost." She can still remember his face as he said it, on the walk home from the bakery that night.

"There weren't camps in Syria?"

Mazna thinks of skin. The cabdrivers in Damascus. The men who bagged groceries and trimmed hedges and swept the classrooms at her school. The housekeepers for wealthier families. The woman who ran the tailor shop in her old neighborhood. They had become like trees or signposts. Of course there were Palestinians in Syria. There were so many. They didn't all live in camps, but some did, neighborhoods in Yarmouk, Hama, Deraa — she'd just never seen them.

"There were," Mazna says, ashamed. "There were camps everywhere." Without thinking, she cradles her stomach, and Kit's face changes, a question she doesn't ask, and the two women look away at the exact same second, busying themselves with their hands, unable to speak any more painful, careful words aloud.

❖

Mazna gives birth on the twentieth of April. It's horrible and messy and humiliating, but it doesn't take as long as she feared it would. There is a moment during the crowning when she nearly screams everything — Zakaria's name, their lovemaking on the bakery floor. It is a pain so deep, it seems specific, like a color, something that can be smeared on a canvas and hung in museums. She wants to yell at Idris that everything's his fault, and then she actually does; as the doctor is pulling the shoulders out, she's screaming that she hates California and him, that she's a nobody, a nobody, until that's the one word she's screaming out, surrounded by nurses and Idris: *Nobody, nobody, nobody.*

"Ava," she says when the nurses ask her. The body begins to forget almost immediately. Already the unimaginable pain is muted. Idris wanted to call her Hana, after his mother, but he doesn't say anything.

He coos over the baby and rocks her to sleep at night. Once, Mazna walks in on him talking to her. "And there are almond trees. They turn pink and white in the spring," he is saying. She feels a distinct moment of misery. It revisits her often throughout the months of early motherhood, the sanitary pads and pediatricians, Ava's weeks-long ear infection. Her mother visits her for two months and talks often about what a good father Idris is. Ava's skin is the shade of Gulf honey, darker than both hers and Mazna's, and Lulwa comments that Ava has her own mother's coloring. But Mazna sees Zakaria in the furrowed brow, the eyes, the complexion. It makes her want to slip out of the apartment in the middle of the night. It makes her want to wrap her arms around Ava and never set her down.

But it isn't all misery. Those early months, she zooms between a reckless joy that's almost painful and something approaching gloom, rocking the baby, listening to her perpetual breathing. Her love of the baby is inevitable, something outside of her; it feels like theft. She loves her gurgles, her toes and little square fingernails, the sighing sound she makes when she falls asleep. But also, coiled within her organs and sinews, is a secret, and that secret now has lungs and eyebrows and a love for sweet applesauce.

Janet gives her four months off, but Mazna returns after six weeks. Her legs are still aching and her back twinges every morning with a pain she's starting to recognize as permanent. There is a fight with Idris about returning to the greenhouse, the biggest they've ever had; he calls her selfish, greedy.

"She needs her mother," he roars. He's speaking of Ava, of course. He's always speaking of Ava now. His attention is unbroken and possessed. "That's you, in case you've forgotten!"

In the end, Mazna gets her way. She straps Ava onto her chest and takes her with her. Entering the greenhouse, she takes a full breath for the first time in months. She cleans the descriptive panels while Ava sleeps in her carrier. Sometimes, a weird tremor passes through her, like she's waking in a foreign room after a night of travel, a disorientation about where she is and how she's gotten there. She is in California. Her baby sleeps under the large saguaro. Her baby and hers alone. In the evenings, Idris will read her American stories. The schoolchildren will visit the greenhouse and ooh and aah over the bromeliads. She has gotten away with it.

Encore in the Wings

1982

IDRIS WANTED THE Chinese place, even though the Indian restaurant is bigger, with a banquet room specifically designed for parties. "We've had many graduation parties," the Indian host tells Mazna sadly, as though she is picking the wrong husband.

"We'll do something here soon," she promises him, although there isn't really money for that; there's barely money for Idris's graduation party, and she's had to cajole the Chinese host to lower the price, feeling ashamed as she negotiates down the cost per drink by a dime. But she's gotten good at it. She shops at the cheaper supermarket, saves coupons. When Ava turned three last month, Mazna filled out the lengthy paperwork and stood in line for three hours to get her enrolled at a free daycare.

Idris's parents visited last year and they'd seemed taken aback by the small apartment. One day, they'd shooed Idris and Mazna out to watch a movie, and when they returned, Mazna thought they'd walked through the wrong door: their old furniture was gone. Hana and Issa had had the university take it away, and then they'd gone to a home-décor store and bought them all new furniture. Both of them — but especially Hana — seemed pleased with their surprise.

"The wood is pine!" Hana said, showing her the new crib for Ava. Mazna nearly cried. The old one was a hand-me-down from one of the neighbors; Ava was going to outgrow a crib soon. It was like setting good money on fire. That's what she kept seeing for weeks after, every time she caught sight of the new couches: price tags disintegrating into flames, all the good meat and health-insurance upgrades and winter coats that the money could've bought. But it wouldn't have occurred to Hana to offer the money up front, and Idris would never ask.

But finally they have their own money coming in. Real money. Unattached money. Idris has been accepted to the cardiothoracic-surgery residency at the hospital at a salary twice his current stipend. Mazna nearly cried when he told her the number. They could move into a new apartment, send Ava to a better preschool. There would be about two more years of training, and then, she's told, much more money, and for the first time in her life, Mazna understands her mother. Lulwa always used to speak of money as though it were a savior, scoffing when Mazna's father would admonish her. *You're too poor to be this expansive,* Mazna once overheard Lulwa tell Bassel when he insisted on paying for everyone's dinner at a gathering.

For Idris's graduation from his general-surgery residency, Mazna has saved up for a nice watch, one she saw him admire on a wealthy-looking man in the mall. They still fight constantly, but there are nice moments too — spreading blankets near the greenhouse on the Fourth of July and naming the colors of the fireworks for Ava. It's difficult when they get calls from Beirut; information travels slowly in this part of America, the television occasionally reporting the bigger bombings but nothing more. Every time there's a large attack, the news pervades the house like humidity, Idris falling into a predictable rut, becoming moody and storming around, singing Fairuz while he showers. Mazna's nerves often feel shot on those days, her nails bitten to the quick. She wants to help, but there's no right thing to say.

We could go back, she always suggests.

That's ridiculous, he always replies.

And so the years pass.

❖

The party is on a Friday night and the weather is perfect, the slow heat of early May in Southern California. Mazna has strung some lights around the table, and the owner of the restaurant has agreed to hang a sign reading CONGRAT-ULATIONS above the table. His English is poor and broken and Mazna feels shamefully elevated talking to him; her own English has improved, but it's nowhere near as good as Ava's — her daughter speaks with the clean, precise sounds of the native tongue.

"I want to try some!" she says while Mazna applies lipstick in the restau-rant's bathroom. Ava stands on her tiptoes, reaching.

"No, Ava," Mazna responds. She's trying to perfect the lip liner. All the women in the magazines are wearing blue eyeshadow and feathered hair this season, and she found a perfect turquoise shadow at the drugstore for two dol-lars. It's greasy and cheap, but the color is good.

"But it's Baba's party!" Ava howls. "I want to look pretty like you!"

Mazna relents. She often does, although the parenting books say not to; it requires energy she simply doesn't have to constantly say no, to meet the tantrums with resolve. She sometimes sees those kinds of women in stores, the ones who coolly look on while their children are melting down at their feet. They're often white, and Mazna wonders if that's meaningful, if women like her are just more easily embarrassed. Whatever it is, she's taught her child to yell louder.

"Purse your lips," she instructs Ava, lifting her onto the counter. The girl does and Mazna kisses her lips firmly, as though she's blotting her own. She can smell her daughter's Dorito breath, and for a second the kiss feels a little trans-gressive, as much of motherhood does. There's so much nakedness: cleaning the soft folds of a child's labia, taking baths together, her nipples in and out of Ava's mouth for nearly a year. There were times when breastfeeding was almost sexual, something she's never told anyone for fear of getting arrested. Her body and Ava's often feel like one — she swipes carrots from her daughter's plate, licks sauce from her cheek; Ava pats her hair when she's on her lap. She turns Ava around to see her reflection and the girl is so excited, she pees a little, and she needs a fresh pair of underwear.

The guests trickle in and Mazna feels a brief embarrassment at the restaurant's shabby carpet, the other patrons in their everyday clothes (she's wearing a lacy dress, the one she wore to her engagement in Damascus; it's definitely tighter, but the zipper closed), talking in their loud, intimidating language. But most of the guests are their newer Arab friends or nurses and residents from the hospital, like Eddie, who whistles when he sees her.

Kit and Cal arrive early with a beautifully wrapped bottle of expensive wine. They look great, energetic and tan from a recent trip to Costa Rica. Kit stands on her toes to fix the banner, and her skirt rises appealingly. When Cal hugs her, Mazna sucks in her stomach, wishing she'd just bought a dress in her size.

"It's been a lifetime!" Kit exclaims.

Their exchange is light and jovial, but their friendship has changed since Ava's birth. It was a graceless time, the excess flesh and bleeding and sleeplessness. She was suddenly at the epicenter of a world of discount shopping and split nipples. She couldn't bear to be around their perfect lives. Kit would bring good wine over and ask if she was okay, and Mazna would chew her lip raw trying not to cry. It was so much easier to see the Arab women, who had equally small apartments and got into screaming matches with their husbands in front of her like she was family. Her friendship with Kit had taken on a different rhythm, a dinner every few months, Kit telling her to audition and Mazna ignoring her. She sees Cal maybe once a year.

Still, they can read each other well. "How are you?" Mazna asks Kit. "You look different."

"We have news." Kit glances at Cal warily. People continue to trickle in. "Later, later." She waves her hand.

All the guests are standing in a throng, talking over one another, and they miss Idris's arrival. When they see him, they shout, "Surprise," though he knows about the party. Still, he acts surprised and twirls Ava around, kisses Mazna on the cheek. Somebody snaps a photograph and Mazna knows that later, she'll marvel at how happy they look.

"Please, sit, sit." Mazna waves the guests to their seats, noticing the manager's frown. The Arabs — she knows she shouldn't think of them this way, but she can't help it, they always move in a group, taking up sidewalks and stores, the women with their teased hair and overdone eyes pulling out snacks for their screaming children — were already friends with one another when Mazna met them; it was like getting ten for the price of one. She is friendly with them. They go to parks together, drove once to the zoo in San Diego. Arabs find each other, she's learned. Maybe all people do. They speak different dialects of Arabic, come from wildly different families back home, but here it doesn't matter. America is the great equalizer.

"To the cardiac surgeon," Cal says, and the guests lift their glasses obediently, moved by his baritone voice. "Cheers."

"Teers!" Ava calls out.

Idris cries when he opens Mazna's gift and sees the watch. The other presents are books and clothes and, from Kit and Cal, a golden lapel pin, a beautifully realistic rendering of a human heart, the perfect gift, clearly custom-made and more expensive than any of the others. Idris fastens it to his dinner jacket and hugs Cal affectionately. "To the man who fixes hearts!" Kit calls out, and everybody cheers again. She seems a little drunk, unusual for her. Her eyes are misty.

"How's the greenhouse, Mazna?" Lamis asks. The Arabs all work, the women running daycares out of their living rooms or cutting hair.

"She can quit now!" Idris says.

"It's good," she says coolly, as though she hasn't heard him. The greenhouse is still a raw subject. *At least go to school,* he'd told her for years, and finally, last September, she had, enrolling in a teaching program at the community college. But she'd walked into the classroom that first day and nearly wept; everything reminded her of theater — the smell of chalk, the scuffed wooden floors, even the instructor's eagerness. She hadn't gone back to the college. The greenhouse reminds her of nothing but itself, but she could never explain that to Idris.

Kit and Cal stay to help Mazna and Idris tidy up the wrapping paper and decorations. There are bits of tinsel on the scraped plates of leftover broccoli chicken. A piece of confetti floats in a water glass, and the sight depresses Mazna; the party took weeks to plan, and there's something existential about how quickly it passed.

"You had news," Mazna remembers. She's tipsy. Earlier she glanced down and saw the black lace of her bra peeking out under the dress, and since then she's been making a point of leaning in front of Cal. He's looked twice. To Idris, she repeats, "Kit has news."

"Well." Kit glances at Cal. "We have news."

"We're moving to New York." Cal unpins the banner. There's an eerie silence, and Mazna is shot with a strange panic. She feels like a schoolgirl who did something wrong.

"Why?" Her voice is froggy. Ava hears it and cocks her head like a dog.

"What New York?"

"It's a city, baby," Kit says. To the adults: "Cal was asked to shoot a series there."

"That's rad!" Idris says, sounding ridiculous. He loves American idioms, but they're often from the wrong generation.

Kit links her arm through Mazna's. "You know what this means?" Her breath is a little sour. "You have to let me do a session." To Idris, she says, "I've been trying to get her to try hypnosis for years, but she's too stubborn. No more excuses, though."

"She always says no. That's always her first answer," Idris offers.

Mazna removes her arm discreetly. "What sort of series?" She hates every cell in her body that stands at attention at the mention of the word *series*, the prospect of cameras and script readings. Kit and Idris are busy talking now, but Cal catches the question.

"A Western," he says ruefully. "Mostly male cast, with a couple of women in smaller parts." He lowers his voice. "I would've called you otherwise." He glances at Idris. "I thought you'd quit."

"I did," she says. Her cheeks flush.

He leans in. "Once an addict," he says, but he doesn't finish the sentence, and before she knows it, Kit and Idris are toasting Manhattan and Broadway, and Mazna has no choice but to find a half-filled glass and raise her own.

That night, they make love. Idris kisses her breasts gratefully and moans when he comes, and she feels small and mean, like she often does when they fuck.

It feels okay enough, but it's not what she wants; it reminds her of a paint-ing she saw once — a fair-haired woman spread-eagled, a large swan bent over her. They have sex once every few months, like owners turning on an over-looked car a few times a year to keep the engine alive. When he's done, she pads to the kitchen in her socks and drinks a glass of water while watching the stovetop clock. If she squints, the numbers dissolve into squiggles of red neon and dance. He doesn't love her like he used to, Idris. Ava has usurped her place in many ways, and his life is full and busy now. She never thought she'd miss it, the doglike devotion. She doesn't, but also she does.

❖

She has a nagging feeling after the party that Cal will reach out and he does just that, while she's teaching Ava how to somersault on the carpet.

"The party was great," he says, his voice warm in her ear. She can hear Ava talking to herself in the other room.

"Thanks for coming," she says automatically. Then, without meaning to, she adds, "I can't believe you're leaving."

"Well, that's partly why I'm calling. We're throwing a goodbye party. It's next month, on the fifth. We'll be doing it at our place."

"Partly," she says. It's like this with Cal, simple, upfront.

"Yes." He laughs. "The other part is a proposal. I was at a dinner in LA the other day, and I met this director. He's doing this indie, a love story. It's a small film, but with great actors. That girl from the last Scorsese is in it. The one with the black bob."

"Yes," she says, even though he hasn't asked a question yet, and she can barely listen to him as he describes the film more. Ava appears in the kitchen, glances at her. *Go on,* Mazna mouths, shooing with her hands.

"You're interested?" Cal finally asks. "There's a party he'll definitely be at next week, but it's in LA. I can meet you near our place, and we'll drive over together. I already told him about you and he sounds interested." *I. You.* No mention of Kit or Idris.

"Yes," Mazna says again. When she hangs up, she does a little shimmy in front of the refrigerator, then runs to the living room. "Come on, baby," she calls. "Show Mama how you do it." When the girl tumbles upside down, Mazna shouts like a cheerleader.

⁂

Idris seems a little wary of the party. "Could've invited both of us, couldn't he?" he grumbles, and she mumbles something about the industry and networking. He drops it pretty quickly, though, and she takes the car to San Bernardino, an Italian restaurant they've gone to with Kit and Cal before. The seats are soft and leathery and Cal always pays. She's used to driving now, the highways familiar, but she still flinches at the eighteen-wheelers gliding by like metal dinosaurs.

"I guess I could've just driven to LA myself," she says sheepishly after they hug in the parking lot, and Cal waves the comment away.

"I could use the company." The ride is a little over an hour, and she feels anxious the entire time, crossing her legs, fidgeting with the door handle. She's worried she wore too much makeup, and while he's watching the road, she wipes at the lipstick surreptitiously with her fingers, then smears it under the seat. Cal keeps glancing over at her.

"That dress," he says, and an awful realization hits her: Kit, years ago, bringing a bag of clothes, shirts, and the slinky dress she's wearing now, black as oil. She'd completely forgotten.

"Kit gave it to me," she says miserably, adjusting the red scarf around her neck.

He snaps his fingers. "I knew I'd seen it before. It looks good on you." He doesn't say any more, but when they pull into the large, winding driveway littered with new cars, she catches him glancing at her as she steps out. The dress is backless; for years it's languished in her closet, too fancy for the Arab gatherings but too beautiful to throw away, and she regrets wearing it now — it's too bold for her.

The house *exudes Los Angeles,* a phrase she's overheard people saying and is starting to understand after multiple trips to the city, shopping and sightseeing. *Exuding Los Angeles* means tall, slouchy women in leather jackets. Electric-blue dresses that dust the floor. Pearl earrings and four-hour traffic jams. Men with hands more beautiful than hers.

"Who lives here?" Mazna hates herself for whispering. She is still scared of wealth; that never went away. It's like being in the presence of fame, a thing that erases and constructs at the same time. She is still her mother's daughter, greedily calculating the cost of skylights and stealing touches of the glass vase in the foyer. It's the biggest house she's ever been inside, and her first impression is of light and glass, angular slopes of the ceiling like cheekbones, one room pouring into the next.

"Claire and Scott Nelson." He smiles. "They're over there by the fireplace." Cal glides her to the gray-haired couple, the woman with a waist so small, Mazna hates her.

"An actress, how lovely," Claire says tolerantly as Cal introduces her. She has the smile of a woman who has known many actresses.

"It's been a while." Mazna pats her hair.

"Mazna has been in several projects I've supervised at the university." Cal's lie surprises her, as does his eager tone.

"Student films are a great way to start," Claire says kindly to her, and Cal flushes. He is not the most powerful man in this room, and witnessing his diminishment is unpleasant. It's like seeing a peacock plucked bare.

The sun lowers beyond the hill, and certain parts of the house have nothing overhead except spotless glass. There's a half-moon visible in the blue sky. They each drink a flute of champagne, then another. More than once, they are stopped by people who call her Kit, and there is a strange frisson in those moments, a glance with Cal. The third time, she doesn't correct the woman.

"Nice to see you again," she says instead. Cal looks surprised.

"You changed your hair," the woman says. "I like it. Very modish."

Mazna smiles at Cal. She remembers something Kit said years ago after she'd asked a cashier a question and the cashier had answered Mazna. *All brown women look alike,* she'd told the man coolly. It had never occurred to Mazna before that she resembled Kit, but after that, examining the woman's features, she noticed how if she turned her head really quickly and took in her face — black hair, dark eyes, arched eyebrows — they were similar.

The woman chatters on and then Cal brightens, waving his hand. "Adam! I was hoping you'd be here." To Mazna, he whispers, "That's him," and she feels a rush of nerves so strong she nearly throws up.

It doesn't last long. Adam is tall and ugly, with large ears. He's visibly tipsy.

"Hi, hi," he trills. His voice is a little high-pitched.

"Adam." Cal claps his shoulder. "This is Mazna. I told you about her, remember?"

Mazna smiles at him, her most pleasing smile, and then, unintentionally, glances back at Cal, just in time to catch him give Adam a meaningful look that's met by a quick, imperceptible nod from Adam. It's brief and chilling and over so quickly she's almost certain she imagined it.

"I watched your film," Adam says. He places an arm around her shoulders like they're old friends. His breath is sour. "You've got a real Sophia Loren thing going on."

"That was her first time onscreen too," Cal says.

"It was a shit movie," Adam says. "But you were good." Cal goes to get them more drinks, and Adam asks her about Blythe. "I stopped there for gas once."

This isn't how she anticipated the conversation going. In her bathroom back in the apartment, she rehearsed lines about acting, theater anecdotes, while Ava babbled in the bath. The champagne makes her bold. "What's yours about?"

"Mine?"

Mazna flushes. "Your film."

"My film." Adam smiles. "We're still finalizing the script."

"There you are!" A woman wearing mini-disco-ball earrings and a backless dress drapes an arm around Adam. "I told you Dana was here! He's over by the bar."

"I'm coming, I'm coming." Adam kisses Mazna's cheek. "I'll get your number from Cal, we'll do an audition. We'll be running them through June."

"I—" There's a wet smudge on her cheek from his kiss. She can make out Cal by the bar, laughing with a woman. Just like that, the director is gone.

There's an animal in Mazna's chest. It roars at the sight of the beautiful women, the overheard snippets of industry conversation. A photographer snaps a photo of two young girls and she wants to smash their perfect white teeth.

Everyone in this room is closer to a movie screen than she is and it makes her want to keel over. This is what she dreamed of in Syria, wandering around a beautiful house in Los Angeles, talking to photographers and directors, only in those dreams she was the beautiful woman lounging on the couch or the one with her heels kicked off, ankle tattoo out for display, or the one who just walked in, wearing a fur coat and army boots.

"I really can't get over that dress," Cal says, appearing by her side, and the animal whimpers. She wants Cal. She wants New York and all of Kit's dresses. The photographer comes over and lifts his camera, and the two of them move toward each other like dancers, graceful, rehearsed. Her right breast mashes up against his chest and she feels her nipple harden.

"How about a headshot?" He nods at the photographer. "We've got golden hour for miles."

The photographer smiles tightly. "That's a separate gig."

"My treat," Cal says, and before Mazna can protest, she's being led to the backyard. The photographer seats her at the patio table and asks her to lift her head. She can tell he's pleased by the effect.

"Nice," he murmurs as the shutter clicks. "Can you just fix that scarf?"

"I'll do it." Cal approaches her and Mazna understands that the past four years have been foreplay for this, a prelude to the glass and champagne and Cal's finger against her neck, undoing and retying the red scarf — *Also Kit's, my God*, she thinks — grazing the divot between her collarbones.

She is trembling for the remaining shots and the photographer is ecstatic now. "Yes! Exactly that. Turn this way just a hair." He flits around like a hummingbird, and Mazna thinks about Janet Leigh in that Hitchcock movie, how appealing a scared woman can be on film. The camera loves her. "I'll send you the prints in a couple of weeks," he tells Cal. Cal gives the photographer his own address, not Mazna's, and she lets him.

"Thank you."

Cal tells her not to thank him and leads her to the pool, where a group of people are drinking and talking loudly about someone they know. Peals of laughter. Mazna might be a little drunk. She wonders if Idris remembered to feed Ava — she can't help it, it's like a clock programmed into her skin — but at the same time, she doesn't really care. They could be on Jupiter right now. She glances back toward the house. It's like nothing she's seen before, two stories, uneven, top-heavy, and glass.

"You want to see inside," Cal observes.

She flushes. "I always feel naked around you." The word flies out before she can stop it.

He takes her to a room on the second floor with an entire wall of windows overlooking the backyard; anyone below could glance up and see them. Beyond the lawn, the nearby hills glitter in the early evening. There's a painting of a coastline on the wall and she stares at it until she feels Cal approaching her and her breath quickens and she'd be lying if she said she didn't know what was going to happen next, which is what does happen next. Cal pulls her to him. He kisses her and it's not particularly good, his lips rubbery and unrelenting, but there's something unbearably sexual about that as well, the not-goodness of it. It reminds her of Omar, that night in Damascus decades ago, how for years she'd flush just thinking about it, how the revulsion and desire had lived right next to each other, like matching dolls.

"The people," she manages. They're visible below; she can make out a woman's expensive earrings. They look like lurid insects, jeweled, colorful.

"They think you're Kit," he reminds her. The words seem to turn him on, and he says it again, pushing her against the glass, his arm snaking against the window and touching her bare back. Mazna lets his tongue part her lips, and she is Kit; she is elegant and rich, she gave up singing for a different life, this is her husband, they are playing a naughty game, they do this in every house they visit, find the quietest room and touch each other in it. This will be her life.

When he puts his hand against her pubic bone, she parts her legs like a puppet. She thinks of Zakaria. He's in the room. He's always in the room. She's tired of it and the only way she can banish him is to focus on Cal, Cal kissing her neck, Cal worrying a finger inside her and rubbing urgently, expertly, so that her knees start to buckle and waves of goodness shake her. Her mind splinters and rotates into a kaleidoscope as it always does on the brink of orgasm. The rust on the playground slide in their complex. An argument with Idris about the weather. Zakaria, again.

Cal rubs harder and she realizes distantly that she is coming, but he stops just before and she nearly cries with frustration.

"Back up against the dresser," he tells her, his voice high and unrecogniz- able. He unbuttons his pants and she wants to tell him to stop, but it seems im- possible now; they've already entered a contract. He's paid for her headshots. She's met the director. She's wearing his wife's dress, and she is wet from his fingers, and there's nothing to do but back up against the dresser, cry out as he enters her, her legs instinctively clenching, but his fingers pull them apart ex- pertly, almost wearily, like he's done this dozens of times, and he pounds into her until he lets out a cry that sounds unnervingly like Idris's and then stum- bles back.

He turns away from her as he straightens up. He kisses her temple and it's sweet and gentle and she feels oddly grateful to him. He was the first thing she'd wanted in America. "Pretty thing," he says, and she knows again it's not his first time, and suddenly it's as though Kit's walked through the door. She can almost smell the expensive perfume.

The drive back to San Bernardino is long and quiet. He offers her their guest room once they reach the city, but she mumbles something about Ava and drives herself east on I-10 instead, drunk and stunned. The highway is endless, street lamps shining menacingly down at her. She recites Qur'an, then tries to listen to the radio. She screams once, loud, and then again, louder, and her face is so contorted, so ugly, in the rearview mirror, that she scares herself.

When she gets to the apartment, the rooms are dark and for a moment, she is reminded of the House, Idris's family house, four years ago, standing in a dark foyer, her body racked with sex. But she wasn't someone's wife then. She didn't have a child.

Her underwear smells disgusting. She wraps it in paper towels and buries it in the kitchen trashcan under coffee grounds and wet orange peels. In the bathroom, she brushes her teeth so hard the gums bleed, then she washes her makeup off. She can't bear to sleep next to Idris, but any alternative would raise questions. He doesn't stir as she gets into bed, and the familiarity of his simple, boyish smell, the worn sheets and the light from the street lamp, make her wish she were dead. She's fantasized about hurting him, of doing something terrible to ruin his life, when they're arguing or when she hates America, but this feels like her own skin is being scraped off. Every time she shuts her eyes and her breath begins to even, she is back against the dresser, Cal's fingers inside her, the strange, deadened way he'd straightened the straps of his wife's dress on her before returning to the party. She digs her nails into her forearms to keep from falling asleep and listens to Idris's breathing, praying for sunrise and Ava's accompanying call, for the terrible hangover that will nauseate her all day, for the rain predicted for late morning, for something to do.

❖

There's nothing to say but yes when Kit calls her the next week to say she'll be driving over that Saturday for the hypnosis session.

"I already spoke with Idris and he's taking Avey out for the afternoon."

The thought of them speaking is jolting, transgressive, almost, and for a second Mazna imagines Idris and Kit locked in an embrace, having a years-long affair. But of course not.

Kit mistakes her hesitation for nervousness. "Honey, I'll see you at noon. Clear the living room."

The day arrives and Mazna wears a thin white dress. It feels like what a person wears to a hypnosis. She has no idea what to expect. Her only other point of reference for this sort of thing, for any sort of intervention of the mind or spirit, is a woman her mother once brought to the house. Mazna was a child at the time. Her sister, Nawal, had refused two suitors in a row, and her mother was worried about jinn. The woman had made both Nawal and Mazna strip naked in the tub, then scrubbed their skin raw while reciting Qur'an. Nawal had refused the four suitors after that too.

But Kit arrives with nothing but her usual white Dior bag. Her hair is pulled back in a ponytail and she looks a little more tired than usual. Mazna braces herself for their first look, and for an alarming instant, it does seem like there's something there, a caginess in Kit's eyes, but it evaporates quickly; her lips are soft on her cheek.

"I've missed you," she says quietly, and Mazna feels the same punch from that night, listening to Idris's breath. She's ruined something and even if nobody ever finds out, she knows. It's a familiar feeling.

"Me too," Mazna says honestly. She wants to fall into Kit's lap and tell her everything, beg for forgiveness, ask her to stay in California, move with her to Los Angeles, but a different one — the Los Angeles she's caught glimpses of during her visits, the graffitied walls and generous bougainvillea trees, brown women in cutoff shorts selling fruit.

"Cal came back blindingly drunk after that party," Kit says as she sits, bending a leg beneath her. It's impossible to read her tone.

"I wish you'd come," she says.

Kit smiles. "He said the same thing. I told him that I've had my fill of those parties. Let the new blood in."

That's all either of them says about it. Kit has her lie down on the couch, a small pillow beneath her neck. Kit tells her to close her eyes, and picture a long staircase leading down to a pool of water. She begins to count.

"When I get to ten," Kit says, "you'll step into that water. It'll be as warm as a bath." A few minutes pass. An hour.

Mazna sleeps, or thinks she does. When she opens her eyes, she's in an airy room with marble floors and faucets, like a Turkish bath. There's only one other person there, sitting to her right, a small dog in his lap.

"You came," Zakaria says.

She's already crying, trying to stand to reach him. She expects snakes to appear or her legs to fail like in half-dreams, but there's nothing hypnagogic in how easily she rises, the marble clicking beneath her sneakers. When she reaches him, he touches her face and she can feel him, smell him.

"I always hated seeing you cry."

"You've seen me cry only once before."

Zakaria smiles like she's wrong, but he doesn't say anything. "How's Iddy?"

She clears her throat, startled. The question is so casual, so expected. It's the kind of conversation the living have. "You have a daughter." She says it in Arabic, then again in English. She wants to say it over and over, the words that she's rehearsed thousands of times in her mind. She needs him to know.

There's a knot in her hair and Zakaria starts to loosen it. He won't meet her eyes.

"Did you hear me?" she asks. She suddenly remembers this too, how he can go cold, as though stepping into another room within himself. "You have —"

"I heard you," Zakaria says evenly. "Idris deserves a son too."

Her temper rises. She swats his hand away. "God, I can't escape Idris, not even for a minute." There are no doors in the room, she notices for the first time, just large, rectangular windows streaming sunlight. She grunts in rage. "You know what's in California, Zakaria? Mostly lettuce," she hisses. "Miles of it. And strip malls and taco stands and a shitty greenhouse where I spend most of my time. We're nowhere near Los Angeles, and even if we were, I'd never end up in a movie, because I'm shit at it." She loses momentum. "I'm not special," she says simply. "I spend my days watching cartoons. You want to know how your *Iddy* is? He's great. He talks to hearts, Zakaria. He literally talks to them. He's about to make a lot of money and he loves this country and he thinks your daughter is his."

She pants. Zakaria is looking at her now, his expression pained, and she is thrilled by it. She didn't know the dead had feelings to hurt. The back of her neck tickles and she starts to remember Kit and the blanket; she knows what he's about to say.

"I'm sorry," he says, and everything ends and begins, and she forgives him, and, somewhere in the distance, the earth starts to rumble and the windows start shaking. "I never meant to leave you behind. We're in London now," he says earnestly, and they're both crying, "we're living in a little studio above a Balinese restaurant and a yarn store, and the heaters are always broken in the winter, but we love the view of the river, and we take the train to the countryside in the summers and nobody asks anything of us."

The rumbling is closer now and the windows are melting and the sun is brightening into whiteness; Zakaria is clasping her closer to him. She's gripping his shirt so tightly it hurts and she's trying to speak quickly, but she can't say it all in time, she's telling him incoherent, unrelated things, how she hates the mailman and how Ava loves carrots with brown sugar and also the Muppets, especially the pink one with the bonnet, and Mazna's favorite month in America is February and he's whispering back, but she can no longer hear him, the earthquake is here now, the walls are falling on them, they're dying, they're already dead.

Kit is holding Mazna's hands when she comes to, a beatific expression on her face. *I can't, I'm drowning,* Mazna gasps, then realizes that she hasn't spoken it aloud, she can't, she's crying too hard. She clasps Kit's shirt, which reminds her of Zakaria's shirt, and she clutches more, sobbing harder than she ever has before.

"Yes," Kit says, over and over. "Yes, yes, let it out. Yes." She strokes Mazna's hair like she's a cat, runs her fingernails from her widow's peak all the way back to the base of her neck. "Yes, sweetheart."

It takes a long time for her to calm down. The room returns to her slowly — Ava's toy lamb on the sofa, the hum of the air conditioner. She's in California. It's May. Her white dress is damp under the arms.

"I need water," she says. Her head is throbbing from crying. "Where did I go?"

Kit cocks her head. "I don't know," she says gently. "A lot of people start to dream."

"I wasn't dreaming!" Mazna can hear the hysteria rising in her voice again, and she takes a breath. There's a glass of water she doesn't remember pouring, and she drinks. "I wasn't," she repeats. "I went somewhere else. I saw someone who —" Here she pauses. His face had been scratchy with an unshaved beard. His hands. "He's dead. But I was touching him."

"You can travel," Kit says quietly. "We all can. Some people sleep. Some people travel to other times or places. Some people visit the dead. You were crying the whole time." Kit's eyes are damp as well. "You had your hand on your throat."

The world is resumed once more, and dull. Mazna sits up properly and stretches her toes. Perhaps she was just dreaming. Her headache is worsening with every minute. She wants Kit out of the house, wants to draw the curtains and watch sitcom reruns. Instead, Kit puts a hand on her shoulder, and Mazna feels her body start to hum again. She was wrong. She doesn't want Kit out. She wants her never to leave. *All brown women look alike.* All deserts look alike. All dreams look alike.

"What does it mean?" she asks. "My hand on my throat."

"It depends. I've heard Reiki healers say we carry our guilt there," Kit says. "The guilt of what we've done and the guilt of what's been done to us. But it means something is coming. A small atonement." She looks away. "I wouldn't be surprised if it came to you in your vision."

"Really?" Mazna tries to remember, but only conjures the shaking.

Kit finally smiles. "Nobody knows for sure." She starts to gather her purse, and Mazna is filled with sorrow. She's being left again. She wishes she had told Kit about Zakaria that first day they'd met, after she'd eaten that sad plate of clams. Kit drains the rest of the water in the glass. All brown women look alike. She imagines all the brown women in the world lined up in a row, like soldiers or flowers, a line long as the horizon. She wonders how many of them have hurt one another, and for nothing. For a white man. For a photograph by the pool.

"You taught me I was brown," she says, and Kit looks startled.

"What?"

"I didn't know I was, before."

At this, Kit laughs for the first time all afternoon. It's genuine; she looks ten years younger. "Honey, I'm just reporting back what I've heard." She laughs harder, the bottom row of her teeth visible, and Mazna laughs as well, but she isn't sure she gets it.

❖

The going-away party is filled with people Mazna has never met. Her mouth is so dry that she keeps swallowing. It's been four weeks since the LA party and every day she both wills the phone to ring, the director on the other end, and prays it won't. It never rings, and it bothers her and doesn't. The night after the hypnosis, she'd dreamed she got the part and woke up so happy, floating, as though it had already happened. It will happen. She's certain of it now. It's the same certainty she felt when the doctor asked about Ava's gender, something impossible to put into language. Mazna will atone, as Kit says. She'll spend her life making it up to Idris if only she gets the part.

At Cal and Kit's house, she and Idris spend most of their time with Eddie and Bernice, his date, eating hors d'oeuvres in the corner. They'd left Ava with a babysitter, an extravagance that Mazna understands will soon become commonplace with Idris's new job. Eddie and Idris seem young, drinking too much champagne, mocking Cal's too-nice art. Eddie is doing the same cardio-thoracic residency as Idris, and they're giddy as schoolboys.

Mazna sips her champagne miserably. Much of the house has already been packed away, making the rooms seem more cavernous than usual. Someone has hung a blank canvas in the living room for people to sign. She barely sees either Kit or Cal, and it reminds her of her wedding, how she hardly had more than a minute or two with each guest. Every now and then, Kit catches her eye and waves or pops over and kisses her cheek, but Cal barely looks at her. She'd worn a different dress, riskier than usual, in case the director came, but she doesn't see him.

"To three weeks' vacation!" Idris says to Eddie. He holds up his flute like an idiot, and the two of them clink.

"Excuse me." Mazna stands and makes her way through the crowd. She doesn't recognize anybody. Who are these people? Since when do Kit and Cal have a hundred friends? The guests move easily through the house, popping open the refrigerator, commenting on the bare walls. They'd all been here before and Mazna envisions dinner parties, holiday parties, fireworks parties. She has been to the house only a few times over the years; usually Kit comes to her. She can picture Kit and Cal having tense conversations about inviting them. *They won't have anything in common.* She's not sure if it's Kit or Cal saying that in her imagination.

She finds Cal on the deck with two other men. It's early evening, still hot, but the moon is already bright enough to make out between the clouds. An airplane weaves its way above them and Cal sees her.

"Have you all met Mazna?"

The men perk up when they see her, as men always do, and she straightens her back, sucks in her gut. She smiles her favorite smile, like she knows an excellent joke. "What a beautiful evening," she says, then looks up at the sky, giving them the chance to admire her profile. But the gesture feels dead. One day she won't be beautiful anymore, and for one brief, mad moment, she wishes that day were today so she could stop pretending she'll be beautiful forever.

One by one, the men take their leave, making excuses about empty glasses.

When she and Cal are alone, he finally looks at her. "I'm so glad you and Idris could come." His tone is expansive. He could be talking to a stranger.

"It's sad, seeing the house packed up."

He considers this. "I'm ready for a change. I've been on the West Coast for twenty years. I miss winter. Have you been to Manhattan?" She shakes her head. The city seems like one of Ava's fairy tales, somewhere fabled and unreal, like Narnia. "There's the best theater in the world."

Her heart quickens. "I was wondering—" She hesitates.

Cal sighs. "I knew you'd ask." He seems disappointed with her, and she recoils like a child. Was it breaking some code of etiquette to ask? She wants to kick the deck railing and yell that nobody ever taught her anything.

"I'm sorry." She hates the words coming from her. They taste rotten in her mouth. "I just — I never heard back —"

"Adam went with someone else." Cal's words are clipped. "Some actress he'd worked with before."

"Oh." Mazna's cheeks burn. *Don't cry,* she silently screams at herself.

"You know how these things are." He waves his hand ruefully. She remembers the look Cal and Adam exchanged at the party.

"Of course," she says. She imagines lying down in that Turkish bath with Zakaria and telling him, *There was no part. There was no movie,* she'd say. *I'm a fucking idiot.*

Cal snaps his fingers. "I have something for you," he says. "Wait here."

He's gone for a long time. Mazna cries a little, then reties her hair. When he returns, he's carrying a cardboard box. He flips the top open and angles it so she can see. "Look."

It's her face. Perfectly made up, crimson lipstick, the red scarf around her neck. The photograph from the party, a stack of headshots, dozens of them, a comical amount. She looks like she's in a magazine. Cal seems pleased. More than that. Handing her the box, she can tell he's finished.

Later, Idris hoists it under his arm as they say their goodbyes on the front lawn. Kit cries as she hugs her, and Cal shakes Idris's hand. The party is still raging inside, but Mazna's head is pounding. They get in the car and Idris backs out of the driveway, Kit and Cal waving to them from the front stoop. Mazna waves back, and they're gone.

❖

It's nearly two in the morning when they get back home. The babysitter is a college student and she has her own car. Ava's sleeping soundly in the bedroom, her hair in a long braid — she loves braids these days. Mazna sits at the edge of her daughter's bed, listening to her breath, then tucks the box under the bed. Nobody cleans under there except for her. She goes into the kitchen, where Idris is eating leftover chicken straight from the Tupperware. His belly is starting to protrude over his underwear.

She remembers how quietly Zakaria had said the word *son.*

"Would you like to have another child?" she asks, and Idris keeps chewing for a moment, clearly half listening. She watches his face change. He cuts his eyes sharply at her.

"You're pregnant?"

"No." She remembers crying in the doctor's office that afternoon she found out about Ava. The prospect of doing it all over again — the pain, the endless fatigue, the hourlong sobbing fits — is daunting, but it feels right. A debt paid. *Idris deserves a son too.*

Idris sets the fork down. "You want another baby?" Her question ricocheted back to her sounds farcical. He doesn't wait for her to respond. "The timing is *excellent,*" he says in that ridiculous whisper voice of his, as though he's sharing rich gossip.

"I'd like a different doctor."

"Of course. Remember when you told me about Ava?" he asks, his voice quiet with the memory. "After your movie screening, and I cried? Look how the days turn. We'll have plenty of money now, a new house soon. Inshallah." He doesn't mention Zakaria.

Mazna nods. He hasn't asked her about acting in years. It was now something she once did, she understands, the way some people studied anthropology in college or wore their hair short for a while. Something interesting to talk about at parties. How many times can you swear off something? She'll find out.

"We'll move to a different neighborhood, of course," Idris is saying.

She remembers that night too. Idris crying into his hands, the way her heart constricted so tight, it never truly loosened again. They'd nearly gotten into an accident on the way home afterward. A truck fishtailed in front of them slightly — the driver working a double shift, on his way back to Phoenix, his eyes briefly fluttering closed during an insurance commercial on the radio — and she'd cried out, *Idris!* and he'd swerved and grazed the gravel instead. She'd shut her eyes out of instinct, and for a split second she'd thought of her grandfather in Damascus, all that life turned rotten. It was no better than Zakaria dying on his knees in the camps, and it all seemed pointless, and yes, there was a leaping within her, small and unfaithful, at the prospect of a blinding light and hot metal, but then, at the last minute, something snapped inside her like a tree branch, a prayer, an incantation to keep living. When she opened her eyes, they were back on the road safely, the incident quickly forgotten. She almost never thought of it. It was a betrayal to Zakaria, but she wanted to live — when given no room to waver, her heart had still chosen life. Hotly, violently. It still did.

The American Dream

1987

THEY RETURN TO Damascus twice after Mimi is born — a son, all dark hair and Idris's smile, named Marwan after an old uncle — once for a family wedding and once after her grandfather's death. Ava's nearly seven the second time, Mimi only three, and the journey is a mess, Mazna and Idris taking turns walking each child to the tiny airplane bathroom, settling them to sleep. Her trips back to Damascus always feel anticlimactic. She'd spent years daydreaming about coming home to a Syria transformed. Celebrated. Instead, when she arrives, her father's house feels tight as a matchbox, though the city itself seemed larger, crowded with mopeds and pedestrians, after Mazna's years of flat, small-town living. At her grandfather's funeral, she couldn't even cry, she was so tired from jet lag and the children.

"Remember those shows Mazzy used to do?" her aunt asked during a dinner, everyone reminiscing about old times.

"It was nothing," Mazna had mumbled, turning to wipe Mimi's nose. Her neck was hot.

"And those arguments we had over London," her father said, amused. Mazna crumpled the tissue in her fist. "She took it so seriously."

"She was good." Her mother's sharp voice cut through the others'. She met Mazna's gaze, surprising her. "She was very, very good." Mazna hears the pride in her mother's voice, the faint note of sadness; she has to look away first, her vision swimming.

On both trips, Idris's family came to visit them in Damascus and then took him back with them for a few days in Beirut.

"The children," Mazna would say whenever Hana mentioned visiting Lebanon. "The war." The truth was that people still drove into Beirut regularly. The war continued to chug along like a faithful engine, destroying the city. *It's like background noise,* Sara said once — Sara, who's grown up knowing nothing else, who's getting her master's at the university. Ava and Mimi call her Rara and love her intensely, which irritates Mazna, especially when it comes to Ava, who is increasingly embarrassed by her mother when they're in California. Ava finds her mother too loud, too beautiful; her English is not fluent enough. She hadn't anticipated this, how her children's schools would become minefields — mispronounced words, incorrectly packed lunches — how outdated and clumsy she'd feel among the fluent blond mothers.

In Damascus, she and Sara treat each other like strangers, polite and aloof, and sometimes Mazna remembers the letter she drowned, the ink running until it was unreadable. But too many years have passed; they're basically strangers now.

"You should visit us sometime," Mazna says, which is what she says over the phone during Ramadan and Eid when they talk, and Sara smiles tightly.

"America doesn't interest me," the younger woman replies, and there's a haughtiness in her voice, pride at being raised in a war, at never leaving her country. Sara looks down on her and Idris, Mazna knows, on their American lives. Once, she overheard her telling her brother off in a sharp tone, the unspoken accusation hanging in the air: when Idris left, he left *her,* left her their parents.

"America is terrible," Mazna lies, as she lies to her parents and Hana and friends — they're truly adults now, Lara marrying a neighborhood boy and raising a handsome son, Fatima marrying years after her friends, a fellow academic at the university. She repeats how hot it is, how lonely it is, the gossip about the other Arabs. When Tarek visits her parents' house in Damascus, bringing kanafeh for the children, she sees the pity in his eyes as she mocks California. But the truth is she misses it terribly. She lies because she feels obligated to, as though the truth would be worse: she misses the sanctity of the greenhouse, the neighbors who never meddle, the hours of solitude, all those people who expect nothing of her and so have nothing to pity.

✥

Another woman would have given up.

The truth is she *does* give up, for years. It wasn't until Mimi was three and they went to a show in Los Angeles that Mazna finally called the small agency that Cal had recommended to her after he moved. He'd called once, months after they'd left, and said he'd passed along the student film and some headshots — this made her flush; so he'd kept some headshots for himself — to an agent friend, and the agent had told him to give her his number.

Call him, Cal said, and there was a finality in his voice that she recognized. It would be the last time they'd speak. He had paid his debt.

For a long time, she didn't call the agent. Her pregnancy with Mimi was difficult, and then two children were so much harder than one. But she memorized the phone number and sometimes would doodle it on the corner of a paper, the way she and Lara used to doodle boys' names. The tipping point came suddenly. It was a Wednesday, and she'd had a rowdy field-trip group at the greenhouse. Idris was on call and so she'd picked Ava up from school, Mimi from the Mexican daycare. It was one of her better days, the days that she thought of herself as a good mother, and so she'd made *fatayer* from scratch and served it on the nice plates.

"This is how your grandmother used to make it," she told Ava, and she'd felt pleased with herself, raising Arab children so far from home.

But neither child touched the meal. Ava whined for something else and Mimi flung his on the table. Her mood darkened immediately, and she'd thrown a frozen pizza in the oven. When the timer bleated, she forgot the oven mitt and burned her hand, dropping the pizza on the floor. Mimi cried at the clatter. She'd picked up the pizza and slapped a slice down in front of each child, even though it was dirty. She smacked Mimi's hand when he'd asked for Pepsi and then went into the living room, turned off all the lights, and put on *A Streetcar Named Desire;* she watched the movie from beginning to end, then rewound it and watched it all over again. She could hear her children in the other room, the sound of Ava putting Mimi to bed. She didn't care. The phone rang and she didn't pick up. She was in New Orleans, she was Vivien Leigh, she was eighteen again, she had moved to London and done theater for several years before moving to Los Angeles, where she lived in a small studio with a roommate from Cincinnati, who was loud and funny, and it took months but eventually she'd booked a commercial, then another, finally landing a role in a small film. People recognized her on the street, but she often chose quiet, indie projects and won a number of critics' awards. At nearly ten that night, Mazna called the agent's office. Her eyes were starry from so many hours of television. Of course she got the machine, and she left a manic, rambling message, her voice urgent: *I'm Cal's friend, he told me to call, I know it's been years, but I'm ready.*

❈

The auditions are awful. Her agent is a short, hairy man who doesn't mince words and who sends her an audition every couple of months. Mazna knows he's taken her on as a favor to Cal because once, during a meeting, he'd said, *This is a favor to Cal.* Another time: *I can't prioritize clients who don't live in LA.* Still, the phone rings every now and then with a brief summation of a part — always ethnic, often a line or two — and she faithfully goes, not telling anyone, even Idris. The omission isn't defensive; there's something about the secrecy that pleases her, a ritual about it — picking the audition outfit, running lines while she prunes at the greenhouse; it's as though she's having an affair.

She doesn't audition for a single part she truly wants, and she comforts herself with this when she doesn't, in turn, get a single part. They are commercial roles for hijabis or two-liners in movies with terrorist plots, audition waiting rooms filled with women who look like her, carrying their scripts. The headshots litter the directors' tables like sad flowers, and once, she glimpses all the smiling faces quickly, indistinguishable in the blur.

"Nice reading," they'll say, "but let's try it with more of an accent." Or "Now do it like that, but differently."

The directors don't want authenticity. They don't want her accent — they want someone who speaks perfect English and can *do* an accent. She is too pretty for simpler roles, too dark for American parts. Still, she goes, driving for hours on that straight arrow of I-10 until the smog of Los Angeles greets her like a friend. The auditions are like picking a scab that won't heal, but the alternative, the not-doing that she's done for years, is infinitely worse, because there's a desire she recognizes in the other women in the waiting room, a camaraderie in the exchanged eye-rolls. It's like being part of an army. A tribe. Everything is easier with hope — picking up the children, chopping vegetables for soup, fucking Idris. The role might be around the corner. If Tarek were to see her now, she'd return his gaze.

❖

It's 1987 and sometimes Mazna feels a brief panic as the end of the eighties approaches — the decade has felt like one long false start, but she's strangely attached to it, as though the big bangs and pink blazers and plastic bracelets are a person. Ava turns eight and they have a party at a local pizza shop, a gaggle of girls playing while the mothers drift into their groups, Arab or white or Mexican. Mimi chases after the girls, trying to get their attention. His sister is kind to him, draping an arm around his shoulders in an absent, adult sort of way while she talks to her friends.

"What a darling," one of the white mothers tells Mazna, and she thanks her, though privately she worries about the girl. Mimi loves messes and music and cartoons, but her elder child is restrained with an air that sometimes verges on judgmental. *I'm okay, thanks,* she'll say if Mazna tries to get her to paint her nails, preferring instead to watch a nature special.

"She's not like other children," Mazna replies tightly, and there's something about her own tone that nags at her, oddly familiar. She rises to serve some cake and the room suddenly tilts. The Arab mothers crowd her with concerned faces.

"*Shoo fee?*"

"You haven't sat down all day. Have some pizza."

But the pizza is nauseating, and she throws it up later, at home, Ava and Mimi crunching up the wrapping paper from her daughter's presents. There's a pregnancy test in the medicine cabinet, but it's expired, and anyway, she won't think to take it until the following day, sobbing into her hands. For now, she stays on her knees, her hands pressed against the cool porcelain, and suddenly she can place the familiarity of her earlier tone about Ava: she sounded like her mother.

Idris wants to tell the children, but Mazna asks him to wait. "But why?" he asks in his wounded, dopey way. His hair is thinner, and there's a new roundness to his face. The nurses at the hospital love him. "Remember how excited Avey was when Mimi was born?" He's the excited one, she knows. Idris loves the accoutrements of parenting, the Father's Day cards, hoisting Mimi on his shoulders at the hospital, bedtime stories. They are his joy, evidence of the best parts of America.

"It's still early," she says. "The doctor said barely five weeks. It's too early to tell anyone. You never know what'll happen."

She wills her words to be prophecy. The children are exhausting but are finally reaching ages of entertaining themselves. It's Los Angeles, the auditions, I-10; a new baby means starting over. Late nights. Not a moment to herself. The timing feels cursed. When the agent calls her that very afternoon, she isn't even surprised.

"This is a good one," he says. "Frankly, it's a long shot, but they've sent out the call all around town. They want someone who speaks Arabic. It's a bilingual role and they'd rather not rely on pronunciation training."

He mails her the script, which is a rarity — usually the auditions entail a few lines — and she reads the whole thing in the greenhouse in one sitting. She thrills every time she sees the name MIRA and weeps at the end. The script is impeccable. The role is complex and electrifying, the character the quiet backbone of the story. Mazna can see her perfectly — how she'll fall in love, how she'll grieve. *It's like my final supper,* she thinks a few days later, picking out what to wear. She's taken the day off from the greenhouse, and the children are at school. Idris will pick them up today; she's told him she's helping Janet with some new shipments after work. Her waist is still small enough, and she wears a white blouse with small, triangular black buttons. The whole thing feels like an exercise in futility — she should've told the agent no. She should've thrown the script away. She's being masochistic. And yet her hands button the blouse, put on the seat belt, put the key in the ignition.

On the drive over, she does what she always does — murmurs *Don't hope, don't hope, don't hope* under her breath like a metronome — but it doesn't work this time; her spirits rise the further west she drives, like a spell lifting, and the biographies she spent years reading in the greenhouse return to her, the hope slipping into her like wind between bricks: Elizabeth Taylor survived eight marriages to do her films. Lucille Ball was discovered at forty. It was possible. It was all possible.

❈

Later, she'll remember only bits and pieces, glinting like tinsel in her mind's eye. The waiting room is different and nicer and surprisingly empty, with aquamarine carpet and soft chairs, the woman at the front greeting her warmly, asking what she'd like to drink. Mazna chooses sparkling, and the bubbles sit on her lips. There are magazines and she flicks through them — it doesn't do to practice lines up to the last second — but can't concentrate on the words.

Finally, the door to the audition room opens. A pretty, Arab-looking woman emerges. She is carrying a briefcase and looks up on her way past Mazna. They catch each other's eye and the woman does something unexpected.

She smiles warmly.

Good luck, she says in Arabic, startling Mazna so much she doesn't respond, a move she'll regret for years — there were Arabs! In Hollywood! — but the woman walks to the door and is gone. A minute later, the door opens again, and a bespectacled man is smiling down at her.

"Mazna?" He pronounces it incorrectly. They all do. But his voice is warm, and he looks her in the eye when they shake hands. "Please, sit, stand, whatever you like."

The audition room is familiar, at least. White and unadorned, with lots of windows and a bored-looking woman behind the camera. She'll read lines with Mazna, the woman explains. The camera's red light blinks, and it reminds Mazna of Pen's camera, in that lot next to the dumpster, only this time she's in a lemon garden in Baghdad and her name is Mira and her life is starting. She takes a breath, and when the camerawoman asks, *Where will you go, Mira?,* she finds that she's shaking, weeping, furious at the love lost. There's a glass of water in front of the director, likely his, and she grabs it, drinks like she's parched, babbling her lines between sips like she's just that moment thinking them.

After — silence. Then, slowly, so faintly at first that it's half imagined, her senses returning to her in beats, a sleepwalker wakening, self-conscious — *What has she done?* — from the corners of her downcast eyes: applause.

❖

It isn't a decision, not really. The director's name is Sam and he loves her. She repeats these facts to herself on the drive home. He'd spoken so excitedly she'd nearly cried: *I'll need to talk with the producer, can't put anything in writing just yet, but, well, let's just say, stay near the phone.* The next few days, the lines of the pregnancy test drift across her hours like an eye floater. It isn't a decision to call the operator in Irvine and make a list of clinics, nor is it a decision to call each one of those clinics, twice getting yelled at in Spanish. Her voice shakes throughout.

"We don't do that here," one receptionist says firmly before hanging up the phone.

She has a hasty longing to call Lara, who had once confessed to accompanying her older cousin to one. The thought buoys her — even in Damascus, even in Damascus. *Women have been doing it since the beginning of time,* she remembers Fatima saying matter-of-factly, but Mazna wonders what her old friends would tell her. They'd probably be aghast. It's one thing to do it out of desperation, without wedlock or money, but not if you're the wife of a doctor, a mother. It wasn't a contingency plan. Her friends had been unruly in college, but there were rules. The line from the Qur'an: *Your mother, then your mother, then your mother.* She loved her children as much as Lulwa always said she would.

But those children have already been born. They have favorite colors and birthdays and loose teeth. Her heart soars when the sixth clinic says yes, they do, but she'll need to come tomorrow, because they've had a last-minute cancellation, otherwise they're booked until June. Mazna tries to imagine the woman who canceled. Maybe she was painting a baby room right now. The procedure will cost an exorbitant amount of money without insurance, more money than she has saved, more money than she can take out of the joint account without explaining. There is a pawnshop near the highway and she stops there. Two pieces of her wedding gold — a necklace and a bracelet.

"Great quality," the man says before quoting her a price that is half their worth but enough.

The waiting room couldn't be more different from the audition room in Los Angeles. There is chicken wire in the windows and the receptionist must buzz people inside. Mazna had been afraid of protesters, but there are only two bored-looking older women carrying signs that say ONE HEART STOPS, ANOTHER BREAKS. On the table, there are old copies of cooking magazines. The other women don't look at each other, but Mazna looks at all of them, trying to determine a pattern. There isn't one. Older, young, Black, white. The only commonality is a certain grim set to the mouth, a recognition of the task awaiting them, of being the only ones who can do it.

❖

There is pain. The doctor gives her a pill, then remarks how early on Mazna is, as though she's been a good girl. *I can just scrape it out,* the doctor says cheerily and Mazna immediately thinks of a shovel scraping ice from pavement. She doesn't sleep, but she isn't exactly awake, and when she asks sleepily, *Are you done?* the doctor laughs kindly and says she hasn't started yet.

That night, she goes to Ava's talent show and changes pads in the bathroom between acts. Mimi is cranky and wants to be held only by her. Afterward, as Idris strikes up conversations with the other parents and Ava giggles with her friends, she hates her family for their loud voices and outstretched hands and eternalness. She hates herself for accepting a compliment from a stranger all those years ago, a stranger who became Idris, and for now being stuck with this for the rest of her life. It's only when she remembers the sparkling water in the audition's waiting room, the carpet soft as a tongue under her feet, that she can breathe again. How the director had tugged at his hair until it stood on end, saying, *I mean, that's exactly how I wanted it.*

She showers once they get home, then puts the children to bed. Twice she wakes up with cramps and rushes to the bathroom. There aren't any thoughts. She just sits on the toilet, and there isn't anybody she wants to call except Kit, who would understand, who would tell her what to do, but she hasn't spoken to Kit in four years, she doesn't even have her number anymore. It's just her, petting her own thighs when the cramps come, waiting for her body to finish what she started.

It happens two weeks later. The cramps stopped after a few days, and her singular focus is redirected to the telephone. It rings. It doesn't ring. It's never the director. On the first weekend after the doctor, she refuses to leave the apartment, claiming a headache, but the next Saturday, Mimi has a cold and she takes him to the doctor. He gets his tonsils swiped and some antibiotics, and on the drive back, he starts crying that he's hungry.

"I just want McDonald's." He sniffles. Her heart softens. For weeks, she's barely noticed her children — the wastebasket filled with bloody pads — snapping at Ava and asking Mimi to play in the other room. Her son wipes his crusty nostrils on his sleeve in the back seat, and she relents. She eats his left-over fries while he swims in the plastic balls. She called the agent yesterday, and for the first time he'd taken her call right away, greeted her warmly.

"How are you feeling?" he asked, like she was a boxer. "Nervous, right? Tense, right? Any day now, I promise. Sam told us you were phenomenal."

"It's been weeks," Mazna frets.

"These things take months sometimes. Especially with an unknown. I promise everything is on track. They liked you. Let's trust in that. Just hang in there. I have a good feeling about this one."

Mazna and Mimi listen to music on the drive back home. Mimi sings along to "Jessie's Girl" like he's a middle-aged man. She pulls into their driveway. The light is dappling the side of the house in a way that makes her arms tingle, like a suddenly remembered dream. Idris is waiting for them in the kitchen. He asks Mimi to go watch television.

"What is it?" she says. Her father is the first to come to mind, a funeral.

"You got a call," Idris says neutrally.

"Baba?" Mazna asks, but she already knows — it's not Damascus, it's not her family. *Let's just say, stay near the phone.*

Idris places his palms on the counter.

"Tell me," she says, sharper than she intended, and Idris narrows his eyes in kind.

"You're auditioning again," he accuses her. "When were you going to say something?"

"It's just one part," Mazna says. She can barely get the words out, her throat is so dry. She grips the edge of the counter to steady herself. *Stay near the phone. Stay near the phone.* "An old friend of Cal's. Who was on the phone?"

"It was the director. Some director."

She smiles. She starts to laugh. The director doesn't call with bad news. The agent does. Her mind spins with people to call: Lara, her mother, Madame Orla. "What did he say?" She isn't trying to hide anything anymore, her voice high and breathless. "Idris." She laughs. "I'm going to faint, tell me, hurry!"

He lowers his head. His shoulders hunch. There is a waft of cartoonish laughter from the living room, Mimi babbling to his sister. Mazna looks at her husband. Her voice breaks: "No."

"He said —" Idris says quietly. "That you were great, but they went with someone else."

"Who?" Mazna thinks of the woman that day. *Good luck.* "Did he say who?"

He looks at her strangely. "I'm sorry, Mazzy. It surprised me, that's all. It's good for you to audition again. I know it'll be rough the next year or two, but after the baby is a toddler, you can —"

Mazna drops her purse with a clatter. She hasn't forgotten. She was going to wait until she got the part, then explain all of it, beg for forgiveness. Instead, she feels her fingertips tingle, like she's losing circulation. The pain is startling. She had wanted it. She had hoped. Her heart is broken and she wants to share it.

"I miscarried," she says coldly. "A few days ago. I was waiting to tell you, but you're always chattering on about your stupid hearts." His face crumples and it's like feeling sun on her face. She's out of the room before he starts to cry.

She gets drunk one night. There's a bar near the community college and she tells Idris she's seeing their friend Sama but instead she flirts with the bartender and shoots tequila. It's nearly three a.m. when she stumbles to the phone booth and leaves a drunk message for the agent, calling him a loser and a charlatan, the worst thing that ever happened to her. *Don't ever call me again,* she snarls. He doesn't.

Exit Cue

1995

NAJLA IS BORN the year before the war ends, 1989. It wasn't planned, but Mazna doesn't cry at the pregnancy test. Three is a nice number, she thinks numbly as the doctor hands her the ultrasound picture. There are no more auditions. The other two children are in school during most of her pregnancy, Ava already in elementary school. Three is a nice number, and they've moved into an even larger house, one with a large backyard and driveway and a refrigerator with an icemaker, but never out of Blythe; she understands now they'll never leave Blythe. This is home: Albertsons with the seasonally decorated cupcakes. Bake sales at the children's schools. Trick-or-treating in a drugstore witch's hat.

And yet, during her labor, while the cramps wrung her lower back like a dishrag, she'd suddenly thought, *Four,* the number coming to her like a ghost, her unborn child, the cells scraped out of her. *Four, four, four,* her mind panted, and Naj entered the world, screaming and red as an apple.

The war ended as inanely as it began. Four Arab countries create a peace treaty, which is confusing to Mazna, since many of those countries had been involved in the war in the first place. It reminds her of Tarek's maps. The parliament pardons all the people involved of their crimes, and just like that, fifteen years of war are over. The blockades dissolve. The borders open. And Mazna has no more excuses; they pack their suitcases and take Najla, Ava, and Mimi to the House, the children sleeping in Sara's old room, she and Idris sharing his. Zakaria's cot is gone. The first summer back, Mazna kept dreaming of fires starting in peculiar places: kitchen sinks, gardens, Hana's closet. She was still breastfeeding, and her nipples leaked into every bra she owned, her misery taunted by the beautiful weather and bars playing loud music, every street in Beirut like the first note of a song, bursting and joyous and reckless. People looked at each other and raised their eyebrows as though in on an outrageous secret. The war was over.

"But they *were* the war," Mazna complains once to Tarek, who has moved back to Beirut. He visits them in the House once or twice, and they eat watermelon and feta cheese and complain about the heat.

"They'll never believe that. Everyone thinks they're the bigger man."

"It's a country of microscopic men." They laugh together. He's an old friend now, which surprises them both. He never brings up her acting.

They return every summer. Hana throws dinner parties for distant cousins, and the children get tan and their Arabic recovers, and Mazna stays in the House until she cannot bear it anymore, then pretends her parents need her and takes a car to Damascus. It's like visiting a graveyard, she wants to tell Idris, but he's so happy to be back, teaching the children to climb his favorite tree. At least she has Damascus, her mother now bad-tempered and fat, her days spent bickering with Mazna's father. Mazna's grandmother died in the late 1980s, so soon after her jiddo that it was almost cathartic, combining the two griefs into one. Khalto Seham surprised all of them and moved to Sweden with Nawal, whose husband had gotten a good job there. *It only took forty years,* Lulwa once said, her voice acid, but Mazna knows her mother misses her Seham; the days are long and hot and dull. Sometimes she goes to Damascus with the children, other times alone, curling in her childhood bed like a teenager, staring at the old posters of movie stars. If she covers their smiles, she can see sadness in their eyes.

In Beirut, the jet lag morphs into a persistent insomnia and she is shaken and tired during the day, curiously energized at night. She wanders the House while everyone sleeps, picking up knickknacks, staring at the old portrait of Hana. A few times, she quietly goes through the VHS collection until she finds the bright orange spine, then watches herself on the television screen. She keeps the sound muted, and her younger face is vibrant, contorting into every imaginable emotion; she watches and rewinds herself. She sits where Zakaria sat.

During her pregnancy, she'd gotten a book about depression out of the library. The author called it the black dog, then listed symptoms like lack of appetite and dullness of mind. Mazna would call it more like suffocating, the feeling of a coat too tightly pinched at her waist, a breath she can't catch. She is perennially uncomfortable after the failed part, too hot or too cold, her legs pins and needles. Her body wakes her from deep sleep like another child, achy and complaining. She cries during commercials and when Mimi practices his music.

It's better after Najla is born. The infant's needs are something tangible to focus her attention on. The movie comes out when the baby is four months old, and Mazna can't help herself. She sits in the dark theater and stuffs her nipple into the baby's mouth, watching her replacement onscreen. It is the woman from the waiting room, Leila Souzan, and the movie propels her into a gentle but resolved fame. She has a supporting role in a blockbuster, then does a series of successful indies. The baby fusses in the theater and some people shush them, so Mazna walks her up the aisle, going backwards so she doesn't miss a second, then down again. Every scene is perfectly shot, every expression captured — the streets of Baghdad, the river, the sounds.

She sees it three more times. This is more to confirm than revel; she knows she could have done it better.

One Saturday when Najla is four, Mazna goes to the grocery store with her. Najla complains in the car for her music, some cartoon soundtrack, and Mazna relents too quickly. Sometimes she forgets about Najla, is surprised to hear her little, demanding voice. With Ava she'd been fearful, superstitious, muttering prayers every time she saw a milk carton with a child's face on it, but the fear has been scrubbed off a little with each child, like glitter. Mimi is moody but well liked, and Najla is downright spoiled.

The parking lot at the grocery store is nearly empty, that nothing hour of one p.m. There is a line of shopping carts glinting in the sunlight. Something is caught in the first one's wheel and she shakes it loose. Najla is kicking an empty Bud can across the lot.

"Stop that," Mazna tells her in Arabic. "Let's go inside."

Najla stops. "You're not fun," she says in her blunt way.

"And you're a mouthy brat. *Yalla,* move it."

"I'm sorry," a male voice says. "But I remember you."

Mazna turns around. There's an older, vaguely handsome man returning a cart, a bag of groceries in one hand. His angular mouth nags at her memory. They stare at each other for a moment.

"Oh my God," she says. It's the director. Sam.

"I thought that was you." He smiles. "I'm sorry, remind me of your name."

"I'm Najla," her daughter offers. "She's Mama."

He laughs this time. "I see that." He kneels down. "The apple landed real close to the tree on this one, huh?" he says, glancing up at Mazna with an expectant smile.

"Mazna," she says. Her hands are shaking, and she grips the cart handle to steady them. She doesn't know what he means by apple or tree, so she nods, as she always does when Americans talk about hitting roads or early birds.

"She's adorable." He rises, dusting off his thighs.

"Thank you," Mazna says automatically.

"My sister-in-law's family lives here," he says, as though they are in midconversation. He shakes his head. "I couldn't believe that was you."

"I live here," she says idiotically.

"So you came back?" He waits expectantly, but she doesn't know how to answer this. "Your audition was brilliant," he says, his eyes misty with remembering.

It is a cruel thing to say. "Thank you," she says quietly. Her own eyes are hot. If there were a button that would swallow her from the earth, erase every tendril of her DNA, she would push it.

"And are you back for good?" he asks casually. He shifts the bag of groceries to the other hand, and she can tell it's heavy. "It's funny, I still remember it was Damascus," he says, almost to himself. "Because I called for you the same week that one of my producers returned from Baghdad. He'd gone to Damascus for a few days while he was there. Brought back the most delicious sweets."

It's like her veins have filled with ice water. A terrible thought comes to her, but she can't look at it directly. The blood rushing in her ears makes it hard to hear. "Mama's mad," she can hear Najla whisper, but her daughter feels miles away. There's a weird buzzing and Mazna swats her hair as though to clear it.

"Say that again, please." Her voice is hoarse. She wishes she had water in her bag. She always forgets to hydrate. "What you just said about Damascus."

He looks at her, hard. "About you returning?" he asks, his voice puzzled now. "The man who answered the phone. He told me you'd gone there and that you weren't coming back."

❋

She breaks the hinges on the front door opening it. Najla scrambles into the house without being told. Mazna storms through, throwing her purse in the hallway. Ever since the director uttered *Damascus,* her vision has a red aura, and it vibrates as she charges into Idris's study. She feels murder at the sight of him at his desk.

He smiles at her. "This year's tax return is going to be brutal."

"I've always regretted marrying you," she says. The words are hot and delicious, and his eyes widen, but she doesn't stop. "I did it because I was terrified. I thought I had no other choice. You came *into my father's house* when I was blind with grief and fed me bullshit about Hollywood. Then you bring me to this town, you go off and build yourself a life, and the *one time* —" Here she doubles over. A sound escapes her lips. That woman in the audition waiting room. The director clapping. "The one chance I got. You slaughtered it."

While she speaks, Idris drops his head into his hands. He lifts it slowly, and his eyes are devastated. "How did you find out?" he says tonelessly.

"So you did it." There's a headiness to their exchange, and Mazna realizes it's the most truthful conversation they've had in years.

"Mazna, it's not what you think."

"*Why,* then?" She pants. "Why?" She repeats the word until he puts his palm up. For a moment, they stare at each other. Then he finally begins to speak.

"With the baby coming," he says, then stops again. "I knew how difficult a decision like that would be for you. How hard it would be to turn it down."

She stares at him, open-mouthed. *They're all strangers to me,* she'd once heard a character say in a film about her lovers, and here he was, her stranger. This man who didn't know her at all. Her mind flashes back to all the auditions, the chalky smell of the stage, the hot lights, the pity in Tarek's eyes, and the realization crushes her — she was so aware of what she wanted, she never spoke it aloud. Not once — at no dinner, during no tipsy evening, her mind screams at her now — had she told Idris she still wanted to act. Not since that night in the university auditorium when she'd told him she was pregnant with Ava. She was his stranger as well.

"I wouldn't have turned it down," she says, her voice hoarse and strange.

"Then when you miscarried" — Idris frowns — "you seemed so sad. I couldn't tell you. It felt too much to put on you."

In another life, she tells him about the abortion. About Cal pushing her against the window, her wet panties. Zakaria and his sugar-powdered hair. In this life, she cries and he cries. Then she turns to leave. He hugs her and whispers something that she can't make out. She doesn't speak to him again for seven months.

It had been winter. Mazna had just told him about the pregnancy, and privately Idris was relieved. She'd always seemed better during the early years of the children, and lately, as they'd been getting older, she'd been so jittery, her unhappiness pickling the house. Ava had been watching television in the living room when the phone rang; he picked up, and there was a strange man asking to speak with his wife.

She's not here, Idris said truthfully. His heart had already sunk. For years he'd suspected affairs and here it was. *Is there something I can help with?*

The man spoke happily. *I probably should just wait to talk to her but* — he assumed Idris knew. The words flew so quickly Idris could barely follow them: Mazna had auditioned for something. A film. This was the director and — here the man's voice burst open with excitement — they loved her, they wanted her. She'd gotten the part.

Can you have her call me back?

While the man spoke, Idris thought of the first time he'd seen his wife. The Damascus auditorium, a gorgeous young woman on the stage, her face luminous with anticipation. She looked like a concept of a woman. The performance was flawless, her tone, the tiny gestures. She was wild and rehearsed at the same time and he wanted everything about her. He would marry her, he knew, and he did, but it was like a fairy tale or a Greek myth — always half wrong, a caveat to every happiness.

I can't, Idris told the man before he could stop himself. The Mazna that had walked across that stage would never have married him. Never have moved to the desert and done this. He'd caught her when she was broken and — he hated himself for the truth — that was why she had stayed. All those years later, he had lied to her in the study; he'd remembered the pregnancy only afterward. When he had, he was relieved — it was a practical reason to have done what he did. But what actually steered him at the time was the idea of Mazna walking onto a red carpet, then her face on a screen. Her return to herself. He'd lose her in an immutable, final way. *She's not here anymore. I'm so sorry.* The lie came swiftly and compellingly, as good lies do: His wife wasn't here. There had been a family emergency. She'd left for Damascus earlier that week. He'd appreciate it if the man didn't call here again.

An evening in August when the house is empty except for her and Najla. In the kitchen cabinet, there's a forgotten bottle of red wine from a party, and Mazna fills a mug. It's already been a long year. She and Idris speak through the children, and at night, she sleeps with a pillow between them. There's been a primal, charged tension in the house for months now — *Don't say that; you know how bad things are with Mama and Baba,* she overheard Ava tell Mimi last week, like the adult she'd been for years — and everyone feels it except for Najla. Her youngest is almost five and all she can talk about is her birthday party.

"I want swans as well," she informs Mazna as she draws a bath. "Maybe golden ones, but silver is okay too."

"You have to share the party favors with your friends," Mazna says. "Or else everyone is going to say you're greedy."

Najla shrugs. "They can say that."

Mazna watches her daughter as she bathes. She takes big sips of the wine. Najla is going to be more beautiful than her, a fact Mazna is confronting for the first time. Ava is too self-conscious to be striking, but Najla already looks like a younger version of herself, starkly dark hair, caramel skin, limbs that are long and clumsy. There's something disconcertingly sexual about her gaze, the way her legs lock, one over the other.

"Okay, Barbie," her daughter is saying to herself, moving the doll through the water, "time to take a dip." Najla laughs at her own joke.

"Is she a mermaid?" Mazna asks gamely. Her daughter looks at her suspiciously.

"Why do you want to know?" she says, dunking the Barbie under the water. The golden hair fans out like silk. "You don't like playing."

"That's not true," Mazna cries. She leans forward, and a little wine sloshes out of her mug. Oops. She's tipsy. "I love games."

"No, you don't!"

"I do!"

They eye each other, a stalemate. Mazna suddenly remembers the night her mother had been waiting for her in the closet. The discomfort of performing for her. She crouches near the tub. "You want to see one of my games?" she asks quietly. Najla nods.

Mazna tosses her hair. "Why, yes, David," she says loudly, startling even herself. Her voice is crackling and brittle. Najla looks at her with interest. She lets the Barbie drown. "That's right. When I first heard about the role, I drove for the better part of an afternoon to the audition." There's a pause and Mazna nods at her imaginary companion to her left. "Yes, I lived in Blythe at the time . . . I *know,* how random, right? I told my husband and kids — hi, honey —" She waves at the shampoo bottles. Looking a little concerned, Najla waves back. "I told them I just had a feeling . . . That's right, a few months later we were all in LA."

Mazna gestures for Najla to tip her head back. She rubs the shampoo into her hair until it froths. "I found the accent to be the most difficult. We filmed on location in Paris and Prague. To be honest," she says, laughing, "I only ever practiced the accent on cabdrivers in Europe." She scrubs Najla's head harder, and the girl lets out a sharp cry as Mazna's fingers tighten.

There are two little half-moons of blood where her fingernails dug in, near her daughter's temple.

"Oh! I'm sorry, baby." She covers her mouth. "I'm so sorry." She reaches out to pet her head, but Najla glides away like a cat.

❈

In May of 1995, the phone rings in the middle of the night, and Idris shoots up like an arrow and leaves the room to answer it. Mazna waits with her heart pounding. They still haven't had a single conversation. *Not Baba, not Baba,* she prays. She hears Idris's footsteps return. He looks dazed in the doorway.

"My mother is dead," he says.

The two of them wake up the children with their wailing. Mazna is surprised by her own sobbing, the deep sorrow rustled up in her — that floral soap, her perfect hair — that night gathering her children into her arms like flowers as Idris explains the heart attack. Hana was the closest thing she'd known to a movie star, the most glamorous person she'd ever met. Dead. Issa had found her naked on the bathroom floor. The indignity of it made her weep harder.

"I'm sorry, Baba." Ava hugs her father. She turns to Mazna and kisses her forehead. "You too, Momsy."

For a strange, depersonalized second, Mazna wonders if Ava is the true wife here. Her daughter is so unknowable, disappearing every day into the foreign world of American high school (just visiting the school during parent-teacher conferences makes Mazna anxious, that smell of microwaved food and dirty socks, senior boys laughing loudly like grown men) and reemerging to do homework in their kitchen. She speaks to her father now in murmuring tones, absently brushing away her own tears. Ava is the changeling, fatherless and not knowing it, and yet also the nucleus of their family. Mazna wants to kiss her hands and apologize for everything, for avoiding her eyes for a decade now, since the girl turned six and became unmistakably his.

"Thank you, *habibti*," she says formally, as though Ava is a stranger, but when her daughter hugs her, she bursts into tears again. Everything is terrible and Hana is dead and her eldest's arms are sturdy with youth. She cries and cries and her daughter murmurs, and something changes, a light warmth spreads through her, and she looks around the bed with wonder. Her family. She remembers Kit's words: *A small atonement*. This is her debt and her repayment, the life she has made for herself. (She'll feel it again when her mother dies and then, years from now, her father. She'll feel it when Najla performs onstage for the first time, and she recognizes what her daughter has. When — the same afternoon — she realizes her son doesn't have it, and so she takes him out for burgers and ice cream and buys him a beautiful watch, because she sees how difficult it will be for him. When, years from now, she watches the stream of Syrian refugees flooding Beirut on the television, sees the shabby tents, the fancy women complaining of their smell, a loyalty she'd long assumed gone will kick inside her like a child: *We don't choose what we belong to. What claims us.*)

Idris meets her gaze and tilts his head, his eyes red and small, and she nods, and he hugs her across their children. You soften in the end because they're all you have. It's not right and it's not what you wanted, but here you are.

She'll never tells Idris this, but she'd laughed when the director told her. She'd laughed so hard, she'd scared him. He'd asked if she needed water, and when she said no, he'd gotten her a bottle anyway, and they'd both sat on the curb, Najla now kicking the can with abandon.

I really needed that, she finally told him, wiping her eyes.

His face softens. *Listen.* He'd fished a business card from his wallet. *I'm working on a couple of projects. There's a role in one of them.* It was a middle-aged woman, he explained, a widow. A firecracker. He gave her his card and she promised she would call, then he walked to his car and drove away, and Mazna stayed in the parking lot under the plain Californian sun. Her daughter stepped on the can. Mazna bit the corner of the business card. There was an embossed star on the back. For a moment, her mind wandered into it, the drives to Los Angeles, the thick script, running lines with Ava.

Finally, she dusted her knees off. *Let's go,* she told Najla and grabbed her elbow when the girl began to complain. They went inside and bought a box of Ho Hos and a bag of Ruffles chips, and years later, it would be one of the girl's earliest memories — the sun-bleached parking lot, a friend of her mother's, so much sugar she felt sick afterward. Mazna drove them home quietly. It was over. She would never be Audrey or Vivian. She let the card drop from her fingers into the open mouth of the car window.

❈

In Idris's arms later that night, after the children have gone back to their bedrooms, she shuts her eyes and sees the House. Her mother's unhappy mouth. The airport south of Beirut. It's the trips that make it worse, the hot summers in Beirut, places of her youth. Walking the same streets. Beirut was where her life had cracked like a thin ankle, neatly splitting into before and after.

But the past remains the past, Beirut the thumbtack that holds it together. She thinks of Zakaria on the veranda, the city alive before them; her life was in front of her, it was bottled in that city like a captured insect. Mocking her with her past. The memories wreck her. When Idris breathes into her neck that night, their bodies interlocking in grief, she tells him she'll go to the funeral, of course, but after that, she's never returning to Beirut.

Part

V

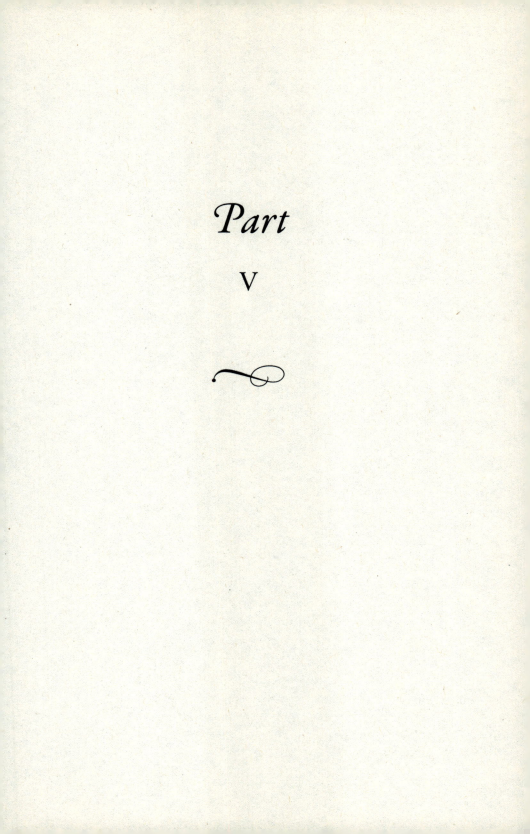

Deus Ex Machina

WHEN AVA TEACHES undergrad biology, she always tells her students to imagine that each cell has been programmed with its own self-destruct button. Cancer, missing chromosomes, assassin molecules, every organism comes into existence with a set of codes to undo it. This is what she thinks about when she swallows Naj's pill, a chalky aftertaste on her tongue. The act is impulsive, her body still thrumming from Emily's voice — *He lied, he lied, my marriage is over* — a kick as close to panic as reprieve. The pill goes down. Almost immediately, she regrets it.

"I regret this," she says aloud.

"Me too," Harp says.

"Such theatrics." Naj splits a second pill and swallows another half, then pockets the other. "Such small, small lives."

The drug doesn't work for what feels like forever. They pile into a cab, giggling nervously, exchanging updates.

"My hands feel tingly," Mimi reports.

"Is this going to give me a heart attack?" Harp asks Naj, who buries her face in her hands.

"Can I just say" — her voice muffled — "how much I regret wasting good drugs on you three?"

"I've never been great on hallucinogens," Mimi says.

"This isn't about you," Naj says sharply. "It's about Avey having a good night." Her sister hooks her arm through hers. Ava can feel her trying to catch her eye, but she keeps looking out the window. There is a hurt growing, like a bruise, in her chest, but if she sits entirely still, it passes.

"I think I feel something," she says, and just like that, she does, a whisper in the back of her head, as though someone is stroking her hair with long fingernails.

"Hey, we were young once," Harp tells Naj. "I was a teenager. I did the drugs."

"You must've worn Keds," Naj says, and this strikes them all as hilarious.

❈

The bar is at the edge of Gemmayzeh, past a row of modern apartment buildings and a Maronite church. Naj had said it was a small dive bar, so of course the nightclub they enter is loud and disheveled and cavernous.

There is a long, dark hallway and at the end, Naj twirls around like a girl in a movie and grins at them. "You're going to *hate* this place!" she shouts gleefully, and the hairs on Ava's arms stand up as though she is already remembering this moment, her sister's messy hair and grin. *I don't know any of them,* Ava thinks suddenly. Not Nate or Mimi or Naj. She imagines herself inside an igloo and knows the image is borrowed from some film or book but can't pinpoint where, so she keeps imagining it until it's too sad. She wants her mother. She wants Zina.

Their foursome is pressed between the crowd. The space is large and narrow in certain spots. In another incarnation, it could've been a garage or a storage space — concrete floors and walls and four massive pillars, one at each corner of the room. It looks like coked-up art students were given an hour to decorate it. The music is aggressively loud, bass-heavy and animated; tons of Christmas lights circle the pillars; ornaments dangle from the ceiling. There's a gunmetal-blue evil eye graffitied on one of the walls. The DJ table overlooks the partygoers, a brunette wearing sunglasses and a white bikini playing music.

Naj says something to Mimi, who repeats it to Harp. "They said to tell the bartender you know Naj!" Harp shouts to Ava.

"Do I have to?" Ava shouts back and they both laugh.

"Your sister is like some Mafiosa." They watch Naj kiss the bartender, then one of the waiters. From the corner, she waves toward a group, and Jo appears from the crowd, a comely woman by his side.

"I was just thinking," Ava says, lowering her voice, Harp leaning in to catch it, "that I don't know anyone. This whole summer, we've been sleeping under the same roof, but it feels like we're all lying. Nate is with Emily right now. My mother's lying about her past. Who knows what Baba's been doing."

Harp is quiet. Then: "There's something I've wanted to say."

"What?"

"I'm not sure it's my place."

There's a pinch behind Ava's eyes. "Tell me."

"Do you think that maybe your parents could use some privacy? That they're owed that?" She looks hesitant. "It's been a weird summer, I get that. Everyone's tense. Your father's hell-bent on selling the house. But it seems like the three of you are so fixated on uncovering your parents' past. It just feels — I don't know. Intrusive?"

"You don't think they're lying?" Ava feels an unexpected irritation. Harp has been on the inside for a few weeks. Even she has an opinion now.

"I think people deserve to have their secrets."

Ava feels that same shiver from earlier. There's the slightest flicker of blue light near Harper's temple. The drug is hitting her in earnest.

"Maybe you guys are just using their past as a way of —" Harp shrugs, but Ava gets the rest.

"What do you think we're avoiding?"

Harp averts her eyes. "I can't answer that for you."

They're rescued by Naj, carrying a plastic cup in her teeth and a beer bot-

tle in each hand, Jo and his friend behind her. "You two are such wallflowers."
She gives them each a beer. "You remember Jo?" she says slyly to Ava like she
always does.

Jo shakes his head. "Don't ever tell Najla anything," he says, kissing Ava's
cheek. His lips are warm and tickling, and for the hundredth time she remembers Emily's voice.

"I don't," she replies. They smile at each other, the undercurrent of flirtation. It's always been put on by her, performative, but tonight she feels a
rare pull. She wants to be terrible. Naj introduces her to the woman, someone
named Fee.

"It's nice to meet you," Fee says, and Ava replies the same, but her attention is split. The shiver is mushrooming, and there's a nest in her throat, and
she keeps swallowing. The woman and Naj huddle near the bar, gesturing as
they talk. They both seem so unhappy, Ava thinks, and the thought surprises
her. There's something in the body language that is familiar, in their hunched
shoulders, their bent heads, a weird buzzing in the back of her mind, like
the beginning of a song, but she can't seem to catch it. Mimi and Harp have
started dancing, and Ava can tell from the way Harp is moving that she's starting to feel it too.

People deserve to have their secrets. Jo asks if she'd like some weed, but she
says no, then pushes through the crowd for the bathroom. Time elongates and
starts to vibrate, and Ava sits on the toilet reading the graffiti. Much of it is in
Arabic. It feels like an hour or ten minutes, and she stays in the bathroom for a
long time, unable to pee. In the hallway, she runs into the woman, Naj's friend.
Her eyes are puffy.

"Hey," Ava says, then regrets it. She has nothing to follow up with.

"I'm okay," Fee says. She tries to smile.

"Where's Naj?" Ava cranes her neck for her sister.

Fee gives her a sad look. "It was nice to meet you," she echoes from earlier.
She pushes past into the bathroom.

The only person Ava can spot is Harp, sitting at the bar. She's fanning
herself with a napkin and looks out of place. At the sight of Ava, she waves
her over a little desperately. Harp's face is red. With her pale hair and flushed

cheeks, she looks as American as apple pie, as one of the girls from the Little House books. "I feel sick," she admits. There's an abandoned drink nearby and she scoops out some dirty ice to hold to her neck. "I should go home."

"Where's Mimi?"

"He went off with Naj." She shakes her head. "I can't believe I took that pill. Thirty-five years old and I'm still trying to look cool."

"I know. Me too. My head feels terrible." Harp's eyes are bloodshot. "Should I get him?"

She shakes her head. "I'll order an Uber," she says. "All summer he's been sulking like a teenager." She waves around her. "This shit is his medicine. I should leave him to it." There's an edge to her words, a saltier Harper. Ava recognizes it from nights out, a cousin's wedding in California, Harper getting nasty after several vodkas. It makes Ava like her more. She imagines a little Harp, angry and gutsy, nested within this one, like a Russian doll.

"I think you're right," Ava says. "What you said about secrets."

The bartender puts a bowl of nuts and some salted carrot slices in front of them. There are beads of water on the carrots. Ava eats one and it's good, lemony. She imagines one of the thousands of teeming microbes that wriggle from sea trout into the ocean, ultimately getting sucked up into sewage and gulped through the intestines of the city, then merging with other microbes and multiplying, whirling through the underground pipes, plopping from the faucet onto the carrot. She crunches.

Ava thinks of the mug slipping from her mother's hand, the blue glass on the veranda. In elementary school, she'd sometimes slip into her parents' bedroom in the middle of the night, not to sleep with them, but just to watch her mother sleep. She always slept neatly — her body a single comma, a pillow tucked under her arm — while her father was flung across the mattress like a mess. When she got older, Ava would sometimes encounter a problem while reading novels — no matter what the era or description was, certain characters became her mother in her mind's eye: Mazna wearing a corset, Mazna raising champagne at Gatsby's party. She was a stranger, which meant she could become anybody. How had that worked its way into Ava's DNA, changing her, making her more watchful, suspicious, grudging from afar?

The bartender brings more carrots. They glitter under the lights. Her mother had knocked a glass out of Zina's hand when they first arrived in Beirut. *The water,* she'd cried. *If you don't drink it every two years, you won't build up immunity.* Ava had never heard that statistic in all her years of academia. And yet she believed her mother; she always did. Every embellishment, every lie about the world or their family, her mother worked on them like prayers, turned over and over like polished river stones in her mouth, the tasting rendering them a truth.

Harper leaves, and Ava can't find her siblings. In the center of the crowd, Jo's bright white shirt flashes between people, like a little sun. The partygoers dance like their city is full of trash and fire and electricity cuts — wild, loose hair, flailing limbs — and Ava hates her Orientalist thoughts. The nest in her throat is dry now. She can't drink enough water. The bartender mishears her and gives her a vodka and 7 Up and she drinks that too, feeling an alien electricity in her fingertips as the two drugs meet. Her phone buzzes.

Come dance.

The caller is unknown, but she knows who it is. Naj must've given Jo her cell number while she and Mimi went off to do God knows what. Ava sneaks a glance at the crowd, but she can't see him. Another buzz.

I know you haven't forgotten how.

The phrasing makes her blush. She rises, a little unsteady, and walks as fast as she can to the door, ducking behind an exiting couple. She jogs to the corner, where the street gets quieter. There's a small *dikaneh* with a neon chicken sign, a couple of men smoking outside. They're her father's age but still snap their eyes up and down her body, and she feels that dizziness again, the drug making little flickers of light ricochet as she turns her head. She stops at the next building, empty, boarded up, and pulls out her phone.

It rings once. Twice. It seems like a lifetime ago when she called alone in her bedroom, the phone ringing, her breath stopping at the sound of the woman's voice. Then her own voice, ragged, yelling for Naj. Five rings. Ava waits. Finally, she hears the click and freezes. *Yes,* she thinks.

"Hello," Emily's voice says for the third time.

Ava's mind blanks. There's a plastic grocery bag hanging from a tree across the street. Behind it, the word *Al-mustaqbal* is graffitied on the building wall in Arabic. *The future.* She doesn't remember there being graffiti here in her youth. But there must've been.

"Hello! This isn't funny." There's a breeze and the plastic bag rustles like a dress.

"Room service, you tragic bitch," Ava says savagely, and hangs up.

❖

The men at the chicken place seem wary of her. She doesn't blame them. Her eyes are narrowing of their own volition, and she hears her jaw pop. She buys gum and water, then drinks the whole bottle in front of the store. Another murmur of light floats in her periphery, glittery and perfect. She wants to go swimming. In Portland a woman half her size is naked, her nipples pressed against Nate; he's moaning in that breathy way that has become ancillary to her, like tying the garbage bags left to right, another symptom of their ordinary life.

Her phone feels warm in her pocket. She goes to Jo's texts, types quickly. *Come to the neon chicken place.* But even looking at the word *Come* makes her blush, so she deletes it, just texts, *Neon chicken place.*

It takes him a perfect amount of time to show up. Long enough for her to brace herself and chew some gum and breathe. His shirt is ripped in the sleeve and he saunters up to her like he owns the city, his lanky limbs swinging cheerfully. She almost cries at the sight of him, so happy and untethered. There's a song blasting from his cell phone.

"The thing about trance music is you have to half ignore it," he calls casually to her, as though they are in the middle of a conversation.

"You're weird," she says. He reminds her of her sister, which is fucked up but also strangely hot, everything sexy and glittery, hangovers and druggy nights and music.

"Good evening," he says to the men, then takes her by the elbow. They walk to the corner of the street, where there's a little bench facing nothing.

She lets herself lean against him as they walk. The music vibrates between their bodies like an animal. He sets his cell down and takes her arm and snaps her toward him, and she surprises herself by leaning at the right moment; her hips move against his as they dance ridiculously in the empty street. "I knew you wanted to dance," he says. He's high too, she can tell from his pupils, but it seems more relaxed on him.

"I didn't," she counters. "I still don't."

"You don't, huh?" He shakes his hips, then abruptly twirls her, and she falls against his chest, palms first. She lands a little hard, and he lets out an *oof,* which makes her laugh. "So what do you want to do?"

Ava meets his gaze. Every cell is bristling at attention. "I don't know," she says. "I'm the tourist."

There's a silence he breaks by laughing. He's handsome. So dark and hairy and lanky, an exact replica of the boys she harbored secret crushes on in high school. Jo stretches his arms above his head like a yogi. She steps into him, and all the men of her twenties come rushing back, the flirting, the anticipation, the pre-kiss. A guy who knows nothing about her, hasn't seen her shit herself on the delivery table at St. Luke's or scream about paper-towel brands or gain twenty pounds. The image of Freckles flashes in her mind. Her polished toe-nails at the Hamptons party. The miracle isn't cheating. The miracle is that people aren't doing it all the time.

"You're no tourist," he says and kisses her, soft and young and close-mouthed. He's being respectful, she thinks, which makes her want to cry. She can feel his erection like glass against her thigh, and it confuses her, makes her feel aroused and tender at the same time. For one second, just to be bad, she cups it, and his grip on her arm tightens, and there it is — dangerous and luscious, the sex everyone is always on the brink of, panties tossed on a street bench, sex in a stranger's doorway. It's reassuring to know it's still there.

They pull apart. It's impossible to know who pulls away first, but there's something warm and amicable in the air between them; he hums as he resumes his stretching. She watches him pee. He turns away from her slightly, but he's exposed enough that she can see. He is striking and young, sleek like Naj.

"Can I ask you something?"

He shakes his dick. "Sure."

"Do you love my sister?"

"Ah." He sits next to her. There's tinsel in his hair, but it feels strange to touch him now. The moment has passed. This, too, is recognizable from her youth — how a sexual encounter could suddenly click shut, like a bathroom drawer, the same person whose face was buried between your legs now politely ordering a cab, a stranger once again. Jo doesn't look at her. "That question."

"Everyone is in love with her," Ava confirms.

"She's a force of nature." His voice is strangely neutral.

"So that's a yes." Her ears are burning. She feels like she's naked and needs to cover herself. The drug is making her second-guess everything. "But then . . ." She hesitates, not sure how to ask. "Why not — why haven't you two —"

Jo looks at her. "Don't be jealous of her, Ava."

"I'm not," she says, but her throat is burning like she might cry.

"Everyone is," he says. "But it's not easy for her."

She thinks for a second. "Who's that Fee girl?" she finally asks.

He doesn't answer. "She wrote a song about you. Naj did. We played it a few times, but I think she lost her nerve to show you."

"I didn't know that." Ava shakes her head.

"I'll send it to you. It was called 'Decade.'"

"'Decade'?"

"Yeah. Like —" He starts humming, his foot tapping. He sings, *"You leave every room I enter, you're June when I'm in winter, you leave every decade I enter."*

"I never heard it." She's crying now, a little, but it's dark and she wipes her face before he stops singing.

There's a long silence. "It's a good song," he finally says.

❖

They don't kiss again. For a few minutes — five, fifteen — she leans against him, breathing him in. He smells like sweat and pistachios. She wants to talk about Nate, about the invisible bruise in her chest, but the streetlight hits the trees in such a pretty way, and she keeps forgetting what she wants to say, a vertiginous feeling that stops only if she focuses on the light. They finally walk back to the party, and this time the men greet Jo back, a merriment in their voices; this too is familiar, the universal back-patting of men. As they near the club, familiar voices drift toward her.

Across the street, Mimi and Naj are screaming at each other. She can see Naj's rings glint as she gestures.

"I'll be a minute," she tells Jo at the door.

"You sure?" He hasn't seen Naj yet.

She nods. "We'll dance." As soon as he disappears inside, she rushes across the street. Her siblings look furious, their arguing fast and intertwined, so snarled it takes her a minute to figure out who is saying what.

"I never needed your handout!"

"For the thousandth time, it wasn't a fucking handout!"

"It was!"

"Fine! You know what? It was. And you should've taken it! Because then, maybe, just maybe, you wouldn't be burying all this resentment, then taking it out on me by *burning my fucking apartment down!*"

"Guys." Ava is dismayed at how soft her voice is, but it interrupts them. Naj turns to her, a wild-eyed expression on her face.

"Did you know?" she snaps. "Since you two always tell each other everything?"

"I — what?"

"Did you know?"

Ava touches her sister's shoulder. It's sweaty. "Know what?" She faces her sister, who studies her.

"Harper," Naj says, her expression ugly. "On her way out, you know what she said to me?"

Ava shakes her head. She wants to go back to the bench. She needs the tree light again.

"He set my apartment on fire!"

"That is *wildly* misleading." Mimi looks desperate. "My cigarette must've set it off while I was sleeping, that's all."

"My God," Ava says. She remembers the way Harper looked earlier when she was talking about Mimi, hard and set.

"I lost half my closet," Naj wails. "My guitar, my favorite painting."

"You can afford another one," Mimi mutters.

This silences them all. Naj shakes her head. "You jealous fuck," she says sadly.

"I'm not — I'm not *jealous*," Mimi sputters, "of your bullshit." He turns to Ava like a lifeline, but she finds she cannot speak.

"Exactly," Naj finally says.

They're silent for several minutes. Her sister sniffles. Then:

"I took those music lessons first," Mimi says suddenly. His voice sounds hollow.

"This might come as a shock to you." Her sister's face is tired. "But I was five years old, Marwan. It wasn't some calculated career move. I wanted to be like my older brother."

"Don't pretend like you've ever cared about me."

This strikes a nerve even Ava can feel. "Mimi —" she starts to say, but Naj is already kicking the tire of a nearby car, and Ava can tell it hurts. She reaches out to touch her sister, then curbs her hand. Naj is turning toward their brother in fury.

"Who calls you from all the way across the world? Who invites you to shows? Who tells you —" Her voice drops and there's something quiet and brutal about it. "Mimi. Who tells you everything? Mimi, *everything*." The word is hoarse, a magic code, and Mimi's face collapses. It's like he's been punched. What happens next stuns Ava.

Her brother lets out a sob. He moves, his face stricken, toward Naj, so quickly Ava winces at first, but when he reaches their little sister, he embraces her, so hard she lets out a huff of air, and lifts her slightly; Naj pushes him, kicking his shins, her thin shoulders straining, but Mimi doesn't let go, holding her tightly, whispering something to her, and Ava is remembering a game they used to play, her and Mimi with Naj, Ava and Mimi pretending they were asleep so Naj would giggle in delight when she woke them.

"What do you mean, *everything*?" Ava's tongue is thick.

Naj peeks at her over Mimi's shoulder. Her eyes are damp and scared and Ava knows what she is going to say the millisecond before she says it. "I'm gay."

They are all suspended in the moment together. Ava's first thought: *Oh.* It makes sense, but she's not sure why. There's something at the edge of her subconscious, flickering like a light, something about Naj's perpetual singleness, her decision to stay in Beirut, the intensity of her lyrics. It's like watching a year march by, and Ava is trying to think of the right thing to say. At Rayan's school, they had a meeting about this, about questions and comments if your child comes out. *Say you love them no matter what,* the teacher had encouraged them. *Ask what they need from you in terms of support.* But this isn't Brooklyn and Naj isn't a second-grader and Ava says the first thing that comes to mind. "Baby Naj," she says. "Is that why you have that stupid haircut?"

"Jesus," Mimi says.

They laugh so hard someone opens the window above to tell them to shut up and fuck their mothers back to America.

They leave abruptly, without saying goodbye to anyone, and Ava is too shy to text Jo. She wonders if he's searching for her on the dance floor, if he's forgotten about it. In the cab, she leans against the car door, wondering if her lipstick is smeared, if her siblings can smell the adultery on her, but they're too busy together, talking over each other about the past. Ava suspects cocaine, but she's too tired to ask. The cab drops them off at the corner of their street, and they tiptoe into the courtyard, sneaking around like when they were teenagers, only no, they never got to be teenagers at the same time, the three of them too far apart in age. One leaving the decade just as the other entered.

"You have to listen to this song," Naj is whispering to her brother, playing something fast and trippy-sounding on her phone. Her face is tear-stained and puffy, but she starts dancing in front of the house.

"It sounds like Hendrix," Mimi says.

"Exactly, but with some electronica over it."

"God, I wish I had my guitar," he says mournfully.

"*Yeah,*" Naj says pointedly, "me too." But the bite is gone, and she plays another song, then another, and she and Mimi are singing along and Ava's head is spinning; she's remembering the first time Nate kissed her neck, remembering an old family trip with her parents, decades ago, when Naj fell in Joshua Tree and cried until Ava sang the Candy Mountain song for her, the entire song from start to finish, while her mother dabbed peroxide on her cuts. She understands something.

"That woman," she calls out. "From the club tonight." Her sister stops dancing.

"Yeah."

That's all she says. Then the music starts up again, and Naj is gyrating, and for the first time Ava sees how much her sister looks like her, the wide eyes, though Ava's are darker. How ordinary she is made by love. And one realization opens the door for another, the date on the videotape, that faraway summer — *July 1978* — the way people used to sing and mourn at the same time in the old days. They probably still do. In places of God. In places without money. In the refugee camps. Naj extends her arm and for the second time that night, Ava rises to dance. She thinks of the woman, Zakaria's mother, the memorial tomorrow. The phone number is still in her pocket. She doesn't believe in heaven, but it seems impossible that her grandparents aren't watching this. *The lemonade springs, where the bluebird sings.* Zakaria's mother had seemed so sad. The fingernails-shiver is stronger now, making her scalp prickle, the drug rushing blood to her palms and temples, something knocking against her like a door — her mother's face on the veranda, her mother telling them to stop the tape, the young man's dark eyes. She shudders and exhales and lets herself see it.

Naj wants to see the children. Mimi has fallen asleep on the couch unceremoniously, and Naj is tugging at her sister's arm as they stumble through the house. Ava no longer feels high or drunk or anything but a singular, unadorned clarity. The air is cool in the house. The strap of her sandal is digging into her ankle. Near the couch, Naj knocks over one of the picture frames and dissolves into giggles. A minute later, Merry appears in the entryway, squinting and wearing a hairnet.

"This is how we honor your grandfather," she says dryly. Ava helps her fix the frame.

"I'm taking her to bed," she says.

Merry gives her a hard look. "Take yourself to bed."

Down the hallway, Naj slips her head into the children's room before Ava can stop her. "Najla, stop!" she hisses. Naj holds a finger to her lips.

"Look at them," she whispers.

Ava looks. Her son has flung a leg over the covers in his sleep. She again sees Nate in him, the sloping cheeks, the winged eyebrows. In the other bed, Zina sleeps demurely. She feels a strange, powerful desire to wake her daughter, the same thing she used to feel as a little girl watching her mother sleep. Her mother was always different with her than with her siblings, something wary. Ava's mind tinkles with mathematics. There is a melancholia to numbers. They are nonnegotiable. She will never be the same age at the same time as her mother and daughter. This strikes her as unspeakably sad. The day will come when her daughter too is thirty-nine, but by then she'll have moved on, drifted to another decade, another set of worries. *I'm always leaving the decade.* If only Zina were her age now. If only Mazna were. If only she could tell them everything.

"I'm about to pass out," Naj says.

Ava guides her sister to the other room, where Harp is already asleep. Naj collapses next to her. There's an old coverlet, faded blue flowers, that's been there since childhood.

"I love them," her sister mumbles. "Zina is my spirit animal."

"They love you," Ava says, her mind racing. She wonders if she's having a heart attack. She imagines the pill laced with PCP, arsenic, fentanyl constricting her arteries. Her sister sighs. "Ten months," Ava whispers.

"Mmm."

"Everyone says nine months, but it's actually ten."

"Mmm."

"I was born in April, Naj."

The truth dances for Ava, like a slide under a microscope. The label on the video: *July 1978.* She was born in April. In California. Her parents married in September. Everything is mathematics.

"We have to go to the camps," she whispers. "We have to see that woman."

Naj is already asleep.

There are certain things we do instinctively, an orchestra of cells waking up and coordinating themselves. The way her sister's fingers knew how to curve against the violin's neck all those years ago, her ear acting of its own accord, catching and replicating the notes expertly. Ava wasn't there, but she's heard about it dozens of times since, mostly from her father, how the music teacher seemed shaken. *Like she'd seen a ghost. She kept telling me my daughter was a true talent!* It was how her brother knew when a baking crust was about to burn, how her mother knew when a plant shoot was going to bloom, how her father knew what to whisper to organs. It's in her life too. The time Zina had choked on a Lego and Ava had known what to do, scooping the toy out of her throat without any training. That split second while Nate was in the bathroom on their second date and she'd blown the nearby candle out, sweeping her hair across the smoke as though she'd been told to. The tingle before the river card in poker. She feels that calmness now, her body acting as its own agent. She goes to her bedroom and quietly changes into a long dress, then pees and gargles mouthwash. There is some leftover cold coffee in the kitchen, and she drinks it straight from the carafe.

The rental car is an Audi and she forgets to change shifts, like she's been forgetting all summer. She props the address on the dashboard and pulls up Google Maps on her phone. It's a small miracle that someone mapped the unnameable streets of Beirut, sketched even the smallest alleyways. She likes the thought of the city being captured in this way; she could open the map in Brooklyn, and Beirut would be waiting for her, unpacked and christened. It makes the place feel both more and less real.

"Turn left," the phone chants. "In one hundred meters, turn left."

It's dawn. Ava can feel the remnants of the drug in her fingertips and her bottom lip, brief electricity. She drives slowly though the light-stained streets. If she were pulled over and given a Breathalyzer, she'd fail, but she won't be pulled over and she doubts there's a single Breathalyzer in the entire country. The city is different at this hour, quieter, prehistoric somehow, with the hulking palm trees and undulating sea; the older buildings appear abandoned. When she reaches downtown, she sees some early protesters setting up; there is smoke drifting from an old fire. She drives past a building with another evil eye on the side of it — a serial graffiti artist, a pleasing thought, someone prowling all over Lebanon to protect it from *7asad* — and thinks of Jo, how he'd gripped her arm.

She presses the phone with one hand, goes to her recent calls. She clicks Nate's cell. It rings and rings, and finally the voicemail beeps.

"I don't care, Nate," she says into the receiver. "You can fuck her later. Just pick up. I need to talk to you."

It's near Saida that she begins to panic, the calmness giving way, as though matching the chaotically colored town. The moneyed skyscrapers of downtown Beirut are gone; this is poor country, ramshackle houses overlooking the water, stretches of ugly huts selling fruit and cheap furniture. This part of the country is already awake and working even though it's barely seven. She wipes her palms on her dress. The phone tells her to turn right, then left. She has arrived.

There are different kinds of camps. The ones that get flooded in January, with cloth walls and UN lettering — they're the newer ones, Syrians from Homs and Aleppo. The unlucky ones without electricity or running water. The older camps are depressing in their own way. She's visited only twice, once at sixteen and once during her trip with Nate. Those camps are all Palestinian, and anchored in a way that's deeply gloomy — there's no pretense of impermanence here. The tents aren't tents at all; they're oatmeal-colored buildings, concrete exteriors with shredded awnings. The families have been here for generations now. She is ashamed driving inside, ashamed talking to a man smoking outside, who tells her where to go. He seems excited she is here, points her in the direction of the apartment address. The camp is like a tiny town, a new country.

And yet. The drive took all of forty minutes. She'd been so close all summer.

Her hands have stopped shaking. The ink has run a bit and she initially reads the seven as an eight, but eventually she pulls in front of the right building. Ava parks the car and exhales slowly. The car starts heating up the second she kills the engine. It's going to be a long, hot day.

The apartment is on the second floor. When she reaches the second landing, she sees something: There's already someone at the door. Not ringing the doorbell.

Ava recognizes her. The hunch of her back. The plain brown ponytail. Black blazer.

"My God," she says aloud, and before the woman has even turned, Ava speaks her name.

"You found the address," Sara says, more comment than question. She doesn't look surprised to see her.

❖

They stare at each other for a long moment. Her aunt looks different somehow in the dirty hallway, younger, her face beaded with sweat.

"I was born in April," she says.

Sara's mouth is a small *O*. "She told you?" she whispers. "Mazna told you?"

Ava thinks of the police-procedural shows she watched obsessively in her twenties, how the detective in the interrogation room invariably answered something like that with *No, but you just did.* She shakes her head.

"You knew her address all along." She gestures at the front door. As though commanded, it opens.

The woman from the videos, from the street corner and the old albums, stands there. Zakaria's mother. Hayat. She crosses her arms. Her face is tired but, like Sara's, unsurprised. It's like she's been expecting them all night.

"Well," she says. "I guess I've been waiting forty years to hear what you two have to say. Come in."

❖

The apartment is humble, a beige sofa covered in plastic and old-fashioned lace doilies everywhere. The room smells like a thousand cigarettes. There's some Qur'anic decoration hanging above the door, words too calligraphied in Arabic for Ava to decipher. There's a large framed photograph of the hand-some young man from the videos. Hayat kisses her fingertip and presses it to the glass, and Sara does the same.

"How did he die?" Ava is surprised to hear herself ask this but more surprised that none of them have asked all summer.

"An accident," Sara says immediately.

The woman grunts. "Your father and my boy were involved with bad people during the war. Those people found my boy."

Ava can't think of a reply. The woman's matter-of-factness unsettles her.

"My goodness, Birdie. It's been years," Hayat says, turning to Sara.

Her aunt looks like she might cry. "I meant to come."

"Forty — no, forty-two years. You still look about sixteen and skinny as a minute."

Ava turns to her aunt, mouth agape. "You haven't seen each other in over forty years?"

"Well, now," Hayat says. "She came to Zuzu's funeral. You remember that, honey?" she asks gently. "We had to get you a new dress; you cried through the first one."

Sara nods.

"And every year," Hayat tells Ava, "around Eid and the new year and my birthday, a package miraculously appears on my doorstep. Filled with fruit and chocolates and the most beautiful *tatriz.*"

"You knew?" Sara looks astonished.

"Honey, who else would it have been? You see any angels around here? Either you or your mama, and when God took her soul to rest and the packages kept coming, I knew." There is already a pot of tea, and Hayat pours them each a cup, adding two spoonfuls of sugar without asking.

"You're here about the memorial?" she says. "I can't go. God rest his soul." She turns to Sara. "You understand. I haven't stepped foot in that house since —"

"I understand." Sara's voice is hoarse.

Hayat looks from Sara's face to Ava's. "Seems like you two have some words for each other."

"I don't have anything to say to her," Ava says roughly. She can't look at her aunt. *She knew, she knew, she knew.*

"Ava."

"Don't."

Hayat chuckles. "I expect you will."

There is a long, taut silence. Ava sips her tea. It's too sweet but she doesn't say anything. The woman's hands are calloused. She wants her to like her.

There are photographs on the mantel, dark, black-eyed women and fat children. Ava was always the darker one in the family. Bedouin, her father called her. Her father.

"You knew my mother?" Ava says uncertainly. She still can't look at Sara.

Hayat shakes her head. "Never met her. I didn't have to. Something changed that summer. I could see it in Zakaria; he became even quieter than usual. Mopey. Once that Dee woman he worked for mentioned something to me, said there was some Syrian girl visiting, that she was spending a lot of time with the boys. Dee said she was dating Idris but that she and Zakaria seemed —" The woman pauses. "Well. I remember how she said it, like it was a joke, like it was all games. People get older, they forget how brutal youth is. How dangerous it can be."

There is the sound of their sipping.

"Three weeks." The words are abrupt. "That's how long before I got a call from your mother, Sara. Telling me Idris was engaged. Some girl from Damascus. She tried to dress it up, saying Idris was finishing his schooling in America, but I knew. It all made sense."

Ava wants her to stop talking. She leans forward to hear more.

"I knew when Idris ran off like that," she says. "The two of them skulking off in the middle of the night to America. Him, I understood. His heart broken for my boy. And he'd always been hungry for America. But her?" Here she looks directly at Ava. "What would she be running from?"

"You knew," Sara says.

"It was just a thought for a long time. But then I got your letter, Sara. About your father passing. The mail here is terrible. I got it months later. I say to myself, *I'll just go by the house. See if you're there.* And I see this young man. And you." Ava squirms. "You don't look like him so much."

"A minor blessing," Sara says. She looks like she might cry.

The woman smiles. "No, you buried it deeper than that. Your mother must be grateful. There isn't much Zakaria, not in a way that's obvious." She waits a beat. "But, my God, if you aren't a spitting image of my sister Halma, God rest her soul."

"Your sister," Ava says faintly. There are different kinds of knowing. Some let the flood in more easily. Her mother slept with some man forty-one years ago and now that man is dead and she is in a living room in Lebanon coming off an ecstasy trip. She thinks of the foyer of her childhood home in California. Her father would always leave his enormous shoes upended. Her father. She'd clomp around the house in them.

"If Mazna didn't tell you," Sara says tentatively, and Ava feels her vision sharpen, the murmuring lights no longer blue but red, "how did you —"

"Who told *you*?" she fires back. "How many years ago, Sara? How many birthdays and anniversaries and visits?"

Sara looks away. Hayat says her name. She lifts her head miserably. "Honey," Hayat says. "You tell this girl everything she needs to know." There is a noise from the street below them, a boy calling. The three of them look toward the window. The voice stops calling.

"I knew her too, you know," Sara finally says. "Mazna. I was this gangly kid, and our lives were pretty quiet. There was the war, of course, but it had always been there. It was only after it was over that I could see what it had done to all of us. I think it was like that for everyone. I remember my mother once said she didn't know anyone who could sleep through the night. Even years later. But at the time, I thought I had this boring life, studying with my friends, sometimes sneaking out for a beer at night. Zakaria —" Her voice catches. "He was my brother too. I had these two older brothers who teased me and taught me to play soccer. I had two brothers.

"Then Mazna arrived. This beautiful stranger. She was from Damascus and she was poor. It's vulgar to say now, but she was, or at least poorer than we were, and she was like this magnet. The whole house changed. My father loved her. Idris and Zakaria spent every second with her."

"You must've hated her," Ava says bitterly. She thinks of the years of tension between her aunt and mother.

Sara looks at her in surprise. "I loved her. I wanted to talk like her, to wear the same clothes. She was kind to me. I fantasized about her being my older sister." She pauses. "She'd ask little questions about Zakaria sometimes when we were alone. I saw the way they looked at each other when no one was paying attention, and I'd see her look at Idris in a different way. Then there was this one weekend Idris got sick. She was sleeping over and we spent the day together, just the two of us. She seemed off. Sad. At the end of it, she went for a walk by herself." She speaks quietly. "I followed her."

It was late summer. The World Cup was over, the heat impossible to escape. Sara ducked between the buildings every time Mazna looked around, seemingly lost, but once they reached the neighborhood, she knew where Mazna was going. Dee's. The bakery was closed. The restaurant across the street had made some fresh fatayer, and Sara ate one, the dough salty and dry, as night fell. The metal grates of the bakery were lowered. She waited. It was hard to remember what she'd felt. Her brother was in love with Mazna, anyone with eyes could see. And Sara loved her brother more than anything. But there was that other, more hidden picture that had been forming all summer, something small and sexy between Mazna and Zakaria, those little stolen moments that Sara caught because nobody was ever watching her.

The restaurant owner started to shut down. It was nearly nine and she needed to go home. But she couldn't help herself — there was a small window into the bakery, above the dumpsters. She crossed the street, pressed her face against the glass. It took only a second. She couldn't look at them longer than that, their bodies twisted like a snake. She ran home like she'd been branded. The house was quiet and her mother was watching television, but she hadn't talked to anyone, just sat on her bed, heart pounding. She could hear her parents moving through the house, her brother coughing — the sound like a knife in her chest — then, one by one, the noises settled. Midnight arrived. She didn't sleep one wink. She was listening, and when the door clicked open, she crept to the hallway. They were kissing. At the landing, she stepped on a creaky wooden board, then ran back to the room.

In the end, she told her brother only about the kissing. She couldn't bring herself to describe the rest. He was devastated and cried like a boy, which made her hate Mazna and Zakaria and herself, but it was more complicated than that. There was a big fight. She could hear it from her bedroom, the boys saying terrible things to each other. It had sent Zakaria back to the camps. The man had always had his pride. He refused to stay another day in the house, and Mazna didn't come back. Sara thought it was all over, and then Zakaria had been killed a week later.

He was supposed to have stayed with them all summer.

For the rest of her life, Sara had reminded herself of that.

"Auntie," Sara says, looking at Hayat.

Hayat nods at her to continue. "Keep going, honey. I can see your color coming back."

"When Zakaria died, I felt terrible. I couldn't stop thinking about your mother, Ava."

"My mother," Ava repeats. Mazna. Mazna, who used to perform on the stage. Mazna, who spent a summer sneaking into Beirut during the war.

Sara wrote Mazna a letter, apologizing, telling her she loved her, that she was her sister and they'd grieve Zakaria together. She never heard back. The next time she saw Mazna, it was at the engagement party, and the other woman was cool and aloof with her, and Sara knew she'd read the letter and didn't feel the same way, that Sara's words had meant nothing to her. Their relationship cracked like an egg and never recovered. Then America. Then the children. Then their lives went where they went. She was the only one who knew about the bakery, that it was more than kissing. She also understood mathematics.

❖

Their tea is cold now. Nobody has finished her cup. Sara is crying quietly, her face in her palms, and Ava is thinking about Mazna watching that VHS tape. Hayat is wiping her eyes.

"Sara." Ava touches her throat as though touching her mother. The anger is gone. Sara knew. Sara had known for years, had been burdened with that secret since girlhood, the way she'd been burdened with Beirut and the war and everything her parents left behind for her. "How did no one figure it out?"

"Mazna said you were premature. I don't know. We were all so far away, her family, her friends. There was no need to question it. Your father was working constantly. He used to tell me sometimes he'd hallucinate, the days were so long."

The shoes in the foyer. Ava's mind skips like a record. "Baba," she pants.

"He never knew." Sara is crying before the words come out. She is rising from her chair, and suddenly Ava is enveloped by her, and Hayat is hugging

Sara, and everyone is crying. "Ave, he never knew." Sara is shaking her shoulders. "I've known that man my whole life, you can see everything on his face. I watched him like a hawk. You lit him up, Ava. You were his everything. You have to believe that."

She doesn't, but she has no choice, so she does.

❖

Outside, in the dazing heat, Sara wipes her face. There's a parcel under her arm, a Tupperware of food Hayat insisted on giving her. Hayat had kissed Ava on the cheek lightly at the door, told her to come back.

"I'll see you at the house," Sara says awkwardly.

"Sara."

Her aunt turns.

"Naj." Ava clears her throat. "You knew about her too. I know you did."

Her aunt's face crumples. "Ava, I couldn't," she says painfully. She opens her mouth to say more.

"I know," Ava says, stopping her. "We deserve our secrets."

❖

She is so tired now, it's a different intoxication. The drive back is longer, the roads congested with traffic and mopeds, and she's sweating through the air conditioning. There's a rank smell coming from somewhere, and it takes her ten minutes to realize it's her, her armpits trickling the alcohol and heat. Her phone buzzes with texts from Naj and her mother; the memorial has started. There isn't enough ice. Can she bring some juice? She drives by four, five supermarkets but doesn't stop at any. Her jaw pops so many times it's sore.

Her father is dead. Her father is a dead Palestinian who was killed in the camps, knifed like an animal. And her father, her *father*-father, the one who speaks with hearts and loves tiramisu, is a few miles away lying to all of them about why he's selling the house, the way her mother has been lying about Zakaria, the way everyone lies about everything. The news is simply too much, an evening saturated to the point of collapse with its kissing and Freckles and music and death, and she can feel her hands begin to shake. It's a strangely familiar feeling, and she finally locates it: childbirth. The digging in, the body splitting in two, the terrible work to do and no other body to do it.

Her phone rings. She puts it on speaker.

"Eleven calls." Nate's voice fills the car. He's angry. "That's the number of missed calls I had, Ava. At two in the morning. And then you turned off your phone. My first thought was the children! I had to call your mother —"

"I can't talk to you right now," Ava says.

"— who then tells me you've been out all night. *Like a street girl.* Her words. Well, maybe mine as well."

"Your first thought." Ava starts to laugh an ugly laugh. There's a McDonald's to her right and she pulls up to park. Rests her head on the steering wheel.

There's a pause. "Ava. I need you to start talking right now."

"It wasn't the children. Your first thought is always about you. Your dick and your vacations and your room service."

"Room — Ava, what are you saying?"

"I called your hotel room," she snarls. It feels so good, beautiful, a place to pour the hot rage. "Since you're so impossible to reach. I called three times and every —"

"Oh God."

"Single."

"Ava, wait. You have to wait."

"*Time,*" she shrieks, "that *bitch* picked up. Must've been washing your dick in the bathroom."

"Oh, Avey," he says sadly.

"You lied to me." Her hands are shaking so badly she balls them up.

"I lied to you," he echoes, surprising her. *Say it,* she says silently, almost exhilarated. *Say our life is over. Say the word.*

"I stayed in Brooklyn."

Her mind trips like a bad fuse. She frowns at her reflection in the rearview. "Wait. What?"

There's a pause. Nate sighs. The car crinkles with the static. "I'm sorry, Avey. I'm so sorry. I lied to you about everything. The summer, the Portland office."

"There was no Portland office?" Her brain is like a marathoner who has given up. But the number. Emily in the hotel.

"No, no. They offered it to me. I told you I took it. But I didn't. I told Alice no. I never went to Portland."

"I . . ." She can't speak anymore. There's an old lady walking out of McDonald's with a greasy plastic bag. Her nails are fuchsia. She catches Ava's eye and waves. Ava waves back. "I don't understand."

She can hear him breathing. "I needed a break," he says finally. "I didn't know how to say it. I just wanted some time alone. In the house. I've been going for runs after work. I have so much time now to just catch up on things. I see Jeremy and the guys sometimes. I've reached Prestige on Call of Duty."

"Call of Duty?" She wishes Naj were here. The image of her husband licking Emily's freckled breast disappears. She can see him, clear as day: his headphones in, a dirty bowl of cereal on the table. His left leg stretched on the coffee table. Her shoulders start to shake.

"Don't cry, Avey. Please."

"Call of Duty," she chokes out.

"Are you —" He pauses. "Are you *laughing?*"

She howls. "You irresponsible, you immature —" She laughs so hard her face hurts. The old lady cocks her head in concern. Ava waves her away. Her face is streaming with tears. "You've been hiding from us all summer."

"I can't believe that room number was Emily's," he says wonderingly.

"This is as bad as an affair." She giggles. "You realize that, don't you?"

"Is it?" He's laughing now too; their laughter turns into hysteria, then tears. He never cheated on her. He's talking quickly now, about how sometimes he has a vision of a small apartment in Midtown with a view of the Hudson when the children are driving him crazy or when she's being cold, how this wasn't the life he'd expected, but he hates himself for being so predictable. He repeats it, *I'm so predictable,* and she can hear the grief in his voice, the heartache as he says he loves her more than anything.

God.

Something catches, like a nail catching lace.

God. She cheated on him.

"What?" he finally says to her silence.

She could say nothing. She thinks of her mother as a young woman, the handsome young man in the photographs in Hayat's house. The glass smudged with fingertips and lips. She has a grandmother again. She had a father. She has another father. This is all wrong. Her mother never said anything. There must've been a million moments just like this one in her life, moments where Idris looked at Mazna with a question he never asked or Ava unwittingly mimicked Zakaria as a child, millions of moments where her mother never broke her silence.

"I kissed somebody."

There's a violent silence. Nate whimpers. "Don't say that."

But she says it again. She tells him everything, about Jo and the dancing and Emily's voice on the phone, and he cries but also listens. And as he listens, she talks more, and oddly, it's as if he's the one talking, because something strange is happening, she's seeing everything differently. She can hear and see herself as though she's in a film, the wife of somebody else, through the eyes of Nate. She can hear the trouble of his life. The parents who trapped him in their money. The children he didn't want to have but whom he has fathered well, the eclipsed career. The brief flirtation, the wife who's always angry. She isn't happy, she realizes. She is grateful, but that isn't the same as happy. And she has now broken something, chinked the life they've built. He wasn't the villain. She wasn't either, or she was, but it didn't matter anymore. After she told him about Jo, she and Nate had cried like children for an hour, talking through their tears as if they were afraid to hang up, afraid of what would come next.

It's nearly eleven when she reaches the house, and there are already several cars in the driveway. The two almond trees that are still alive are strung with black ribbons. Naj's handiwork. Sara's car is near the entrance. The memorial has begun. As Ava parks, she sees people at the door, Sara talking to a couple and some woman.

Not talking. Yelling. The woman has bleached hair. Mirabel.

Ava can hear Sara from the closed car. She's screaming, her car keys jangling around in her hands as she gestures.

"I deeply cannot," Ava says aloud, then kills the engine. She needs to sleep. Every act is like lifting a barbell. She exits the car.

"Sara," she calls. Then, remembering, she covers her mouth.

It's like watching a train wreck in slow motion. This is how a secret unfolds. Sara turns to her, wild-eyed. *Do you hear this shit?* The front door opens and her father walks outside. He sees Ava first.

"You're late," he tells her. "Did you get the juice?" He sees Mirabel, starts to smile, then freezes. "I thought I told you about today," he whispers.

"I know," Mirabel says. "But this is Sami and Lana." She touches his forearm. "They're *very* serious," she says conspiratorially.

"Idris! You did this?" Sara's voice cuts through the rest.

"Why don't we go inside?" Idris says in his doctor voice. "We can talk inside." But Sara isn't his patient.

"You two-faced, duplicitous asshole. This lady is telling me that she's selling the house. This house. Our house?" Her voice pitches higher. "The house *you* left?"

Idris's eyes dart around. Behind him, Naj and Mimi and Harp are peering through the doorway. Naj catches Ava's eye and mouths something unintelligible. Ava shrugs.

"You'll have to burn this house with me in it," Sara is saying.

"Careful around Mimi," Naj mocks in a whisper.

Mimi glares at Harper. "I hope you're happy."

She glares back. "Read the room, Mimi. Not the time."

"Sara, come inside," Idris says.

"My God, if you touch me —" Sara steps back.

"Am I hallucinating?" Mazna is hissing at them. Her hair is pulled back tightly and she's wearing a simple sleeveless black dress, a string of pearls around her neck. She's beautiful, and Ava can't stop looking at her. She feels parched for her, longs to see everything with what she now knows. "Is this godawful woman showing the house right now? Is my elder daughter skulking around like a bum in the front yard? Are you two" — she jerks her chin toward Idris and Sara — "fighting like children when there are guests *who can hear you?* Everyone, *in the house now.*"

"That's a good idea," Mirabel says. She turns to Idris and says cloyingly, "I was thinking we'd just pop in real quick, you won't even know we're here, just take a look at the veranda." She starts moving toward the house.

"Get your grubby hands off that door!"

Harper, her hair a mess, clearly hungover, steps toward the woman with a sudden violence that shuts everyone up. She waves a finger menacingly at Mirabel. The prospective buyers take a step back. Harp's eyes are blazing. Her Texan accent is murder.

"You're like a plague, aren't you? You just keep coming back. I don't know how else to say this." Harper cups her hands around her mouth like a megaphone and shouts directly into Mirabel's face, "These people *lost* someone, you prissy vulture."

Mirabel is speechless. Sara is still staring daggers at her brother. Mazna clamps a hand over her mouth. In the most astonishing moment of the day, Ava sees her mother shake with laughter.

***

Mazna ushers them all into the house. "Be polite," she snaps at her children. Ava feels a bony finger in her back. "You look like a drifter." They all plaster smiles on their faces. There are a dozen people or so already in the room, mostly older. Merry is seated with the children on one of the couches. Their hair is freshly combed, and Zina is wearing a navy dress Ava hasn't seen before.

"You spend too much time with Najla," Merry tells Ava. "Now you smell like her."

Mazna frowns at Merry. "This isn't the time." She sniffs around her eldest. "You're right, but this isn't the time."

"Mama, I'm going to go change. Oh, honey, I missed you." Zina presses her face into Ava's stomach. Mazna shakes her head.

"You say hello to these people first." There's an older woman looking at the pictures in the frames. "Ava, you remember your auntie Darine? She went to school with your grandfather."

"Of course," Ava says, shaking the stranger's hand.

"The remainder in your life, my dear. The remainder in your life."

"Thank you."

The older woman's hands are papery, and she peers into Ava's face in a way that is unnerving. "My goodness, if your mother didn't spit you from her mouth."

Ava can feel her mother's gaze on her. Her eyes start to burn. She remembers Hayat's words about her long-dead sister. "Thank you," she says again. There are so many people, so many strangers and half-remembered relatives, and by the time she finishes greeting all of them, several more have arrived. She and her siblings go from one to the next, smiling and nodding like children, answering the same questions about their lives, thanking the guests for coming. From the next room, Sara's and her father's voices rise and fall like water. She finally returns to the children. They are balancing plates on their laps. "My babies," she says. She buries her face in their necks. "Mama's had a big day." They smell like glue and shampoo.

Rayan scans her face. "Today we're sad," he pronounces.

"Why's that, honey?" She feels a brief panic, but he can't know about Freckles or Jo or the camps.

He looks at her like she's an idiot. "Your jiddo." He lowers his voice like an adult. "He's dead."

She exhales. "Of course. I know that, baby." She looks behind her. "You two don't have to be sad, though," she says conspiratorially. "It's okay if you're not, I mean. You didn't know him."

"We're still sad," Rayan says.

Zina looks at her brother. "We're sad," she confirms.

"Well, he would've loved you." She knows it's true as she says it. How horrible, never to have brought Jiddo the children. Never to have returned.

"*. . . left for America!*" Sara shrieks in the next room.

They get louder. Ava catches her mother's eye. Mazna's lips are thin. She nods. Ava excuses herself and the two of them push the door open, find her father and aunt facing each other like boxers. The déjà vu is immediate: Mimi and Naj in front of the nightclub some twelve hours ago, screaming about their past.

"I wanted to tell you before," her father is saying, "but you made it impossible."

"I made it *impossible* to share your betrayal? Am I meant to apologize for that?"

"Our parents are dead, Sara. God rest their souls. This house is empty and —"

"This isn't your house." Sara is wild-eyed. "You don't get to sell our inheritance to ease your guilt."

Ava sucks in her breath.

Idris notices them. He looks a little relieved at the sight of Mazna and turns to her as if for help. Her mother crosses her arms.

"She's right," she says quietly. "About all of it." Idris looks dumbfounded. The doorbell rings. More guests. "But right now, there are people out there gathered around photographs of your father. They came all the way here to see you two. This is your father's memorial," Mazna continues. "Both of you. Have some respect." Her aunt and father bow their heads.

"Baba," Ava says as they're walking out of the room. He looks at her. She searches his face. She has to tell him. He hugs her. He smells like coffee. Caramel. Her father.

In the living room, a few guests enter. An older couple, the woman carrying a tray of Turkish sweets. There's someone behind them, looking somber. She is gazing around the house in wonder.

Zakaria's mother. Hayat.

Ava sees her first. Her mind doesn't grasp; it reacts. She rushes to Mazna and tugs at her sleeve, an old memory rising up to her of childhood, trying to get her mother to look at something, some landscape or person. "Mama. Look."

"What?"

"*Look.*"

Her mother's face tells the truth. All of it lives in the second she looks at this woman whom, Ava realizes, she's never seen in person before. But she knows. She knows her. She has seen the same photographs, watched the same videos. Her mother clutches her arm.

"Avey," Mazna moans like a child.

"It's the woman from before," Ava says numbly. It's a decision that takes place in a split second. She barely makes it. Her words restore the secret, rebuild it like a house. There was a moment of recognition, she knows, when her mother clutched her arm. But she'll give her grace instead. She keeps her voice steady, pretending. *People deserve their secrets.* "She must've decided to come."

Her father looks up with a practiced smile, ready to greet the guests. Ava watches him see Hayat. He turns white.

"Ibni," she calls. "My son." Idris gasps, grips the chair in front of him.

Her father bends over. He calls out the thing that is his currency, his English failing him, so that he says the word in Arabic. *"Albi,"* he rasps, clutching his heart, then collapses to the floor.

Fever Pitch

MIMI HAS ALWAYS hated hospitals. They remind him of the worst parts of childhood — the waiting and tension, being at the mercy of others. He's a little embarrassed at how much the niceness of the hospital surprises him; Beirut is an unkempt city, but the hospital is shiny and new. The doctor is a young woman; the tag on her coat reads L. QIBLAWI. She speaks calmly, enduring his father's interruptions from the bed, where he's linked to a thousand machines, wires and thin tubes fixed onto him like a squid. It's early evening, the day spent in the waiting rooms and cafeteria, crying and panicking and praying, waiting for news. The family had run out on the guests, leaving the children with Merry; some of them went in the ambulance, the rest of them followed in the rented car.

They are all crowded in the small hospital room, Naj and Mimi and Ava and Sara and Harp and Mazna, and in the corner, looking immovable as a brick house, Zakaria's mother. *I'm coming,* she'd said when the ambulance arrived, and nobody argued with her.

"He has had a heart attack, a myocardial infarction," she explains. "One of the major coronary arteries is —"

"A little clogged up!"

"Well, yes. More than a little. But occasionally these things can be triggered by environmental causes. Some shock or fall?"

Five heads swivel toward Hayat.

She smiles. "Forty years of absence will do that to a person."

"Are you scolding me?" Idris demands. He sounds like a boy talking to his mother. "I'm strapped to a machine."

"Ibni, you put yourself in that machine."

"Amen," Mazna says, but there's no bite to it. She's been pale ever since he dropped, and in the ambulance over, Mimi heard her whispering something. Prayers. As soon as the doctor said the word *minor,* she'd turned to the trashcan in the hallway and vomited.

"The good news," the doctor continues, "is that most of the other coronary arteries are completely clear."

"That's as good as a clean bill of health right there!" Idris says triumphantly. He starts removing the IV catheter.

"It is not." The doctor sounds amused. "It's a warning bell. Lifestyle changes. Exercise. Better nutrition. You're going to have to clean up your act."

"I live well," his father cries.

"Your favorite food is fried cheese," Mazna counters.

"Still?" Hayat says, but Mazna doesn't answer. She seems terrified of Hayat, hasn't looked at her once.

"You were very lucky today," the doctor says. She leaves, and most of them busy themselves discussing the news, arguing with Idris about finishing his pudding. Only Ava is still. She watches them all. She'd told Mimi and Naj everything; they'd cried down in the cafeteria as she described the visit to Hayat's house, how Sara had been there, everything the two women had told her.

He was my father, she'd said, and the words were both impossible and not, a funhouse mirror on everything Mimi known about his life, changing the axis of their family. As they'd gone back up to the room, he caught his sister looking in the mirror of the elevator, scanning her face, as though seeing for the first time the miracle, the lie, that she was.

Visiting hours end at eight, but every time the nurses come in, Hayat or Sara charm them into giving them another half an hour. The room is littered with food wrappers. Mimi sees Zakaria's mother lean down and say something to Idris, sees his father's face lighting up in an almost painful smile. Most surprising of all, Mazna and Sara set up camp near the window, talking in low, urgent tones, their faces animated, barking at anyone who tries to get close.

"Do you not see us having a private conversation?" his mother snaps at Naj.

"What I see," Naj grumbles, "is the world turned upside down."

Finally, the nurse kicks them out. "Only one person can sleep here," she says, and when Mazna nods, Sara puts a hand on her shoulder.

"Let me stay instead," she says. "We have some talking to do."

Mazna looks around. "Are you sure?"

"Yes. It's about time."

"She's going to smother me with a pillow," his father jokes.

Sara punches his arm, and Mimi can see how they must've been as children. "Only you," she says fondly, "would almost die to get out of apologizing."

The siblings kiss their father. In the hallway, they wander to the elevator, their strange group. Hayat humming under her breath. They wait for the elevator. Finally, Hayat sighs.

"Are you going to look at me, daughter?" she says gently.

Mazna twitches like she's been shot. She slowly lifts her eyes. "I don't know what to say."

Hayat moves so close to her that their noses are almost touching. She lifts a hand and cradles Mazna's face, then does the most unexpected thing: She kisses her forehead. Lightly, tenderly. Mazna begins to cry. Her shoulders shake with it. Mimi averts his eyes; it's like walking in on a private moment. He sees Naj start to cry and turn away as well.

They remain like that for a long minute, Hayat's hand still cradling his mother's face, spattered with her tears. The two women look like they've known each other a lifetime. Hayat finally speaks, her voice low and kind.

"You have as much to forgive as anyone, daughter," she says cryptically, and Mazna shudders, throws her arms around the older woman, buries her face in her shoulder, and weeps as she's waited forty years to do.

It is late now and the chaos of the day has wiped them out. They stand in the hospital lobby. Zakaria's mother needs a ride back to her car, and Naj and Ava take her. Mimi waits for a taxi with Harp and his mother. Nobody says anything. Mazna keeps chewing her lip. Harper looks around at the atrium, the spotless glass.

"This place is so nice," Harp finally says. "It sounds bad, but I didn't expect it to be."

He tries to look weary. "Don't be racist, Harp."

His mother rolls her eyes. "Shut up, Mimi," she says companionably. There's a thaw between her and Harp. "Put him in Beirut for a week and the boy thinks he's an Arab nationalist. I saw you gawking at this place when we came in."

She and Harp exchange a quick, almost infinitesimal smile.

Harp's flight back to Austin is booked for the day after the memorial. He drives her to the airport alone, and as they go through the Salim Salam tunnel, she clicks off the radio. "I can stay, you know. If you want me to."

He glances at her. It's noon, and nobody slept much the night before. Her eyes are bruised underneath, a beautiful lavender. "I know, Harp. He's okay, though. You heard the doctor. Sara said he'll probably be released in a couple of days."

Harp nods. "That Nate thing is crazy."

That's all he told her about Ava, how Nate was in Brooklyn all these weeks. Nothing about Hayat. Nothing about Zakaria. In a few months, this summer will be a wild, feverish time in Harp's life, full of unanswered questions that she'll eventually forget she ever had. It wasn't his story to tell, the way Mazna's wasn't Ava's to tell; a natural order has been disrupted and he doesn't want to continue it.

"That he would lie about something like that," Harp continues, and Mimi knows what's coming. "You remember what I said?" she asks quietly.

He doesn't answer.

"About not telling me?" She takes a breath. "I changed my mind. I want you to tell me if it's going to change my life." She leans back on the headrest.

Mimi lets himself think. A minute passes, two. It doesn't matter. He wants what he says to be true. He imagines the Igloo, their storage room filled with sleeping bags and an air mattress and that old bike. The stuff they've spent a decade amassing. He thinks of Allie, whom he remembers less and less these days, the way he remembers Dulcet less and less, that humid night, his hand against her thigh. He feels sorry for that person. How hungry he must've looked outside that bar. How pathetic. Jacob had done the right thing. He is glad Harper told Naj about the fire. He is glad Naj yelled at him. For years he's been a liar, and he wants to stop.

"I want you to give me that ring back," he says. Harp stares at him, stunned.

"You asshole." Her breath is uneven.

"I want to ask you again," he says. "I want to ask you properly, not as an afterthought. Not because I'm trying to fix things." He finally turns to her. Not deserving something wasn't the same as not wanting it. "Please, Harp. You could leave me right now, and I wouldn't blame you. But if you're not going to, give me that ring back."

She gives him the ring. At the terminal, he watches her walk into the departing crowd, but right before she does, she turns and gives him one final, radiant smile.

He'd thought what he knew would make it impossible to look his parents in the eye. The truth is, he has to remind himself of what he knows. His mother picks up a dishrag in the kitchen and he thinks, *She loved Zakaria.* But it is a small mercy, how time distills what we know, how it fictionalizes it. The hospital discharges his father after a week, and the children cut up paper flowers with Merry. Whatever it is that he and Sara discussed that first night in the hospital goes unmentioned until he's back. They are all gathered in the living room, even Merry. She has all but stopped doing chores and nobody asks her to anymore.

"We have an announcement," Sara says. "About the house."

Mimi and his sisters exchange a look.

"Your father and I talked for a long time that night," she continues, "and I think we reached an agreement." She turns to Merry, who is braiding Zina's hair. "Merry," she says nervously. "Would you stay? Here, I mean. You can bring your family if you'd like. I have a friend who can help with the visas."

The woman freezes. After a second, her face fills with a smile. "Absolutely not," Merry says.

"What?" Sara asks, stunned.

Merry dusts her hands off on her thighs. She kisses the crown of Zina's head. "Your father," she says to the room, "was kind to me, and I spent good years in this house. We never talked of him dying. But he always understood I would leave. The only thing he asked of me was to keep his trees alive."

The white, blooming almond trees. Mimi walks by them every morning. The largest tree dead now, the saw still embedded in its heart.

"What?" his father says.

"Do you know why he asked that of me?" she says to the room. Nobody answers. "Because he knew his children would be too busy fighting. That's how it always is. But I did what that good man asked of me. I kept those trees alive the best I could. I stayed here all summer."

"You can't leave," Sara says childishly.

Merry looks at her with rare tenderness. "I had a life before Beirut and I'll have one after. Somehow it worked out," she continues, gesturing around the room. "All of you gathered here. It would have made him happy." She smiles again and walks out.

There is a long silence after she leaves. "Who'll keep the almond trees alive now?" Ava finally asks.

Sara and Idris look at each other. "We'll figure something out," Sara finally says.

His father stretches his arm on the couch and Mazna falls back into it. "No more Mirabel," she says.

"No," Idris says. He leans his head against hers. Mimi watches his mother not move away. He thinks of Harp smiling in the airport. Things can look so different depending on where you're standing. His father clears his throat. There's a dreamy look in his eyes.

"Here it comes," Naj says.

They all recognize it: His sage face. His proverb face. The one after they've failed exams or lost soccer games, the one Mimi knows from years of mediocrity. His father raising a family on new soil, with nothing but dead words as armor against America. Idris speaks in Arabic.

"A house divided cannot stand."

Mimi doesn't ask what he means. He's within touching distance of the people that love him, in spite of everything.

⁂

It is the third week of August and Naj finally tells them about her show. It's a big one, he knows from her tone, and she spends a lot of time telling them not to come, but he can see how pleased she is when they do. She takes them around backstage before the show, then kisses them, and they go back outside. Their parents are dressed in jeans, his mother's hair in a bun. They look absurd. Ava left the children with Merry and seems nervy with energy.

"You're in the front row," Naj says, and they're all excited, laughing and calling out as they find their seats, even Mimi. All day he's had a terrible knot in his stomach, but there's deliverance at the sheer size of the crowd, the professional light displays, the logo with NOJA emblazoned in hot pink on the stage; it's a whole other level. He wants it, but he also wants a million dollars and tropical vacations, and these are all concepts. What is real is the music, the light hitting the glossy guitar, the way his fingertips begin to itch when Jo plays, the recoil of bass in his throat. All around them, tweens bounce up and down in miniskirts and ripped shirts, dazzling creatures screaming the lyrics together. There's a lot of kissing. A lot of hands and naked shoulders and drugs.

He keeps waiting for his parents to say something, but they seem shell-shocked.

"Am I awake?" his mother yells to Idris.

"I've never felt so old in my life," he calls back.

They dance anyway. There are Styrofoam cups of bad beer being sold and Mimi buys one for everyone, then another round. Ava dances alone, turning in circles until she knocks into a beautiful woman, who nonchalantly takes his sister's hand and dances with her. There's a look of relief on Ava's face as she dances, and he almost cries thinking of Nate and Zakaria. But he can't do anything about it, so he dances too, first with his father, who hops back and forth to the beat, then his mother, who surprises him by dancing well, differently than she does at gatherings or weddings, her hair shaking loose from her hair tie. The beautiful woman moves on to Mazna, who knocks her hips in return.

"You're *gorgeous,*" the woman tells his mother.

"You're about twelve and a half," his mother returns, and both women laugh so hard they almost cry.

"Remember me?" Idris says and the women laugh again.

Mimi dances like he's fourteen. He dances the good, ugly dance of real dancing, letting his face contort, flailing his arms around. He was never very good at it, which is different than being bad at it. Naj soars around the stage like a meteor. It's like looking at an alien, her skin bright purple under the lights, her voice hungry, gravelly. She's aware of them in the crowd, she's showing off, but she should. He would too if he could do that with his instrument. He strums his fingers on his chest like an invisible guitar. He screams the lyrics he knows.

Listen, Mimi commands himself. He listens. To the music and the voices around him. But underneath that, to California twenty-five years earlier, to the sound of his sister's playing that day in the music school, the magazine cover of her and Jo. There was grit and there was timing and then there was the simple, divine matchstick of pure talent.

And he didn't have it.

Listen.

He stops dancing, panting. It was more than that. Naj at eleven, thirteen, missing her junior prom for a recital in Los Angeles. The hours she'd lock herself in her room and play. Devotion. Devotion like Harper listening to hundreds of recordings, like Ava writing a two-hundred-page dissertation about sea microbes. He suddenly knows in a flash, in his bones, that if she hadn't been successful in music, Naj would've found something else to devote herself to. His mother dances by his side and it is twenty-three years ago and she is on the telephone still trying to audition.

"Mimi!" Ava shouts. She tugs his arms. "She's calling for you!"

He looks toward the stage. His sister is flapping her arm like a bird, her hand outstretched to him, the violin dangling from it. "Get your ass up here," she screams, and the crowd goes wild.

At first there is rage. Humiliation. It burns him like a brand, but before he can form a single thought, his father's hands are pushing him toward the stage, a uniformed bouncer moving him up the stairs, and the feeling gives way to fear and exhilaration, his sister running up to him and kissing him on the cheek.

"You made me do it this way," she whispers in his ear, irrepressibly smiling.

Someone hands him a guitar. It's expensive and hefty and he knows it's perfectly tuned, the strap falling predictably against his body like an embrace. Jo hands him a pick. At the microphone, his sister is talking.

"From Beirut," she screams into the microphone, "by way of Austin by way of California! Give it up for my big bad wolf of a brother, Mimi!"

They howl for him. They cheer and he glimpses Ava in the front row, clinging to their mother, both of them grinning like cartoons. He turns to his sister and Jo in terror. He has no idea what to do next. Jo smiles at him and starts playing. The air is plunged into noise, familiar, haunting noise.

"Pink Rabbits." The National.

It was one of the last songs he'd sent to Naj. He'd listened to it for a summer straight, and he had to send it to her, even though everything was already broken between them by then, because she was the only one who would understand. She grins at him, and her eyes are glittering, but before he can say anything, she's already growling into the microphone. *I couldn't find quiet.*

I went out in the rain, the crowd screams back.

Mimi shuts his eyes. *Listen.* Everything is a single, purring roar. He can smell the crowd, weed and gasoline and the smoke of a million cigarettes. Everything is smaller than he thought it would be from up here. Bigger too. *Listen.* There's a restaurant. Like Olive, but different. Cordelia will front him the money. They'll do a sister restaurant. The second the thought arrives, it's perfect, it's so perfect he does finally begin to cry, playing along with Naj and Jo, singing into the same microphone. He'll work in the kitchen this time. There will be *umm ali* and *mansaf* and freshly baked pita and he'll serve entrées based on the month, the way his grandmother used to. He won't paint shitty murals on the wall. It'll be simple Arabic food, and he'll cook all of it. There will be recipes on the napkins and he won't open in Downtown or Old West, but in Dove Springs, where the Arabs live, the Mexicans and Guatemalans. Everything will be cheap. They'll never serve brunch.

But before that, he has a show to do. He and his little sister have to make a thousand people sing. The strings meet his trembling fingers. He plays his fucking heart out.

Intermission

MAZNA CRIES, WATCHING her children. Mimi's face plain with joy. Najla dancing across the stage. She cries as the beautiful woman twirls her around and when her children sing into the same microphone. She cries when Idris crushes her to him and says hotly in her ear, *She's the spitting image of you,* reminding her of the woman's words about Ava at the memorial, as their youngest glows in front of the microphone, blowing a kiss toward her brother, toward them, taking every bit of applause like she's owed it. There's an intermission and Mazna tells Ava and Idris she's going to the bathroom, but instead she sneaks out. The parking lot is filled with concertgoers doing this and that. There's a blue-haired boy rolling a cigarette, and she taps him on the shoulder.

"May I?" she asks.

He looks her up and down, then smiles. He hands her a cigarette and she smokes it greedily. There are children dipping in and out of the crowd, like the children she's seen all summer at cafés and in front of stores. Back in the 1990s, they were Palestinian, hawking roses and cigarettes with their rough accents. The roses are still here, but now the children are Syrian. They have her mother's accent. A couple of young girls crowd her and beg.

"Auntie, just a dollar, Auntie."

"Please, Auntie."

She digs up the change she has, and they thank her perfunctorily, a strange dignity in how they take the coins.

"Bless you, Auntie," the younger girl says, like a grandmother. It makes Mazna want to kneel down. To take the girl and make a room for her in their house in California, teach her to pot azaleas.

Zakaria had once said something outside the bakery. They'd just walked by a refugee child poking into the stores. A shopkeeper had called him Palestinian trash. Zakaria had clenched his fists and given the boy a wad of cash. *May you never see your people like this,* he'd said to her. *Even one of them. That's all it takes. Then it might as well be all of you.*

He's been dead now for forty-one years. The anniversary of his death came and went earlier this month. This year, she knows, she and Idris will talk about him. Only the dead don't change. Or only the dead do. He could be anyone. She knows only the twigs of facts she collected over those months: He disliked tangerines. He loved her. She'd taken those twigs and created a man out of them, and she has missed that man every day for decades. He could be anyone. He has become Damascus and Palestine, all of it, everything that aches between her chest and teeth, all the unnamed things that she had to lose to know what she loved, the time she thought she had so much more of.

In this way, she got what she wanted. She has been married to him for over forty years as much as Idris.

❖

Zakaria's mother had given her a piece of paper. It was her number, an address, even an e-mail account. She'd make her dinner, Hayat promised, and Mazna will keep the paper, but its very keeping is futile. She'll never go to the camps. It would be cruel. To treat Hayat like a plot device. Someone who could answer her questions. Mazna was poor once too. Her children forget that. Why

wouldn't they? It was a lifetime ago, long before they knew her. But she understands how people can use you. How the wanting can empty you out. Idris
did it to her and she did it to Zakaria. That was the beginning of everything
— wanting more, stealing Hana's soap. Hadn't she wanted Idris as well? If she'd
met Hayat that summer, when she was a poor Syrian girl pretending to be
more, it might've been different. But too many years have passed. She's the
wife of a doctor now. She might spend her days turning soil, but there's the
unmistakable smell of America on her, abundance, slackened rope. If she visits
her, it'll only be to take more, and Hayat has given enough. The woman deserves to be left alone.

She misses the rest of the show. The parking lot fills with people from the concert, a hot, swirling mess of bodies and smoke. Finally she sees Ava and Idris
and Mimi. They're all sweaty and beautiful, her son's face rosy from playing.

"I saw you," she tells him before he can ask, and he flushes.

"It was fun." He rubs his father's shoulder. "I can't hear anything." He's
speaking too loudly.

Ava puts a hand out. "Are you okay, Mama?"

That's when she realizes she's crying again. She nods. Her daughter hugs
her so hard, it hurts her ribs. Mimi and Idris move toward them. They're all
clucking over her, and she feels like a child, wiping her running nose. Ava's reli-
able, solid frame. If she could tell her everything, she would. But she'd lose her.
You can cry, her daughter whispers in her ear. Or that's what she hears.

They meet Naj in a private lot. She and Jo are hectic with energy, also talking
too loudly, and Mimi jumps in, all three recounting the night like veterans.

"Did you see them at the end?"

"When Jo played the first chord, I swear I nearly passed out. I played on
pure muscle memory."

"You were good," Idris says. "All of you." Then, slyly, "But I've seen better." He lifts an eyebrow in Mazna's direction.

"Shut your mouth," she tells him. But his words warm her anyway. Ava is still by her side, their arms linked.

"I've heard the rumors," her daughter says with humor.

"Apparently Mama was an amazing actress," Naj tells Jo.

"I believe it."

"Do the scene from that play. Tarek's play," Idris says. He is grinning. *Silly man,* Mazna thinks, *with his fat stomach, his hair needing a cut, silly man with a bad heart and fantastical ideas.* But suddenly Mazna is twirling around, suddenly she is fanning herself with an invisible magazine. The beer and cigarette and music are tipping her head back, extending her arm.

"'You meet me in July,'" she drawls, "'and I'll meet you in Ramleh.'"

Her little audience bursts into cheers and hoots, their applause as generous as any.

Those City Lights Are Yours

LATER, PEOPLE CALLED it Noja's best show. Jo had been right; having her family there — especially Mimi — had opened something vulnerable and girlish in Naj.

But she had also been playing for Ava. Her sister dancing at the lip of the stage. Every now and then, they'd catch each other's eye and Ava would dance harder and Naj would howl into the microphone. Her sister, half a stranger. Her sister, talking with Nate late into the night all week after the memorial, the conversations sometimes punctuated with unlikely laughter. *I feel like myself for the first time in ages,* she confides to Naj, and even that she understands, the way pain can wake you up, how Naj hasn't looked twice at another woman all summer, how she sometimes walks around the city wondering where the past decade has gone. Right before their last song, she'd thrown her sweaty towel at her sister, and Ava caught it neatly, wore it around her neck for the next two hours.

Her mother had been drunk enough after the show to act for them. Jo went to the after-party, but Naj headed back to the house. Their father insisted on finding the VHS tape. They were all in a good mood, happily tipsy.

They watched the tape, Mazna ruthlessly young, her hair longer than Ava's. Naj felt a brief, irrational envy — her mother was more beautiful than her once, and that seemed unfair. The tape was old and the camera blurry, but her mother was unmistakably talented; the camera followed her around the stage obediently. "You're a fox, Mama," Ava said. Her mother snorted.

"Right here!" their father said. He'd been watching the screen like a magnet. They all were. "This here, that's when I couldn't take my eyes off her."

I'll wait all night by the telephone, their mother said dozens of years ago, and they watched their father fall in love.

It was late by the time the film ended. Their parents kissed each of them and giggled down to their bedroom. Naj could hear her mother asking if Idris remembered the time they drove to Byblos during the war. Mimi had fallen asleep on the couch, and Ava was gathering the glasses.

"Leave it, Ave. It's so late."

"You want to sleep in my room?" Ava asked, but Naj said no, she had to get home. Her apartment was finally hers again, and she'd been sleeping there the past few nights, alternating between crying into the plants and calmly watching the street below.

Fee had left the week before. She wasn't at the show, but of course she was, in the purple lights and singing voices. She'd sent a photograph of some bridge in Copenhagen with a setting sun behind it, and Naj replied with a pineapple emoji, and Fee understood. There were no more photographs.

For the first time, both sisters are heartbroken simultaneously. They huddle on the couch watching sitcoms. Naj tells her everything. Almost everything. About Fee and the fox tattoo. The night of the x-rays, Fee looking up at her in the ghostly light, the summer like an exquisite string of pearls, each one a moment of Fee's presence.

But Ava was wrong about one thing. They hadn't been fighting in the club that night. They'd been talking about the past. Apologizing and forgiving. She'd seen her once after that; they'd met at the Roadsters in Hamra. Just the two of them. They ordered a plate of fries and picked at it.

Naj felt the tears come. "What are we supposed to do now," she asked plaintively.

Fee brought Naj's knuckles to her lips. In front of the whole restaurant. Fee with the husband. "Everything we were already doing. But different."

Naj walked alone afterward, all the way to the water. It was the same as the last time and also not. Her face ran with tears. There was no longer Hady's at the corner, with the fire whiskey he served with pistachios. Her favorite restaurant had shut down. The club where she did her first hit of ecstasy. The bar she and Fee first kissed in. Prague. All replaced by new, expat money — spas, pottery bars, the city a reverberation of its former self, but to the young, this was it, the city they'd always known. What was the same was the feeling of being left.

It had been 2008. They were both sophomores and everything felt illicit. They once kissed in an empty classroom on campus. They slipped into the same bathroom at parties, pretending to do each other's makeup. Naj texted Fee all the time and one day Fee's brother looked at her phone. He was older; the things Naj knew about him formed a half-coherent thought: he loved Metallica, had memorized the Qur'an, believed himself responsible for his sister.

He'd threatened Fee.

But Naj wasn't generous at the time. She was cruel. *You're a coward,* she'd taunted her, both of them crying after Fee told her she was moving back to Damascus. *You're just doing what you're told.*

He'll tell my parents, Fee said. *My life will be over. He'll tell everyone.*

In the end, Fee moved back and he didn't do any of that. He didn't tell her parents. What he did do was rent a car and drive from Damascus. Naj was walking back from a night out. He was waiting in front of the apartment building for her.

He'd started screaming terrible, ugly things to her, things that he wanted to do to her, saying that she should stay away from his sister, that he knew men who would stitch her pussy shut, that she was an ugly dyke and he'd kill her if she ever spoke to Fee again.

She struck him first. Right after the word *dyke* had clunked from his mouth like a gumball-machine toy, she swung her purse at his head. It was the first time she'd ever hit someone, and when he swung back, that was a first as well, a shock of pain against her mouth, and she realized in that moment how naive she was — for all her mouthiness and bluster, she lived in a world where women didn't get hit.

He didn't stop until she was unconscious. It was a rattle of punches and kicks and she'd started crying, which she hated herself for after, begging him to stop, but he must've been as terrified as he was angry at her bleeding lip, her bent body, and every sob made him hit her harder until she was lying on the floor covering her face, trying to breathe. He stomped on her rib cage. Somebody from an upstairs building started screaming at him. He tossed her legs apart. There was one final, brutal kick between her legs. She passed out.

Fee didn't find out for months. But Naj didn't know that then. She wept and hugged Jo and spent that time writing Fee out of her life. When the e-mail from Fee arrived, full of apologies and typos, begging her to meet, she read it once and deleted it.

❖

Seven stitches. A fractured nose. Lacerations on her vagina. A single rib broken, three more bruised. She'd bitten her tongue when the brother punched her the first time, and Jo had to feed her soup for weeks.

She couldn't tell her siblings about it. It's still too tender. It belongs to her.

❖

Leaving Jiddo's house now, Naj pictures her mother's image of California, the sexy California, not the desert highways and nosy neighbors of Blythe, but the palm trees, rooftop pools, hot-pink drinks. Movie stars and limos and famous hotels. She's been to Los Angeles for shows, of course, and trips in childhood, each time feeling a chime of longing, and for a moment she imagines herself stepping onto the tarmac and never leaving.

But Beirut is all she knows. Her staying was something to prove. The streets named after martyrs. Heaps of trash on the curb like plants. The music. In every bar. Every balcony. She suddenly remembers her conversation with her father that night in early June, right after she met Fee. *Maybe it's haunted*, he said. He'd said it lightly, but now, in the remembering, she can hear the strain in his voice, how tired he'd sounded. She thinks of her younger mother performing, this woman who'd leave everything and everyone for a man she barely knew, for a life she wanted but wouldn't have, a decision so brave and enormous it makes Naj's head spin. She knows it's time to leave Beirut.

She walks east, to Gemmayzeh. It's begun to cool in the evenings, and there's the faintest contract of autumn in the air. She passes the Orthodox cathedral. The mosque on Khoury Street. There's a small residential street, and she walks to the third building. She has a key. They always do this, swap keys whenever they move. The apartment is on the fourth floor and she makes her way through the dark living room. She half expects the bed to be empty, but Jo is already asleep. He's wearing gray boxers, his legs akimbo over the sheets. There's the sound of light snoring. She slips off her T-shirt and jeans. She kneels on the side of the bed, the mattress sinking beneath her, and he stirs.

He blinks. "Hey."

"Sorry," she says.

He opens his arms wordlessly, already shutting his eyes again, and she crawls in, wishes for the millionth time that it could be different, that she could open her mouth against his and feel something, could force this love into a different one. Instead, she burrows against him, feeling his meager erection, his breath, his wholeness. He doesn't smell very good — slept in. She loves him like atoms. Like Ava's microbes. In his half-sleep, he strokes her hair and she shuts her eyes. When she first woke up in the hospital, she'd wished she were dead, was certain she'd never laugh again, but life was sneakier than that.

She won't tell Jo about leaving Beirut right away, but she knows he'll go with her; he's more her wife than anybody will ever be, although someday one of them will fall in love again, and it'll be fucked. Noja will eventually die — all bands do — but she's okay with it; they'll find a way to fix things, to meet in airports and for Christmases and children's birthdays. But first Los Angeles. First an actual first. The reverse migration of her family. She'll return, for the second time in her life, to a place made of her. She'll look out at the same desert as her mother and she'll try to make something there, art films or photographs of rainstorms or more music, a jolt of light on a stage and, below her, dancing people. It's not unheard of. It's not impossible. People have been doing it for eons.

Once a Wife

ZINA AND RAYAN want to bake Naj a cake. It's her thirtieth birthday and the family wants to take her out, but Naj refuses, so Ava helps the children ice the words *Happy 30th Najy* onto the cake while Mimi bakes cheesy biscuits. The kitchen smells incredible and she lets the children lick the batter from the wooden spoon, only momentarily envisioning the pinkish specks of salmonella wiggling through. Mimi has hollowed out the biscuits and he's spooning something inside.

"Figs and goat cheese," he explains.

Ava applauds. "What did Cordelia say?"

"I think she's into it." He ducks his head, and she can see him smile the way she has seen him smile about Harp and Dulcet. "She's fighting me on the neighborhood, but I think I'll get my way." Rayan is dancing around for a bite of the stuffing. "I want it to be casual. Set up like a living room. For people to come in their pajamas if they want."

"It sounds like a dream." He'd drawn the floor plan for the family the day before, his eyes lighting up as he brainstormed decorations. Their parents got into a fight about the name. Idris wanted Fennel or Thyme. Mazna wanted Beiti — "my house" — which Ava privately thinks is perfect, but she's still quiet around her mother, nervous in a way she knows Mazna has noticed but, to her surprise, says nothing about.

The weather is finally beautiful, as if Beirut has relented at last. Merry and Mazna set the table, fill little water glasses with flowers. The almond trees. Merry walks around them absently, but Ava knows she sees them. She's flying home on Tuesday, but she is unsentimental about it, and Ava understands. This was her job, she reminds herself. Two of the trees are alive. The family is speaking. Her grandfather didn't get the best memorial, but he got the one most like them, and there's something strangely satisfying about it. *It's exactly what he would've expected,* Nate joked on the phone, but tentatively. So many people are tentative now.

They've worked out something, her and Nate. He's coming in a couple of days to see the children, and they'll talk more. In fact, they'll talk for two days straight and at the end of it, what they come up with is both surprising and expected. She'll stay in Beirut with the kids for the fall semester. A sabbatical, she'll tell the university. One of her colleagues puts her in touch with a friend of a friend who is running a lab at the American University here; there is extra funding and for two months, she'll blink in the dark at microbes and wonder what life she'll have after all. Then the fires will begin, then the protests. They will be different than the ones that have come before. It won't be dozens of people on the streets now, but thousands, millions even. She will press her body against everyone else's, her voice raw from shouting through the night everything they tell her to shout. The politicians begin to resign. The banks begin to buckle. Something deep and ancient within the country begins to awaken. There is a sudden hope in the streets, a hope that become weariness and rage by the time she returns to Brooklyn, watching the country from thousands of miles away. She will watch the currency fall. She will watch the price of bread rise like a fever. She will watch — her fist pressed against her heart as she sobs — the very face of the city be rearranged forever, plunging it and everything it carries into uncertainty. But before that, during those autumn evenings, the weather will be perfect, cool but never cold; still she'll buy her coffee from the same *dikaneh* every day. Some evenings, Nate will call her from Brooklyn, and they'll joke gently with each other. They might get a divorce. They might work it out. Either way, they've reclaimed something precious. In the end, she's the one who will watch over the almond trees for those months, and certain evenings, she'll feel so lonely it will be a certain kind of death, sitting among the portraits and belongings of the departed while the city burns on the television. Other days, she and Rayan and Zina dance on the bed. The children are young enough. They'll enroll at the American school near the university, and when they're teenagers, they'll refer to it as their Beirut Year. The Year of the Protests. The Year of the Revolution. The truth is that Rayan will remember only odds and ends, breakfasts with his grandparents, who stay until October; scoring a winning goal at his new school; the snaking traffic and people yelling all around them. He'll remember the floods that season that will wash the trash into the ocean. A stretch of protests, smoke smudging downtown, bodies packed together so densely they resemble a sea, a single flag waving from hands, how on certain days his mother would roll their car windows up because of the air. Zina, of these months, will remember nothing.

They sing to Naj in English, then in Arabic, and she directs them like an orchestra conductor. Merry unearths some party poppers from a long-forgotten party, and they crack them. The children hop around, trying to catch the bits of confetti. The biscuits are delicious, opening like suns in her mouth, and Mazna and Idris bicker again about the name.

"I think Fennel sounds more elegant."

"Idris, if you have another slice of that cake, I'm going to call your doctor."

"I'm living under house arrest."

"You're living," Mazna counters.

Naj sighs. There's icing in her hair. "I'm thirty," she groans.

Ava can't help laughing. *You leave every decade I enter.* "Welcome." She kisses Naj's forehead. "We've been waiting."

They settle into the living room afterward. Mimi puts on the Cartoon Network, for the children, he says, but he laughs as loudly as Rayan. There is wrapping paper everywhere. Her mother and Naj are lying head to foot on the sofa, but Idris has vanished.

"I will bet my last dime," her mother says, "that that man is hiding in some closet somewhere wolfing down cakes."

"Nobody's going to take that bet, Moms," Naj says.

Ava finds him on the veranda. The sun is beginning to set, pinkening the sky. He's sitting, looking up. There's a half-finished cake slice on the ground. She laughs without meaning to. In that moment, she wishes she could give him every slice of cake in the world. All his fried cheese and tiramisu. Every greasy fingertip. Let him eat it all.

He startles at the sound, then relaxes when he sees it's her. "This is my last one," her father says. "Scout's honor." He winks at Ava. He pats the seat next to him and her heart is plucked like a string. He drapes an arm around her. "Come, sit with me. Take in this sight."

The city is muted from here, as quiet as it will get. The car honks and street noises seem faraway, a string of birds hooting at each other from branches. She watches it like a television. A moped revs somewhere. Between the buildings, there is water, and beyond that, more land. From here to there, however — an entire galaxy. The camps flooding in the winter. Her new grandmother making dinner. Music and lesbians and, up to the north, an entire country wolfed from the inside. Her mother's house. Her theater school. Her first stages. They can't know this, but there are new people in that house now. The windows have been cracked for two years. And in the south is Palestine. A land so unknown to her it feels like a concept. Something she half belongs to now.

"Penny for your thoughts," her father says. He loves his American sayings. This is the moment to tell him everything, the first time they've been alone since the memorial.

"Baba," she says. In graduate school, they'd taught her that the best microbes were the ones that could camouflage themselves as something else. Germ as host. Virus as sister cell. That was the only way to survive. But how did the microbe know when to reveal herself? Science was an incomplete story; they all were. She remembers her mother smiling the night of Naj's show, her head against Idris's shoulder. One cannot be picky about love. She leans against her father's shoulder. What will it help to speak now? What will it save? She turns her closed mouth against his sleeve. He's her father. The only one she has.

The Heart Teller

IDRIS CONTINUES TO sit on the veranda after his daughter goes inside. There's something prickly and muted about Ava these days that reminds him of her childhood, the weeks she'd sometimes go silent. Interior. Her face would quiet, something sad and urgent in her features.

He exhales slowly. The urge to tell her is always strongest after joy — birthdays and celebrations, the dinner he took her to after her PhD graduation. Each missed opportunity feels like a failing. But to tell her would be to tell Mazna. When Ava fell in love with biology, he'd dreaded that she'd find out on her own, but people are funny in that way: *Sometimes we never see what we aren't looking for*.

It was the most basic science. The truth was on his daughter's face the entire time. At four, five months, a small dimple started to form on her right cheek. Every time she smiled he stared at her in wonder. Tenth-grade biology class, Mr. Abadi forcing them to memorize dominant and recessive traits. Dimples, dominant. He got it right on the exam. It was impossible to have dimples without at least one parent having them.

Gotcha.

He'd spent his childhood staring at his friend's face. Zakaria with his curly hair and dark eyes. His lopsided smile. His dimple. In some ways, the truth was easier than he'd thought. There was an unremitting guilt those first few months in Blythe, that tiny apartment, realizing how he'd lied to bring Mazna here. The dimples settled some score. They made it strangely easier to breathe. When that director had called all those years later, Idris had thought of his daughter's face.

The heart had been real. It was a six-hour surgery. The recipient had been young, dark-haired, and handsome. He looked for all the world like Zakaria. Idris had knelt before the heart and heard it. It was his own voice, or not, or the whir of air conditioning, telling him what to do. *Let the past die.* He'd made an ordinary life at that point. Unhappy wife. Late-night drive-throughs at McDonald's. His children sprinkled around the world. Whenever he shut his eyes after a particularly long day, he saw Beirut, Ava's dimples, Zakaria's body at the *azza*.

He'd killed his friend. The love of his life. During the fight, Idris had brought up their childhood, the years spent in his house, had said it just like that, *My house,* because he knew that Zakaria wouldn't forgive that, had too much dignity to stay, and it worked, his friend packing his bag that very night. He was dead six days later. It didn't help that Zakaria's mother had kissed his hands at the funeral, called him her second son, or that Tarek kept reminding him they'd all been brothers. Brothers fought.

The country was poisoned for him. Everything terrible he'd done or had had done to him had happened in that house, and when Mazna stopped visiting, he wanted to thank her; she was just another witness to it. Then his father died, and the heart told him to sell.

It made sense only afterward. These past few days, he's felt released. *You were never going to sell the house,* Sara told him that night in the hospital. *You just wanted to believe you could. That you could erase the past like that.*

The sun has set now, and whatever light is left is dying, leaving to be reclaimed tomorrow. He can't hear the birds anymore. He'd seen his father when his heart failed. The ground had buckled beneath him, his hands flailing out, and Mazna caught them. Another bird lands on the telephone wire and cocks its little head at him. They forgave each other because. Because.

He whispers it aloud: "I'm sorry." Again: "I'm sorry." Zakaria laughing in the bakery. Throwing the couch pillows into the air with joy when Pelé scored a goal. The thing that made him return to Beirut, that heart saying, *Sell*. Maybe what it was really saying was *Repent*. You saw it in the hospital all the time, the way people's prayers got tangled with their fears. He'd wanted the girl on the stage more than he'd wanted love. He wanted America, all of it, children who rubbed the country into their skin like perfume. He wanted to be done with Beirut. That's the thing about fortunes — the one you believe is the one you get.

From inside the house, his wife's voice: "Idris, if you're out there with more cake . . ."

His heart is healing with each beat; there will be a scar, invisible to everyone, but Idris will know it's there, the dead tissue that will never regenerate. It will outlast him, with his memories and stories, his last delicious bite of cake.

The light is gone. It is evening. His father's almond trees are bright as stoplights. *I'm sorry.* The city stalks herself like a lioness. The city wants him to remember. The city wants him to forget. And so he does both.

Acknowledgments

I'm deeply grateful for the wonderful people at Houghton Mifflin Harcourt. Enormous gratitude to Jenny Xu, Liz Anderson, Taryn Roeder, Lisa Glover, Lori Glazer, Martha Kennedy, and the rest of the warm, magnificent team at HMH. In particular, thank you to the fantastic Naomi Gibbs for being such a thoughtful and generous editor. Thank you to Tracy Roe, Greta Sibley, and Phyllis DeBlanche for their meticulous work on the book. I continue to be grateful to Lauren Wein, who helped shape this book when it was just an idea. As always, unending gratitude to my brilliant agent, Michelle Tessler.

Thank you to Yardenne, Iris, Karen, and Madeline for being such lovely readers and friends. I'm beyond grateful to all the incredible poets and writers who have inspired and supported my work over the past decade: Randa, Fady, Marwa, Zeina, Susan, Deema, Nomi, Cyrus, Aja, Safia, Mira, Etaf, Rumaan, George, Jason, Courtney, and my darling Zeina, among countless others.

I couldn't have constructed a more loving, eccentric, perfect family if I wrote them myself. I am grateful to Reem, to my uncles, aunts, and cousins.

Thank you to my beloved grandparents, who taught me so much about the world, and whose ancestry I am proud to carry on.

Mama: you are the fierce matriarch of this family, and I love you for it. Thank you for the example you set, for your ability to adapt and re-create your life on so many different soils; I've learned so much courage from you.

Baba: thank you for always being the first to read my writing. I'm so grateful for the storytelling I inherited from you, for the ways you've taught me to respect myself and all I have to say. I love you kteer.

Talal ya Talal: thank you for helping me find this book's heart in the span of an elevator ride. Nobody but you could do that. You know the rest.

Miriam: habibit albi. Thank you for all the ways you've inspired me these past few years, for everything you've taught me about the world.

Layal: I am always writing with you in mind. Thank you for being my sister and friend and witness.

Omar: you were one of the first readers, and I know I'll never hear the end of it. Thank you, habibi.

Massive gratitude to Yara and Tara for being such unexpected joys and additions to our family. To Lisa and Kip and Jamie, and the beloved Perkins and Heiserman families, who are the antithesis of the in-laws in this book.

An enormous thank you to Michael Page, Dalea Alawar, Karam Hider, Andre McGlashan, and Kiki Ghossainy, for knowing me since Beirut (and miraculously still sticking around).

To Atheer Yacoub: thank you for the constant lifeline that you've been. So much heart and gratitude for the beauties that are Alexis Buryk, Ashlyn Chesney, and Sara Akant.

Thank you to the phenomenal Arab women/blessings in my life, first and foremost Sahar Ghaheri, Olivia Shabb, and Darine Hotait.

Thank you to the wonderful communities I work with at NYU and the Islamic Center, and to my profoundly inspiring clients and students.

Johnny: I love you and I'll never stop seeing you. Your patience and support and growth have been such a light over the years. Thank you for all the chances you've taken on this life of ours, and for always championing my writing.

Listen: I'm so grateful. Forgetting is worth the pleasure of remembering. الحمد لله.